◉ 普通高校专业英语教程系列

# 旅游专业英语实用教程 第二版

马 飞 司爱侠 编著

清华大学出版社

北 京

# 内 容 简 介

本书是"普通高校专业英语教程系列"中的一本，为切实提高读者的专业英语能力而设计。

本书分13个单元，每个单元包括对话、阅读、词汇、缩略语、难句讲解、习题、技能训练、旅游小百科、著名景点介绍等。本书还提供配套的音频，能够帮助提高读者的听说能力。

本书既可作为高等本科院校、高等专科院校旅游相关专业的专业英语教材，也可以作为旅游从业人员自学或者相关行业的培训教材。

**图书在版编目（CIP）数据**

旅游专业英语实用教程 / 马飞，司爱侠编著. –2 版. – 北京：清华大学出版社，2016（2022.8重印）

（普通高校专业英语教程系列）

ISBN 978-7-302-43414-6

Ⅰ.①旅…　Ⅱ.①马…②司…　Ⅲ.①旅游—英语—高等学校—教材　Ⅳ.① H31

中国版本图书馆 CIP 数据核字（2016）第 075219 号

责任编辑：徐博文
封面设计：平　原
责任校对：王凤芝
责任印制：刘海龙

出版发行：清华大学出版社
　　　网　　　址：http://www.tup.com.cn, http://www.wqbook.com
　　　地　　　址：北京清华大学学研大厦 A 座　　　邮　　编：100084
　　　社 总 机：010-83470000　　　邮　　购：010-62786544
　　　投稿与读者服务：010-62776969, c-service@tup.tsinghua.edu.cn
　　　质量反馈：010-62772015, zhiliang@tup.tsinghua.edu.cn
印 装 者：三河市天利华印刷装订有限公司
经　　销：全国新华书店
开　　本：185mm×260mm　　　印　张：19.5　　　字　数：489 千字
版　　次：2005 年 5 月第 1 版　2016 年 6 月第 2 版　　　印　次：2022 年 8 月第 8 次印刷
定　　价：78.00元

产品编号：067921-04

# 普通高校专业英语教程系列
## 编 委 会

主　编　司爱侠

成　员　宋德富　姜彦君　张强华　吕淑文

　　　　马占青　古绪满　张美兰

# 序

　　我国人才发展总体目标是：培养造就规模宏大、结构优化、布局合理、素质优良的人才队伍，确立国家人才竞争比较优势，进入世界人才强国行列。努力造就数以亿计的高素质劳动者、数以千万计的专门人才和一大批拔尖创新人才，建设规模宏大、结构合理、素质较高的人才队伍。开发人才资源必须优先发展教育。要通过发展各级各类教育创造丰富的人力资源，努力构建人人享有学习和成才机会的学习型机会。这些目标既指明了我国人才培养的方向，也指明了我国英语教育的发展方向。

　　随着全球化的不断发展，我国的英语教育规模不断扩大，也取得了显著的成就，但同时也面临着许多新的课题。英语教育的根本目标是培养人，培养各行各业人员实际应用英语的能力，使英语成为提高人才能力的助推器。随着英语基础教学水平的日益提高，市场对从业人员英语运用能力要求的不断攀升，专业英语教学得到空前的重视。尽管英语教学界对此还有种种争论，但现实却无视这些争论，"看不见的手"有力地推动了专业英语教学的进程；各个高校专业英语课程越开越多，社会上各种专业英语培训班日益火爆，从业人员急切地自我充电。正是为了满足这些需要，我们编写了这套"普通高校专业英语教程系列"。

　　本丛书主要遵循以下原则：第一，实用。我们在兼顾理论体系完整性的同时，尽可能多地从应用角度取材。读者在学过本丛书后，会感觉工作中的材料就像是本书的一个单元；第二，新颖。我们对各专业的最新发展都给予充分的关注；第三，本丛书以网络学习理念为指导，构筑开放、互动的教学体系。作者在本书的前言中留有电子邮件地址，读者在学习中遇到问题可以与作者及时联系。我们希望通过与读者的互动，努力把本丛书打造成精品系列教材。

　　本丛书的作者都是在教学一线的优秀教师，有着丰富的教材编写经验，其中一些作者还有从事行业工作的实际经历。因此，本套教材更加贴近读者。

　　本丛书既可作为普通高校专业英语教材，也可作为相关行业的各种短期培训班使用，个人也可以使用本丛书作为工作充电使用。

　　由于时间仓促，编者水平有限，书中难免有疏漏和不足之处，恳请广大读者和同行提出宝贵意见，以便再版时进行修正。

司爱侠

# 第二版前言

　　本书自第一版出版以来，深受广大读者的欢迎，被许多学校选作教材。在此，编者对读者的厚爱致以衷心的感谢。本次修订内容如下：

　　1. 修正了第一版中的个别错误。

　　2. 新增附录 1，包括全书的词汇。读者既可用来记忆单词，也可作为小词典长期使用。

　　3. 新增附录 2，包括导游员和中级导游员英语考试模拟题。读者可借此了解此类考试的题型和难度，也可通过自测评价自己的水平。

　　4. 制作了配套的音频，读者可以从出版社网站下载。编者相信此举对提高读者的听说能力大有裨益。

　　本书由马飞和司爱侠担任主编，张强华、张千帆参加部分编写工作。

　　欢迎广大读者通过邮件与编者进行沟通（zqh3882355@163.com）。

编　者

# 第一版前言

对于旅游从业人员而言，专业英语水平的重要性不言而喻。专业英语的水平直接关系到专业能力及业务水准，最终影响事业成就。本书的目的在于提高读者专业英语实际使用的能力。

本书在结构上以单元为单位，每单元由以下几部分组成：对话——注重实用性，每篇对话围绕一个主题，内容简单且易上口；课文——选材广泛、风格多样、切合实际；单词——给出课文中出现的新词，读者由此可以积累旅游专业的基本词汇；词组——给出课文中的常用词组；缩略语——给出课文中出现的、业内人士必须掌握的缩略语；难句讲解——讲解课文中出现的疑难句子，培养读者的阅读理解能力；习题——可有效巩固学习成果；技能训练——包括实用口语句型背诵、实用表格填写以及实用写作；旅游小百科——介绍一些旅游方面的知识；著名景点介绍——介绍中外著名景点，进一步扩大读者的视野。

本书选材新颖，包含大量的实用内容，让读者可以学习到目前最常用的、最新的基本知识，以便学以致用。

本书提供电子教案及参考答案，读者可以在清华大学出版社网站（www.tup.com.cn）下载。

本书既可作为高等本科院校、高等专科院校旅游相关专业的专业英语教材，也可作为从业人员自学或者相关行业的培训教材。

编　者

# Contents

## Unit 8  Cruise  *131*

## Unit 9  Hotel  *151*

## Unit 10  Restaurant  *171*

# Unit 1

# Introduction to Tourism Industry

## Part One Dialogues

### Sample Dialogue 1

👥 **Situation** ▶ Jack has just come back from China and he is talking with Lily about his travel.

**Lily**: Hi, Jack. I haven't seen you for a long time. How is it going?

**Jack**: I've just come back from China. It is really an exciting trip.

**Lily**: Really? That must be very interesting.

**Jack**: You are right. As I recall these good memories, once again I have the pleasure of the past experience.

**Lily**: Traveling seems to appeal to you wonderfully.

**Jack**: Yes. It broadens my perspective and I can learn a lot from it.

**Lily**: But travel is costly. I can't imagine a person working hard the whole year and then spending his savings within a couple of days just for seeing landscape and meeting people of different colors and races.

**Jack**: I agree with you on that, but we can choose a cheaper way of traveling.

**Lily**: I'm afraid I can't afford long trip with my salary. If I work in a travel agency, I could find some chances to travel cheaply or even without pay.

**Jack**: Good idea. Why not give it a try?

## Sample Dialogue 2

**Situation** ▶ Lily Lee is going to graduate from her university and now she is having an interview for a tour guide at a travel agency.

**Interviewer**: Good morning, Miss Lee.

**Lily**: Good morning!

**Interviewer**: Please take a seat. I see you are studying Travel and Tourism. Could you tell me why did you choose this major?

**Lily**: Well. I love traveling and this major will enable me to see the world.

**Interviewer**: Good idea. Do you have any real experience of being a tour guide?

**Lily**: Yes. I have been a part-time tour guide for almost three years. And I even guided the foreign guests to Xi'an, Beijing and Luoyang.

**Interviewer**: Impressive experience. What do you think of the work of being a tour guide?

**Lily**: It is hard work, but rewarding, and the potential for advancement is very likely for the dedicated and determined employee.

**Interviewer**: Wonderful point. I can't agree with you any more. OK. You will get a reply in a couple of days.

**Lily**: I'm looking forward to a positive reply. Thank you very much.

**Interviewer**: You are welcome.

## Useful Expressions

1. I went on a package tour.
   我参加的是一个旅行社代办的旅行。

2. What famous sights have you been to?
   你去了哪些著名的景点？

3. It is really a wonderful experience to see Paris with your own eyes.
   用自己的眼睛去看巴黎真是绝妙的经历。

4. Could you give a brief introduction of yourself?
   请简单地介绍一下你自己。

5. I major/specialize in Tourism English.
   我的专业是旅游英语。

6. I'm from Xi'an, Shaanxi. / I come from Xi'an, Shaanxi.
   我来自陕西西安。

## Task Dialogue 1

**Situation** ▶ Sam has just traveled around Europe, and he is talking with his best friend Lucy about his experience.

## Task Dialogue 2

**Situation** ▶ You are the manager of Personnel Department of a Travel Agency, and you are interviewing a new graduate.

## Part Two  Text A

### Tourism Industry

Tourism is a distinctly modern phenomenon. Historians have traced the emergence of tourism to industrial England, attributing its growth to the burgeoning of a "middle class" and the availability of inexpensive modes of transportation such as trains, automobiles and steamships. With the post-WW II establishment of commercial airlines and the subsequent development of jet aircraft, the sphere of tourism rapidly expanded to a global scale.

After so many years' development, the tourism is now viewed as one of the most important and fastest growing industries in this rapidly changing world, which generates more jobs and benefits more people than most other industries throughout all levels of local, national, regional and international economies.

There are quite a few reasons that contribute to its rapid development and reversibly it also benefits the society greatly.

First, tourism is a great source of tax revenue. Often the public is not aware of how much tax revenue the tourist industry generates. Every time a tourist buys a product and pays a sales tax, he (or she) is adding extra money to that city's or state's coffers with minimal use of city facilities. In communities where there is a motel or hotel or restaurant tax, this effect is even greater.

Second, this industry accounts for more than $3 trillion in global spending every year and employs about one out of every ten workers in the world. The World Travel and Tourism Council (WTTC) expects 119.5 million new jobs world wide between now and 2015. Therefore it has become one of the world's foremost economic activities.

Third, it stimulates enormous investment in infrastructure, most of which helps to improve the living conditions of local people as well as tourists. Most new tourism jobs and business are created in the developing countries, helping to equalize economic opportunities and keep rural residents from moving to overcrowded cities.

Fourth, tourism is a multi-faceted industry, which is supported by many other smaller industries such as accommodations, travel agencies, convention facilities, casinos, restaurants, libraries and education. Tourism also has an especially strong dependency on culture-based industries such as museums and arts, gaming, movies and cultural heritage resources. The way that tourism impacts on the community's economic well-being is by the amount of money it generates for a host of secondary or support industries. For example, tourists may contribute an extra 10% to a gas station's or restaurant's business. At times, this extra income may make the difference in that business showing a profit or a loss.

Fifth, a tourism industry with a cultural basis is expected to become the strongest industry in the region. A graft between tourism and cultural resources produces synergetic exchange of resources. Taking Republic of Korea (hereinafter referred to as Korea) for example, Korea's image abroad was improved by the 2002 World Cup and by its outstanding IT industry. These cultural and industrial factors are not only affecting tourism and cultural development, but also serving as an economic growth engine in other industries by upgrading brand value of Korean products. It is believed that a country's competitiveness can be determined by its cultural creativity and cultural infrastructure, which can be incorporated with tourism and other industries.

Another important reason for further developing tourism in a country is that there is a great need for leisure and cultural activities to improve the quality of life. The domestic tourism climate needs to be improved to match the increased incomes of the people and an increase of leisure time due to introduction of the five-day workweek. Tourism and cultural activities are directly related to quality of life, they are diversifying to fulfill tourist needs and they need rapid, continuous growth in the near future.

Last, the effect of multiplier effect is also a great contribution to the local economy. The multiplier effect is a concept, which has been borrowed from Economics, and used within the tourist industry. It is an effect in which an increase in spending produces an increase in national income and consumption greater than the initial amount spent. Simply stated, the multiplier effect signifies that every dollar spent by a tourist circulates in the community a number of additional times before it leaves the community. For example, if a tourist spends a dollar on an attraction, then part of that dollar pays an attendant's salary. The attendant then may use his portion of that same dollar to buy food at the local supermarket. There is no one magic number for how many times the multiplier effect works until the dollar leaves the community, however, common estimates range from 3 to 7 times.

As a result, tourism has been seen as the economic cornerstone of many communities around the world. While a thriving tourism industry can provide a better livelihood for local people, it should not, and cannot, be at the expense of the environment and local culture. Hence sustainable tourism is put forward in an aim to avoid the threats it poses. Sustainable tourism, in its purest sense, is an industry which attempts to make a low impact on the environment and local culture, while helping to generate income, employment, and the conservation of local ecosystems. It is responsible tourism that is both ecologically and culturally sensitive.

At the new millennium, tourism is firmly established as the number one industry in many countries and the fastest growing economic sector in terms of foreign exchange earnings and job creation. International tourism is the world's largest export earner and an important factor in the balance of payments of most nations. And as well intercultural awareness and personal friendships fostered through tourism has become a powerful force for improving international understanding and contributing to peace among all the nations of the world.

## New Words

**tourism** ['tuərizm] *n.* 旅行，旅游，观光

**distinctly** [di'stiŋktli] *ad.* 清楚地；明显地；截然不同地；独特地

**phenomenon** [fə'nɔminən] *n.* 现象

**emergence** [i'məːdʒəns] *n.* 出现

**convergence** [kən'vəːdʒəns] *n.* 会聚，集中

**burgeon** ['bəːdʒən] *vi.* （迅速）成长，发展

**availability** [ə,veilə'biliti] *n.* 可用性；有效性；实用性

**inexpensive** [,inik'spensiv] *a.* 便宜的，不贵的

**mode** [məud] *n.* 方式，模式；样式

**transportation** [,trænspɔː'teiʃən] *n.* 运输，运送

**establishment** [i'stæbliʃmənt] *n.* 建立，成立

**subsequent** ['sʌbsikwənt] *a.* 随后的，后来的；继起的

**sphere** [sfiə] *n.* 领域；范围

**expand** [ik'spænd] *vi.* 扩大

**global** ['gləubəl] *a.* 球形的；全球的，全世界的

**scale** [skeil] *n.* 范围；比例

**industry** ['indəstri] *n.* 工业；企业

**regional** ['riːdʒənl] *a.* 地区性的，地域性的

**reversibly** [ri'vəːsibli] *ad.* 可逆地

**benefit** ['benifit] *vt.* 有益于，有助于

**generate** ['dʒenəreit] *vt.* 产生，创造

**revenue** ['revənjuː] *n.* 国家的收入；税收

**coffer** ['kɔfə] *n.* 保险箱

**facility** [fə'siliti] *n.* （常作 facilities）设施，设备

**motel** [məu'tel] *n.* 汽车旅馆

**community** [kə'mjuːniti] *n.* 社区；团队

**employ** [im'plɔi] *vt.* 雇用；用，使用

**foremost** ['fɔːməust] *a.* 最重要的；主要的

**stimulate** ['stimjuleit] *vt.* 刺激，激励

**infrastructure** ['infrə,strʌktʃə] *n.* 基础设施，基础建设

**investment** [in'vestmənt] *n.* 投资

**equalize** ['iːkwəlaiz] *vt.* 使相等；补偿

**culture-based** ['kʌltʃə beist] *a.* 基于文化的

**museum** [mjuː'ziːəm] *n.* 博物馆，博物院

**multi-faceted** ['mʌlti 'fæsitid] *a.* 涉及多方面的

**catering** ['keitəriŋ] *n.* 公共饮食业

**entertainment** [,entə'teinmənt] *n.* 款待；娱乐；娱乐表演

**recreation** [,rekri'eiʃən] *n.* 消遣；娱乐

**accommodation** [əˌkɔmə'deiʃən] *n.* 膳宿

**casino** [kə'siːnəu] *n.* 娱乐场；赌场

**heritage** ['heritidʒ] *n.* 遗产；继承权；传统

**gaming** ['geimiŋ] *n.* 赌博；赌胜负

**well-being** [ˌwel'biːiŋ] *n.* 康乐，安宁；福利

**graft** [grɑːft] *n.* 嫁接；移植

**engine** ['endʒin] *n.* 发动机；机车，火车头

**upgrade** ['ʌpˌgreid] *vt.* 使升级；提升

**brand** [brænd] *n.* 商标，牌子

**creativity** [ˌkriːei'tivəti] *n.* 创造力；创造性

**synergetic** [sinə'dʒetik] *a.* 协同的，协作的；协同作用的

**incorporate** [in'kɔːpəreit] *vt.* 合并；一体化

**domestic** [də'mestik] *a.* 家庭的；国内的

**improve** [im'pruːv] *vt.* 改善，改进

**match** [mætʃ] *vt.* 匹配，相配

**diversify** [dai'vəːsifai] *vt.* 使多样化；变化

**signify** ['signifai] *vt.* 表示；意味

**fulfill** [ful'fil] *vt.* 履行；实现；完成（计划等）

**contribution** [ˌkɔntri'bjuːʃn] *n.* 贡献；捐献

**concept** ['kɔnsept] *n.* 观念；概念

**income** ['inkʌm] *n.* 收入，收益

**consumption** [kən'sʌmpʃən] *n.* 消费

**initial** [i'niʃəl] *a.* 最初的；词首的

**attendant** [ə'tendənt] *n.* 服务员

**tourist** ['tuərist] *n.* 旅行者，旅游者

**cornerstone** ['kɔːnəˌstəun] *n.* 基础；基石

**thrive** [θraiv] *vi.* 兴旺，繁荣

**livelihood** ['laivlihud] *n.* 生活，生计

**environment** [in'vairənmənt] *n.* 环境；外界

**employment** [im'plɔimənt] *n.* 雇用；工作；职业

**sustainable** [sə'steinəbl] *a.* 可持续发展的

**conservation** [ˌkɔnsə'veiʃən] *n.* 保护；保持；保存

**ecosystem** ['iːkəuˌsistəm] *n.* 生态系统

**ecologically** [ˌiːkə'lɔdʒikli] *ad.* 生态地

**sensitive** ['sensətiv] *a.* 敏感的；灵敏的

**millennium** [mi'leniəm] *n.* 一千年

**foster** ['fɔstə] *vt.* 养育，培植；促进

 # Phrases and Expressions

attribute... to...　归因于
view as　认为；把……看作是
contribute to　贡献
commercial airlines　商业航空公司

jet aircraft　喷气式飞机
account for　说明……的原因
be aware of　知道，明白；意识到
tax revenue　税收

| | |
|---|---|
| sales tax 销售税 | multiplier effect 乘法效应，倍增效应 |
| have dependency on 依靠；信赖 | local economy 地方经济 |
| a host of 一大群，许多 | at the expense of 以……为代价，在损害……的情况下 |
| cultural heritage resources 文化遗产资源 | attempt to do sth. 企图做某事，尝试做某事 |
| impact on 影响 | |
| gas station 加油站 | |
| be expected to 期待，盼望，指望；预期 | be established as 被确定为 |
| serve as 充当…… | in terms of 在……方面；根据，按照 |
| be determined by 由……决定 | balance of payments 贸易差额，国际收支，收支差额 |
| leisure time 空闲，空闲时间 | |
| due to 因为；由……引起 | intercultural awareness 跨文化意识 |
| be related to 与……相关的；与……有关系 | |

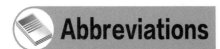

## Abbreviations

| | |
|---|---|
| WW Ⅱ (World War Two) 第二次世界大战 | IT (Information Technology) 信息技术 |
| WTTC (The World Travel and Tourism Council) 世界旅游业理事会 | |

## Notes

**1** Historians have traced the emergence of tourism to industrial England, attributing its growth to the burgeoning of a "middle class" and the availability of inexpensive modes of transportation...

　　本句中，trace... to... 的意思是"上溯，追溯到"。attributing its growth to... 为现在分词短语作原因状语。

**2** Its central goal is to work with governments to realize the full potential economic impact of the world's largest generator of wealth and jobs.

　　本句中，to work with governments 是一个动词不定式短语，作表语。动词不定式短语 to realize the full potential economic impact of the world's largest generator of wealth and jobs 作目的状语，修饰 to work with governments。

**3** ... it stimulates enormous investment in infrastructure, most of which helps to improve the living conditions of local people as well as tourists.

　　本句中，most of which helps to improve the living conditions of local people as well as tourists 是一个由 most of + 关系代词引导的定语从句，修饰先行词 infrastructure。as well as 表示"也、又"之意。

注意：most 也可换成其他名词或代词，如：many, some, a lot, all 等。如果先行词是物时，用 which；如果先行词是人时，用 whom。请看下例：

He has visited many places in the world, some of which are in Europe.

This travel agency has several tour guides, all of whom are dedicated.

**4** While a thriving tourism industry can provide a better livelihood for local people, it should not, and cannot, be at the expense of the environment and local culture.

本句中，while 为连词，意思是"虽然"。短语 at the expense of 意为"以……为代价，在损害……的情况下"。

**5** It is responsible tourism that is both ecologically and culturally sensitive.

本句是一个强调句型：It is + 所强调的部分 + that…。所强调的部分 responsible tourism 在句中作主语。

注意：在 It is + 所强调的部分 + that... 句型中，所强调的部分是主语时，该主语可以是人，也可以是物。是人时，既可以用 who 也可以用 that。但是，如果强调的是时间或地点时，则只能用 that，而不能用 when 或 where。

请看下例：

It was the manager of the travel agency that/who told them the news.

It was in China that they met for the first time.

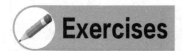 # Exercises

**EX. 1** **Answer the following questions.**

1. What has given the first push to the great development of tourism?

2. In what aspects has tourism made contributions to the society?

3. Could you explain "multiplier effect"?

4. What is sustainable tourism according to your understanding?

5. Please explain with examples how tourism benefits the economy of the city you are living in.

**EX. 2** **Write out the English words according to the definitions given below.**

| definitions | words |
|---|---|
| the business of providing services, such as transport, places to stay or entertainment, for people who are on holiday | |
| to take goods or people from one place to another | |
| the income that a government or a company receives regularly | |

(continued)

| definitions | words |
|---|---|
| a hotel by the side of a road, usually with spaces for cars next to each room | |
| the business of serving food | |
| a period of 1,000 years | |
| making or becoming larger | |
| world-wide | |
| the people living in one place, district or country, considered as a whole | |
| the way of using nature products so that no damage is caused to the environment | |

**EX. 3** **Complete the following sentences with appropriate words or expressions from the text.**

1. Tourism is a great source of tax _____.

2. Tourism employs about _____ out of every _____ workers in the world.

3. Tourism stimulates enormous investment in _____.

4. Tourism is a _____ industry, which is supported by many other smaller industries.

5. A tourism industry with a _____ is expected to become the strongest industry in the region.

6. One important reason for further developing tourism in a country is that there is a great need for leisure and cultural activities to improve _____.

7. _____ signifies that every dollar spent by a tourist circulates in the community a number of additional times before it leaves the community.

8. _____ is put forward in an aim to avoid the threats the tourism poses.

**EX. 4** **Translate the following sentences into Chinese.**

1. Historians have traced the emergence of tourism to industrial England, attributing its growth to the convergence of a burgeoning "middle class" and the availability of inexpensive modes of transportation such as trains, automobiles and steamships. With the post-WW II establishment of commercial airlines and the subsequent development of jet aircraft, the sphere of tourism rapidly expanded to a global scale.

2. The tourism industry accounts for more than $3 trillion in global spending every year and employs about one out of every ten workers in the world.

3. A tourism industry with a cultural basis is expected to become the strongest industry in the region.

4. Sustainable tourism，in its purest sense, is an industry which attempts to make a low impact on the environment and local culture, while helping to generate income, employment, and the conservation of local ecosystems.

5. At the start of the new millennium, tourism is firmly established as the number one industry in many countries and the fastest growing economic sector in terms of foreign exchange earnings and job creation.

## Part Three  Text B

## Tourism in China

China is a vast land, rich in tourism resources. It comes out in front in the world in scenic spots and historical sites, spectacular landscapes, and colorful and varied national customs. At present, there are two major tour routes in China: One is the "S"-shaped traditional tour route, containing famous political and cultural cities such as Beijing, Xi'an, Shanghai, Suzhou and Hangzhou; the other one is the crescent-shaped tour route containing coastal open regions, such as the Liaodong and Shandong peninsulas and the Yangtze and Pearl River deltas.

Following the "S"-shaped tour route, tourists may climb the Badaling Great Wall and visit the Imperial Palace and Temple of Heaven in Beijing, and view the Terra Cotta Warriors and Horses excavated from the Mausoleum of the First Qin Emperor, the Stele Forest and the Great Wild Goose Pagoda in Xi'an, wander along the bustling Bund and Nanjing Road and through the Pudong New Zone in Shanghai, enjoy Suzhou's gardens and the sights of the West Lake in Hangzhou. Following the crescent-shaped tour route, visitors may get some idea of the enormous changes which have taken place in the open coastal cities since the initiation of reform and opening to the outside world, and appreciate the charming seaside areas in North and South China. Moreover, the coastal towns all have holiday villages and various recreation facilities.

With so many attractions, China is sure one of the most attractive tourism attractions in the world. Furthermore China has tried hard to develop this industry and attract tourists.

Ever since the policy of opening and reform was adopted in 1978, the tourism industry in China, thanks to the great importance attached by the governments at various levels, has become a new but most dynamic and potentially strong factor in the tertiary industry. It has been serving as a new growth point in China's national economy. And in many parts of the country, tourism has been regarded as a pillar, superior or priority industry in bringing up the local economic development. The position of tourism in the national economy continues to be enhanced and upgraded.

From January 2015 to June 2015, China reported 123.6 million tourist arrivals from overseas. Major sources of tourists include Korea, the Philippines, Indonesia, Thailand, Malaysia,

Mongolia, Singapore, Japan, Australia, Great Britain, the United States and Canada.

Meanwhile, the number of Chinese tourists traveling abroad will continue to record double-digit growth, with Australia, New Zealand, Korea and Japan among the most attractive destinations. At the end of 2015, about 140 million people have travelled around the world.

As China integrates with the global economy, its tourism industry is expected to continue to boom in the next five years. It is forecasted that China's tourism industry will still develop with an annual growth rate of about 10 percent. Moreover the sustained growth in China's gross domestic product is expected to further stimulate the growth of the tourism industry, and the number of domestic tourists is expected to increase by about 5 percent annually in the next few years.

Accordingly the booming tourism industry has played a vital role in increasing consumption, reducing poverty and creating job opportunities.

The World Tourism Organization predicts that by 2020, China will be the largest travel destination and the fourth largest source country, overtaking traditional destinations such as France, Spain and the United States.

In that year, there will be 137.10 million international travelers to the country, making up 8.6% of the global share, and 100 million outbound Chinese visitors, taking 6.2% of the worldwide outbound visitors.

In the next few years, China will develop various tourism products including ecological ones and leisure ones to satisfy the soaring international markets. Moreover Chinese government is already paying attention to ecological sustainable development and protecting the environment. They vow to combine the cultural heritage with the modern society.

 **New Words**

**spectacular** [spek'tækjulə] *a.* 壮观的；引人注目的

**landscape** ['lænd,skeip] *n.* 风景；山水画；地形

**custom** ['kʌstəm] *n.* 风俗；习惯

**crescent-shaped** ['krezntʃeipt] *a.* 新月形的

**coastal** ['kəustl] *a.* 沿海的；海岸的

**delta** ['deltə] *n.* 三角洲

**excavate** ['ekskəveit] *vt.* 挖掘

**mausoleum** [,mɔːsə'liːəm] *n.* 陵墓

**bustling** ['bʌsliŋ] *a.* 熙熙攘攘的；忙碌的

**bund** [bʌnd] *n.* 堤岸；码头

**initiation** [i,niʃi'eiʃən] *n.* 开始，启动

**dynamic** [dai'næmik] *a.* 有活力的，精力充沛的

**potentially** [pə'tenʃəli] *ad.* 潜在地

**pillar** ['pilə] *n.* 支柱，柱子

**superior** [su'piəriə] *a.* 较高的；较好的，出众的

**priority** [prai'ɔrəti] *n.* 优先；优先权

**enhance** [in'hɑːns] *vt.* 增加；提高

**Philippines** [,filə'piːnz] *n.* 菲律宾

**Indonesia** [,indəu'niːzjə] *n.* 印度尼西亚

| | |
|---|---|
| **Thailand** ['tailænd] *n.* 泰国 | **boom** [buːm] *vi.* 繁荣，兴隆 |
| **Malaysia** [məˈleiʒə] *n.* 马来西亚 | **forecast** [ˈfɔːkɑːst] *vt.* 预测，预报 |
| **Mongolia** [mɔŋˈɡəuliə] *n.* 蒙古 | **sustained** [səˈsteind] *a.* 持续不变的 |
| **Singapore** [ˌsiŋɡəˈpɔː] *n.* 新加坡 | **overtake** [ˌəuvəˈteik] *vt.* 赶上；追上 |
| **double-digit** [ˈdʌbl ˈdidʒit] *a.* 两位数的 | **ecological** [ˌiːkəˈlɔdʒikl] *a.* 生态的 |
| **integrate** [ˈintiˌgreit] *vt.* 使成整体，使一体化 | **vow** [vau] *vi.* 发誓，立誓 |
| | **combine** [kəmˈbain] *vt.* 联结；结合 |

 # Phrases and Expressions

| | |
|---|---|
| scenic spot　风景点 | the Stele Forest　碑林 |
| Imperial Palace　故宫 | the Great Wild Goose Pagoda　大雁塔 |
| Temple of Heaven　天坛 | tertiary industry　第三产业 |
| the Terra Cotta Warriors and Horses　兵马俑 | gross domestic product　国内生产总值 |

## Notes

**1** Following the "S"-shaped tour route, tourists may climb the Badaling Great Wall and visit the Imperial Palace...

　　本句中，Following the "S"-shaped tour route 是现在分词短语作方式状语，其逻辑主语为主句的主语 tourists。

**2** Ever since the policy of opening and reform was adopted in 1978, the tourism industry in China, thanks to the great importance attached by the governments at various levels, has become a new but most dynamic and potentially strong factor in the tertiary industry.

　　本句中，tourism industry... has become a... factor... 是句子主干。ever since 意思是"从那时起，自那时以来"，引导了一个时间状语。thanks to the great importance attached by the governments at various levels 是原因状语。thanks to 的意思是"由于，多亏"。

**3** Meanwhile, the number of Chinese tourists traveling abroad will continue to record double-digit growth, with Australia, New Zealand, Korea and Japan among the most attractive destinations.

　　本句中，traveling abroad 为现在分词短语作定语，修饰 tourists。with 引导的介词短语作补足语。

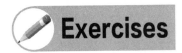 **Exercises**

**EX. 5** **Answer the following questions.**

1. What are the two major tour routes in China? And what does each route contain?

2. What was the condition of foreign tourists to China in 2015?

3. According to estimation, will China's tourism industry be prosperous in the next five years?

4. Is there a possibility that one day China become one of the world's leading tourism destinations?

5. What is China's plan to further develop the tourism industry?

**EX. 6** **Decide whether the following statements are *true* or *false*.**

1. There are two major tour routes in China. One is the "S"-shaped traditional tour route; the other is the crescent-shaped tour route.

2. Following the crescent-shaped tour route, visitors may view the Terra Cotta Warriors and Horses, the Stele Forest and the Great Wild Goose Pagoda in Xi'an.

3. Ever since the policy of opening and reform was adopted in 1978, the tourism industry in China has become a new but most dynamic and potentially strong factor in the tertiary industry.

4. The number of Chinese tourists traveling abroad will fall down in the coming years.

5. The sustained growth in China's gross domestic product is expected to further stimulate the growth of the tourism industry.

6. Chinese government is aiming at developing tourism industry without considering ecological sustainable development and protecting the environment.

# **Part Four** **Skill Training**

## **Forms**

The following is an online ENQUIRY FORM from a travel and tourism website—*Yes Tourism* (http://www.yes-tourism.com). If you want to consult some tourism information, you can fill in this form and send it online. You will get a very prompt response.

### ENQUIRY FORM

**Please complete the relevant sections of the Enquiry Form as fully as possible and press the "*Submit*" button to transmit your enquiry.**

| NUMBER OF GUESTS: | ☐ adults<br><br>☐ children (under 12 years)<br><br>☐ infants (up to 2 years) |
|---|---|
| DATE OF - ARRIVAL:<br>DATE OF - DEPARTURE: | 01 ▼ January ▼ 2003 ▼<br><br>01 ▼ January ▼ 2003 ▼ |
| ACCOMMODATION: | Please complete if enquiring about **Accommodation**<br>please complete<br><br>type ... ▼ type of accommodation<br><br>featured ... ▼<br>featured properties, else...<br><br>☐ other named hotel/villa, etc. |
| | rate ... ▼ room/villa rate, per night<br><br>basis ... ▼ room basis/meal plan<br><br>☐ Air-Conditioned<br>☐ Fan<br>☐ Cable/Satellite TV<br>☐ Swimming Pool<br>☐ Close to Beach<br><br>☐ Preferred Location |
| **TOURS:** | Please complete if this is a **Tour** enquiry.<br>☐ Safari Tour ☐ Culture & Market<br>☐ Rain Forest ☐ Around the Island<br>☐ Little Tobago ☐ Trinidad Excursion<br>☐ Union Island |
| **REMARKS:** | Other remarks, comments, questions, requests or information<br><br>☐ |
| **Your Name:**<br>**Your E-mail Address:** | Please provide you name and E-mail address for our reply.<br><br>☐<br>☐ |

Submit Form   Reset Form

### Essential Parts of Business Letter

Every well-constructed business letter is made up of six essential parts, namely the heading, the inside address, salutation, the body of the letter, the complimentary close, and the signature. See the example below:

|  |  |
|---|---|
|  | June 18, 2015 |
| (1) Heading | Mr. Zhang Wei |
|  | 105 Xichang'an Ave. |
|  | Xi'an 727000, China. |
| (2) Inside address | Mr. Karl Bruce |
|  | Deputy Director |
|  | Dept. of North America and South Pacific |
|  | Youth International Travel Service |
|  | 1088-1090 East Georgia Avenue |
|  | Vancouver B.C. |
|  | Canada V6E 3K5 |
|  | Tel. (604) 688-8341 |
| (3) Salutation | Dear Mr. Karl Bruce: |
| (4) Body | Would you please proceed with land arrangements in Canada for the group, according to the itinerary enclosed and the following items: |
|  | Members: Eighteen (18) paying members and one free tour conductor. |
|  | Rooms required: Nine (9) double rooms and one single room, each with a private bath. |
|  | Hotels: Holiday Inn |
|  | TR./SS: By an air-conditioned motor-coach for transfers and sightseeing. |
|  | Meals: As given in the itinerary. |
|  | Airport tax: Not included |
|  | We look forward to receiving your confirmation for the group at your earliest convenience. |
| (5) Complimentary close | Yours truly |
| (6) Signature | Zhang Wei |
|  | Manager |

👥 **Simulate and create** ▶ Draft a letter using content that you are most familiar with. Be sure your letter contains all the six essential parts.

# Part Five　Related Information

| Text | Notes |
|---|---|
| **The World Tourism Organization** | |

The World Tourism Organization[1] had its beginnings as the International Congress of Official Tourist Traffic Associations set up in 1925 in The Hague. It was renamed the International Union of Official Travel Organizations (IUOTO)[2] after World War Ⅱ and moved to Geneva. IUOTO was a technical, non-governmental organization, whose membership at its peak included 109 National Tourist Organizations (NTO) and 88 Associate Members, among them private and public groups.

[1] 世界旅游组织

[2] 官方旅行组织国际联盟

As tourism grew and became an integral part of the fabric of modern life, its international dimension increased and national governments started to play an increasingly important role—their activities covering the whole spectrum from infrastructure to regulations[3]. By the mid-1960s, it became clear that there was a need for more effective tools to keep developments under review and to provide tourism with intergovernmental[4] machinery especially equipped to deal with the movement of persons, tourism policies and tourism's impacts.

[3] 规定，规章

[4] 政府间的

In 1967, the members of IUOTO called for its transformation into an intergovernmental body empowered to deal on a worldwide basis with all matters concerning tourism and to cooperate[5] with other competent organizations, particularly those of the United Nations' system, such as the World Health Organization (WHO)[6], UNESCO[7], and the International Civil Aviation Organization (ICAO)[8].

[5] 合作

[6] 世界卫生组织
[7] 联合国教科文组织
[8] 国际民航组织

A resolution to the same effect was passed in December 1969 by the UN General Assembly, which recognized the decisive and central role the transformed IUOTO should play in the field of world tourism in cooperation with the existing machinery within the UN. Following this resolution, the WTO's Statutes were ratified in 1974 by the States whose official tourist organizations were members of IUOTO.

Thus IUOTO became the World Tourism Organization (WTO) and its first General Assembly[9] was held in Madrid[10] in May 1975. The Secretariat[11] was installed in Madrid early the following year at the invitation of the Spanish Government, which provides a building for the Headquarters.

[9] 代表大会
[10] 马德里（西班牙首都）
[11] 秘书处

| | |
|---|---|
| In 1976, WTO became an executing agency of the United Nations Development Program (UNDP)[12] and in 1977, a formal cooperation agreement was signed with the United Nations[13] itself. In 2003, the WTO was converted into a specialized agency of the United Nations and so even reaffirmed its leading role in international tourism. | [12] 联合国开发计划署<br><br>[13] 联合国 |
| Since its early years, WTO's membership and influence in world tourism have continued to grow. By 2003, its membership included 141 countries, seven territories[14] and some 350 Affiliate Members, representing the private sector, educational institutions, tourism associations and local tourism authorities. | [14] 地域 |
| **World Tourism Day** | |
| Since 1980, Members of the World Tourism Organization have been celebrating World Tourism Day[15] every year on September 27. Events include parades, concerts, tourism fairs, seminars, dinners, dances, and free entrance to museums—anything and everything that draws attention to the important role that tourism plays in the local community. | [15] 世界旅游日 |

# Part Six  Guide to World Famous Sight

| Text | Notes |
|---|---|
| **The Forbidden City** | |
| Lying at the center of Beijing, the Forbidden City[1], called GuGong in Chinese, was the imperial palace during the Ming and Qing dynasties. Now known as the Palace Museum[2], it is to the north of Tian'an Men Square[3]. Rectangular[4] in shape, it is the world's largest palace complex and covers 74 hectares. Surrounded by a six-meter deep moat[5] and a ten-meter high wall are 9,999 buildings. The wall has a gate on each side. Opposite the Tian'an Men Gate, to the north is the Gate of Devine Might (Shenwu Men), which faces Jingshan Park. The distance between these two gates is 960 meters, while the distance between the gates in the east and west is 750 meters. There are unique and delicately[6] structured towers on each of the four corners of the curtain wall. These afford views over both the palace and the city outside. | [1] 紫禁城<br><br>[2] 故宫<br>[3] 天安门广场<br>[4] 矩形<br>[5] 护城河<br><br><br>[6] 优美地 |

The Forbidden City is divided into two parts. The southern section or the Outer Court was where the emperor[7] exercised his supreme power over the nation. The northern section or the Inner Court was where he lived with his royal family. Until 1924 when the last emperor of China was driven from the Inner Court, fourteen emperors of the Ming dynasty and ten emperors of the Qing dynasty had reigned[8] here. Having been the imperial palace for some five centuries, it houses numerous rare treasures and curiosities.

Listed by UNESCO as a World Cultural Heritage Site[9] in 1987, the Palace Museum is now one of the most popular tourist attractions worldwide.

[7] 皇帝

[8] 统治

[9] 世界文化遗址

# Preparations Before Tour

**Dialogues**

**Sample Dialogue 1**

👤 **Situation** ▶ Bill is asking his friend, Celia to spend the coming weekend with him and they are discussing their holiday plan.

**Bill**: Hi, Celia, would you like to do something with me this weekend?
**Celia**: Sure. What shall we do?
**Bill**: I don't know. Do you have any ideas?
**Celia**: Why don't we go traveling?
**Bill**: That sounds good to me. Where shall we go?
**Celia**: Let's go to the Great Wall.
**Bill**: I'd rather not. I have been there before. How about going to the Summer Palace? I hear it's a wonderful place.
**Celia**: OK. Let's go to see it. When shall we depart?
**Bill**: How about eight o' clock on Saturday morning?
**Celia**: Great! I'll meet you then at the station.

**Sample Dialogue 2**

👤 **Situation** ▶ Ken Beare is enquiring about traveling to China after seeing the advertisement of a travel agency.

**Ken**: Hello, this is Ken Beare. May I speak to Ms Sunshine, please?
**Office clerk**: Hold the line a moment. I'll check if she is in her office.

| | | |
|---|---|---|
| **Ken**: | Thank you. | |
| **Office clerk**: | (after a moment) Yes. Ms Sunshine is in. I'll put you through. | |
| **Ms Sunshine**: | Hello, this is Ms Sunshine. Can I help you? | |
| **Ken**: | Hello, my name is Ken Beare and I'm calling to enquire about traveling to China. Can you arrange for this? | |
| **Ms Sunshine**: | Yes. We have been doing this for many years. | |
| **Ken**: | Well. I'd like to go to your company for some details. | |
| **Ms Sunshine**: | Welcome. Shall I wait for you here? | |
| **Ken**: | Yes, please. I'm coming soon. | |
| **Ms Sunshine**: | See you then. | |
| **Ken**: | Bye. | |

## Useful Expressions

1. Would you like to go to China with me this summer vocation?

   今年暑假和我一起去中国怎么样？

2. Let's go to Tibet for a change.

   我们换换花样去西藏吧。

3. Why don't we go to Paris?

   我们为什么不去巴黎呢？

4. How about/What about going to Tokyo?

   去东京怎么样？

5. May/Can/Could I speak to Miss Lee?

   请李小姐接一下电话好吗？

6. I'm calling from New York.

   我是从纽约打电话的。

7. Hold the line, please.

   请不要挂断。

8. Can you put me through to this number?

   你能给我接通这个电话号码吗？

9. Who's calling?

   是哪位？

## Task Dialogue 1

**Situation** ▶ The summer vocation is around the corner. Martin wants to travel in Tibet and he also wants his girlfriend Lucy to go with him together. Now he is talking about this with Lucy.

## Task Dialogue 2

**Situation** ▶ Kevin is traveling in Paris, France, and now he is making a phone call to his best friend Jack about his wonderful experience there.

## Part Two  Text A

### Prepare for a Tour

Whether you are traveling overseas for business, pleasure or study, the best way to ensure a carefree and relaxing trip is to prevent problems before they happen. The more you learn about passports, visas, customs, immunizations, and other travel basics, the less likely you are to have difficulties during your travel.

Before you go, there is much that you can do to prepare for your trip abroad:

*Learn About the Countries That You Plan to Visit*

Read as much as possible about the countries in which you plan to travel. Informing yourself about a nation's history, culture, customs and politics will make your stay more meaningful. Such information can be found in most libraries, bookstores and tourist bureaus. Although English is spoken in many countries, it is a good idea to learn what you can of the language of the country in which you will travel.

Travel agents can provide brochures and tourist information about the countries that you wish to visit. Foreign embassies or consulates also can offer up-to-date information on their countries.

*Get the Required Documents*

Travel document requirements vary from country to country, but you will need the following: a passport or other proof of citizenship, plus a visa or a tourist card, if required by the country or countries that you will visit. Sometimes you may also need evidence that you have enough money for your trip and/or have ongoing or return transportation tickets.

Your passport is the most valuable document that you will carry abroad. It confirms your citizenship. Please guard it carefully. Do not use it as collateral for a loan or lend it to anyone. It is your best form of identification. You will need it when you pick up mail or check into hotels, embassies or consulates. A citizen needs a passport to depart or enter his country and to enter and depart most foreign countries.

Certain countries will not permit you to enter and will not place a visa in your passport, if the remaining validity is less than six months.

A visa is an endorsement or stamp placed in your passport by a foreign government that permits you to visit that country for a specified purpose and a limited time, for example, a 3-month tourist visa. It is advisable to obtain visas before you leave your country because you may not be able to obtain visas for some countries once you have departed. You should apply directly to the embassy or nearest consulate of each country that you plan to visit, or consult a travel agent.

If the country that you plan to visit requires a tourist card, you can usually obtain one from the country's embassy or consulate, from an airline serving the country, or at the port of entry. There is a fee for some tourist cards.

### Ensure Your Immunizations

Under international health regulations adopted by the World Health Organization, a country may require international certificates of vaccination against yellow fever and cholera. Typhoid vaccinations are not required for international travel, but are recommended for areas where there is risk of exposure. Smallpox vaccinations are no longer given. Check your health care records to ensure that your measles, mumps, rubella, polio, diphtheria, tetanus, and pertussis immunizations are up-to-date. Medication to deter malaria and other preventative measures are advisable for certain areas.

### Change Foreign Currency

Before departing, you may wish to purchase small amounts of foreign currency to use for buses, taxis, phones, or tips when you first arrive. Foreign exchange facilities at airports may be closed when your flight arrives, so it will be better if you do it beforehand.

Some countries regulate the amount of local currency that you can bring into or take out of the country; others require that you exchange a minimum amount of currency. For currency regulations, check with a bank, a foreign exchange firm, your travel agent, or the embassy or consulate of the countries that you plan to visit.

Local banks usually offer better rates of exchange than hotels, restaurants, or stores. Rates are often posted in windows. Above all, avoid private currency transactions. In some countries, you risk more than being swindled or stuck with counterfeit currency—you risk arrest. Avoid the black market. Learn and obey the local currency laws, wherever you go.

### Take Traveler's Checks or Credit Cards Instead of Large Amounts of Cash

It is wise not to carry large amounts of cash. You should take most of your money in traveler's checks and remember to record the serial number, denomination and the date and location of the issuing bank or agency. Keep this information in a safe and separate place. If you lose your traveler's checks, you can quickly get replacements.

Some credit cards can be used worldwide, even for cash advances. Keep track of your credit card purchases so that you do not exceed your limit. Travelers have been arrested overseas for mistakenly exceeding their credit limit! Leave all unnecessary credit cards at home. Record the numbers of the credit cards that you do bring, and keep the list separately from the cards. Before leaving on your trip, you may wish to check with your bank to see if the country or countries that you plan to visit have Automated Teller Machine (ATM) service. The bank should be able to tell you if you can use your ATM card during your trip abroad or not.

### Try to Make Lodging Reservations in Advance

Many travelers wait until they reach their destination before making hotel reservations. Some train stations and airports have travel desks to assist you in finding lodging. However, when you arrive, you may be tired and unfamiliar with your surroundings, and could have difficulty locating a hotel to suit your needs. Therefore, when possible, reserve your lodging in advance and confirm your reservations along the way. During peak tourist season, it is important to have a hotel reservation for at least the first night that you arrive in a foreign city.

### Customs and Customs Pre-registration

Customs is a mandatory element in the movement of goods across borders. It is important that you learn about the customs of the country you go and your own country. You should know what articles (and what quantities of that) you can take across a border without paying customs duty. Keep all receipts for items you buy overseas. They will be helpful in making your Customs declaration when you return.

It is a good idea to be informed about the Customs regulations of your own country. Foreign-made personal articles taken abroad are subject to Customs duty and tax upon your return, unless you have proof of prior possession such as a receipt, bill of sale, an insurance policy, or a jeweler's appraisal. If you do not have proof of prior possession, items such as foreign-made watches, cameras, or tape recorders that can be identified by serial number or permanent markings, may be taken to the Customs office nearest you, or to the port of departure for registration, before you depart your country. The certificate of registration provided can expedite free entry of these items when you return to your country.

 **New Words**

| | |
|---|---|
| **passport** ['pɑ:spɔ:t] *n.* 护照 | **embassy** ['embəsi] *n.* 大使馆；使馆官员 |
| **visa** ['vi:zə] *n.* 签证 | **consulate** ['kɔnsjulət] *n.* 领事馆 |
| **immunization** [,imjunai'zeiʃən] *n.* 免疫 | **vary** ['vɛəri] *vi.* 变化；不同 |
| **customs** ['kʌstəmz] *n.* 关税；海关 | **confirm** [kən'fə:m] *vt.* 确定，确认 |
| **bureau** ['bjuərəu] *n.* 局；办事处 | **collateral** [kə'lætərəl] *n.* 抵押品，担保物 |
| **brochure** ['brəuʃə] *n.* 小册子 | |

**identification** [ai,dentifi'keiʃən] *n.* 身份证明

**validity** [və'lidəti] *n.* 有效性；合法性

**endorsement** [in'dɔːsmənt] *n.* 背书，签署文件；认可

**obtain** [əb'tein] *vt.* 得到，获得

**certificate** [sə'tifikət] *n.* 证书

**vaccination** [,væksi'neiʃən] *n.* 接种疫苗

**cholera** ['kɔlərə] *n.* 霍乱

**typhoid** ['taifɔid] *n.* 伤寒症，伤寒

**smallpox** ['smɔːl,pɔks] *n.* 天花

**measles** ['miːzlz] *n.* 麻疹

**mumps** [mʌmps] *n.* 腮腺炎

**rubella** [ruː'belə] *n.* 风疹

**polio** ['pəuliəu] *n.* 脊髓灰质炎；小儿麻痹症

**diphtheria** [dip'θiəriə] *n.* 白喉

**tetanus** ['tetənəs] *n.* 破伤风

**pertussis** [pə'tʌsis] *n.* 百日咳

**medication** [,medi'keiʃən] *n.* 药物治疗；药物

**deter** [di'təː] *vt.* 阻止，防止

**malaria** [mə'lɛəriə] *n.* 疟疾

**tip** [tip] *n.* 小费

**currency** ['kʌrənsi] *n.* 货币

**transaction** [træn'zækʃən] *n.* 交易；办理

**swindle** ['swindl] *vt.* 诈骗

**counterfeit** ['kauntəfit] *a.* 伪造的，假冒的

**arrest** [ə'rest] *n.* 逮捕，拘留

**denomination** [di,nɔmi'neiʃən] *n.* 面额，票面金额

**advance** [əd'vɑːns] *n.* 预付，预支

**exceed** [ik'siːd] *vt.* 超过，超出

**lodging** ['lɔdʒiŋ] *n.* 住宿

**reservation** [,rezə'veiʃən] *n.* 预订

**registration** [,redʒi'streiʃən] *n.* 注册；登记

**mandatory** ['mændətəri] *n.* 法定的；强制的

**prior** ['praiə] *a.* 预先的；在前的

**receipt** [ri'siːt] *n.* 收据，收条

**appraisal** [ə'preizəl] *n.* 评估证明；鉴定书

**permanent** ['pəːmənənt] *a.* 永久的，持久的

**marking** ['mɑːkiŋ] *n.* 记号，标识

**expedite** ['ekspədait] *vt.* 促进，加速

 # Phrases and Expressions

up-to-date 最近的，最新的
World Health Organization 世界卫生组织
yellow fever 黄热病
rate of exchange 兑换率
traveler's check 旅行支票

credit card 信用卡
keep track of 保持联系；明了
in advance 提前
be subject to 未独立的，受制于……的
bill of sale 抵押证券

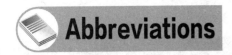

## Abbreviations

ATM (Automated Teller Machine) 自动取款机

## Notes

**1** The more you learn about passports, visas, customs, immunizations, and other travel basics, the less likely you are to have difficulties during your travels.

"The + 形容词比较级，the + 形容词比较级，"表示"越……越……"之意。本句意为你对护照、签证、关税、免疫及其他旅游基本知识了解得越多，在旅行中你遇到困难的可能性将越小。又如：

The angrier he became, the more she laughed at him.

他越生气，她就越是嘲笑他。

**2** You should apply directly to the embassy or nearest consulate of each country that you plan to visit...

本句中，that 引导的定语从句修饰先行词 country。apply to 的意思是"向……申请"。

I want to apply to that company for the job.

我想向那家公司申请这份工作。

**3** In some countries, you risk more than being swindled or stuck with counterfeit currency.

本句中，risk 意思是"冒……之险"，后接动名词作宾语。又如：

He risked losing his life when he saved the child from the fire.

他冒着生命危险把孩子从火中救出。

**4** Many travelers wait until they reach their destination before making hotel reservations.

本句中 until 和 before 搭配起来使用，可理解为"直到……才"，本句可翻译为：许多旅游者等到了目的地才订房间。又如：

He waited until the volcano became quiet before returning home.

他一直等到火山平息下来才回家。

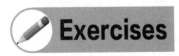

## Exercises

**EX. 1** **Answer the following questions.**

1. To travel abroad, what documents does a person need?

2. Can you bring into or take out of a country the local currency as much as you wish?

3. What diseases may a country require international certificates of vaccination against?

4. Why is it wise to reserve lodging in advance?

**EX. 2** Write out the English words according to the definitions given below.

| definitions | words |
|---|---|
| protection given against particular disease by introducing special substances into the body, esp. using an injection | |
| money paid to the government when you take particular articles from one country to another | |
| the group of people who represent their country in a foreign country, or the building they work in | |
| a small amount of money given to someone who has provided you with a service, in addition to the official payment and for their personal use | |
| the money in use in a particular country in a particular time | |
| the proof of receiving money or goods | |
| stamp or signature put on a passport to show that it has been examined and approved by the officials of a foreign country which the owner intends to visit | |
| to seize (sb.) by the authority of the law | |
| to secure possession of, or the right to use, e.g. by advance payment | |
| going on for a long time; intended to last | |

**EX. 3** Complete the following sentences with appropriate words or expressions from the text.

1. Your _____ is the most valuable document that you will carry abroad. It confirms your citizenship.

2. A _____ is an endorsement or stamp placed in your passport by a foreign government that permits you to visit that country for a specified purpose and a limited time.

3. Certain countries will not permit you to enter and will not place a visa in your passport, if the remaining validity is less than _____ months.

4. Concerning foreign currency changing, local banks usually offer better _____ than hotels, restaurants, or stores.

5. It is wise not to carry large amounts of cash. You should take most of your money in _____.

**EX. 4** Translate the following sentences into Chinese.

1. Under international health regulations adopted by the World Health Organization, a country may require international certificates of vaccination against yellow fever and cholera. Typhoid vaccinations are not required for international travel, but are recommended for areas where there is risk of exposure.

2. Local banks usually offer better rates of exchange than hotels, restaurants, or stores. Rates are often posted in windows. Above all, avoid private currency transactions. In some countries, you risk more than being swindled or stuck with counterfeit currency—you risk arrest.

3. Foreign-made personal articles taken abroad are subject to Customs duty and tax upon your return, unless you have proof of prior possession such as a receipt, bill of sale, an insurance policy, or a jeweler's appraisal.

## Part Three  Text B

## A Guide to China Tour

### *Procedures and Visa*

According to the Law of the People's Republic of China concerning the Administration of Foreigners Entering and Leaving the Country, foreign tourists must apply for visas at China's foreign affairs offices, consulates or other organizations authorized by the Ministry of Foreign Affairs. A group of five tourists or more can apply for a group tourist visa. This is usually handled by a travel agency organizing groups. People coming to China from countries which have visa agreements with China (such as agreements which exempt tourist groups from visas) are treated in accordance with these agreements.

If you want to go to Tibet for a visit, you can apply for a visa only with the consent of the Tourism Administration of the Tibet Autonomous Region or any one of its foreign representative offices. A passport is required for visa application; the passport shall be valid for at least six months beyond the duration of the tour.

For Canadian and US passport holders, visa is not required for Hong Kong of China if your stay is less than 90 days as a tourist. For other passport holders, please consult with your nearest PRC embassy or consulate.

### *Customs Regulations*

*Entry*

Tourists must fill out a baggage declaration form (in two copies) and hand it in to customs, retaining the carbon to show upon exit.

Personal belongings will be admitted duty free, including food, two bottles of liquor and two cartons of cigarettes. Wristwatches, radios, tape recorders, cameras, movie cameras, and similar items may be brought in for personal use but cannot be sold or transferred to others and must be brought out of China.

Gifts for relatives or friends in China, or articles carried on behalf of other, must also be

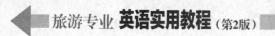

declared.

Visitors can bring in an unlimited amount of foreign currency and Chinese Renminbi (RMB) traveler's checks, and the unspent portion can be taken out.

*Exit*

On leaving China, tourists must again submit the baggage declaration form for customs inspection (the second copy). Travelers by ship are exempted.

Items purchased in China with RMB converted from foreign currencies may be taken out or mailed out of the country after receipts are presented for customs inspection. In cities where a Customs Office does not exit, this can be arranged through the local Friendship Store.

### Quarantine & Immunizations

Those who carry such special articles as microorganisms, human body tissues, biological products, and blood and its products, should declare to a quarantine department, and subject these articles to quarantine inspections.

Passengers from yellow fever-infested areas should, when entering China, display to the quarantine department effective certificates showing that they have been inoculated against yellow fever. He who does not have such a valid certificate shall be retained for observation for six days beginning from the day he left the infested area, or he shall be inoculated and retained until the certificate comes into effect. It is the task of the Chinese quarantine authorities to prevent foreigners suffering AIDS, venereal diseases, leprosy, mental diseases and open tuberculosis from entering China.

### Currency

The Chinese currency is called Renminbi, and is issued by the People's Bank of China. The abbreviation for Chinese currency is RMB. Many hotels and stores accept major credit cards. At present, the following credit cards can be used in China: Master Card, Visa Card, American Express, JCB, Diners Card. Holders of these cards can draw cash from the Bank of China, buy goods and pay for purchases at exchange centers of the Bank of China, appointed shops, hotels and restaurants.

For the convenience of tourists, the Bank of China can cash travelers' checks sold by international commercial banks and travelers' check companies in the United States, Canada, Australia, Japan, Britain, France, Switzerland, Germany and other countries and regions. Also the Bank of China sells travelers' checks for such banks as American Express, Citibank, Travelex, Sumitomo Bank of Japan, the Swiss Banking Corporation and others.

### Foreign Exchange

Foreign currency cannot be circulated within the People's Republic of China or used to determine the price and settle accounts. At present, China will accept and convert into Chinese Renminbi such foreign currencies as the US dollar, British pound, Euro, Japanese yen, Australian dollar, Austrian schilling, Belgian franc, Canadian dollar, Swiss franc, Danish Krone, Singapore dollar, Malaysian ringgit, Italian lira, and Finnish markka. Exchange rates are issued every day by the State Administration of Exchange Control. Before leaving China, unused Chinese Renminbi can be converted back into foreign currency with a "foreign exchange certificate" which is valid for six months.

## Climate

China has a continental and seasonal climate. Most parts are in the temperate zone but southern areas are in the tropical or subtropical zone while northern areas are in the frigid zone. Climates in different areas are complicated. For instance, northern Heilongjiang Province has a winter climate the year round without summer, while Hainan Province has a summer climate the year round without winter.

China can be visited throughout the year because of the stretch of its territories and sites and activities it can offer. Deciding when to visit China depends on which places you wish to visit, what type of weather you enjoy, and how much a bargain you want. China is a huge country with many different climates and types of landscape. Traveling along the Golden Route (Beijing, Xi'an, Shanghai, Guilin) is like visiting New York, Chicago, Santa Fe, and Jacksonville, Florida all in one trip.

April, May, September and October are the peak tourist months at China's most popular destinations when the weather is the most comfortable. Prices drop a bit in the shoulder season, which runs from November through March and from June through August. However, the winter months are peak season for trips to China's Hainan Island and to the Northeast Harbin for its world-famous ice-lantern festival. These months are also packed with New Year holidays, Chinese Spring Festival and other national or local happy fairs. Summer months are great time to explore Northeast China.

## Baggage Limits on Flights

For China domestic flights, you are allowed to check one piece of luggage. The limitation is 20 kilograms (44 pounds) total. A fee may be imposed for extra piece or excessive weight. You can also take one hand carry-on plus a backpack or tote bag, all of which should fit in the overhead compartment or under your seat.

## Electricity

The electricity used in China is 220 volt AC. Many middle and high-class hotels' washrooms have transformer plugs for electric shavers and hair dryers, but it is better to be prepared with an adapter plug.

## Telephone and Postal Service

In towns and cities, IDD service is provided at all hotels. Phone cards are available in post offices inside hotels or in the streets. Even more conveniently, most newsstands in major cities also carry phone cards. Telephone booths in the streets are mostly for local calls.

Tourist hotels provide postal services. If you want to send important items such as antiques and cultural relics that are under customs control, you will have to ask for the help of the local branch of the international post office, instead of the small post office in a hotel.

### Tipping Practice for Visitors to China

It is a common practice for visitors to tip the tour guide and driver in recognition of their good service. Hotel bellboy expects your tips as well. It is not customary to leave tips at hotel or local restaurant as the bill usually includes 10%-15% service charge.

### Some Useful Numbers

110—Police

114—Inner-city telephone number inquiries

119—Fire

120—Ambulance

121—Weather forecasts

## New Words

**concerning** [kən'sə:niŋ] *prep.* 关于，涉及

**administration** [əd,mini'streiʃən] *n.* 管理，经营；行政部门

**authorize** ['ɔ:θəraiz] *vt.* 批准；授权

**exempt** [ig'zempt] *vt.* 免除

**Tibet** ['tibet] *n.* 西藏

**consent** [kən'sent] *n.* 同意；赞成

**representative** [,repri'zentətiv] *n.* 代表

**valid** ['vælid] *a.* 有效的

**duration** [dju'reiʃən] *n.* 持续时间；期间

**baggage** ['bægidʒ] *n.* 行李

**declaration** [,deklə'reiʃən] *n.* 申报；宣布

**carbon** ['kɑ:bən] *n.* 副本

**submit** [səb'mit] *vt.* 提交；递交

**convert** ['kɔnvə:t] *vt.* 兑换；转变

**quarantine** ['kwɔrənti:n] *n.* 检疫

**microorganism** [,maikrəu'ɔ:gənizm] *n.* 微生物

**tissue** ['tisju:] *n.*（人、动植物细胞的）组织

**infest** [in'fest] *vt.* 大量滋生

**inoculate** [i'nɔkjuleit] *vt.* 预防注射，接种疫苗

**retain** [ri'tein] *vt.* 保留；保持

**venereal** [və'niəriəl] *a.* 性病的

**leprosy** ['leprəsi] *n.* 麻风

**tuberculosis** [tju:,bə:kju'ləusis] *n.* 结核病，肺结核

**Citibank** ['sitibæŋk] *n.* 美国花旗银行

**circulate** ['sə:kjuleit] *vt.*（使）流通

**Euro** ['juərəu] *n.* 欧元

**schilling** ['ʃiliŋ] *n.* 先令（奥地利的货币单位）

**franc** [fræŋk] *n.* 法郎

**Danish** ['deiniʃ] *a.* 丹麦的

**Krone** ['krəunə] *n.* 克朗（丹麦、挪威的货币单位）

**ringgit** ['riŋgit] *n.* 林吉特（马来西亚的货币单位）

**lira** ['liərə] *n.* 里拉（意大利的货币单位）

**markka** ['mɑ:kɑ:] *n.* 马克（芬兰的货币单位）

**climate** ['klaimət] *n.* 气候

**temperate** ['tempərət] *a.*（气候）温和的

**tropical** ['trɔpikl] *a.* 热带的

**subtropical** [ˌsʌb'trɔpikəl] *a.* 亚热带的

**frigid** ['fridʒid] *a.* 寒冷的

**complicated** ['kɔmpliˌkeitid] *a.* 错综复杂的

**stretch** [stretʃ] *n.* 伸展，延伸

**territory** ['terətəri] *n.* 领土，版图

**Jacksonville** ['dʒæksənvil] *n.* 杰克逊维尔（美国佛罗里达州东北部港市）

**impose** [im'pəuz] *vt.* 征税

**backpack** ['bækˌpæk] *n.* 背包

**compartment** [kəm'pɑːtmənt] *n.* 行李柜

**volt** [vəult] *n.* 伏特（电压单位）

**transformer** [træns'fɔːmə] *n.* 变压器

**plug** [plʌg] *n.*（电源）插座

**shaver** ['ʃeivə] *n.* 剃须刀

**adapter** [ə'dæptə] *n.* 适配器

**available** [ə'veiləbl] *a.* 可得到的；可利用的

**newsstand** ['njuːzˌstænd] *n.* 书报摊，书报亭

**relic** ['relik] *n.* 遗物，古物

**tip** [tip] *n.* 小费

**bellboy** ['belˌbɔi] *n.* 行李服务员；侍者

**ambulance** ['æmbjuləns] *n.* 救护车

 ## Phrases and Expressions

apply for　申请

Tibet Autonomous Region　西藏自治区

fill out　填写

subject... to...　使服从；使遭受

Master Card　万事达卡

Visa Card　维萨卡

Diners Card　大莱卡

American Express　美国运通公司

Travelex　通济隆公司

Sumitomo Bank of Japan　住友银行

tote bag　手提包

hair dryer　吹风机

telephone booth　电话亭

weather forecast　天气预报

 ## Abbreviations

PRC (People's Republic of China)　中华人民共和国

AIDS (acquired immune deficiency syndrome)　艾滋病（获得性免疫缺损综合征）

JCB　JCB 信用卡（JCB 为日本国际信用卡公司）

AC (alternating current)　交流电

IDD　国际直拨长途电话

# Notes

**1** According to the Law of the People's Republic of China concerning the Administration of Foreigners Entering and Leaving the Country, foreign tourists must apply for...

本句中，concerning the Administration of Foreigners Entering and Leaving the Country 是现在分词短语作定语，修饰 law, 意为有关外国人出入境管理的法律。

英语中，现在分词短语可作定语。请看下例：

The girl sitting besides Jack is his girlfriend.

坐在杰克旁边的那个女孩是他的女朋友。

**2** On leaving China, tourists must again submit the baggage declaration form for customs inspection.

本句中，on 为介词，意思是"当……的时候，在……时"。leaving China 是动名词短语，做介词 on 的宾语。请看下例：

She fainted on hearing that her son had been dead.

当听到她儿子已经死了的时候她就昏倒了。

**3** Northern Heilongjiang Province has a winter climate the year round without summer, while Hainan Island has a summer climate the year round without winter.

本句中，while 为连词，意思是"然而；但是"，表示对比。while 也可以表示让步，意思是"虽然，尽管"。请看下例：

You like tennis, while I'd rather read.

你爱打网球，但我爱看书。（表示对比）

While I understand what you say, I can't agree with you.

虽然我理解你的意思，但我还是不同意。（表示让步）

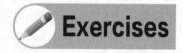

## Exercises

**EX. 5** **Answer the following questions.**

1. How can foreigners who want to visit China get the visa?

2. What articles can foreign visitors bring duty free when entering China?

3. Can a person with mental diseases enter China?

4. Shall the visitors tip the guide and the driver? How about the waiter at a restaurant?

**EX. 6** **Decide whether the following statements are *true* or *false*.**

1. For Canadian and US passport holders, visa is not required for Hong Kong of China if your stay is less than 90 days as a tourist.

2. Personal belongings should also be declared upon going through China's customs.

3. It is the task of the Chinese quarantine authorities to prevent foreigners suffering AIDS, venereal diseases, leprosy, mental diseases and open tuberculosis from entering China.

4. Travelers' checks can't be used in China.

5. Foreign currency cannot be circulated within the People's Republic of China or used to determine the price and settle accounts.

6. It is customary to leave tips at hotel or local restaurant in China.

## Part Four   Skill Training

### Forms

If you want to visit a foreign country, you must get the visa from the consulate/embassy of that country. The following is a visa application form of Ethiopia.

申请人须填写签证申请表格，一式两份。

申请人需在申请表格上粘贴两张标准的护照照片。

## VISA APPLICATION（USE BLOCK LETTERS）
### 入境签证申请表（请用大写字母填写）

1 MR. MRS. OR MISS（姓氏）

2 PLACE AND DATE OF BIRTH（出生地和日期）

3 NATIONALITY（国籍）

4 PROFESSION（职业）

5 PERMANENT ADDRESS（永久性地址）

6 PASSPORT NO.（护照号）

7 ISSUING AUTHORITY（发证机构）

8 VALID（有效期）

9 ESTMATED LENGTH OF STAY IN ETHIOPIA（计划在埃塞俄比亚的逗留时间）

10 PURPOSE OF VISIT（旅行目的）

11 ADDRESS IN ETHIOPIA（IF ANY）（在埃塞俄比亚的联系地址）

12 PERSONS ACCOMPANYING ON SAME PASSPORT（同一护照的随行人员）
_____

NAME（姓名）　AGE（年龄）　RELATIONSHIP（关系）
1）_____　_____　_____
2）_____　_____　_____
3）_____　_____　_____
4）_____　_____　_____

I HEREBY CERIFY THAT THE ABOVE STATEMENTS ARE TRUE TO THE BEST OF MY KNOWLEDGE AND THAT I SHALL NOT DURING MY STAY IN ETHIOPIA ACCEPT ANY EMPLOYMENT FOR REMUERATION.
（本人在此担保以上声明情况属实，而且到埃塞俄比亚以后不因报酬而接受聘用）
APPLICANT'S SIGNATURE
申请人签名
_____
REMARKS FOR OFFICIAL USE ONLY
（以下由签证官填写）
VISA NO.（签证号）_____ ISSUING AUTHORITY（发证机关）_____
DATE.（时间）_____ FREE / PAID（免费／交费）_____ RECEIPT NO.（收据号）_____
OFFICIAL SIGNATURE & SEAL
（签证官签字盖章）

## Practical Writing

*Sample Template for a Memorandum*

To: Jack Clinton　　　　Copies to: Peter McCarthy
From: Bill Murphy　　　Susan London
Date: March 10, 2004
Subject: **Boldface the line and use words to allow filing the memo correctly**

The purpose of this memo is to provide a model. Generally, you should clearly state your purpose at the beginning of the memo and request the action you want at the end. Confine your memo to a single purpose. If you have two purposes, write two memos. Take the time to analyze your reader; that is, consider how he or she (always a single reader) wishes to be approached with your message. Consider the tone or language that will appeal to the reader. Because your organization pays you to think and to communicate that thinking to others, be sure to include the following content:

- I am writing because...

- The facts are...
- I will, or I propose that you...

**The following formatting devices will add to the attractiveness of your memos:**

- Use 1-inch margins all around (1-inch left margin if the memo will be 3-hole punched and inserted in a binder). Do not justify the right margin.
- Use block-style paragraphs.
- Single-space your memo, and add six points above paragraphs—three points above the items in a list. Double-space a very short memo.
- Use 12-point Times New Roman as the default.
- Do not add a complementary close (e.g., sincerely). Do not sign memos at the bottom.
- Add initials beside your name to indicate that you have read and approved the memo (optional).
- If the "copies to" list is longer than ten names, place it at the end of the memo. If your memo is addressed to a distribution list, name the list.
- In a footer, add the date and number the pages of the memo, for example "1996-02-23, page 2/4". In the footer, you may choose to use smaller type.
- Begin long memos with a paragraph that functions as an executive summary. Your reader determines what long is.
- Use the spell-check function.
- Break long lists of bullets into several clusters.
- Read your memo out loud to discover awkward rhythms and phrases.
- Proofread it carefully for mistakes and missing words.
- Sleep on it for five minutes or overnight.
- Finally, ask someone whose competence and wisdom you value to read it and to give you feedback.

**Simulate and create** ▶ Suppose you are the secretary of a foreign trade company. One of your very important customers has called you and wants to discuss a co-operation project with your boss. Write a memo to your boss based on the above information.

## Part Five  Related Information

| Text | Notes |
|---|---|
| **International Travel and Health** | |
| *Health risks and precautions[1]—general considerations* | [1] 预防 |
| People in their home environment live in a state of equilibrium[2] with the locally occurring strains of microorganisms[3] and with the altitude[4] and climatic conditions of the region. | [2] 平衡 [3] 微生物 [4] 海拔，高度 |

However, this is an unstable[5] equilibrium that can be upset[6] even in the home environment by factors[7] such as the arrival of an unfamiliar microorganism, seasonal changes in climate[8] and unusually stressful situations. The many physical and environmental changes encountered[9] during international travel may upset this equilibrium to an even greater extent: sudden exposure[10] to significant changes in altitude, humidity[11], microbial[12] flora[13] and temperature, exacerbated[14] by stress and fatigue[15], may result in ill-health and an inability to achieve the purpose of the journey. The risks associated[16] with international travel are influenced by characteristics[17] of the traveler (including age, sex and health status) and by characteristics of the travel (including destination[18], purpose and duration[19]).

Forward planning, appropriate[20] preventive measures and careful precautions can substantially[21] reduce the risks of adverse[22] health consequences[23]. Although the medical profession and the travel industry can provide a great deal of help and advice, it is the traveler's responsibility[24] to ask for information, to understand the risks involved, and to take the necessary precautions for the journey.

*Key factors in determining the risks to which travelers may be exposed*

Destinations where accommodation[25], hygiene[26] and sanitation[27], medical care and water quality are of a high standard pose[28] relatively few serious risks for the health of travelers, unless there is pre-existing illness. In contrast, destinations where accommodation is of poor quality, hygiene and sanitation are inadequate[29], medical services do not exist, and clean water is unavailable[30] may pose serious risks for the health of travelers.

The duration of the visit and the behavior and lifestyle of the traveler are important in determining the likelihood[31] of exposure to many infectious[32] agents[33] and will influence decisions on the need for certain vaccinations or antimalarial[34] medication[35]. The duration of the visit may also determine whether the traveler may be subjected to[36] marked changes in temperature and humidity during the visit, or to prolonged[37] exposure to atmospheric pollution.

The purpose of the visit is critical[38] in relation to the associated health risks. A business trip to a city, where the visit is spent in a hotel and/or conference center of high standard, or a tourist trip to a well-organized resort[39], involves fewer risks than a visit to remote[40] rural[41] areas, whether for work or pleasure. However, behavior also

[5] 不稳定的
[6] 颠覆，扰乱
[7] 因素
[8] 气候
[9] 遇到
[10] 暴露
[11] 潮湿
[12] 微生物的
[13] 植物群
[14] 使加剧
[15] 疲乏
[16] 相关的
[17] 特性，特征
[18] 目的地
[19] 持续时间
[20] 正确的
[21] 相当大地
[22] 不利的
[23] 结果
[24] 责任

[25] 膳宿
[26] 卫生
[27] 公共卫生设施
[28] 引起，造成
[29] 不充分的
[30] 不可得到的

[31] 可能性
[32] 有传染性的
[33] 介质
[34] 抗疟的
[35] 药物处理
[36] 遭受
[37] 长时期的
[38] 重要的

[39] 度假胜地
[40] 偏僻的
[41] 乡下的

| Text | Notes |
|---|---|
| plays an important role; for example, going outdoors in the evenings in a malaria-endemic[42] area without taking precautions may result in the traveler becoming infected[43] with malaria. Exposure to insects, rodents[44] or other animals, infectious agents and contaminated[45] food and water, combined with the absence of appropriate medical facilities, makes travel in many remote regions particularly hazardous[46]. | [42] 地方性的疟疾<br>[43] 传染<br>[44] 啮齿动物<br>[45] 污染<br><br>[46] 危险的 |

## Part Six  Guide to World Famous Sight

| Text | Notes |
|---|---|
| **Museum of Qin Terra Cotta**<br>**Warriors and Horses** | |
| The Terra Cotta Warriors and Horses[1] are the most significant archeological[2] excavations[3] of the 20th century. Work is ongoing at this site, which is around 1.5 kilometers east of Emperor Qin Shi Huang's Mausoleum[4], Lintong County, Shaanxi Province. It is a sight not to be missed by any visitor to China. | [1] 兵马俑<br>[2] 考古学的<br>[3] 出土文物<br>[4] 陵墓 |
| Upon ascending[5] the throne[6] at the age of 13 (in 246 BC), Qin Shi Huang, later the first Emperor of all China, had work begun on his mausoleum. It took 11 years to finish. It is speculated[7] that many buried treasures and sacrificial[8] objects had accompanied the emperor in his after life. A group of peasants uncovered some pottery[9] while digging for a well nearby the royal tomb in 1974. It caught the attention of archeologists immediately. They came to Xi'an in droves[10] to study and to extend the digs. They had established beyond doubt that these artifacts[11] were associated with the Qin Dynasty (211 BC—206 BC). | [5] 攀登；继承；占领<br>[6] 王座<br>[7] 推测<br>[8] 牺牲的<br>[9] 陶器<br><br>[10] 成群结队<br>[11]（有考古意义的）<br>　　人工制品；史前<br>　　古器物 |
| The State Council[12] authorized[13] to build a museum onsite[14] in 1975. When completed, people from far and near came to visit. Xi'an and the Museum of Qin Terra Cotta Warriors and Horses have become landmarks on all traveler scenery. | [12] 国务院<br>[13] 授权<br>[14] 现场 |
| Life size terra cotta figures of warriors and horses arranged in battle formations[15] are the star features at the museum. They are replicas[16] of what the imperial[17]guard should look like in those days of pomp[18] and vigor[19]. | [15] 编队<br>[16] 复制品<br>[17] 皇帝的<br>[18] 盛况<br>[19] 活力 |

The museum covers an area of 16,300 square meters, divided into three sections: No. 1 Pit[20], No. 2 Pit, and No. 3 Pit respectively. They were tagged[21] in the order of their discoveries. No. 1 Pit is the largest, first opened to the public on China's National Day, 1979. There are columns[22] of soldiers at the front, followed by war chariots[23] at the back. No. 2 Pit, found in 1976, is 20 meters northeast of No. 1 Pit. It contained over a thousand warriors and 90 chariots of wood. It was unveiled[24] to the public in 1994. Archaeologists came upon No. 3 Pit also in 1976, 25 meters northwest of No. 1 Pit. It looked like to be the command center of the armed forces. It went on display in 1989, with 68 warriors, a war chariot and 4 horses.

The Terra Cotta Warriors and Horses is a sensational archaeological find of all times. It was listed by UNESCO in 1987 as one of the world cultural heritages.

[20] 一号坑
[21] 做标记

[22] 纵队
[23] 战车

[24] 公之于众

# Travel Agency

## Part One   Dialogues

### Sample Dialogue 1

👤 **Situation ▶**   Alice is looking for a Travel Agency. However she can't locate it, so she is asking a policeman for directions.

| | |
|---|---|
| **Alice**: | Excuse me. Is there a Travel Agency nearby? |
| **Policeman**: | Yes. There's one nearby. |
| **Alice**: | How can I get there? |
| **Policeman**: | Go along this street and turn left at the traffic lights. You can't miss it. |
| **Alice**: | Is it far? |
| **Policeman**: | Not really. It is within walking distance. |
| **Alice**: | Thank you. |
| **Policeman**: | Don't mention it. |

### Sample Dialogue 2

👤 **Situation ▶**   Alice is consulting a travel agent about a city tour.

| | |
|---|---|
| **Alice**: | What kinds of tours are there? |
| **Agent**: | Here's the tour brochure. Please have a look. |
| **Alice**: | How long does the sightseeing tour of the city take? |

**Agent**: It takes around seven hours.

**Alice**: Do we have dinner on this tour?

**Agent**: Certainly. It's included in the price.

**Alice**: That will be fine. Can you recommend a hotel? I want something cheap and near the beach.

**Agent**: How about Holiday Inn?

**Alice**: It is wonderful.

## Useful Expressions

1. Excuse me. Is there a travel agency nearby?
   请问附近有一个旅行社吗？

2. It's on the corner/on the left.
   在拐角处 / 在左边。

3. Go straight ahead until you see the traffic lights.
   一直往前走直到你看见红绿灯。

4. Is it far?
   远吗？

5. What sights do you suggest?
   你能推荐一些景点吗？

6. Do you offer any discount?
   有打折吗？

## Task Dialogue 1

**Situation ▶** Jane is visiting Beijing. She wants to change some currency but she can't find the Bank of China. She is asking a passerby for the direction.

## Task Dialogue 2

**Situation ▶** Mike wants to travel to Japan. He is asking the information at a travel agency.

# Part Two    Text A

## Introduction to Travel Agency

*Definitions*

A travel agent sells either individual parts of or complete holiday packages to the customer.

The main function of the travel agency is to sell the temporary use of transport (air, rail, coach, car), accommodation (hotel, motel, lodge), tours (packages) and other associated services (insurance, foreign exchange). This means that they are involved in the planning, booking, organization and documentation of travel arrangements for their clients. Often, this also involves advising, reassuring, explaining and encouraging the customer. However, they generally do not operate vehicles or accompany tourists themselves.

Travel consultants (the people in a travel agency who deal with the public) are expected to gather information on travel destinations and be capable of giving advice on travel products. Travel consultants require good inter-personal and organizational skills and the ability to deal with unexpected situations.

### Different Kinds of Travel Agent

Experience in the travel industry and a love of travel are some of the best training grounds for individuals wishing to enter the travel agency business. There is a clear distinction between those travel agents who sell air tickets and those who do not, and this choice is influenced by the qualifications of the travel agency consultants and the availability of start-up funds.

If you do not wish to be involved in the sale of air tickets, but wish to make arrangements for clients in terms of accommodation, transport and excursions, the International Air Travel Association (IATA) Diploma is not compulsory. However, it has become a benchmark for quality training in the travel industry, and would provide the travel agency with a mark of integrity and credibility which is critical in the early years.

If you wish to be involved in the sale of air tickets, you must be registered with IATA which requires the completion of an IATA/UFTAA (universal air travel) Standard Diploma. The IATA/UFTAA Diploma will provide a broad understanding of travel agency and airline operations, and enable you to advise clients, make appropriate travel arrangements and reservations, calculate airfares, and complete international travel documents in accordance with IATA rules and procedures.

### Licensing and Registration

Approach the Local Municipality to register your business. If you wish to be involved in the sale of air tickets, you will need to be registered with IATA. Compliance with the Consumer Code for Travel Agencies is necessary.

### Structure of Your Business

You may be registered as a Sole Proprietor, or your business may be registered as a Private Company (Propriety Limited or (Pty) Ltd Company), or Close Corporation (cc). Chamber of Commerce is a good contact through which to obtain details of organizations that can give advice on the structuring of your business. Advice may also be obtained from Business Advice Centers.

### Space and Infrastructure

Sufficient space is needed where the public can sit and discuss their needs with the travel consultant. Access to basic office infrastructure is needed, including access to electricity, telephones, fax and E-mail. Access to quite expensive computer equipment and software is required if the travel consultant is to be involved in the booking of air tickets. Registration with IATA will allow the keeping of airline ticket stock and the use of a ticket printer. The operational costs of an IATA registered travel agency are therefore likely to be higher than a business which is not registered.

### Amenity Value

An attractive or appealing tourism office environment may be created with posters and maps and will be supported by being located in attractive, clean and well-kept surroundings.

### Accessibility/Roads

Is the site easy to be found for those people using their own or public transport? The Local Municipality has controls for the erection of any signs. If new access onto streets is needed, the Local Municipality will usually construct them, at the cost of the developer. Permission must be obtained from the Provincial Department of Transport to construct new access points onto main roads outside of Local Municipality areas.

### Marketing and Advertising

Marketing and advertising may be done through a variety of media such as through printed brochures, Internet, television and word of mouth. It is important to enter your business into the tourism assets database for the Province which provides freely available information to the public on tourism facilities. The District Municipality has a copy of the same database. Publicity Associations should be approached to help disseminate your information. Any brochures produced to advertise your establishment should include an easily readable map showing your location.

### Job Outlook

Projected employment growth stems from increased spending on tourism and business travel over the next decade. With rising household incomes, smaller families, and an increasing number of older people who are more likely to travel, more people are expected to travel on vacation—and to do so more frequently—than in the past. Business travel also should grow as business activity expands. Further, professional and related workers, who are projected to be the fastest growing occupational group, do a significant amount of business travel.

Several other factors also will lead to more business for travel agents. For example, charter flights and larger, more efficient planes have brought air transportation within the budgets of more people, and the easing of air fares and routes has fostered greater competition among airlines, resulting in more affordable service. In addition, travel agents now organize more tours for the growing number of foreign visitors. Also, travel agents often are able to offer various travel packages at a substantial discount.

The travel business is sensitive to economic downturns and international political crises, when travel plans are likely to be deferred. Therefore, the number of job opportunities for travel agents fluctuates.

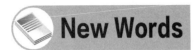

## New Words

**definition** [ˌdefiˈniʃən] *n.* 定义；解说

**coach** [kəutʃ] *n.* 长途汽车

**associated** [əˈsəuʃieitid] *a.* 关联的，相关的

**insurance** [inˈʃuərəns] *n.* 保险

**documentation** [ˌdɔkjumenˈteiʃən] *n.* 证明文件的提供

**client** [ˈklaiənt] *n.* 顾客，客户

**reassure** [ˌriːəˈʃuə] *vt.* 安慰，使安心

**ground** [graund] *n.* 场所；基础，根据

**distinction** [diˈstiŋkʃən] *n.* 区别；差别

**influence** [ˈinfluəns] *vt.* 影响

**qualification** [ˌkwɔlifiˈkeiʃən] *n.* 资格，条件

**excursion** [ikˈskəːʃən] *n.* 远足；短途旅行

**diploma** [diˈpləumə] *n.* 证书，文凭

**compulsory** [kəmˈpʌlsəri] *a.* 必须做的，强制的

**benchmark** [ˈbentʃˌmaːk] *n.* 基准

**integrity** [inˈtegrəti] *n.* 完整性；正直

**credibility** [ˌkredəˈbiləti] *n.* 可靠，可信

**critical** [ˈkritikəl] *a.* 关键的，决定性的

**license** [ˈlaisəns] *vt.* 准许；发给执照；批准

**municipality** [mjuːˌnisiˈpæləti] *n.* 市政当局

**register** [ˈredʒistə] *vt.* 登记，注册

**access** [ˈækses] *n.* 使用；接近

**amenity** [əˈmiːnəti] *n.* 宜人；礼仪

**accessibility** [əkˌsesəˈbiləti] *n.* 易接近，可到达

**marketing** [ˈmaːkitiŋ] *n.* 销售，市场营销

**media** [ˈmiːdiə] *n.* 大众传播媒介

**asset** [ˈæset] *n.* 资产，财产

**database** [ˈdeitəˌbeis] *n.* 数据库，资料库

**publicity** [pʌbˈlisəti] *n.* 公开；宣传，广告

**disseminate** [diˈsemineit] *vt.* 散布，传播（消息、观念等）

**projected** [ˈprəudʒektid] *a.* 预计的，计划中的

**frequently** [ˈfriːkwəntli] *ad.* 常常，频繁地

**budget** [ˈbʌdʒit] *n.* 预算

**affordable** [əˈfɔːdəbl] *a.* 能支付得起的

**substantial** [səbˈstænʃəl] *a.* 大量的，可观的

**discount** [ˈdisˌkaunt] *n.* 折扣

**downturn** [ˈdaunˌtəːn] *n.* 低迷时期

**defer** [diˈfəː] *vt.* 推迟，延期

**fluctuate** [ˈflʌktjueit] *vi.* 波动，起伏

**Phrases and Expressions**

| | |
|---|---|
| travel agency　旅行社 | Propriety Limited or (Pty) Ltd Company　有限责任公司 |
| holiday package　假日旅行整体计划 | close corporation　封闭式公司 |
| be involved in　涉及 | chamber of commerce　商会 |
| deal with　处理，应付 | stem from　源于，基于，出于 |
| in accordance with　与……一致，依照 | charter flights　包机 |
| sole proprietor　个人业主 | result in　导致 |

 **Abbreviations**

IATA (International Air Travel Association)　国际航空运输协会

## Notes

**1** With rising household incomes ... more people are expected to travel on vacation ...

　　本句中介词短语 with rising household incomes 作伴随状语，意为"随着家庭收入的提高……"。

　　英语中，with 后接名词、动名词构成的短语作状语，可表示原因、伴随、方式等。又如：

The minister received the bad news with surprising equanimity.

部长听到这个坏消息时，镇定得令人吃惊。

With his help, we finished the task ahead of time.

在他的帮助下，我们提前完成了任务。

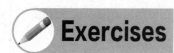 **Exercises**

**EX. 1**　**Answer the following questions.**

1. What is the function of the travel agency?

2. If a travel agency wishes to be involved in selling air tickets, what procedures should it undergo?

3. What infrastructure does a travel agency need to be a qualified one?

4. If you were a travel agent, how would you do your marketing and advertising?

5. What will stimulate the growth of employment of the travel agency industry according to this text?

**EX. 2** **Write out the English words according to the definitions given below.**

| definitions | words |
|---|---|
| a comfortable bus used for long-distance travel or touring | |
| a place to live or work in; house, flat, hotel room, etc. | |
| agreement by contract to pay money to someone if something, esp. a misfortune, such as illness, death, or an accident, happens to them | |
| a person who buys goods or services | |
| an official paper, card, etc., showing that permission has been given to do something | |
| mass communication, e.g. television, radio, the press | |
| a reduction made in the cost of buying goods | |
| short, usu. descriptive, printed article in a paper cover; pamphlet | |
| point of difference; that which makes one thing different from another | |
| anything owned by a person, company, etc., that has money value and that may be sold to pay debts | |

**EX. 3** **Complete the following sentences with appropriate words or expressions from the text.**

1. A _____ sells either individual parts of or complete holiday packages to the customer.

2. _____ (the people in a travel agency who deal with the public) are expected to gather information on travel destinations and be capable of giving advice on travel products.

3. _____ and _____ may be done through a variety of media such as through printed brochures, Internet, television and word of mouth.

4. The travel business is sensitive to _____ and international _____ , when travel plans are likely to be deferred.

**EX. 4** **Translate the following sentences into Chinese.**

1. The main function of the travel agency is to sell the temporary use of transport (air, rail, coach, car), accommodation (hotel, motel, lodge), tours (packages) and other associated services

(insurance, foreign exchange).

2. If you do not wish to be involved in the sale of air tickets, but wish to make arrangements for clients in terms of accommodation, transport and excursions, the International Air Travel Association (IATA) Diploma is not compulsory.

3. An attractive or appealing tourism office environment may be created with posters and maps and will be supported by being located in attractive, clean and well-kept surroundings.

4. For example, charter flights and larger, more efficient planes have brought air transportation within the budgets of more people, and the easing of air fares and routes has fostered greater competition among airlines, resulting in more affordable service.

## Part Three Text B

## How to Choose the Best Travel Agency

(The regulations for travel agencies may vary slightly from country to country. This text is mainly using US system for reference.)

A good travel agency can provide you with a broader and more complete range of services than that can be found in the internet. And the ability to conveniently talk with a real person can make all the difference when you have a problem, or need some special advice or assistance.

Although travel agencies are generally keen to avoid any complicated qualification procedures that would control the establishment of travel agencies, the lack of any formal quality controls has meant that there is an enormous variation in the quality of service provided by travel agencies.

Here are some issues to consider when choosing an agency.

### *Agency Affiliations and Accreditations*

If an agency is able to issue airline tickets itself and print for your travels, the agency might have been accredited by IATA, the International Air Transport Association, to allow it to issue tickets on behalf of most foreign airlines. However, because issuing airline tickets is no longer profitable, many agencies have withdrawn from IATA accreditation, cutting down on their overheads and reporting costs considerably.

Most other suppliers of travel products e.g. hotels, cruise lines, rental car companies, tour operators, don't have any requirements at all for who they will recognize as a travel agency. For example, CLIA, the Cruise Line International Association, will basically allow anyone with a business license and who pays a joining fee then sell cruises for their member cruise lines. An agency's membership in CLIA is accordingly meaningless one way or the other.

Agencies sometimes belong to franchise groups or consortia. These groups negotiate better rates for their members with key suppliers. In some cases, an agency that is a branch of a mega-agency, or that belongs to a franchise group, or that is a member of consortia will be able to get better deals for you than an agency with no affiliations at all. Ask agencies who they are affiliated with, and perhaps even research the group they belong to and confirm that it is a helpful group that will translate into better deals for you.

### What Type of Travel Help Do You Need?

Travel is usually split into two broad categories — "corporate" or business type travel, and "leisure" or personal, vacation type travel.

Although agencies will be pleased to help you with all types of travel, most agencies tend to be generally stronger either in corporate type travel services or in leisure type travel services. Ask a travel agency "are you primarily corporate or are you primarily leisure"?

If your needs are mainly for business travel, obviously a corporate focused agency is your better choice. In such a case, sometimes it even makes sense to buy your personal travel from a different agency that specializes in leisure travel.

### Specialty Agencies

In addition to generic "corporate" or "leisure" type travel agencies, it is increasingly common to see very specialized travel agencies.

For example, it is possible that an agency might specialize only in selling cruises. Another type of specialization might be an agency that sells only one destination (perhaps the South Pacific).

Other agencies concentrate on a particular type of travel—maybe singles travel or gay travel or perhaps golf or ski trips.

Still more agencies specialize in areas such as disabled travel or family travel, or school group travel, or probably just about any other distinction you could think of.

If you have special rather than generic needs, see if you can find a specialist travel agency that is experienced in helping people like you.

### Agency Size—Big or Small?

Travel agencies range from very small two or three employees, "mom and pop" type stores to enormously large offices that belong to national chains of hundreds of outlets and thousands of employees.

Bigger is not always better. Although, in theory, large agency groups should be able to negotiate better rates with suppliers, and should have more infrastructure and support and added-value services, this is not invariably the case.

Furthermore, it is quite common that the best agents will leave their employment at a mega-agency and choose instead to manage or own their own, smaller agency, and perhaps to create a more friendly environment both for their clients and also to get and keep good staff.

Small agencies may belong to buying consortiums that can give them effectively similar purchasing power and negotiating clout to that enjoyed by the mega-agencies.

If you're a small sized client, then the similarity in size between you and a small agency might make for a compatible match. If you're managing the travel needs for 1,000 people, then you might find a larger size agency is more suitable for your more complicated needs.

### Added Value Services and Assistance

Even in this Internet age, we all find an old fashioned brochure one of the best ways to evaluate a potential tour or hotel or other travel activity. A good agency that provides comprehensive leisure travel services will have a comprehensive range of up-to-date brochures on most major travel products and destinations, and will be able to get in other brochures to meet your interests if asked.

In addition, some agencies will also have a library of travel books and/or travel videos, which they may loan out to you.

A good agency will also have a wide range of their own reference material, such as probably various hotel directories, tour operator directories, and other information to help them find suitable products for your travels.

Some agencies even sell various travel accessories—power adapter plugs, headrest cushions, and other minor items that you often need but might find difficult/inconvenient to purchase elsewhere.

Ask the simple question—What else can you do for me that other agencies can't or won't do? The answer might surprise you.

### Other Issues

Of course, many of the comments about how to choose a travel agency also apply to how to choose a travel agent. In particular, recommendations from friends can be very helpful.

Here's an interesting suggestion: If you are meeting with an agent in person, see if you can watch how they use their computer screen. If they are looking for flights for you, do they just look at one screen full of information, or do they flip through two or three screens of flight information? Assuming you have indicated some flexibility in your travel arrangements, and that there is more than one screen of flight options, a good travel agent will look through multiple screens of flight options. A bad agent will only look through the first screen of flights (perhaps as few as four or so different flight choices).

Subjectively, do you like the agent? If the agent is someone that you feel comfortable with, that will help you to relax and interact with them a great deal more.

Is the agent easy to contact, and does she always spend as much time as you need when you call her? Does she return calls promptly, and always have sensible answers to your questions?

### Creating a Win-Win Relationship

If you want a travel agent to work hard and well for you, you need to incentivize them accordingly. You need to explain to them that you are indeed seriously committed to dealing with them and their agency, and that their time and effort spent researching travel products for you will indeed be rewarded by your subsequent purchase of travel through them.

These days travel agents can spot a "shopper" a mile away — a person that picks their brains for free advice, but who then does not reward the free advice with their business.

Expect to pay a good travel agent for their time, advice, and assistance. You didn't think the best agent in town would work for nothing, did you?

 **New Words**

| | |
|---|---|
| **assistance** [ə'sistəns] *n.* 帮助，协助 | **outlet** ['aut,let] *n.* 出路，销路 |
| **affiliation** [ə,fili'eiʃən] *n.* 联系；从属关系 | **invariably** [in'veəriəbli] *ad.* 不变地，总是 |
| **accreditation** [ə,krediteiʃən] *n.* 委派；鉴定合格 | **compatible** [kəm'pætəbl] *a.* 协调的，一致的；兼容的 |
| **accredit** [ə'kredit] *vt.* 信任；授权 | **accessories** [ək'sesəriz] *n.* 辅助设备，附件 |
| **profitable** ['prɔfitəbl] *a.* 有利可图的，可赚钱的 | **recommendation** [,rekəmen'deiʃən] *n.* 推荐；介绍 |
| **withdraw** [wið'drɔː] *vt.* 退出，离开 | **flip** [flip] *vi.* 用指轻弹；翻 |
| **overhead** ['əuvə,hed] *n.* 日常开支 | **assume** [ə'sjuːm] *vt.* 假定；设想 |
| **franchise** ['fræntʃaiz] *n.* 经销权，专卖权，特许 | **indicate** ['indikeit] *vt.* 指出；表明 |
| **consortium** [kən'sɔːtiəm] *n.* 国际财团 | **flexibility** [,fleksə'biləti] *n.* 灵活性 |
| **negotiate** [ni'gəuʃieit] *vt.* 商定，达成（协议） | **subjectively** [səb'dʒektivli] *ad.* 主观地 |
| **mega** ['megə] *a.* 巨大的 | **promptly** ['prɔmptli] *ad.* 迅速地，敏捷地 |
| **primarily** [prai'merəli] *ad.* 首先，主要地 | **win-win** [win win] *a.* 双赢的 |
| **generic** [dʒə'nerik] *a.* 普通的，一般的 | **incentivize** [in'sentivaiz] *vt.* 刺激，激励 |
| **range** [reindʒ] *vi.* 在……范围内变化 | **committed** [kə'mitid] *a.* 承诺……的 |
| | **spot** [spɔt] *vt.* 认出；发现 |

 **Phrases and Expressions**

| | |
|---|---|
| be keen on  喜爱，喜欢 | make sense  合理 |
| mom and pop store  夫妻店 | specialize in  擅长于，专攻 |
| on behalf of  代表 | in addition to  除了 |
| one way or the other  从某种意义上来说；以某种方式；无论如何 | |

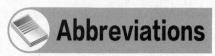

CLIA (The Cruise Line International Association)　国际游船协会

## Notes

**1** Although travel agencies are generally keen to avoid any complicated qualification procedures that would control the establishment of travel agencies, the lack of any formal quality controls has meant that there is an enormous variation in the quality of service provided by travel agencies.

　　本句中 Although 引导了一个让步状语从句，在该从句中，that would control the establishment of travel agencies 是一个定语从句，修饰和限定 any complicated qualification procedures。that there is an enormous variation in the quality of service provided by travel agencies 是一个宾语从句，作 has meant 的宾语。在该宾语从句中，provided by travel agencies 是一个过去分词短语，作定语，修饰和限定 the quality of service。

**2** If you have special rather than generic needs, see if you can find a specialist travel agency...

　　rather 常与 than 连用，表示"比起……更……"。例如：

These shoes are comfortable rather than pretty.

这双鞋不好看，但是舒服。

We would rather receive money than the usual gifts.

比起寻常的礼物，我们更愿意收到钱。

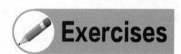

**EX. 5** **Answer the following questions.**

1. Why have many agencies withdrawn from IATA accreditation?

2. If you are planning a business travel, what kind of travel agency will you look for?

3. Does bigger travel agency always offer better service?

4. How to create a win-win relationship with a travel agency?

**EX. 6** **Decide whether the following statements are *true* or *false*.**

1. Not all travel agency is able to issue airline tickets itself.

2. Travel is usually split into two broad categories —"corporate" or business type travel, and "leisure" or personal, vacation type travel.

3. It is possible that an agency might specialize only in selling cruises.

4. Bigger agency is always better than small one.

5. Even in this Internet age, we all find an old fashioned brochure one of the best ways to evaluate a potential tour or hotel or other travel activity.

6. If you want a travel agent to work hard and well for you, you need to incentivize them accordingly.

## **Part Four** **Skill Training**

**Forms**

*Trip Registration Form*

TIBET TRAVELS & TOURS (P) LTD.

Lucky Plaza Shopping Arcade (2nd floor), Thahity Road, Thamel,

P.O. Box-7246, Kathmandu, Nepal.

Tel.: 977-1-249140/250748/250611    Fax: 977-1-249986

**Non-Credit Card    Trip Registration Form**

**Please complete this form online and then print the results.** After you print this information, mail it with your non-refundable deposit of $100 along with a copy of the front page of your passport (with photo). Make checks payable to Tibet Travels & Tours (P) Ltd. Full payment is due fifteen days before departure. Be sure to read the **General Terms and Conditions** prior to filling out this application. Your registration is not complete until you have read and agreed to the General Information, Terms and Conditions; **Limitation of Liability**; and Release and Assumption of Risk form. Whether you complete this registration online, mail or fax it, we must have a printed copy with your signature.

Trip Name or Code* [ ---Select your tour-- ▼]

Departure Date* [ ]

Journey Extension [ ]

Class of hotel* F.A.Q.

○ Super Deluxe      ○ Deluxe

○ Standard      ○ Budget

No. of Travelers* [ ]

Your First/Last Name* [ ]

(F)[　　　　]　(L)[　　　　]

Company Details with Address (If applicable)

[　　　　　　　　]

Zip Code* [　　　　]　　　Country* [　　　　]

Phone (day)* [　　　　]　　Fax [　　　　]

E-mail* [　　　　　　　]

## GENERAL INFORMATION

Name (as it appears on passport) [　　　　　　]

Passport Number [　　　　　]

Place of Issue [　　　　　]

Date of Issue [　　　　]　　Expiration [　　　　]

Birth date* [　　　]

Birthplace [　　　　　]

Citizenship/Nationality* [　　　　　]

Other Details

Age* [　　]

Sex* ○ Male　　　　○ Female

Height* [　　]　Weight * [　　] (mention kg/lb)

Smoker*　　○ No　○ Yes

Tee Shirt　　○ L　○ XL

## EMERGENCY INFORMATION

Contact Person* [　　　　　]

Their Full Address*

```
┌─────────────────────┐▲
│                     │█
│                     │█
│                     │█
│                     │█
│                     │▼
└─────────────────────┘
```

Zip* [                    ]          Their Telephone No. (s)* [                    ]

## DIET, HEALTH, TRAVEL

Food Preference

○ Non-vegetarian          ○ Vegetarian

If vegetarian, please specify [            ]

☐ No Red Meat          ☐ No Fish

☐ No Chicken           ☐ No Dairy

### Health*

Please alert us to anything and everything.

```
┌─────────────────────┐▲
│                     │█
│                     │█
│                     │
│                     │
│                     │
│                     │▼
└─────────────────────┘
```

### Allergies*

Please specify drug or food allergies.

```
┌─────────────────────┐▲
│                     │█
│                     │█
│                     │
│                     │
│                     │
│                     │▼
└─────────────────────┘
```

Please describe your outdoor background and regular physical activity.

```
┌─────────────────────┐▲
│                     │█
│                     │█
│                     │
│                     │
│                     │
│                     │▼
└─────────────────────┘
```

I am willing to share Double Room. ⊙ Yes    ⊙ No

Tent    ⊙ Yes    ⊙ No

Prefer Single Room (Additional fee applies). ⊙ Yes    ⊙ No

Any other information/instruction you might like to add.

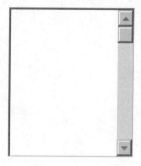

(For the convenience of reading, *the General Information, Terms and Conditions; Limitation of Liability; and Release and Assumption of Risk form* are attached as appendix 1)

I agree with the terms of this contract*: ⊙ Yes    ⊙ No

I agree that in the event any part or portion of this Trip Member's Agreement Regarding Complete Assumption of Risk of Travel and Release of Tibet Travels Tours (P) Ltd. Liability is found to be void or unenforceable, then such part or portion will be stricken, but the rest of the Agreement will be given full force and effect. * ⊙ Yes    ⊙ No

Date                 _____

Signature        _____

                        Parent or Guardian must sign if applicant is under 21 years of age.

Print This Form

## Practical Writing

### *Resume Writing*

A resume is a written presentation specifically targeted toward landing the job you want. It should reflect the experience and skills you have which are relevant to the job you seek. A resume shouldn't look like a laundry list of job titles and duties. Remember, it's an overview of what you offer as an employee, not an autobiography.

Here are a few tips for resume writing:

Be clear, direct, effective and professional. Make your resume easy to read. Use bullet statements to facilitate skimming. Avoid long paragraphs and large blocks of text.

Try to keep it to one or two pages. If you have less than 10 years of experience, a single-page resume is a good rule-of-thumb. You should be able to skim your resume in 25 to 30 seconds.

Determine a format and stick with it through the resume i.e., ensure section headings have the same placement and font treatment throughout the resume.

Information about your most recent job may use current or past tense depending on your current status, only use past tense to describe previous accomplishments, since they are completed actions.

Accurately use up-to-date terminology relevant to the industry you have targeted.

Spell out terms. Avoid abbreviations and acronyms.

Identifying information should be listed on the first page in a balanced, organized layout, including:

- Name (should stand out, i.e., bold, capital letters etc.)

- Street Address

- City, State and Zip Code

- Home, Mobile and/or Cell Phone (include 10 digit telephone numbers with area code)

- Work Phone

- E-mail address (include personal not work)

If your resume is more than a single page, be sure to place name and page number in upper right hand corner of the second page.

*Sample*

**Jimmy Zitbolli**

Gettysburg College
Campus Box 4303
Gettysburg, PA 17325-4303
zitbolli@gettysburg.edu

**Education**

*Bachelor of Arts*, Gettysburg College, Gettysburg, PA, May 2014

Major: Digital Arts
Minor: Marketing
Specialization: Information Systems

**Experience**

*Director of Marketing*, Web Solutions Inc., Gettysburg, PA, summer 2014

Organized and attended NRA and Comdex 02 trade shows.
Sold Web site service to Central Pennsylvania companies.

Designed various Web sites.

Coordinated seminars discussing the Internet.

***Advertising Specialist and Consultant***, Gettysburg College, Gettysburg, PA, Nov. 2012/present

Directed marketing for the 2008 Gettysburg Tennis Team.

Created 2012 and 2013 Career Fair posters.

Designed and maintained Web sites for various college departments.

Coordinated 2014 Summer Business School Abroad Program.

***Kitchen Positions***, Restaurant Industry, NJ, 2005/2011

Seasonally employed as a chef to finance education:

Catering Chef, The Manor, West Orange, New Jersey, summers 2010, 2011

Assistant Chef, La Primavera, West Orange, New Jersey, 2007, 2008, 2009

Prep Cook, Il Tulapanos, Cedar Grove, New Jersey, summers 2005, 2006

## Achievements & Activities

***President and Founder***: Managerial Events Committee, Gettysburg College

Led committee in organizing and implementing First Annual Career Development Conference attended by more than 20 of North America's top companies, including Johnson & Johnson, Oracle, Silicon Graphics, New York Life, Utility Partners, and Bank of America.

Established organization as a member of Students In Free Enterprise (SIFE).

**Fund Raiser**: Personally raised more $1,200 in food for the Red Cross.

**Vice President of Communications**: American Marketing Association, Gettysburg College chapter.

**Representative**: Student Government Association.

## Computer Skills

Windows NT, Microsoft Office, Next step, HTML/Web Publishing, Macintosh, True Space, Visual Basic, Adobe Photoshop, Systems Development, Corel Draw, Macromedia Director, Dun & Bradstreet Marketplace

## Language Skills

Reading and speaking knowledge in Spanish

## Honors

Gettysburg College Honor Roll, Fall 2012

Citizen Scholarship, Gettysburg College, Fall 2011

John Bishop Scholarship, Gettysburg College, Fall 2013

Culinary Scholarship, Johnson and Whales University, Fall 2010

👤 **Simulate and create** ▶ Suppose you are going to graduate from your university and wanting to find a good job. Write a resume for yourself.

## Part Five  Related Information

*Locations of Major Tourists Cities*

| Text | Notes |
|---|---|
| **A Brief Introduction to China's Major Tourists Cities** | |
| Without **Beijing**, any tour itinerary[1] to China is incomplete, especially for first-time travelers. As the capital of China, Beijing is one of the world's truly imposing[2] cities, with a 3,000-year history and over 11 million people. Covering 16,808 square kilometers in area, it is the political, cultural and economic center of the People's Republic of China. Beijing adjoins[3] the Inner Mongolian[4] Highland to the northwest and the Great Northern Plain to the south. Five rivers run through the city, connecting it to the eastern Bohai Sea. Administratively[5], the Beijing municipality[6] equals the status of a Province, reporting directly to the central government. | [1] 旅行计划<br><br>[2] 壮丽的<br><br>[3] 毗连<br>[4] 内蒙的<br><br><br><br><br>[5] 行政管理上<br>[6] 市政当局 |
| **Xi'an** was one of the most important cradles[7] of Chinese civilization[8]. The famous "Silk Road" that linked China with central Asia and the Roman Empire started in Xi'an in the east. The city served as the first capital of a unified China and capital of 11 dynasties[9] periodically from the 11th century BC to the early 10th century AD. | [7] 发源地<br>[8] 文明<br><br><br>[9] 朝代，王朝 |
| **Dunhuang**, a small city in Gansu Province, is located near the crossroads of the ancient Silk Road. It is made famous largely by the Buddhist[10] Grottoes[11], known as the Mogao Grottoes, which are one of the world's most important sites of ancient Buddhist culture. The grottoes, also known as Caves of the Thousand Buddhas, preserve[12] nearly a thousand years of Buddhist cave-temple architecture, clay sculpture[13], mural paintings, and manuscripts[14], dating from the 5th to the 14th centuries. | [10] 佛教的<br>[11] 石窟<br>[12] 保存<br>[13] 雕刻品<br>[14] 手稿，原稿 |
| **Chengdu**, the capital of Sichuan Province in the southwest, has been the economic and cultural center of China's most populous[15] province since 400 BC. | [15] 人口稠密的 |
| Situated in the northeast corner of the Guangxi Zhuang Autonomous[16] Region, **Guilin** is hailed[17] by many as the most beautiful place in China and is one of the must-see destinations for most foreign tourists. According to a popular Chinese saying, "Guilin's scenery bests all others in the world". Its shapely-rising limestone[18] towers and crystal-clear[19] waters are often portrayed[20] in Chinese artworks. Adding to its natural beauty are many fascinating[21] caves. | [16] 自治的<br>[17] 拥戴<br><br><br><br>[18] 石灰石<br>[19] 像水晶一样清澈的<br>[20] 描绘<br>[21] 引人入胜的 |
| **Haikou** is the capital of Hainan Province and Special Economic Zone, a tropical[22] island just to the south of Guangdong. Separated | [22] 热带的 |

| Text | Notes |
|---|---|
| from the mainland by the 30-kilometer-wide Qiongzhou Channel[23], Haikou is the main port and business center for the island, a tropical city with streets lined with palm[24] trees. | [23] 海峡<br><br>[24] 棕榈 |
| **Harbin** is the capital of Heilongjiang Province, which borders Russia in the north. Situated in the middle reaches of the Songhua River, it is a busy river port. With several highways and railways converging at Harbin, the city is an important transportation hub[25] in northeastern China. | [25] 中心 |
| If Tibet is the "roof of the world", then its capital, **Lhasa**, is certainly the "city of the sun". Standing on a plain over 13,000 feet above sea level, surrounded by towering[26] mountains, Lhasa is a town bathed in sunlight. | [26] 高耸的<br>[27] 显著的 |
| The largest city in China, **Shanghai** contains the most striking[27] blend[28] of oriental[29] and western cultures and of the past and present. In this city, European-style buildings can be seen standing alongside Chinese structures and ancient temples. Modern ocean-going vessels[30] sail past junks[31]. | [28] 混合<br>[29] 东方的<br>[30] 船<br>[31] 舢板船 |
| The last stop on your westward journey along the "Silk Road" is **Urumqi**[32], the capital of the Xinjiang Uygur[33] Autonomous Region, situated at the northern foothill of the snow-capped Tianshan Mountains. | [32] 乌鲁木齐<br>[33] 维吾尔族 |

# Part Six Guide to World Famous Sight

| Text | Notes |
|---|---|
| **The Great Wall** | |
| The Great Wall, a landmark[1] of the earth that can be viewed from the moon, runs 6,700 kilometers from east to west across five provinces. Like a gigantic[2] dragon's body, it winds up and down across deserts, grasslands and mountains. Its history spans[3] more than 2,000 years. The Great Wall is considered one of the greatest wonders[4] in the world. Although some of the sections of the wall are now in ruins[5] or have disappeared completely, it is still one of the most sought-after attractions in the world thanks to its magnificence[6] and significance[7]. In 1987, the Great Wall was enlisted in the World Heritage[8] by UNESCO[9]. | [1] 明显的目标<br>[2] 巨大的<br><br>[3] 跨越<br><br>[4] 奇迹<br>[5] 废墟<br><br>[6] 华丽<br>[7] 意义<br>[8] 世界遗产<br>[9] 联合国教科文组织 |
| ***History of the wall*** | |
| Excitement abounds[10] in the origin, vicissitude[11] and nature of the great wall of the Qin, Han, and Ming dynasties. | [10] 大量存在<br>[11] 变迁兴衰 |

The Great Wall was originally built in the Spring, Autumn, and Warring States Periods[12] as a defensive[13] fortification[14] by the three states: Yan, Zhao and Qin. The Great Wall went through constant extensions[15] and repairs in later dynasties. In fact, it began as independent walls for different states when it was first built, and did not become the "Great" wall until the Qin Dynasty. Emperor[16] Qin Shihuang succeeded in his effort to have the walls joined together to fend off[17] the invasions[18] from the Huns in the north after the unification[19] of China. Since then, the Great Wall has served as a monument[20] of the Chinese nation throughout history. A visit to the Great Wall is like a tour through the history backwards[21]; it brings tourists great excitement in each step of the wall.

*Construction of the wall*

The mystery of the construction of the wall is amazing[22]. The construction of the Great Wall, drew heavily on[23] the local resources for construction materials, was carried out in line with the local conditions under the management of contract and responsibility system. A great army of manpower, composed of soldiers, prisoners, and local people, built the wall. The construction result demonstrates the manifestation[24] of the wisdom[25] and tenacity[26]of the Chinese people.

*Sections of the wall*

Ready to show you an incredible[27] diversity[28] of scenery and ethnic[29] people along its way.

The Great Wall as we see today was mostly built during the Ming Dynasty. It starts from Shanhaiguan Pass[30] in the east to Jiayuguan Pass[31] in the west traversing[32] provinces and cities of Liaoning, Hebei, Beijing, Tianjin, Shanxi, Inner Mongolia, Ningxia, Shaanxi and Gansu.

*Protection of the wall*

The China Great Wall Academy[33] has called for greater protection of this important relic[34].

Following a forty-five day long survey of 101 sections of the Wall in different provinces, the China Great Wall Academy reported on December 12, 2002, that the forces of nature and destruction at the hand of mankind are bringing about the gradual[35] reduction of its extent with the result that less than 30% remains in good condition. The Academy has called for greater protection of this important relic.

*Culture of the wall*

Unfolding[36] a considerable part of Chinese culture beyond the wall.

The Great Wall has long been incorporated[37] into Chinese

| | |
|---|---|
| [12] 春秋战国时代 | |
| [13] 防御用的 | |
| [14] 工事，要塞 | |
| [15] 延长，扩充 | |
| [16] 皇帝 | |
| [17] 挡开 | |
| [18] 侵略 | |
| [19] 统一 | |
| [20] 纪念碑 | |
| [21] 向后 | |
| [22] 令人惊异的 | |
| [23] 利用了 | |
| [24] 显示，表现 | |
| [25] 智慧 | |
| [26] 坚韧 | |
| [27] 难以置信的 | |
| [28] 差异，多样性 | |
| [29] 种族的，少数民族的 | |
| [30] 山海关 | |
| [31] 嘉峪关 | |
| [32] 穿越，通过 | |
| [33] 中国长城研究院 | |
| [34] 遗迹 | |
| [35] 逐渐的 | |
| [36] 显露 | |
| [37] 合并 | |

| | |
|---|---|
| mythology[38] and popular symbolism[39]. The most beautiful of several legends[40] is about the collapse of a section of the Great Wall caused by Meng Jiangnu, who cried bitterly over the death of her husband in the construction of the Great Wall. This legend has been spread widely through textbooks, folk songs and traditional operas. It is well-known in China. | [38] 神话<br>[39] 象征主义<br>[40] 传说 |

### *Travel of the wall*

| | |
|---|---|
| Elaborate[41] tour plans make travel comfortable, memorable, enjoyable and informative. | [41] 精心制作的 |
| If you prefer to see the wall in a relatively natural state, visit Simatai[42], 110km northeast of Beijing. This part of the Wall is the best choice, for it is still in its original state without being developed into a popular tourist attraction due to its distance and little public transportation options[43]. | [42] 司马台<br><br><br><br>[43] 选择 |

# Airport

---

**Part One**  **Dialogues**

## Sample Dialogue 1

👥 **Situation ▶** Oliver is checking in at an international airport.

| | | |
|---|---|---|
| ⚪ | **Oliver**: | Good morning. Do I check in here for Delta Flight 79 to New York? |
| ⚪ | **Ticket inspector**: | Yes. Can I have your ticket, please? |
| ⚪ | **Oliver**: | Here you are. |
| ⚪ | **Ticket inspector**: | Thank you. Would you like a window or an aisle seat? |
| ⚪ | **Oliver**: | An aisle seat, please. |
| ⚪ | **Ticket inspector**: | Do you have any baggage to check? |
| ⚪ | **Oliver**: | Yes. This trunk please. |
| ⚪ | **Ticket inspector**: | Here's your boarding pass. Have a nice flight. |
| ⚪ | **Oliver**: | Thank you. |

## Sample Dialogue 2

👥 **Situation ▶** Sam had a terrible holiday in Portugal last week. Now he is making a complaint to the travel agency.

| | | |
|---|---|---|
| ⚪ | **Agent**: | Good morning. Can I help you? |
| ⚪ | **Sam**: | I'd like to make a complaint about my holiday in Portugal last week. |

**Agent**: I'm sorry to hear that. What exactly was the problem?

**Sam**: First of all, the coach took us to the hotel broke down and we had to wait for over two hours in the sweltering heat before a replacement arrived. Then when we got to the hotel we found our room hadn't been cleaned.

**Agent**: Oh dear, did you complain to the hotel staff?

**Sam**: Of course, but we were told all the chambermaids were off duty. Anyway, that's not all. The people in the room above sounded like they were having all-night parties, every night. I demanded another room but the receptionist told me the hotel was full.

**Agent**: Oh, I see.

**Sam**: And to cap it, all the food in the hotel restaurant was awful. It was so bad we had to eat out all the time despite having paid for meals in the price of our holiday.

**Agent**: I do apologize. I'd like to offer you a 20% discount on the original price as a gesture of goodwill.

**Sam**: A 20% discount? You must be joking. I want to see the manager.

## Useful Expressions

1. Can I see your passport?

   请出示你的护照。

2. Have a nice trip.

   旅行愉快。

3. I'm afraid your flight has already taken off.

   恐怕你的航班已经起飞了。

4. I have a complaint to make.

   我要投诉。

5. My holiday was destroyed.

   我的假期被破坏了。

6. You must compensate for it.

   你们必须为此做出补偿。

## Task Dialogue 1

**Situation** ▶ You are checking in at the Pudong International Airport and the ticket inspector is trying to serve you.

**Task Dialogue 2**

**Situation** ▶ You had beef curry at the Grand Hotel a couple of evenings ago. That night you had stomach ache, sickness and diarrhea. The doctor said you had food poisoning. You're feeling better now and have gone back to the hotel to complain.

## Part Two  Text A

## Procedures of Boarding a Plane

### Airport Tax

Some airports levy airport tax on passengers. Taking China as an example, there are two kinds of fees in China's airport, domestic and international. When one travels within China, RMB 50 yuan is levied at all domestic airports known as airport construction fee. When catching a departure flight to leave China, a departure tax of RMB 90 yuan (about $ 14.00) is charged. All the fees are payable in RMB and in cash only at a special airport tax desk before check-in. So the first thing at the airport is to pay the tax, and you will be given a receipt. Now the tax is usually collected when buying the flight ticket.

### Check-in

Then, you can have your ticket and passport ready while waiting to check in. You will find the check-in counter allocated to your flight from flight information screens.

Check-in procedures vary by airline, but travelers are advised to present themselves at their airline's ticket counter no less than one hour before flight departure. It is recommended that passengers arrive and check in 2-3 hours before their departure.

Adults are required to have at least one current government issued photo ID—such as passports, driver's licenses, military IDs, etc. Expired identification will be rejected. Children traveling alone should also have photo identification.

Only passengers with valid tickets will be allowed beyond screener checkpoints. Persons who are attending to child passengers and travelers needing a medical assistant will be permitted into secure gate areas.

### Checked-in Baggage

If you have luggage to check, arrive at the airport two hours or more ahead of flight time. Longer if you are flying internationally. Check with your air carrier for specific guidelines.

Most airlines allow a total of three pieces of luggage free of charge for each ticketed passenger—one carry-on bag and two checked items. They allow two big bags as checked-in baggage. At the time of check-in they will take these bags and return it to you in final destination directly. You will not see these bags anywhere in between.

International airports determine luggage allowance and luggage charges (if applicable) based on weight and number of pieces. Total linear dimensions (length + height + width) of each checked-in baggage must not exceed 158 cm (62 inches) and weight of each bag must not exceed 32 kg (70 pounds).

Curbside luggage check-in is available through some airlines at some airports. Verify with your departure and arrival airports for their current procedures. This may change during the duration of your trip.

Be prepared to identify your checked luggage and have identity luggage tags affixed to each bag. If your bags are not very strong, tie ropes so that they stand rough handling.

Some airports are now equipped to X-ray check-in luggage. Avoid packing any suspicious items which will trigger further scrutiny and cause delay.

### Hand Baggage

You can carry one piece per person. Important papers and travel documents (passport) should be carried on board by the passenger, because they might be needed at immigration at the port of entry (arrival at first intention airport). Also keep one set of clothing, and other necessary stuff like toothbrush, etc., in it. All items not needed in flight should be checked.

Carry-on luggage must fit underneath the passenger seat or in an overhead compartment. Maximum carry-on dimension is 56 cm × 36 cm × 23 cm (22" × 14" × 9"), and maximum carry-on weight is 18 kg(40 pounds). Passengers traveling in First Class, Business Class, or as a member of frequent flyer programs who already have a lot of miles occurred (like Gold members, Silver members etc.) may be allowed an extra carry-on item. But that depends upon particular airline.

### Security Check

Next you will go for security check. Here they will scan every person and X-ray their hand baggage. Then you have to wait in a hall till they make announcement for Boarding.

### Boarding

Last step is boarding. You will proceed towards the Gate Number they gave at Check-in time. Gate number is also on the Boarding Pass. All gates are on lower level.

You might have a lot of time. There are places to sit. There are lots of shops also, just to look at.

Normally they sit people in following order: Handicapped, First Class, Last rows, Middle Rows, and Front Rows. You keep your boarding pass ready and enter the plane. Air hostesses may help you locate your seat. If not, ask them. Put your hand baggage in overhead compartment.

## New Words

**levy** ['levi] *vt.* 征收，征税
**departure** [di'pɑːtʃə] *n.* 启程，出发，离开
**allocate** ['æləkeit] *vt.* 分派，分配
**military** ['militəri] *a.* 军队的；军人的
**expire** [ik'spaiə] *vi.* 期满，终止
**reject** ['riːdʒekt] *vt.* 拒绝；不接受
**screener** ['skriːnə] *n.* 扫描器
**secure** [si'kjuə] *a.* 安全的
**specific** [spə'sifik] *a.* 明确的，具体的
**allowance** [ə'lauəns] *n.* 允许；容差
**charge** [tʃɑːdʒ] *n.* 费用
**curbside** ['kəːbsaid] *n.* 街道边
**verify** ['verifai] *vt.* 证实；核实
**identify** [ai'dentifai] *vt.* 鉴别，标识
**affix** [ə'fiks] *vt.* 使固定；贴上，粘上

**suspicious** [sə'spiʃəs] *a.* 可疑的；引起怀疑的
**trigger** ['trigə] *vt.* 引发，引起
**scrutiny** ['skruːtini] *n.* 详细检查
**immigration** [,imi'greiʃən] *n.* 移居入境，移民入境
**intention** [in'tenʃən] *n.* 意图，目的
**maximum** ['mæksiməm] *n.* 最大量，最大限度
**announcement** [ə'naunsmənt] *n.* 广播，通告
**board** [bɔːd] *vt.* 让乘客登机（或上船等）
**proceed** [prə'siːd] *vi.* 进行，继续下去
**handicapped** ['hændi,kæpt] *a.* 身体有缺陷的

## Phrases and Expressions

airport construction fee　机场建设费
air carrier　运货飞机，运输机
linear dimension　线性尺寸

Boarding Pass　登机卡
air hostess　空中小姐

## Abbreviations

ID (identification)　身份证明

## Notes

**1** When one travels within China, RMB 50 yuan is levied at all domestic airports known as airport construction fee.

本句中，known as airport construction fee 是过去分词短语作主语 RMB 50 yuan 的补足语，可理解为 "称为机场建设费"。又如：

The parliament of that country enjoys the highest power, known as the House of Representatives and the Senate.

那个国家的议会享有最高权利，它们被称为众议院和参议院。

**2** Check-in procedures vary by airline, but travelers are advised to present themselves at their airline's ticket counter no less than one hour before flight departure.

本句中，to present themselves at their airline's ticket counter no less than one hour before flight departure 是一个动词不定式短语，作主语 travelers 的补足语。本句可理解为：..., but travelers are advised to arrive at the airport no less than one hour before his plane departs.

**3** Most airlines allow a total of three pieces of luggage free of charge for each ticketed passenger—one carry-on bag and two checked items.

本句中，one carry-on bag and two checked items 是对 three pieces of luggage 的补充说明，free of charge 是形容词短语作定语，修饰 three pieces of luggage。free of charge 的意思是 "免费的，不收费的"。

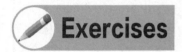 **Exercises**

**EX. 1** **Answer the following questions.**

1. How much tax does a passenger have to pay when leaving from a China's airport?

2. What procedures does a person have to undergo before boarding a plane?

3. What documents does a passenger need when checking in?

4. How much luggage can a passenger take free of charge?

**EX. 2** **Write out the English words according to the definitions given below.**

| definitions | words |
| --- | --- |
| the act of leaving, esp. when starting a journey | |
| (of something which lasts for a period of time) to come to an end | |
| a statement making publicly known something has happened or will happen | |
| to get into a plane, ship or public vehicle | |
| people who have a disability of the body or mind | |
| impose; collect by authority or force | |
| refuse to accept | |
| coming as a settler into another country, not as a tourist or visitor | |
| go forward; go on | |
| purpose, aim or plan | |

EX. 3  Complete the following sentences with appropriate words or expressions from the text.

1. When one travel within China, RMB 50 yuan is levied at all domestic airports known as _____.

2. You will find the check-in counter allocated to your flight from _____.

3. At the time of check-in they will take these bags and return them to you in _____ directly.

4. _____ must fit underneath the passenger seat or in an overhead compartment.

5. Next you will go for _____ where they will scan every person and X-ray their hand baggage.

EX. 4  Translate the following sentences into Chinese.

1. All the fees are payable in RMB and in cash only at a special airport tax desk before check-in.

2. Adults are required to have at least one current government issued photo ID—such as passports, driver's licenses, military IDs, etc. Expired identification will be rejected.

3. Most airlines allow a total of three pieces of luggage free of charge for each ticketed passenger—one carry-on bag and two checked items.

4. Carry-on luggage must fit underneath the passenger seat or in an overhead compartment.

## Part Three  Text B

## Check-in  Online

With tighter security at the airports, checking-in for a flight can take much longer these days. Now, some airlines are allowing travelers to save time, but they have to do something before they get to the airport.

Unless you own your own plane, there is not a fast, easy way to fly these days. As many frequent flyers know, you can save yourself time and a lot of hassle, if you are better prepared before your flight.

The check-in lines at Los Angeles International Airport and other Southland airports can be horrendous. It's not the only line you'll go thru, but airport security checkpoints may be even longer.

Now, there is a new system that let you check in at home. You can check in for your flight from anywhere you have access to the Internet. And several major airlines including American, Continental and Delta are hoping that this new system will make your wait shorter.

Editor Janet Libert of *SkyGuide Go Magazine* says, "You just go right from your car, or from the curb to the security line and then on to the gate. "

The new system saves a minimum of twenty minutes, if you're flying first class. If you're flying coach, it probably saves you well over an hour.

To take advantage of the new system you need a computer and other thing. Libert says, "It does require that you have a mileage number for that particular airline and that you also know your pin code."

So here is how it works. Once you are on the airline's website you log in your frequent flyer number and your pin. Then you can search up your itinerary. Next, you are asked about seating. Then you are ready to print your boarding pass.

Here is a pointer—check your boundaries before you hit O.K. Libert says, "Make sure that when you print out your boarding pass that you can get the whole pass on one eight and a half by eleven sheets of paper. Because the bar code that prints out is very important. "

When you get to the airport, if you don't have any bags to check, just go right to security with your boarding pass.

But, if you do—you need to bring that luggage and your boarding pass to the curbside check-in and they will check your bags. Then you go right to the security line.

If you lose your boarding pass between home and the airport, just talk to a gate agent and they should be able to replace it for you.

"The earliest you can check in for most airlines is twenty four hours", Libert says. Check-in times can vary across airlines, so Libert suggests checking the airline's policies on their website. If you're a procrastinator, Libert says airlines may let you check in up to an hour before your flight leaves. Some airlines even push the limit to thirty minutes before your flight leaves. Check with the airline to make sure you don't miss the cut-off.

To cut that time waiting for your flight, Libert says you can go online to the airline's websites to check the status of your flight. If you see that it's late, you can wait at home instead of at the gate.

You can also check the status of your scheduled flight by calling a day or two before your flight to reconfirm your reservation. Flight schedules sometimes change, so it's wise to double-check. However, most cancellations happen the day of the flight.

## New Words

| | |
|---|---|
| **tight** [tait] *a.* 严厉的；紧的 | **pin** [pin] *n.* 个人识别号，个人身份号码 |
| **frequent** [ˈfriːkwənt] *a.* 经常的，频繁的 | **code** [kəud] *n.* 代号；代码 |
| **horrendous** [hɔˈrendəs] *a.* 可怕的 | **boundary** [ˈbaundəri] *n.* 边界，分界线 |
| **thru** [θruː] *prep.* 经过，通过（美 = through） | **procrastinator** [prəuˌkræstiˈneitə] *n.* 拖延者，拖拉者 |
| **checkpoint** [ˈtʃekˌpɔint] *n.* 检查站 | **cut-off** [ˈkʌtɔf] *n.* 截止点 |
| **minimum** [ˈminiməm] *n.* 最小量，最小数 | **status** [ˈsteitəs] *n.* 情况，状态 |
| | **scheduled** [ˈʃedjuːld] *a.* 预定的 |
| **mileage** [ˈmailidʒ] *n.* 英里数，英里里程 | **reconfirm** [ˌriːkənˈfəːm] *vt.* 再次证实，再次确认 |

**Phrases and Expressions**

Los Angeles  洛杉矶（美国城市）
log in  进入（系统），注册，登录

bar code  条形码

 **Abbreviations**

Curb (curbside luggage check-in)  外围行
李托运

PIN (personal identification number)  个人
身份号码，个人识别号

## Notes

**1** It does require that you have a mileage number for that particular airline and that you also
know your pin code.

　　本句中，does 是助动词，表示强调。又如：

He did come after all!

他毕竟还是来了！

**2** Libert suggests checking the airline's policies on their website.

　　本句中，checking the airline's policies on their website 是一个动名词短语，作
suggest 的宾语。

suggest 后面常接动名词或从句，后接从句时，该从句要用虚拟语气，而不接不定式。如：

I suggest leaving now.

I suggest that we leave now.

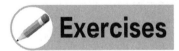 **Exercises**

**EX. 5** **Answer the following questions.**

1. Why check-in online is created?

2. What basics should you obtain if you want to check in online?

3. What do you have to pay attention to when you print out your boarding pass?

4. How do you think of check-in online?

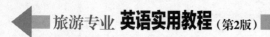
**EX. 6** **Decide whether the following statements are *true* or *false*.**

1. Airport is the only place you can check in a flight.

2. No matter you're flying first class or you're flying coach, checking in online probably saves you well over an hour.

3. After checking in online, if you don't have any bags to check, you can go right to security with your boarding pass.

4. If your boarding pass gets lost between home and the airport, you can talk to a gate agent and they should be able to replace it for you.

5. The earliest you can check-in online for most airlines is twenty-four hours.

## Part Four Skill Training

### Forms

The following is a form that can allow you check in a flight online, which is very convenient and will save you a lot of time. You just need to fill out this form and hit CONTINUE button. The computer will guide you to finish your check-in. Finally you can use your printer to print out the boarding pass.

| **Flight Check-in** |
|---|
| To begin check-in, enter the departure city/airport and a confirmation number, eTicket number or OnePass number and then click Continue. Before you begin, please ensure your printer is ready to print boarding passes. |
| Departure City/Airport: |

Enter one of the following:

| | |
|---|---|
| Confirmation Number: | |
| eTicket Number: | |
| OnePass Number: | |

**General Eligibility Requirements:**

Check-in is permitted between 60 minutes and 30 hours before scheduled departure.

Check-in is currently offered for domestic ticket itineraries that are wholly operated by Continental Airlines, Continental Express and Continental Connection (operated by Cape Air, CommutAir, Gulfstream International Airlines and SkyWest Airlines).

If you have bags to check, you may do so at an airport service center kiosk or with a Continental ticket counter representative up to 45 minutes prior to scheduled departure.

Find more information and help on how to get started with your flight check-in on continental.com.

## Practical Writing

### Writing a Letter of Application

Letters of application are widely needed in business activities for the purpose of applying for a job or study or business, so it is essential to grasp the layout of formal letters and regulation of writing.

Letters of applying for job or study focus on making understood your work history, competency, career achievement, aspiration, educational background, performance, analytical ability and motive for further study, so as to obtain good opportunities. Therefore, a general plan of writing this type of application letters is helpful for you to keep in mind. Take a letter of application for job as an example.

(1) Use a formal greeting.

(2) When you start with opening paragraph, use set phrases to state the position you are applying for and state where or when you saw the advertisement.

(3) In writing main part of this letter you'd better mention your age; describe your qualifications and experience; state your present/previous job if relevant; explain why you believe you are suitable for the job.

(4) Use set phrases to mention that you hope your application will be taken into consideration and mention that you enclose a resume.

(5) In signing off, you should use a formal signature ending. Sign underneath this print your full name below your signature.

### Model Case

#### (1) Job Application

Dear Professor Wang,

I am interested in teaching English in the People's Republic of China. I am qualified to teach reading, writing and literature. An acquaintance of mine, Mr. Liu Yongli of your university suggested that I should write to you.

Presently, I work as a teaching assistant in X College in Los Angles, California, U.S.A. My background is strong in the liberal arts, especially in the English language. I have a Ph.D. degree in linguistics from University of Michigan.

Enclosed you will find a copy of resume. Basically, I am interested in a position as a foreign language expert or as a teacher.

If you have any positions available, please allow me to interview with you.

Thank you for your time and consideration.

Respectfully yours,

(Signature)

#### (2) Further Study Application

Dear Sir,

I left Nanjing University as graduate in economy in Aug. 1998. Now I am a lecturer, working in the Department of International Trade of Progenitor University. To pursue further studies, I wish to enter the Graduate School of Economy of Harvard University to read for the degree of Master of World Economy. Your institute has a long history and a fine tradition of scholarship. It's well staffed and equipped, enjoying worldwide fame. To find an ideal place in such a school of higher learning is indeed a matter of the greatest honor. It is my long-cherished hope that I will be fortunate enough to be admitted into it.

I should be grateful to know the conditions under which the applications are accepted. Would you please send me an applicant form and some related information?

I am looking forward to your early reply.

Yours sincerely,

Brain

### (3) Applying for Business Registration

Dear Sir,

We are going to trade in an import and export firm named "New Century Import and Export Corporation" at Room216, Lian Shui Hotel, Nanning.

Kindly send us a form of application and let us know the registration fee.

Yours faithfully,

Zhu Liang

**Simulate and create** ▶ Suppose you have finished your four-year study in a university and you want to continue your study in Oxford University, UK. Write an application letter for yourself.

## Part Five Related Information

### Worlds Top Airports

The following are the world's top 30 busiest airports ranked by passenger numbers in 2012. The busiest airports are ranked depending on the number of passengers flying to or from each airport. Passenger Number data is related to the Airport Council International estimated full year figures for 2012.

| No. | Airport | Code | Chinese appellation | Total passengers | Change (%) |
|-----|---------|------|---------------------|------------------|------------|
| 1 | Atlanta International | ATL | 亚特兰大（美） | 95,462,867 | 3.3 |
| 2 | Beijing Capital | PEK | 北京首都（中） | 81,929,359 | 4.1 |
| 3 | London Heathrow | LHR | 伦敦希思罗（英） | 70,037,417 | 0.9 |

(continued)

| No. | Airport | Code | Chinese appellation | Total passengers | Change (%) |
|-----|---------|------|---------------------|------------------|-----------|
| 4 | Tokyo International | HND | 东京（日） | 66,795,178 | 6.7 |
| 5 | Chicago O'Hare | ORD | 芝加哥奥黑（美） | 66,633,503 | −0.1 |
| 6 | Los Angeles | LAX | 洛杉矶（美） | 63,688,121 | 3 |
| 7 | Charles de Gaulle | CDG | 戴高乐（法） | 61,611,934 | 1.1 |
| 8 | Dallas Fort Worth | DFW | 达拉斯（美） | 58,591,842 | 1.4 |
| 9 | Soekarno-Hatta | CGK | 哈达（印尼） | 57,772,762 | 12.9 |
| 10 | Dubai International | DXB | 迪拜（阿联酋） | 57,684,550 | 13.2 |
| 11 | Frankfurt am Main | FRA | 法兰克福（德） | 57,520,001 | 1.9 |
| 12 | Hong Kong International | HKG | 香港（中） | 56,057,751 | 5.1 |
| 13 | Denver International | DEN | 丹佛（美） | 53,156,278 | 0.6 |
| 14 | Suvarnabhumi | BKK | 曼谷（泰） | 53,002,328 | 10.6 |
| 15 | Singapore Changi | SIN | 新加坡 | 51,181,804 | 10 |
| 16 | Amsterdam Schiphol | AMS | 阿姆斯特丹（荷兰） | 51,035,590 | 2.6 |
| 17 | John F. Kennedy | JFK | 肯尼迪（美） | 49,291,765 | 3.4 |
| 18 | Guangzhou Baiyun | CAN | 广州白云（中） | 48,548,430 | 7.8 |
| 19 | Madrid Barajas | MAD | 马德里（西） | 45,176,978 | −9 |
| 20 | Atatürk International | IST | 阿塔蒂尔克（土耳其） | 45,124,831 | 20.6 |
| 21 | Shanghai Pudong | PVG | 上海浦东（中） | 44,880,164 | 8.3 |
| 22 | San Francisco | SFO | 旧金山（美） | 44,399,885 | 8.5 |
| 23 | Charlotte Douglas | CLT | 夏洛特（美） | 41,228,372 | 5.6 |
| 24 | McCarran International | LAS | 麦卡伦（美） | 40,799,830 | 0.6 |
| 25 | Phoenix Sky Harbor | PHX | 凤凰城（美） | 40,421,611 | −0.4 |
| 26 | George Bush Intercontinental | IAH | 乔治·布什洲际机场（美） | 39,891,444 | −0.6 |
| 27 | Kuala Lumpur | KUL | 吉隆坡（马） | 39,887,866 | 5.8 |
| 28 | Miami International | MIA | 迈阿密（美） | 39,467,444 | 3 |
| 29 | Incheon International | ICN | 仁川（韩） | 39,154,375 | 11.3 |
| 30 | Munich International | MUC | 慕尼黑（德） | 38,360,604 | 1.6 |

# Part Six　Guide to World Famous Sight

| Text | Notes |
|------|-------|
| **Guilin** | |
| Famous for its wonderful scenery[1], rivers and karst[2] peaks covered in lush[3] greenery, Guilin has a long history as the most beautiful place in China. Established in the Qin Dynasty as a regional power base for the first emperor of China, Guilin's population exploded[4] to around a million during the 1930s when the city was a Communist stronghold[5] against the Japanese. In recent decades, although development and exploding tourism are changing the face of this beautiful city, Guilin has remained one of China's greenest and scenic cities. | [1] 风景，景色 <br> [2] 石灰岩地区常见的地形 <br> [3] 青葱的 <br> [4] 突破，爆炸 <br> [5] 要塞，据点 |
| Guilin is situated along the Lijiang River[6], which is a favorite travel attraction in itself. The beauty of the water and the karst peaks towering[7] into the sky has attracted travelers to this area for centuries. | [6] 漓江 <br><br> [7] 高耸的 |
| Parallel[8] to the Lijiang River runs Zhongshan Road, Guilin's main street. In the middle of the city on both sides of Zhongshan Road are Banyan Lake and Fir Lake respectively[9], each a beautiful park in its own right. To the north stands Solitary Beauty Peak[10], Guilin's most prominent[11] karst peak. Along the Lijiang River are two more peaks, Wave Subduing Hill[12] and Elephant Trunk Hill[13], each proudly showing off Guilin's unique scenery. Elsewhere[14] in the city is the immense Seven Star Park[15] with seven peaks and six caves as well as pavilions[16] and gardens to enjoy. Lastly, on the northwestern outskirts[17] of town is Reed Flute Cave[18], one of the area's wonderful underground sights. | [8] 平行 <br><br> [9] 分别地 <br> [10] 独秀峰 <br> [11] 显著的，突出的 <br> [12] 伏波山 <br> [13] 象鼻山 <br> [14] 在别处 <br> [15] 七星公园 <br> [16] 亭，阁 <br> [17] 郊区，外边 <br> [18] 芦笛岩 |
| While Guilin is a very beautiful place, many travelers simply pass through Guilin on the way to their true destination, Yangshuo[19]. Yangshuo is 83 kilometers along the Lijiang River, settled amongst the most beautiful part of the Lijiang River's karst scenery. Less than two hours by bus, Yangshuo has become something of a backpacker's[20] legend and the relaxed pace of life, good food (including some great western cuisine), friendly people, scenic beauty, flat landscape[21] of rice fields and streams perfect for cycling make it paradise[22] for all those who wish to get a rest from the harsher aspects of life in China. Yangshuo's best sights include Moon Hill[23] with its local villages and caves, Green Lotus Peak[24], and Yangdi Village[25]. | [19] 阳朔 <br><br><br> [20] 背包一族 <br><br> [21] 风景，山水画 <br> [22] 天堂 <br> [23] 月亮山 <br> [24] 碧莲峰 <br> [25] 杨堤村 |

# Unit 5

## En Route

**Dialogue and Broadcasting**

### Sample Dialogue

👤 **Situation** ▶ John is booking a flight to Tokyo at a ticket agency.

**John**: I'd like to book a flight to Tokyo, please.

**Agent**: Which airline would you like to use?

**John**: Which is the cheapest?

**Agent**: When do you want to travel?

**John**: Next week, the 15th.

**Agent**: Would you like a return ticket?

**John**: Yes. I'm coming back on the 30th.

**Agent**: Let me see... ABC costs 550.00, but you have to transfer at Hong Kong. XYZ is the cheapest direct flight at 590.00, and both tourist class of course.

**John**: How long does the ABC flight take?

**Agent**: Total time is 15 hours, and XYZ takes 11 hours.

**John**: I may as well go with XYZ then.

**Agent**: How many seats would you like?

**John**: Just one, and could I have vegetarian meals?

**Agent**: Certainly. There's no extra charge.

## Sample Broadcasting on a Plane

Welcome aboard Delta Airlines.
欢迎搭乘达美航空。

On behalf of Delta Airlines Captain Johnson and his crew welcome you aboard. Our flight to Japan will take approximately four hours. Let us remind you to fasten your seat belts, straighten your seats, and kindly refrain from smoking during the whole flight.
机长强生及全体机员谨代表达美航空欢迎您搭乘本机。本班机抵达日本约需要四小时。在此提醒您系好安全带，竖直椅背，在整个飞行期间请勿吸烟。

Under your seat there is a life vest like this one for each of you.
在各位的座位底下每人各有一件像这样的救生衣。

An oxygen mask will come down from overhead in case of an emergency.
若发生紧急情况，头顶上方会放下一只氧气罩。

Please press the call button whenever you need any help.
有任何需要时，请按呼叫按钮。

We'll take off soon. Please fasten your seat belt.
我们马上就要起飞了。请系好您的安全带。

## Useful Expressions

1. What's the fare to Boston one way?
   去波士顿的单程票价是多少？
2. How long is a round trip good for?
   双程票的有效期为多久？
3. Is Flight 102 to New York on schedule?
   去纽约的 102 次航班准点吗？
4. That flight closed ten minutes ago.
   那个航班 10 分钟前已停止检票。
5. Could you tell me where the men's room is?
   请问男洗手间在哪里？
6. Well, let me know if I can be of any help.
   如需要帮助就通知我。
7. Would you mind putting my bag up on the rack?
   请帮我把包放在行李架上好吗？

## Task Dialogue 1

**Situation** ▶ You are booking an air ticket to Paris at the ticket agent. Making a dialogue with your partner based on the above situation.

## Task Dialogue 2

**Directions** ▶ Read and memorize the Sample Broadcasting to get familiar with the broadcasting on a plane.

## Part Two   Text A

## En Route

### On the Plane

Once you board the plane, there are a lot of things to do to ensure a safe and comfortable trip.

*Pay attention to the preflight briefing*

Pay attention to the flight crew safety demonstration/video. Carefully read the safety-briefing card although the information seems repetitious. The locations of the closest emergency exits may be different depending on the aircraft that you fly on and the seat you are in. Note where the nearest exits are and count the number of rows you are from them. In a survivable crash, smoke can make it difficult, if not impossible, to visually see the exits.

*Keep the overhead storage bin free of heavy articles*

Overhead storage bins may not be able to hold very heavy objects during turbulence, so if you or another passenger has trouble lifting an article into the bin, have it stored elsewhere.

*Keep your seat belt fastened while you are seated*

Keeping the belt on when you are seated provides that extra protection you might need if the plane hits unexpected turbulence.

*Listen to the flight attendants*

The primary reason flight attendants are on an aircraft is for safety, so if one of them asks you to do something like fasten your seat belts, do it first and ask questions later.

*Let the flight attendant pour your hot drinks*

Flight attendants are trained to handle hot drinks like coffee or tea in a crowded aisle on a moving aircraft, so allow them to pour the drink and hand it to you.

*Don't drink too much*

The atmosphere in an airliner cabin is pressurized to about the same altitude as ground, so any alcohol you consume will affect you more strongly than at sea level. Moderation is a good policy at any altitude.

*Food*

Relax during flight, sleep as much as possible. They bring food to you every now and then. You don't have to finish everything. Just eat what you like. You can always ask for something to drink or eat. Normally everything including drinks is free but before ordering anything on board check if you have to pay for it.

*Immigration card and customs declaration card*

When the plane is about to arrive at the destination, the air attendants will distribute the immigration card (I-94 Form) and customs declaration card. Every passenger needs to fill them out even you are not an immigrant or you have no customs to report. You will need them when you are entering the country at the immigration and customs check.

*Misc*

When flight is long, they close windows to make you sleep. Try to sleep. You can walk around once the plane is in the air or just sit in one place. They show some movies and some programs in the flight. Also there is some music. If you want, you can get a book to read or a walkman to listen to music. All the announcements are in English and also in the official language of the country of the airline. If you don't understand anything ask flight attendant or a neighbor.

*Keep your wits about you*

In the unlikely event that you are involved in an emergency situation such as a precautionary emergency evacuation, follow the directions of the flight attendants and flight crew and exit the aircraft as quickly as possible.

### At Intermediate Airport

There can be international stops on your way.

Generally passengers are required to get down at an international stop, which might be for security checkup or cleaning of the airplane. You should take your hand baggage with you when you get down. You will be given a "transit card" or say "transit visa". Normally the halt is for a few hours. Listen to the announcement, which is always made before the international halt. You will hear or see on TV monitor information about departure time, gate number, etc. This information also may be on the boarding pass. Flight attendant also can give you terminal and gate number for your next flight. After getting down at international airport, you can move around in the airport. You may want to get fresh in the toilets located in the airport.

It's always advisable to keep your watch in sync with current time zone.

*Changing flight*

Remember that your airport is mostly very big. It might take longer time to search for terminal and gate number. Airport normally has good directions/maps. You can also ask airport staff about how to go to the gate. Once you locate the gate, you may spend some time looking around. Ideally you won't eat anything outside because you eat in the flight. Be at the gate within 45 minutes of your flight's departure for the onward journey, because they may require checking your tickets, etc.

*Boarding again*

You have to go through Metal Detectors, and have your hand-baggage X-ray again. You might have to wait for sometime before they announce boarding of the flight. Once you get in, you are all set to take off for the final destination.

## New Words

**ensure** [in'ʃɔ:] *vt.* 确保，保证

**preflight** ['pri:'flait] *a.* 飞行前的，为起飞做准备的

**briefing** ['bri:fiŋ] *n.* 简令；飞行前指示

**crew** [kru:] *n.* （船上、飞机上的）工作人员；全体船员；全体乘务员

**demonstration** [,demən'streiʃən] *n.* 示范

**video** ['vidiəu] *n.* 电视，录像，视频

**repetitious** [,repi'tiʃəs] *a.* 反复的；重复的

**exit** ['eksit] *n.* 安全门；出口

**survivable** [sə'vaivəbl] *a.* 可以存活的

**crash** [kræʃ] *n.* 碰撞，坠落，坠毁

**visually** ['viʒuəli] *ad.* 在视觉上地；真实地

**bin** [bin] *n.* 箱柜

**turbulence** ['tə:bjuləns] *n.* 紊流，湍流

**unexpected** [ʌnik'spektid] *a.* 意外的，想不到的

**attendant** [ə'tendənt] *n.* 服务员，乘务员

**airliner** ['εə,lainə] *n.* 大型客机；班机

**aisle** [ail] *n.* 走廊，过道

**cabin** ['kæbin] *n.* 机舱，船舱

**pressurize** ['preʃəraiz] *vt.* 增压；密封

**altitude** ['ælti,tju:d] *n.* （海拔）高度

**alcohol** ['ælkə,hɔl] *n.* 酒精；酒

**consume** [kən'sju:m] *vt.* 吃，喝；消耗

**moderation** [,mɔdə'reiʃən] *n.* 适度

**destination** [,desti'neiʃən] *n.* 目的地，终点

**misc** [misk] *n.* 其他事宜，杂项

**walkman** ['wɔ:kmən] *n.* 随身听

**precautionary** [pri'kɔ:ʃənəri] *a.* 预防的

**evacuation** [i,vækju'eiʃən] *n.* 撤退；疏散

**security** [si'kjuərəti] *n.* 安全

**halt** [hɔ:lt] *n.* 停止，暂停

**monitor** ['mɔnitə] *n.* 监视器，显示器

**terminal** ['tə:minl] *n.* 航站楼

**sync** [siŋk] *n.* 同时；同步

**locate** [ləu'keit] *vt.* 找到……位置

**onward** ['ɔnwəd] *a.* 向前的，前进的

**detector** [di'tektə] *n.* 探测器

## Phrases and Expressions

be about to  将要，快要
keep one's wits about  保持警惕，保持清醒

transit card/transit visa  转机卡

## Notes

**1** The locations of the closest emergency exits may be different depending on the aircraft that you fly on and the seat you are in.

本句中，depending on 的意思是"取决于，根据"。定语从句 that you fly on 和 you are in 分别修饰 the aircraft 和 the seat。

**2** Keeping the belt on when you are seated provides that extra protection you might need if the plane hits unexpected turbulence.

本句中，keeping the belt on when you are seated 是一个动名词短语，作句子的主语，when you are seated 是动名词短语的时间状语，provides 是句子的谓语，that extra protection 是宾语。you might need if the plane hits unexpected turbulence 是一个定语从句，修饰宾语 that extra protection。在该定语从句中，if the plane hits unexpected turbulence 是一个条件状语从句，修饰谓语 hits unexpected turbulence。

**3** When the plane is about to arrive at the destination, the air attendants will distribute the immigration card (I-94 Form) and customs declaration card.

本句中，词组 be about to do sth. 的意思是"就要做某事，将要做某事"。请看下例：

I was about to leave the room when the telephone rang.

我刚要离开房间突然电话铃响了。

**4** Generally passengers are required to get down at an international stop, which might be for security checkup or cleaning of the airplane.

本句中，which might be for security checkup or cleaning of the airplane 是一个非限定性定语从句，修饰主句，对其进行补充说明。

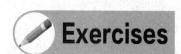 **Exercises**

**EX. 1** **Answer the following questions.**

1. Is it important to locate the closest emergency exits when you board the plane? Why?

2. Can you put very heavy objects in your overhead bins? Why?

3. If you are not an immigrant, you needn't fill out the immigration card. Is this statement correct?

4. Can you stay in the plane at the international stops?

**EX. 2** Write out the English words according to the definitions given below.

| definitions | words |
|---|---|
| an act of giving necessary instructions or information | |
| all people working on a shop, plane, spacecraft, etc. | |
| an act of showing or providing something | |
| (often written over or on a door) a way out | |
| a large storage container | |
| a narrow passage between rows of seats, shelves, etc., e.g. in a theatre, plane, or large shop | |
| a place or set of buildings for the use of passengers joining or leaving a bus, ship, plane, etc. | |
| a device with a screen on which words or pictures can be shown | |
| trademark for a small cassette player, with small headphones, which people use for listening to music when they are walking around, sitting on public transport, etc. | |
| a recording of moving pictures and sound which can be played on a special machine so that it can be watched on a television | |

**EX. 3** Complete the following sentences with appropriate words or expressions from the text.

1. The primary reason flight attendants are on an aircraft is for _____.
2. When the plane is about to arrive at the destination, the air attendants will distribute the _____ card and _____ card.
3. All the announcements are in _____ and also in the official language of the country of the airline.
4. Generally passengers are required to get down at an international stop, which might be for _____ or _____. You should take your _____ with you when you get down. You will be given a _____ or say transit visa.

**EX. 4** Translate the following sentences into Chinese.

1. Overhead storage bins may not be able to hold very heavy objects during turbulence, so if you or another passenger has trouble lifting an article into the bin, have it stored elsewhere.

2. The atmosphere in an airliner cabin is pressurized to about the same altitude as ground, so any alcohol you consume will affect you more strongly than at sea level. Moderation is a good policy at any altitude.

3. In the unlikely event that you are involved in an emergency situation such as a precautionary emergency evacuation, follow the directions of the flight attendants and flight crew and exit the aircraft as quickly as possible.

## Part Three  Text B

## Air  Transportation

### *Nature of the Industry*

The rapid development of air transportation has increased the mobility of the population and created thousands of job opportunities. The air transportation industry involves many activities. Most familiar are the major airlines, which provide transportation for passengers and cargoes; and airports, which provide the many ground support services required by aircraft, passengers, and cargoes. Air taxi companies and commuter airlines also provide commercial transportation, such as passenger and cargo service, often to and from small airports not serviced by the major airlines. Other companies provide air courier services, which furnish air delivery for individually addressed letters, parcels, and packages, and helicopter and sightseeing airplane services for tourists. This industry also includes services related to air transportation, such as aircraft repair, cleaning, and storage.

### *Working Conditions*

Working conditions vary widely, depending on the occupation. Although most employees work in fairly comfortable surroundings, such as offices, terminals, or airplanes, mechanics and others who service aircraft are subject to noise, dirt, and grease and sometimes work outside in bad weather.

Because airlines operate flights at all hours of the day and night, many workers often have irregular hours or schedules. Flight and ground personnel may have to work at night or on weekends or holidays. Flight personnel may be away from their home bases frequently. When they are away from home, the airlines provide hotel accommodations, transportation between the hotel and airport, and an allowance for meals and expenses. Pilots and flight attendants employed outside the major airlines also may have irregular schedules.

Flight crews, especially those on international routes, often suffer jet lag—disorientation and fatigue caused by flying into different time zones. Because employees must report for duty well rested, they must allow ample time to rest during their layovers.

### *Occupations in the Industry*

Although pilots and flight attendants are the most visible occupations in this industry, more than 40 percent of all employees in air transportation work in ground occupations. For example, aircraft mechanics and service technicians service, inspect, and repair planes, and reservation and transportation ticket agents and travel clerks make and confirm reservations and sell tickets to passengers.

Aircraft mechanics and service technicians may work on several different types of aircraft, such as jet transports, small propeller-driven airplanes, or helicopters. Many, however, specialize in one section of a particular type of aircraft, such as the engine or the hydraulic or electrical systems. In small, independent repair shops, mechanics and technicians usually inspect and repair many different types of aircraft.

Many mechanics and technicians specialize in scheduled maintenance, following a schedule based on the number of hours flown, calendar days, cycles of operation, or a combination of these factors. Mechanics inspect the engines, landing gear, instruments, and other parts of aircraft and perform necessary maintenance and repairs.

Other employees interact with the public. Reservation and transportation ticket agents and travel clerks answer telephones, sell tickets, and make reservations for passengers on scheduled airlines. Customer service representatives assist passengers, check tickets when passengers board or disembark an airplane, and check luggage at the reception area and ensure that it is placed on the proper carrier. They also assist elderly or handicapped persons and unaccompanied children in claiming personal belongings and baggage, and in getting on and off the plane. They also may provide assistance to passengers who become ill or injured. Airline security representatives screen passengers and visitors to ensure that weapons and illegal or forbidden articles are not carried into restricted areas.

Airplane cargo agents take orders from shippers and arrange for transportation of their goods. Baggage handlers are responsible for loading and unloading passengers' baggage. They stack baggage on specified carts or conveyors to see that it gets to the proper destination and also return baggage to passengers at airline terminals upon receipt of their claim check. Aircraft cleaners clean aircraft interiors after each flight. Firms supplying air courier services that deliver individually addressed packages, letters, and parcels employ many truck drivers, to deliver and pick up merchandise or to deliver packages within a specified area. The airline industry also relies on many management, professional, and administrative support workers to keep operations running smoothly.

Flight crewmembers make up the remainder—about one-fifth—of air transportation employment, and include pilots and flight attendants. Pilots are highly trained professionals who fly airplanes and helicopters to carry out a wide variety of tasks. Although most are airline pilots, copilots, and flight engineers who transport passengers and cargoes, others are commercial pilots involved in more unusual tasks, such as dusting crops, spreading seed for reforestation, testing aircraft, flying passengers and cargoes to areas not serviced by regular airlines, directing firefighting efforts, tracking criminals, monitoring traffic, and rescuing and evacuating injured persons.

Except on small aircraft, two pilots usually constitute the cockpit crew. Generally, the most experienced pilot, or captain, is in command and supervises all other crewmembers. The pilot and copilot split flying and other duties such as communicating with air traffic controllers and monitoring the instruments. Some aircraft have a third pilot in the cockpit—the flight engineer or second officer—who assists the other pilots by monitoring and operating many of the instruments and systems and watching for other aircraft. Most new aircraft are designed to be flown without a flight engineer.

Most airline flights have one or more flight attendants on board. Their most important function is assisting passengers in the event of an emergency. This may range from reassuring passengers during occasional encounters with strong turbulence to opening emergency exits and inflating escape chutes. More routinely, flight attendants instruct passengers in the use of safety and emergency equipment. Once in the air, they serve meals and snacks, answer questions about the flight, distribute magazines and pillows, and help care for small children and elderly and disabled persons. They also may administer first aid to passengers who become ill.

### Training and Advancement

The skills and experience needed by workers in the air transportation industry differ by occupation. Some jobs may be entered directly from high school, while others require extensive specialized training.

Pilots must have a commercial pilot license with an instrument rating, and must be certified to fly the types of aircraft their employer operates. For example, helicopter pilots must hold a commercial pilot certificate with a helicopter rating. Pilots receive their flight training from the military or from civilian flying schools. Physical requirements are strict. With or without glasses, pilots must have 20/20 vision and good hearing, and be in excellent health. In addition, airlines generally require two years of college and increasingly prefer or require a college degree. Pilots who work for smaller airlines may advance to flying for larger companies. They also can advance from flight engineer to copilot to captain and, by becoming certified, to fly larger planes.

Applicants for flight attendant jobs must be in excellent health. Employers prefer those who have completed some college and have experience in dealing with the public. Speaking a foreign language also is an asset. Applicants are trained for their jobs at company schools; the length of training usually lasts from two to seven weeks, depending on the size and the type of carrier. Training may include crew resource management, which emphasizes teamwork and safety. After completing initial training, flight attendants must go through additional training and pass a safety exam each year in order to continue flying. Advancement opportunities are limited, although some attendants become customer service directors, instructors, or recruiting representatives.

When hiring aircraft mechanics, employers prefer graduates of aircraft mechanic trade schools who are in good physical condition. After being hired, aircraft mechanics must keep up-to-date on the latest technical changes and improvements in aircraft and associated systems. Most mechanics remain in the maintenance field, but they may advance to head mechanic and, sometimes, to supervisor. Most other workers in ground occupations learn their job through a combination of company classroom and on-the-job training. At least a high school education is required for most jobs.

A good speaking voice and a pleasant personality are essential for reservation and transportation ticket agents and customer service representatives. Reservation agents also need some keyboard skills. Airlines prefer applicants with experience in sales or in dealing with the public and most require a high school education, but some college is preferred. Some agents and service representatives advance to supervisor or other administrative positions.

Some entry-level jobs in this industry, such as baggage handler and aircraft cleaner, require little or no previous training. The basic tasks associated with many of these jobs are learned in less than a week, and most newly hired workers are trained on the job under the guidance of an experienced employee or a manager. However, promotional opportunities for many ground occupations are limited due to the narrow scope of the duties and the specialized skills of some occupations. Some may advance to supervisor or other administrative positions.

 **New Words**

**nature** ['neitʃə] *n.* 性质，特性；种类

**mobility** [məu'biləti] *n.* 流动性

**airline** ['ɛə,lain] *n.* 航空公司

**cargo** ['kɑ:gəu] *n.*（船、飞机所载的）货物

**commuter** [kə'mju:tə] *n.*（远距离）上下班往返的人

**courier** ['kuriə] *n.* 信使，送急件的人；旅游服务员

**individually** [,indi'vidʒuəli] *ad.* 个别地；单独地；个人地

**parcel** ['pɑ:sl] *n.* 小包，包裹

**package** ['pækidʒ] *n.* 包裹，包

**helicopter** ['heli,kɔptə] *n.* 直升机

**occupation** [,ɔkju'peiʃən] *n.* 职业

**surroundings** [sə'raundiŋz] *n.* 环境

**mechanic** [mi'kænik] *n.* 技工，机修工，机械工

**dirt** [də:t] *n.* 污垢，泥土

**grease** [gri:s] *n.* 油脂

**irregular** [i'regjulə] *a.* 不规律的

**schedule** ['ʃedju:l] *n.* 时间表；进度表

**personnel** [,pə:sə'nel] *n.* 人员，职员

**pilot** ['pailət] *n.* 飞行员；飞机驾驶员

**disorientation** [dis,ɔ:riən'teiʃən] *n.* 方向知觉的丧失；迷惑

**fatigue** [fə'ti:g] *n.* 疲乏；劳累

**ample** ['æmpl] *a.* 充足的；充分的

**layover** ['lei,əuvə] *n.* 中途的短暂停留，临时滞留，中途下车

**hydraulic** [hai'drɔ:lik] *a.* 水力的，水压的

**maintenance** ['meintənəns] *n.* 保养，维护，维修

**calendar** ['kælində] *n.* 日历，历法

**cycle** ['saikl] *n.* 周期，循环

**combination** [,kɔmbi'neiʃən] *n.* 结合，联合

**interact** [,intər'ækt] *vi.* 相互作用，交互

**assist** [ə'sist] *vt.* 援助，帮助

**disembark** [,disim'bɑ:k] *vt.* 使下（车、船、飞机等）

**proper** ['prɔpə] *a.* 适当的；正确的

**carrier** ['kæriə] *n.* 从事运输业的公司或企业；运载工具

**unaccompanied** [,ʌnə'kʌmpənid] *a.* 没有陪伴的

**screen** [skri:n] *vt.* 筛选，审查

**illegal** [i'li:gəl] *a.* 违法的，不合规定的

**shipper** ['ʃipə] *n.* 托运人，发货人

**handler** ['hændlə] *n.* 管理人，操纵者

**load** [ləud] *vt.* 装载，装填

**unload** [ʌn'ləud] *vt.* 卸货；卸下

**stack** [stæk] *vt.* 堆叠

**cart** [ka:t] *n.* 大车，手推车

**interior** [in'tiəriə] *n.* 内部

**firm** [fə:m] *n.* 公司，（合伙）商号

**deliver** [di'livə] *vt.* 递送

**professional** [prə'feʃənl] *a.* 专业的，职业的

**administrative** [əd'ministrətiv] *a.* 管理的，行政的

**remainder** [ri'meində] *n.* 剩余物；其他的人

**copilot** ['kəu,pailət] *n.*（飞机的）副驾驶员

**dust** [dʌst] *vt.* 撒

**reforestation** [,ri:fori'steiʃən] *n.* 重新造林

**track** [træk] *vt.* 跟踪，追踪

**rescue** ['reskju:] *vt.* 援救，营救

**constitute** ['kɔnsti,tju:t] *vt.* 构成

**cockpit** ['kɔk,pit] *n.* 驾驶员座舱

**supervise** ['su:pəvaiz] *vt.* 监督，管理，指导

**split** [split] *vt.* 分开；分工

**function** ['fʌŋkʃən] *n.* 功能，作用

**encounter** [in'kauntə] *n.* 遭遇，遇到

**inflate** [in'fleit] *vt.* 使膨胀，使充气

**chute** [ʃu:t] *n.* 滑道

**routinely** [ru:'ti:nli] *ad.* 例行公事地

**pillow** ['piləu] *n.* 枕头，枕垫

**advancement** [əd'va:nsmənt] *n.* 前进，提升

**extensive** [ik'stensiv] *a.* 广大的，广阔的，广泛的

**rating** ['reitiŋ] *n.* 等级级别

**certified** ['sə:tifaid] *a.* 被鉴定的

**civilian** [si'viljən] *a.* 民间的，民用的

**degree** [di'gri:] *n.* 学位

**applicant** ['æplikənt] *n.* 申请者

**emphasize** ['emfəsaiz] *vt.* 强调，着重

**teamwork** ['ti:m,wə:k] *n.* 联合作业，协力

**instructor** [in'strʌktə] *n.* 指导者

**recruit** [ri'kru:t] *vt.* 招募

**improvement** [im'pru:vmənt] *n.* 改进，进步

**personality** [,pə:sə'næləti] *n.* 个性，人格

**essential** [i'senʃəl] *a.* 必要的，必不可少的

**keyboard** ['ki:bɔ:d] *n.* 键盘

**guidance** ['gaidəns] *n.* 指导，领导

**promotional** [prə'məuʃənəl] *a.* 升职的

**scope** [skəup] *n.* 范围；机会

# Phrases and Expressions

air taxi  短程小客机，出租飞机

jet lag  时差，时差反应，时差综合征

propeller-driven airplane  螺旋桨飞机

arrange for  安排

make up  组成，构成

in the event of  万一，如果

# Notes

**1** Air taxi companies and commuter airlines also provide commercial transportation, such as passenger and cargo service, often to and from small airports not serviced by the major airlines.

本句中，to and from 为"往复，来回"之意。not serviced by the major airlines 为过去分词短语作定语，修饰 airports。又如：

I took part in the party held for Jean's birthday.

我参加了为简举行的生日聚会。

**2** Because employees must report for duty well rested, they must allow ample time to rest during their layovers.

本句中，report for duty 为上班之意。well rested 为过去分词短语作伴随状语，意为充分的休息。例如：

She attended the banquet well clothed.

他穿着得体的衣服参加了那个宴会。

**3** This may range from reassuring passengers during occasional encounters with strong turbulence to opening emergency exits and inflating escape chutes.

本句中，range from... to... 意思为其工作职责"从……到……变动，从……到……范围"。to 为介词，故后面用动名词。又如：

The leather shoes range from $10 to $100 a pair.

皮鞋售价每双 10 美元到 100 美元不等。

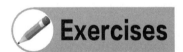

# Exercises

**EX. 5** **Answer the following questions.**

1. The employees of this industry mainly work on regular hours or schedule. Is this statement correct? Why?

2. What occupations does this industry involve according to this text?

3. How many pilots constitute the cockpit crew, generally speaking?

4. What is the main responsibility of flight attendants?

5. What are the basic qualities of being a good flight attendant?

**EX. 6** **Decide whether the following statements are *true* or *false*.**

1. The rapid development of air transportation has increased the mobility of the population and created thousands of job opportunities.

2. Most employees of this industry often work at regular hours or schedules.

3. Except on small aircraft, two pilots usually constitute the cockpit crew.

4. The most important function of flight attendants on board is assisting passengers in the event

of an emergency.

5. Speaking a foreign language is an asset to apply for a flight attendant job.

6. A good speaking voice and a pleasant personality are essential for air ticket agents and customer service representatives.

# Part Four  Skill Training

## Forms

Please fill out the **immigration card (I-94 Form)** and **customs declaration card** before landing, which will save you a lot of time when you are entering the country.

*(Form One)*

### 美国出入境：I-94 表格（I-94 Form）

入境美国的外籍旅客都必须在下机前填写两份表格，一份是 I-94 表格（I-94 Form），一份是美国海关申报表（Custom Declaration）。I-94 表格非常重要，这是美国移民局认可您合法进入美国的证明，同时在到期之前，也能证明您没有在美国逾期非法居留。此表格只是一张小白卡，通常会由美国移民官订在旅客的护照上，等准备离开美国出境时，再由航空公司人员收回，交给移民局，建立您出入美国国境的记录，不然将来有可能被美国拒绝入境。不需要 I-94 Form 的外籍人士，以加拿大人为主。一般而言，加拿大公民进出美国不需要 I-94 Form，墨西哥持越境卡每日进入美国工作的人员也不需要 I-94 Form，另外多次进入的非移民签证持有人也不需要 I-94 Form。

### I-94 FORM
### I-94 表格

US Department of Justice    美国司法部

OMR 1115-4077

Immigration and Naturalization Service    移民局

Welcome to the United State    欢迎来到美国

Admission Number 552738531 01

登记号码（举例说明）552738531 01

### I-94 Arrival/Departure Record-Instructions
### I-94 入境 / 离境记录说明

This form must be completed by all persons except US citizens, returning resident aliens with immigrant visas, and Canadian Citizens visiting or in transit.

除了美国公民、美国海外侨民、永久居民和加拿大公民外，所有访问或过境的人士都必须填写此表。

Type or print legibly with pen in ALL CAPITAL LETTERS. Use English. Do not write on the back of this form.

请用大写字母打字或用笔填写清楚。请用英文填写。不要在此表背面填写任何东西。

This form is in two parts. Please complete both the Arrival Record (Item 1 through 13) and the Departure Record (Item 14 through 17).

此表包括两部分。请填写入境记录（第 1 项至第 13 项）和离境记录（第 14 项至第 17 项）两部分。

When all items are completed, present this form to the US Immigration and Naturalization Service Inspector.

填写完毕后，请将此表交给美国移民局官员。

Item 7: If you are entering the United States by land, enter LAND in this space. If you are entering the United States by ship, enter SEA in this space.

第 7 项内容说明：如果您从陆地进入美国，请在空格内填写 LAND。如果您乘船进入美国，请在空格内填写 SEA。

## I-94 Arrival Record
## I-94 入境记录

1. Family Name _____
   姓氏 _____

2. First/Given Name _____
   名字 _____

3. Birth Date (Day/Month/Year) _____
   生日（日 / 月 / 年）_____

4. Country of Citizenship _____
   国籍 _____

5. Sex (Male or Female) _____
   性别（男性或女性）_____

6. Passport Number _____
   护照号码 _____

7. Airline & Flight Number _____
   航空公司和航班号 _____

8. Country Where You Live _____
   您居住的国家_____

9. City Where You Boarded _____
   您登机的城市 _____

10. City Where Visa Was Issued _____
    取得签证的城市 _____

11. Date Issued (Day/Month/Year) _____
    取得签证的日期（日 / 月 / 年）_____

12. Address While in the United State (Number and Street) _____
    在美国的住址（门牌号及街名）_____

13. City and State _____
    在美国的住址（城市及州名）_____
    Departure Number 552738531 01
    离境号码 552738531 01
    Immigration and Naturalization Service 移民局

### I-94 Departure Record
### I-94 离境记录

14. Family Name _____
    姓氏 _____

15. First/Given Name _____
    名字 _____

16. Birth Date (Day/Month/Year) _____
    生日（日 / 月 / 年）_____

17. County of Citizenship _____
    国籍 _____

假如 I-94 Form 丢掉或损坏了，要向美国移民局申请补发。有意要在美国延期停留，改变原有非移民签证等，都一定要有 I-94 Form，如果入境时没有发给 I-94 Form 则应该向移民局申请补发。以防万一，入境美国后，记得马上把 I-94 表格影印一份，包括正反面，然后和其他重要证件一起妥善保存。

*(Form Two)*

### 美国入境：海关申报表
### Customs Declaration

按照美国法律，如果您携带超过一万美元现金入境，一定要向美国海关申报，否则海关可以没收您的财产。

携带少于美元一百元的礼品入境不需关税。

不可携带任何食物进入美国，尤其是易腐烂食物，包括水果、蔬菜、肉类或农作物。

衣物、专业设备及其他家庭物品，如果已经使用一段时间并不再出售的话，不需付关税，可带入美国。

以某些特定动物为原料的产品禁止带入美国。详情请咨询动物及农产品健康检查服务中心（Animal and Plant Health Inspection services）。

带入美国的金钱数额不限多少，但如果超过一万美元，则必须填写海关申报表。

任何含有麻醉成分的药品或注射药物均须附上医生开示的处方证明。走私麻醉药物入境美国，将受巨额罚款。

**WELCOME TO THE UNITED STATES**
欢迎来到美国
DEPARTMENT OF THE TREASURY
UNITED STATES CUSTOMS SERVICE
财政部 美国海关署
**CUSTOM DECLARATION**
海关申报表
Each arriving traveler or head of family must provide the following information (only ONE written declaration per family is required):
每位入关的旅游者或一家之主必须提供以下资料（一个家庭只须申报一份）：

1. Family Name _____ First/Given _____ Middle _____
   姓氏 _____ 名字 _____ 中间名 _____

2. Birth date
   出生日期
   _____ Day _____ Month _____ Year
   _____ 日 ____ 月 ____ 年

3. Number of family members traveling with you: _____
   与您同行的家庭成员人数：_____

4. U.S. Address: _____
   在美地址：_____

5. Passport issued by (country) _____
   护照发照（国家）_____

6. Passport Number _____
   护照号码 _____

7. Country of Residence _____
   居住国家 _____

8. Countries visited on this trip prior to US arrival _____
   到美国前造访过的国家 _____

9. Airline/Flight No: _____
   航空公司 / 航班号：_____

10. The primary purpose of this trip is business. YES NO
    此次旅程的主要目的是商务？是 否

11. I am/we are bringing fruits, plants, meats, food, soil, birds, snails, other live animals, farm products, or I/we have been on a farm or ranch outside the US
    YES        NO
    我（们）携带水果、植物、肉类、食品、土壤、鸟类、蜗牛、其他动物和农产品，或一直居住在美国以外的农村或牧场。
    是        否

12. I am/we are carrying currency or monetary instruments over $10,000 US or the foreign equivalent.
    YES        NO
    我（们）携带现金或珍贵物品，其价值超过一万美元或相当于一万美元的外币。
    是        否

13. I/we have commercial merchandise. (articles for sale, samples used for soliciting orders, or goods that are not considered personal effects.)

    YES          NO

我（们）有携带商品。（贩卖之商品、订购之样本等任何非属私人之物品。）

    是           否

14. The total value of all goods I/we purchased or acquired abroad and am/are bringing to the US is (see instructions under Merchandise on reverse side; visitors should report value of gifts only): $ _____ US Dollars

您境外购买或获得并带入美国所有物品总价值（参看背面商品栏目；访问者只需要申报礼品价值）：$ _____ 美元

I have read the important information on the reverse side of this form and have made a truthful declaration.

我已阅读过这个表格背面之重要须知，并据实以报。

SIGNATURE _____

签名 _____

Date _____

日期_____

    如果您是随旅行团到美国，有一些旅行社会事先将您的海关申报表基本资料都先打好或写好，您只要再填写某些问题即可，很方便。建议据实以报，因为美国海关人员有时候会抽查入境旅客的行李，如果您所带的东西没有据实以报，被海关抽查到，海关可以没收您的财物，美国海关那边也会留下您的不良记录，之后您要进入美国，可能每次都会被翻箱倒柜地检查行李，得不偿失！

## Practical Writing

### *Making a Name Card*

    It is popular and important to exchange name cards in business activities. It is especially necessary to have a name card of English version in a foreign social intercourse.

    The information on a name card may consist of seven parts:

    1. the name of company

    2. name

    3. position, title

    4. the address

    5. telephone number

    6. fax number

    7. E-mail address

*Sample*

> **Mat Bao Company**
> **Mr. Nguyen Quoc Vinh**
> **Marketing Dept.**
> **(Internet, Web solutions)**
>
> **Address**: No. 26, Zhongshan Road, Shijiazhuang City
> Hebei Province, 050000, P.R.China
> **Tel**: 0311-6081514 6075767
> **Fax**: 0311-6081514
> **E-mail**: 5663@sohu.com
> **Web site**: www.sjzmingying.com

👤 **Simulate and create** ▶ Suppose you are the secretary of a big company. Design a name card for the general manager.

## Part Five  Related Information

| Text | Notes |
|---|---|
| **Travel Tips for Pregnant[1] Mothers** | [1] 怀孕的 |
| Air travel is generally one of the safest and most convenient methods of traveling. Millions of passengers around the world choose to travel by air each year, the vast majority of which experience no ill effects from their journey. | |
| It is generally safe for pregnant passengers to travel, though caution[2] should be exercised about excessive[3] amounts of flying during the early weeks because of hypoxia[4]. Heavy lifting during pregnancy should be avoided, so extra care should be taken with baggage. Please consult your gynaecologist[5] or obstetrician[6] before planning your trip. | [2] 注意，当心<br>[3] 过多的<br>[4] 缺氧<br>[5] 妇科学家<br>[6] 产科医生 |
| We will accept passengers with single pregnancies up to 36 weeks and multiple[7] pregnancies up to 32 weeks. A medical certificate may be required at check-in. | [7] 多个的 |
| Pregnant passengers should make certain that the facilities at the destination country are adequate to cope with any problems with the pregnancy happened during the visit. It is wise to avoid travel to remote locations whilst pregnant. | |
| If you require medications during your pregnancy, please ensure that you have an adequate supply for the journey. Please remember that certain medications, such as some types of malarial[8] prophylaxes[9] and vaccinations[10], cannot be used in pregnancy. If the destination country requires such prophylaxis, it is better to postpone the journey until after your pregnancy. You can obtain further details from your gynaecologist or obstetrician. | [8] 疟疾的<br>[9] 预防<br>[10] 接种疫苗 |

# Part Six Guide to World Famous Sight

| Text | Notes |
|---|---|
| **Notre Dame de Paris** | |
| Notre Dame de Paris, known simply as Notre Dame in English, is a Gothic[1] cathedral on the eastern half of the Île de la Cité2[2] in Paris, France, with its main entrance to the west. It is still used as a Roman Catholic cathedral and is the seat of the Archbishop of Paris[3]. Notre Dame de Paris is widely considered one of the finest examples of French Gothic architecture. It was restored and saved from destruction by Viollet-le-Duc, one of France's most famous architects. Notre Dame translates as "Our Lady" from French. | [1] 哥特式的 <br> [2] Île de la Cité: 西岱岛 <br><br> [3] Archbishop of Paris: 巴黎大主教 |
| Notre Dame de Paris was one of the first Gothic cathedrals, and its construction spanned the Gothic period. Its sculptures and stained glass show the heavy influence of naturalism[4], giving them a more secular[5] look that was lacking from earlier Romanesque[6] architecture. | [4] 自然主义 <br> [5] 长期的 <br> [6] 罗马式的 |
| Notre Dame de Paris was among the first buildings in the world to use the flying buttress[7]. The building was not originally designed to include the flying buttresses around the choir[8] and nave[9]. After the construction began and the thinner walls (popularized in the Gothic style) grew ever higher, stress fractures began to occur as the walls pushed outward. So, naturally, they built supports around the building and later additions continued as such. | [7] flying buttress 飞拱 <br> [8] 唱诗班 <br> [9] 中央广场 |
| At the end of the 18th century, during the French Revolution, many of the treasures of the cathedral were either destroyed or plundered[10]. The statues of biblical[11] kings of Judea (erroneously thought to be kings of France) were beheaded[12]. Many of the heads were found during a 1977 excavation[13] nearby and are on display at the Musée de Cluny[14]. Only the great bells avoided being melted down, and the cathedral was dedicated first to the Cult of Reason, and to the Cult of the Supreme Being. The church interior was used as a warehouse for the storage of forage and food. | [10] 抢劫 <br> [11] 圣经的 <br> [12] 斩首，砍头 <br><br> [13] 挖掘，发掘，出土文物 <br><br> [14] Musée de Cluny: 克鲁尼美术馆 |

# Unit 6

## Arrival

---

**Part One** **Dialogues**

### Sample Dialogue 1

👤 **Situation** ▶ After arriving at the destination airport, Keith is at the customs declaration desk.

| | |
|---|---|
| **Customs inspector**: | Do you have anything to declare, sir? |
| **Keith**: | Just some wine and cigarettes. |
| **Inspector**: | How much wine do you have? |
| **Keith**: | Four bottles. |
| **Inspector**: | That's fine, and how many cigarettes? |
| **Keith**: | I have 20 packets. |
| **Inspector**: | I'm afraid you're only allowed 15 packets. You'll have to pay duty on the rest. |
| **Keith**: | Oh! How much is it? |
| **Inspector**: | A total of 4.10 pounds plus V.A.T. |
| **Keith**: | Here you are. |

### Sample Dialogue 2

👤 **Situation** ▶ Amy just arrived at New York. Her friend Nancy is meeting her at the airport.

| | |
|---|---|
| **Amy**: | I am really glad you can come to meet me. |
| **Nancy**: | It's my pleasure. It has been so many years but you haven't changed a bit. Still as beautiful as before. |

| | | |
|---|---|---|
| **Amy**: | You are the same. |
| **Nancy**: | Oh. How was your flight? |
| **Amy**: | Great. I enjoyed it very much. |
| **Nancy**: | How long did the flight take to New York? |
| **Amy**: | About twelve hours. |
| **Nancy**: | Shall I take you to the hotel now? |
| **Amy**: | Yes. That would be great. |
| **Nancy**: | Did you make a reservation for a hotel? |
| **Amy**: | Yes. I'm booked at the Hilton Hotel. |

## Useful Expressions

1. May I have your customs declaration form?

   请出示你的关税申报表。

2. A total of 4.10 pounds plus V.A.T.

   加上增值税共计 4.10 英镑。

3. Long time no see.

   好久未见。

4. Excuse me, but would you perhaps be Mr. Thorn?

   对不起，请问你是索恩先生吗？

5. Did you enjoy your flight?

   旅途愉快吗？

6. Thank you for picking me up.

   谢谢你来接我。

## Task Dialogue 1

**Situation** ▶ After arriving at Washington International Airport, you are clearing the customs.

## Task Dialogue 2

**Situation** ▶ You haven't seen your close friend Ted for many years. He comes to pick you up at the airport. After seeing each other, you two talk a lot.

## Part Two　Text A

# Entering the Country

*Entering a foreign country follows some similar procedures. This passage mainly takes USA procedure as an example.*

### Before Arrival

Before landing in US port of entry (international airport where you first land ), you will have to fill in two forms, namely I-94 Arrival-Departure Record and Customs Form. Both of the forms will be given by flight attendant prior to landing in US. Fill these forms in only capital letters. Wherever they mention TYPE or PRINT, it means write in capital letters. Fill in one I-94 form for each person. Fill in only one customs form for the whole family.

The lower portion will be given back and it should be kept in passport. It's required while going back. On the reverse side you may have to sign.

Keep your watch in sync with current time zone.

### Arrival

*Getting out of plane*

Take you all the things including carry-on and start walking towards immigration check. Follow the signs for immigration. There will be separate lines for US citizens / Green Card holders and for non-immigrant visa holders. Keep two filled forms filled in the passport. Also keep all other papers ready in case required. Every one in the family can walk together to Immigration Counter.

*Going to immigration counter*

They will ask for passport and filled I-94 forms. They will ask you simple questions like how long you will stay. What's purpose of your trip? Where will you stay? Talk absolutely to the point. Don't try to lie. Make sure that whatever you say is written on the paper. Keep your answers simple and to the point such as "six months", "visiting my son and see tourist places", "with my son". They stamp your passport saying you are permitted for six-month stay (for visitor visa holders) or for three years (H1B/H4 visa holders). They also staple a counter foil of I-94 form (Departure Record) in your passport. It is stamped with a date, which is the day until when you are supposed to stay in the US. Your stay after that day in US is illegal.

Many people who come here on non-immigrant visa are confused regarding the duration for which they can stay legally in the United States. The visa stamp is used just to enter the United States. And you can enter United States at any period during the validity of the visa. (Whether you can enter once or multiple times is dependent whether your visa is single entry or it is multiple entries.) At the port of entry, immigration officer determines the duration for which you can stay in the United States. And that is the legal period for which you can stay. So if you are coming on visitor visa and your visa is expiring next month and immigration officer grants you six months stay, then you can stay here for six months.

*Baggage claim*

Try to acquire some 25 cent coins (called "quarters"), which you may need for getting a trolley cart for your baggage and also for making telephone calls etc. Thereafter move toward the baggage claim carousel assigned to your flight; simply follow the signs directing you to the place. Collect your luggage and look for signs directing you to customs clearance. At the customs clearance they may ask you to open your bags for a security check/verification.

*Baggage tracing*

If any of your luggage is missing or if you notice any damage to your luggage, please contact the luggage-tracing counter in the Arrivals Hall. If there is no this counter, you can contact the airline you are taking.

*Customs*

Push your trolley towards customs. Customs officer is going to ask you what you are bringing in. Your answer would normally be clothes and personal belonging. If they ask to open the bag, just co-operate. They are mainly looking for drugs etc. The officer will stamp on your form and keep it with him. Now you are free to go. Follow signs for Ground Transportation. Walk out of closest door with the baggage and trolleys.

### Domestic Flight

Since the port of entry may not be your final destination in the US and you have to proceed onwards, locate the counter for the domestic airline which will take you to your final destination. Above all don't hesitate or feel shy to ask for help from airport support staff (at information desks) or police officers, if you need anything.

Follow signs directing you to your domestic flight because you will need a boarding pass. If it is far away, take the airport shuttle/bus service that is free. If you don't know where to get down, tell the driver in advance and he will drop you off at the proper place. At the counter check in your baggage and get your boarding pass issued and ready.

On arrival at the final destination, collect your baggage once again and look around for someone who may be there to receive you. If you don't find anyone or you already have specific instructions, follow those, otherwise call up your son/daughter, relatives or friends. Therefore remember to keep phone numbers handy.

Finally, if no one comes to pick you up, try to locate the information counter from where you will get all the information regarding how to call for. Also the Public Transport section of this guide will help you in understanding the travel facilities available in the US.

## New Words

enter ['entə] *vt.* 进入

procedure [prə'si:dʒə] *n.* 手续；程序

capital ['kæpitəl] *n.* 大写字母

portion ['pɔ:ʃən] *n.* 部分；一份

reverse [ri'və:s] *a.* 背面的，反面的

sign [sain] *vt. & vi.* 签名（于），署名
（于）*n.* 标记，符号，记号

holder ['həuldə] *n.* 持有者

absolutely ['æbsəlu:tli] *ad.* 完全地，
绝对地

stamp [stæmp] *n.* 邮票；印花；印，
图章 *vt. & vi.* 在……压印

staple ['steipl] *vt.* 用订书钉订住

single ['siŋgl] *a.* 单一的

entry ['entri] *n.* 进入

multiple ['mʌltipl] *a.* 多次的；多样的

determine [di'tə:min] *vt. & vi.* 决定，
确定

grant [grɑ:nt] *vt.* 同意，准予

stay [stei] *n.* 逗留

claim [kleim] *n.* 认领

coin [kɔin] *n.* 硬币

carousel [ˌkærə'sel] *n.* 传送带

assign [ə'sain] *vt.* 分配，指派

verification [ˌverifi'keiʃən] *n.* 确认，
查证

trolley ['trɔli] *n.* 手推车；电车

belonging [bi'lɔŋiŋ] *n.* 所有物，财产；
行李

co-operate [kəu'ɔpəreit] *vi.* 合作

drug [drʌg] *n.* 麻醉药品，麻醉剂；瘾
性毒品

hesitate ['heziteit] *vi.* 犹豫，踌躇

shuttle ['ʃʌtl] *n.* 往返汽车

issue ['isu:] *vt.* 发给

handy ['hændi] *a.* 手边的，就近的，
唾手可得的，便利的

regarding [ri'gɑ:diŋ] *prep.* 关于

## Phrases and Expressions

in sync with  与……相一致

time zone  时区

Green Card  绿卡

non-immigrant visa  非移民签证

to the point  中肯，扼要

prior to  在……之前

counter foil  存根

trolley cart  手推车

customs clearance  报关，海关结关

Ground Transportation  地面交通

domestic airline  国内航班

boarding pass  登机证

call up  打电话给

call for  要求

# Notes

**1** Since the port of entry may not be your final destination in the US and you have to proceed onwards, locate the counter for the domestic airline which will take you to your final destination.

本句中，since 引导了一个原因状语从句，which will take you to your final destination 是一个定语从句，修饰和限定 the domestic airline。

**2** H1B visa

The H1B Visa Program is the primary method for bringing foreign professionals to work in the USA. This visa entitles your spouse and children to accompany you, and is a "dual intent" visa allowing you to apply for a Green Card and obtain permanent residency.

H1B visas are typically used for the following professions: Computing & IT, Telecoms, HealthCare, Finance & Accounting, Teaching, Legal, PR, Marketing & Advertising, Sales, Management and Engineering.

**3** H4 visa

Spouse and unmarried children under age of 21 of an H1B visa holder are eligible for an H4 visa. A person on an H4 status is not allowed to work unless and until the person gets a Change of Status from the INS (Immigration and Naturalization Service, 移民归化局) from H4 to H1B status. Currently INS is not issuing Social Security Number (SSN) to H4 visa holders. H4 holders can get a driver's license, open a bank account, or even go to college. Children on H4 visas do not need a separate visa to attend school.

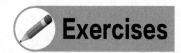 **Exercises**

**EX. 1** **Answer the following questions.**

1. What is the procedure to enter the USA?

2. What two forms should a passenger fill out before entering the USA?

3. How will you deal with the situation if any of your luggages is missing or if you notice any damage to your luggage?

4. Can you refuse when the customs officer ask you to open your bag?

**EX. 2** Write out the English words according to the definitions given below.

| definitions | words |
|---|---|
| go forward; go on | |
| work or act together in order to bring about a result | |
| a continuous moving strip on which airport passengers' bags are put for collection | |
| having many parts or elements | |
| being effective because made or done with the correct formalities | |
| agreeing in time, speeds, etc.; happening at the same time | |
| the back of a piece of paper | |
| to ask for something because you think it belongs to you or because you have a right to it | |
| to pause before you do or say something, often because you are uncertain or nervous about it | |
| a letter of the alphabet in the form and larger size that is used at the beginning of sentences and names | |

**EX. 3** Complete the following sentences with appropriate words or expressions from the text.

1. Before landing in US port of entry, you will have to fill two forms, namely _____ and _____.
2. A _____ of I-94 form (Departure Record) will be stapled in your passport when you come cross immigration check.
3. Whether you can enter a country once or multiple times is dependent whether your visa is _____ entry or it is _____ entry.
4. If the _____ is not your final destination in the US you have to proceed onwards.

**EX. 4** Translate the following sentences into Chinese.

1. Wherever they mention TYPE or PRINT, it means write in capital letters.

2. There will be separate lines for US citizens/Green Card holders and for non-immigrant visa holders such as Visitor visa and H1B visa.

3. It is stamped with a date, which is the day until when you are supposed to stay in the US.

4. Above all don't hesitate or feel shy to ask for help from airport support staff (at information desks) or police officers, if you need anything.

## Part Three  Text B

# Learn About the Airport

### Airfield System

The primary components of the "airside" are those directly related to the arrival and departure of aircraft. These facilities are comprised of the runways and taxiways, navigational aids, and airport lighting and marking.

The development of airport facilities is based primarily on the characteristics of the aircraft, which are expected to use the airport. The most important characteristics are the approach speed and the size (wingspan) of the "design" aircraft expected to use the airport. A "design" aircraft is defined as the most demanding aircraft, which performs regular operations annually at the airport.

Take Vernon Regional Airport (Canada) as an example. Transport Canada groups' aircrafts according to their performance and size. The categories range from Approach Category A, for slower single-engine piston aircraft, to Approach Category E, for supersonic jet aircraft. The "design" aircraft group now using Vernon Regional Airport falls into Category B (approach speed less than 166 knots/wingspan less than 79-feet/wheel base less than 19 feet), which is considered a transport aircraft. Based on the forecasts of aviation demand, and for future long-term airport requirements, the "design" aircraft group will remain within Category B.

Along with the aircraft's approach speed, the airplane's wingspan is another principal characteristic, which affects airport design standards.

### Runway Requirements and Orientation

The runway length, pavement strength, and their orientation relative to area winds should be considered when constructing the runway. Area wind characteristic is a major factor in determining the optimum number and alignment of runways.

The established goal for wind coverage is ninety-five percent (95%); that is, a light plane should be able to operate at an airport ninety-five percent (95%) of a given period without experiencing a crosswind component greater than 10.5 knots. Wind coverage required for larger, transport-type aircraft are 13 knots.

Another factor used to determine necessary airfield improvements is the comparison between demand and capacity. The most common means of measuring airfield efficiency is by determining the airport's operational capacity, or Annual Service Volume. This acts as a reasonable estimate of an airport's annual capacity. Overall, demand/capacity figures establish a time frame for projecting development to preserve and enhance airport operational safety.

### Taxiway Requirements

Taxiways are one of the most important factors in determining and maintaining the operational safety of an airport. As airport activity increases (take-offs, landings, and touch and go maneuvers), faster access from the runways to the taxiway system is required to maintain safety.

Because taxiways are considered critical areas, they should be constructed to the same pavement strengths as the runways they serve.

## Airport Lighting and Marking

In order to obtain the maximum utilization of the airport, lighting is necessary to accommodate aircraft during night and adverse weather conditions. There are several different types of lighting aids recommended to facilitate and enhance the identification, approach, landing, and taxiing operations. Recommended systems include: Runway Lighting, Taxiway Lighting/ Marking and Visual Guidance Indicators.

## Airport Signs

Standard airport signs provide taxiway and runway directional and identification guidance for aircraft movement on the ground. A system of standard signs is expected to distinguish runway, taxiway and aircraft parking destinations. Runway intersections and connecting taxiways should be identified through adequate signage.

## Electronic Navigation

Airport navigation aids (NAVAIDS) are facilities and equipment installed on or near the airport for the purpose of providing pilots with electronic guidance and visual references for executing an approach to the airport and landing on a specific runway. The purpose of installing and/or upgrading navigational aids is to increase an airport's reliability. The use of this equipment depends on the ratings of the pilot and the instrumentation capability of the aircraft. Each facility in the NAVAID development process adds greater reliability but at increasing cost. Progressively, each additional NAVAID allows aircraft to fly during lower ceiling and visibility minimums. The traditional development process is as follows: (1)Non-directional beacon (NDB); (2)VOR or VORTAC; (3)Localizer; and (4)Precision Instrument Landing System (ILS/MLS).

On the forefront of navigational systems for aircraft is the Global Positioning System (GPS). GPS is a navigational system that links on board aircraft receivers to satellite transmitters.

## Terminal Area Requirements

The terminal is defined as that portion of the airport used by itinerant aircraft for flight planning, washroom, and food services. It is also used as a holding area by departing and arriving passengers of charter and possible future scheduled carriers.

The location of the terminal facility is adjacent to the main ramp on the airfield. The terminal facility should be an ongoing concern.

The facility should have the following: six to eight hundred square feet of common area for passenger with furnishings; a restaurant/coffee shop, including a kitchen and an airside outdoor patio; public washroom space, including a handicapped facility; office space to house various businesses. This number may vary depending on the anticipated demand: a flight-planning room; sterile customs search room; airport Managers office; two public telephones, one inside the facility and the other outside for after hour calls; ample parking.

### *Aircraft Rescue and Fire Fighting Requirements*

The regulations and standards are based on the number of aircraft movements handled per day and the type of operation. Types of operations are grouped as follows: air taxis are defined as aircraft authorized to carry fewer than 10 passengers; commuter aircrafts are authorized to carry between 10 and 19 passengers; and airlines authorized to carry 20 or more.

Category A airports, which handle air taxis or fewer than eight commuter aircraft movements per day, would be required to have an alerting system to a community-based fire service, as well as on-site fire extinguishers.

Category B airports, which handle eight or more commuter aircraft movements or fewer than eight airliners per day, would be required to have an alerting system to a community based fire service, along with either an on-site trained emergency responder, vehicle and equipment, or community fire response within 10 minutes.

Category C airports, which handle eight or more airliner movements per day, would be required to have trained emergency personnel, vehicles and extinguishing agents on site, and a communications and alerting system, along with a response capability of three minutes.

 **New Words**

airfield ['eə,fi:ld] *n.* 飞机场

component [kəm'pəunənt] *n.* 组成部分，成分

airside ['eəsaid] *n.* 对空面，机场控制区

runway ['rʌnwei] *n.* 飞机跑道

taxiway ['tæksiwei] *n.* 滑行道

navigational [,nævi'geiʃənl] *a.* 航行的，导航的

lighting ['laitiŋ] *n.* 照明，照明设备

characteristic [,kæriktə'ristik] *n.* 特性，特征

wingspan ['wiŋ,spæn] *n.* 翼展

define [di'fain] *vt.* 定义，详细说明

demanding [di'mɑ:ndiŋ] *a.* 过分要求的，苛求的

annually ['ænjuəli] *ad.* 一年一次，每年

performance [pə'fɔ:məns] *n.* 性能，运行

piston ['pistən] *n.* 活塞

supersonic [,sju:pə'sɔnik] *a.* 超音速的，超声的

knot [nɔt] *n.* 节,海里 / 小时( 航速单位 )

aviation [,eivi'eiʃən] *n.* 飞行，航空；航空学，航空术

**principal** ['prinsəpəl] *a.* 主要的；首要的

**standard** ['stændəd] *n.* 标准，规格

**orientation** [,ɔ:riən'teiʃən] *n.* 方向，方位

**pavement** ['peivmənt] *n.* 人行道

**optimum** ['ɔptiməm] *a.* 最适宜的

**alignment** [ə'lainmənt] *n.* 队列

**coverage** ['kʌvəridʒ] *n.* 覆盖范围

**crosswind** ['krɔs,wind] *n.* 横风，侧风

**comparison** [kəm'pærisn] *n.* 比较，对照

**capacity** [kə'pæsəti] *n.* 容积，容量

**efficiency** [i'fiʃənsi] *n.* 效率，功效

**figure** ['figə] *n.* 数字

**projecting** [prə'dʒektiŋ] *a.* 突出的，伸出的

**preserve** [pri'zə:v] *vt.* 保护，保持

**operational** [,ɔpə'reiʃnel] *a.* 操作的，运作的

**maintain** [men'tein] *vt.* 保持，维持

**take-off** ['teikɔf] *n.* 起飞

**landing** ['lændiŋ] *n.* 降落

**touch** [tʌtʃ] *n.* 触地；碰

**maneuver** [mə'nu:və] *n.* 机动，调动

**utilization** [,ju:təlai'zeiʃən] *n.* 利用，应用

**adverse** ['ædvə:s] *a.* 不利的

**facilitate** [fə'siləteit] *vt.* 使容易，使便利

**visual** ['viʒuəl] *a.* 看的，视觉的

**indicator** ['indi,keitə] *n.* 指示器

**distinguish** [di'stiŋgwiʃ] *vt.* 区别，辨别

**intersection** ['intə,sekʃən] *n.* 十字路口，交叉点

**adequate** ['ædikwət] *a.* 适当的；足够的

**install** [in'stɔ:l] *vt.* 安装

**execute** ['eksi,kju:t] *vt.* 执行，实行

**reliability** [ri,laiə'biliti] *n.* 可靠性

**instrumentation** [,instrumen'teiʃən] *n.* 检测仪表，仪表设备

**capability** [,keipə'biləti] *n.* 能力；性能

**progressively** [prəu'gresivli] *ad.* 前进地，渐进地

**ceiling** ['si:liŋ] *n.* 升限，绝对升限

**visibility** [,vizə'biləti] *n.* 能见度

**beacon** ['bi:kən] *n.* 信标，灯标

**localizer** ['ləukəlaizə] *n.* 定位器，定位信标

**precision** [pri'siʒən] *n.* 精确，精密度，精度

**transmitter** [trænz'mitə] *n.* 发射机，发送器

**itinerant** [ai'tinərənt] *a.* 巡回的

**charter** ['tʃɑ:tə] *n.* 租，包（船、车、飞机等）

**ramp** [ræmp] *n.* 坡道；客机梯子

**furnishings** ['fə:niʃiŋz] *n.* 家具陈设

**patio** ['pætiəu] *n.* 院子；室外就餐处

**anticipate** [æn'tisipeit] *vt.* 预期，期望

**sterile** ['sterail] *a.* 消过毒的，无菌的

**regulation** [,regju'leiʃən] *n.* 规则，规章

**alerting** [ə'lə:tiŋ] *n.* 警戒，告警

**extinguisher** [ik'stiŋgwiʃə] *n.* 灭火器

**responder** [ri'spɔndə] *n.* 回应者；应答器

**vehicle** ['vi:ikl] *n.* 交通工具；传达手段

# Phrases and Expressions

comprise of  由……组成
base on  基于
according to  根据

fall into  属于
time frame  时间范围，时间帧
be adjacent to  相邻的，邻近的

 # Abbreviations

NAVAID (airport navigation aids) ［航空］助航系统
NDB (Non-Directional Beacon) 无方向性信标（归航台）
VOR (Very-high-frequency Omnidirectional Range) 甚高频全向无线电信标
VORTAC (VHF Omni Range Tactical Communications) 甚高频全向无线电信标战术通信

ILS (Instrument Landing System) 仪表着陆系统
MLS (Microwave Landing System) 微波着陆系统
GPS (Global Positioning System) 全球定位系统

# Notes

**1** Along with the aircraft's approach speed, the airplane's wingspan is another principal characteristic, which affects airport design standards.

本句中，which 引导非限定性定语从句，其先行词是 characteristic。along with 意为"与……一起"。

又如：

Along with the letters there are answers written by people who are supposed to know how to solve such problems.

与这些来信的还有对这些问题的解答，这些解答由那些被认为能够解决这些问题的人来撰写。

**2** The established goal for wind coverage is ninety-five percent (95%); that is, a light plane should be able to operate at an airport ninety-five percent (95%) of a given period without experiencing a crosswind component greater than 10.5 knots.

本句中，that is 意思是"简而言之，说得更精确些"。后半句意为：也就是说，一轻型飞机在机场运作时，在给定时限内在 95% 的情况下不会遇到大于 10.5 节的侧风分量。

**3** In order to obtain the maximum utilization of the airport, lighting is necessary to accommodate aircraft during night and adverse weather conditions.

本句中，in order to 作目的状语，意为"为了"。accommodate 此处为"配合"之意。adverse 意为"不利的"，adverse weather conditions 此处可理解为"不利的天气状况"。

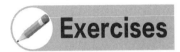 **Exercises**

**EX. 5** **Answer the following questions.**

1. Why is airport lighting important?

2. What's the function of airport signs?

3. What is NAVAID? And its function?

4. What is terminal according to your understanding?

**EX. 6** **Decide whether the following statements are *true* or *false*.**

1. The development of airport facilities is based mainly on the characteristics of the aircraft, which are expected to use the airport.

2. Area wind characteristics are not important in determining the optimum number and alignment of runways.

3. Taxiways should be constructed to the same pavement strengths as the runways they serve.

4. In order to obtain the maximum utilization of the airport, lighting is necessary to accommodate aircraft during night and adverse weather conditions.

5. The terminal is a place that can only be used by itinerant aircraft for flight planning, washroom, and food services.

6. Air taxis are defined as aircraft authorized to carry fewer than 10 passengers.

## Part Four  Skill Training

**Forms**

If you need someone to pick you up at the airport upon your arrival, you can fill in this form.

**Airport Greeting Request**

**If you want to request airport pickup, please send this form AT LEAST 3 to 4 days before you arrive.**

IMPORTANT: Please arrive in Little Rock on a weekday, Monday through Friday between 08:00

and 21:00. **We cannot guarantee pickups on weekends, holidays, or times other than the above.** UALR is closed during the Christmas holidays beginning December 18. Please arrive after January 2. Any arrival date during the summer or fall term is acceptable.

*Family Name* _____    *Given Name* _____

Male _____ Female _____

Date of Birth: _____/_____/_____

          *Month*    *Day*    *Year*

_____    _____

*Country of Birth*    *Citizenship*

Arrival in Little Rock: _____/_____/_____ _____

          *Month*    *Day*    *Year*    *Time*

_____    _____

*Name of Airlines*    *Flight Number*

Your last stop before arrival in Little Rock: _____

Have you confirmed housing: Yes _____    No _____

Your Fax number or E-mail address: _____

Send this form AIRMAIL, E-MAIL, or FAX to:

Mrs. Suzanne Lee

International Student Services

University of Arkansas at Little Rock

2801 South University Avenue

Little Rock, AR 72204-1099

USA

Fax: 501-569-8157

E-mail: msstevens@ualr.edu

NOTICE: If there is a change in your flight arrival time, PLEASE notify us.

## Practical Writing

### Certificate Writing

There are various certificates, such as the Certificate of Work Experience, Certificate of State of an Illness, Certificate of School Work, etc., which are used to prove a person's status, educational background, marital status, health condition, etc. Certificate writing often adopts the letter format and requires briefness. It usually begin with "This is to certify that..."

**Sample 1    Certification of Educational Background**

This is to certify that Mr. Jiang Tao, male, born in Shexian County, Anhui Province, in 1991, was admitted into the Department of Computer Science and Engineering of Nanjing University in September 2010, majoring in Computer Application. He graduated from the University in July 2014 with a degree of Bachelor in Computer Engineering.

Nanjing University

June 25, 2015

**Sample 2    Health Certificate**

This is to certify that Mr. Wang Hongjiang, male, aged 62, professor of Anhui Education College, his health is excellent and capable of going to Japan to attend the 9th Mathematics and Statistics Conference.

Zhang Wang

Physician-in-Chief

Anhui Provincial Hospital

June 18, 2015

**Sample 3    Doctor's Certificate**

This is to certify that our patient, Mr. Thomas, male, aged 41, was admitted into our hospital on June 9, 2015, for acute appendicitis. After immediate operation and ten days of treatment, he has completely recovered and will be discharged on June 19, 2015. It is suggested that he rest for one week at home before resuming his work.

Jack Hopkins

Surgeon-in-charge

June 18, 2015

**Sample 4    Certificate (90) Lu Zi, No. 1130**

This is to certify that Mr. Zhao Qiangwen holds a diploma issued to him in July, 2014 by Shandong University (Diploma No. 064) and that the seal of the said University and the signature by President Zhou Yongsen are authentic.

Jinan Notary Public Office

Shangdong Province

The People's Republic of China

Notary: Wang Fang

May 2, 2015

公证书（90 鲁公证字第 1130 号）

兹证明赵强文先生持有的山东大学于 2014 年 7 月发给他的 064 号毕业文凭上的学校印鉴和校长周永森签字属实。

中华人民共和国
山东省济南市公证处
公证员：王芳
2015 年 5 月 2 日

**Simulate and create** ► Wang Ming, a graduate of your university, who wants to continue his study in the USA. Please write a Certification of Educational Background for him.

## Part Five  Related Information

| Text | Notes |
|---|---|
| **Techniques for Reducing Jet Lag[1]** | [1] 时差综合征 |
| *Pre-flight* | |
| This is one of the most important aspects of combating[2] jet lag. Before departing[3], make sure you have all your affairs, business and personal, in order. Ensure you are not stressed-out with excitement or worry, and not tired or hungover[4] from a function the night before. Get plenty of exercise in the days prior[5] to departure and try to avoid sickness such as the flu, colds and so on. Get a good night's sleep just prior to departure. | [2] 抗击 [3] 起程 [4] 难受的 [5] 预先的 |
| *East or west?* | |
| There is much debate[6] about whether it is better to fly eastward or westward. It may be largely a matter of personal preference[7], but there is some evidence that flying westwards causes less jet lag than flying eastwards. | [6] 争论 [7] 偏爱 |
| *Drinking fluids[8]* | |
| The dry air in aircraft causes dehydration[9]. Drinking plenty of non-alcoholic[10] fluids counters[11] this. Water is better than coffee, tea and fruit juices. Alcohol not only is useless in combating dehydration, but has a markedly greater intoxicating[12] effect when drunk in the rarefied[13] atmosphere of an airliner than it does at ground level. | [8] 饮料 [9] 脱水 [10] 不含酒精的 [11] 抗击 [12] 致毒，致醉 [13] 稀薄的 |
| *Sleeping aids* | |
| Blindfolds[14], ear plugs, neckrests and blow-up pillows[15] are all useful in helping you get quality sleep while flying. | [14] 眼罩 [15] 枕头 |

| | |
|---|---|
| *Exercise* | |
| Get as much exercise as you can. Walking up and down the aisle, standing for spells[16], and doing small twisting[17] and stretching[18] exercises in your seat all help to reduce discomfort, especially swelling[19] of legs and feet. Get off the plane if possible at stopovers, and do some exercises or take a walk. It also helps to reduce the possibilities of blood clots[20] and associated trauma[21]. | [16] 一段时间<br>[17] 扭动<br>[18] 伸展<br>[19] 肿胀<br>[20] 凝块<br>[21] 外伤，损伤 |
| *No-Jet-Lag* | |
| This is a safe and effective remedy[22] for countering jet lag, in the form of easy-to-take tablets[23]. Its effectiveness was proved in a scientific trial of round-the-world passengers and confirmed by long-haul[24] flight attendants in a test conducted in cooperation with their union. | [22] 药物<br>[23] 药片<br>[24] 长途 |
| *Melatonin*[25] | [25] 褪黑激素 |
| This is a controversial[26] and complex treatment[27] for jet-lag. Latest research shows if used incorrectly melatonin will make jet-lag worse! | [26] 有争议的<br>[27] 治疗 |
| *Anti*[28] *jet lag diet* | [28] 反，抗，防 |
| Another method is the anti jet lag diet. Like melatonin this is only for people with lots of time on their hands who can devote[29] several days before and after a trip to looking after themselves. It is complicated[30] and there is little evidence that it works, although it has some passionate[31] devotees. | [29] 投入于<br>[30] 复杂的<br>[31] 充满热情的 |
| *Sleeping pills*[32] | [32] 安眠药片 |
| Some people use this to try to alleviate[33] jet lag. This is a dangerous approach as a report in *The Lancet* in 1988 says "estimated that over three years at Heathrow Airport, 18% of the 61 sudden deaths in long distance passengers were caused by clots in the lungs." Sleeping pills induce[34] a comatose[35] state with little or no natural body movement. Imagine leg veins[36] as bags of blood. When blood doesn't circulate[37] there is a possibility that it will clot. | [33] 减轻<br><br><br><br>[34] 导致，引起<br>[35] 昏睡的<br>[36] 血管<br>[37] 循环；流通 |
| Also many so-called sleeping pills are variants[38] on anti-histamines[39] and they tend to dehydrate[40] significantly adding to the already big problem of dehydration. | [38] 变体，变种<br>[39] 抗组胺剂<br>[40] （使）脱水 |

## Part Six  Guide to World Famous Sight

| Text | Notes |
|---|---|
| **British Museum**<br>The national repository[1] in London for treasures[2] in science | [1] 知识库<br>[2] 珍品，财宝 |

and art located in the Bloomsbury[3] section[4] of the city. It has departments of antiquities[5], prints and drawings, coins and medals, and ethnography[6]. The museum was established by act[7] of Parliament[8] in 1753 when the collection of Sir Hans Sloane, begun in the previous century and called the Cabinet of Curiosities[9], was purchased by the government and was joined with the Cotton collection and the Harleian Library. In 1757 the royal library was given to the museum by George II. The museum was opened in 1759 under its present name in Montague House[10], but the acquisition[11] of the library of George III in 1823 necessitated[12] larger quarters[13]. The first wing[14] of the new building was completed in 1829, the quadrangle[15] in 1852, and the great domed Reading Room in 1857. Later, other additions were built. Long a part of the museum, the British Library was established as a separate entity[16] by act of Parliament in 1973 and moved to new London quarters in 1997. After the relocation[17] of the library, the famous Reading Room underwent extensive renovations[18], including the opening of a surrounding glassed—in Great Court and the installation[19] of a billowing[20] transparent[21] roof. The 1.5-acre space now houses a gallery and a restaurant, as well as two small theaters and an education center beneath the courtyard.

The museum's collection of prints and drawings is one of the finest in the world. The natural history collection was transferred[22] (1881-1883) to buildings in South Kensington[23] and called the Natural History Museum. One of the major exhibits of the Egyptian department is the basalt[24] slab[25] known as the Rosetta Stone[26]. The Greek treasures include the Elgin Marbles[27] and a caryatid[28] from the Erechtheum[29]. The museum's special collections include a vast number of clocks and timepieces, ivories[30],and the Sutton Hoo[31] treasure.

[3] 布鲁姆斯伯格
[4] 区
[5] 古董，古代文物
[6] 人种史，人种论
[7] 法案，法令
[8] 议会
[9] 古董陈列室
[10] 蒙塔古家族
[11] 获得，获得物
[12] 成为
[13] 来源，出处
[14]（主楼）侧楼
[15] 四边形
[16] 实体
[17] 迁移
[18] 革新
[19] 设计，安装
[20] 巨浪的
[21] 透明的
[22] 迁移，移动
[23] 肯辛顿
[24] 黑陶器
[25] 厚片
[26] 罗塞塔石
[27] 埃尔金大理石雕
[28] 女像柱
[29] 厄瑞克修姆庙
[30] 象牙
[31] 萨顿胡

# Unit 7

## Ground Transportation

**Part One**  **Dialogues**

### Sample Dialogue 1

👤 **Situation** ▶ Toby wants to rent a car for the coming holiday. Now he is in the car rental agency.

| | | |
|---|---|---|
| ○ | **Toby**: | I'd like to rent a car for two weeks. |
| ○ | **Clerk**: | Can I see your driver's license? |
| ○ | **Toby**: | Sure. Here it is. |
| ○ | **Clerk**: | What kind of car do you want? |
| ○ | **Toby**: | An economy car, if possible. |
| ○ | **Clerk**: | How will you pay? |
| ○ | **Toby**: | With my American Express Card. |
| ○ | **Clerk**: | Okay. Now just complete this form. |
| ○ | **Toby**: | Do you charge mileage? |
| ○ | **Clerk**: | No. It's a flat rate. |
| ○ | **Toby**: | What make is it? |
| ○ | **Clerk**: | It's a Thunderbird. |
| ○ | **Toby**: | How fast can it go? |
| ○ | **Clerk**: | The top speed is 110 mph. |
| ○ | **Toby**: | Thank you a lot. |

## Sample Dialogue 2

👤 **Information▶** Long-distance travel by train is not as common in the United States as it is in many other parts of the world. Most train travel is in the "Northeast Corridor". Special express trains called "Metroliners" travel between New York and Washington, D.C. All seats on these trains are reserved in both coach (2nd class) and club car (1st class). Sleeping compartments are available on most long-distance trains and must be reserved in advance.

| | | |
|---|---|---|
| ⊙ | **Passenger**: | What time does the train for Boston leave? |
| ⊙ | **Clerk**: | 9:25 on Track 12. |
| ⊙ | **Passenger**: | When does it arrive? |
| ⊙ | **Clerk**: | It should be there at 11:45, but it may be a little late. |
| ⊙ | **Passenger**: | How much is a one-way ticket. |
| ⊙ | **Clerk**: | It's $32.00 coach and $50.00 club car. |
| ⊙ | **Passenger**: | What's the round-trip fare of club car? |
| ⊙ | **Clerk**: | $90.00. |

## Useful Expressions

1. I'll need to see your International License.

   我需要看一下你的国际汽车驾驶执照。

2. How long will you need it?

   你需要多长时间？

3. Fill out this form, please.

   请填写这张表格。

4. What time does it get in?

   什么时候到达？

5. It's scheduled to arrive at 11:50.

   预定 11：50 到达。

6. It's due at noon.

   预定正午时分到达。

## Task Dialogue 1

**Situation ▶** You want to rent a car to travel to Tibet, so you come to the car rental agency.

## Task Dialogue 2

**Situation ▶** You are at the ticket office to buy a round-trip ticket to New York.

## Part Two   Text A

# Transportation Service at International Airport

Almost all International Airports offer many convenient transportation alternatives. As one of the biggest international airports, Washington Dulles International Airport offers various transportation options.

### Washington Flyer Services

The Washington Flyer Ground Transportation services include the Washington Flyer Taxi and the Flyer Coach.

### Washington Flyer Taxi

Washington Flyer Taxicabs serve Dulles International Airport exclusively with 24-hour service to and from the airport. Taxicab Dispatchers are on duty 24 hours a day at the East and West ramps on the lower level of the Main Terminal. Wheelchair mini buses only accommodate one chaired or disabled passenger and three additional non-chaired passengers. Smoking and non-smoking vehicles are available by request.

For information or to arrange transportation for your return trip, call 703-661-6655. Taxicabs accept American Express, Diners Club, MasterCard, Discover Card, and Visa, and provide transportation at metered rates to any destination in metropolitan Washington. Approximate one-way fares to Washington, D.C. range from $44 to $50. A chart listing approximate taxi rates from Dulles International Airport can also be viewed.

### SuperShuttle

SuperShuttle's door-to-door service is available to the Flyer Coach Stops, as well as Union Station. SuperShuttle stops are clearly identified on the Ground Transportation Level roadway outside the Main Terminal at Washington Dulles. Shuttles operate on a shared ride-on demand basis.

### *Washington Flyer Coach Service*

Operated by the Metropolitan Washington Airports Authority, the Washington Flyer Coach Service provides a convenient link between Washington Dulles and the West Falls Church Metrorail station. All coaches are disabled-accessible.

### *Tickets*

*Washington Dulles International Airport*: Tickets for the Flyer Coach can be purchased at Washington Dulles at the Ground Transportation Centers' ticket counter located inside the vestibule of Door Four on the Arrivals Level. You can board the bus at Dulles from the Main Terminal at Door Four located on the Arrivals Level.

*West Falls Church Metrorail Station*: When departing from the West Falls Church Metrorail station, you may purchase tickets on arrival at Washington Dulles.

### *Metrorail*

The Washington Flyer Coach Service provides direct transportation between Dulles and Metrorail, the region's rapid-transit system. Washington Coach Service is available every 30 minutes to link the West Falls Church Metrorail Station and the Airport. Metrorail fare cards may be purchased from machines located at the rail station.

A map of the Metrorail Transit Lines is available, or visit the Metrorail web site for complete fare, schedule, and passenger information.

### *Rental Cars*

Information screens and courtesy telephones are located on the Lower Level of the Main Terminal in the Ground Transportation Centers. Rental car check-in facilities are open 24 hours a day. You may also view a list of car rental companies available at the airport. Rental car patrons are transported to the rental car agencies via shuttle buses. From Baggage Claim (lower) Level, go down any ramp, and proceed out the building to the second curbside.

### *Hotel/Motel Shuttles*

Hotel/Motel courtesy transportation can be arranged by using the phone hook-ups attached to the hotel courtesy boards on the Baggage Claim Level. To meet the hotel shuttle, proceed from the Baggage Claim level down a ramp and out the building to curbside.

### *Disabled-Accessible Courtesy Service*

Courtesy service is available 24 hours a day, seven days a week, between parking lots and the Main Terminal. Service may be requested by using Customer Assistance Call Boxes near selected shuttle bus stops in Economy and Daily two parking lots.

### *Metrobus*

Public bus service is available at the West Falls Church Metrorail Station to areas not served by Metrorail. Washington Flyer Coach Service is available every 30 minutes, linking the West Falls Church Metrorail station and the Airport.

There is also an express bus service offered by the Washington Metropolitan Area Transit Authority operating from downtown Washington, D.C. to Washington Dulles Airport and along the Dulles Corridor.

### Limousine Service

Stretch limousine and executive-class sedans are available with advance reservations through private vendors. Prices start at approximately $42 for downtown Washington and suburban Maryland destinations.

### Greyhound Airport Service

Greyhound connects the airport to multiple locations in Virginia (Warrenton, Culpepper, Charlottesville, Lynchburg, Roanoke, Winchester, and Harrisonburg with connecting service to Richmond, Harrisburg, Baltimore, Philadelphia, and New York). Greyhound has instituted a new toll-free number for travelers using its airport service. The number 888-BUS-N-FLY provides schedule information and reservations, which are recommended but not required.

 **New Words**

**convenient** [kən'viːniənt] *a.* 便利的，方便的

**alternative** [ɔːl'təːnətiv] *n.* 可供选择的办法或事物

**option** ['ɔpʃən] *n.* 选择，选项；选择权

**exclusively** [ik'skluːsivli] *ad.* 排外地，专有地

**dispatcher** [di'spætʃə] *n.* 调度员

**wheelchair** ['wiːl,tʃeə] *n.* 轮椅

**mini** ['mini] *n.* 迷你型，袖珍型；小型机

**accommodate** [ə'kɔmədeit] *vt.* 容纳

**rate** [reit] *n.* 价格，费用

**metropolitan** [,metrə'pɔlitən] *a.* 大城市的

**approximate** [ə'prɔksimeit] *a.* 近似的，大约的

**chart** [tʃɑːt] *n.* 图表

**authority** [ɔː'θɔrəti] *n.* 权力；管理机构

**disabled-accessible** [dis'eibld ək'sesəbl] *a.* 可供残疾人使用的

**vestibule** ['vesti,bjuːl] *n.* 门廊，前厅

**metrorail** ['metrəureil] *n.* 地下铁道

**farecard** ['feəkɑːd] *n.* 月票卡

**rental** ['rentl] *n.* 租赁

**courtesy** ['kəːtəsi] *n.* 谦恭，礼貌

**patron** ['peitrən] *n.* 顾客，老主顾

**attach** [ə'tætʃ] *vt.* 缚上，系上

**lot** [lɔt] *n.* 一块地，地区

**express** [ik'spres] *a.* 急速的

**downtown** [daun'taun] *n.* 市中心区，商业区

**corridor** ['kɔridɔː] *n.* 通道，走廊

**limousine** [,limə'ziːn] *n.* 豪华轿车

**sedan** [si'dæn] *n.* 轿车

**vendor** ['vendə] *n.* 供应者，卖者

**suburban** [sə'bəːbən] *a.* 郊外的，偏远的

**Maryland** ['mɛərilænd] *n.* 马里兰（美国州）

**greyhound** ['grei,haund] *n.* 美国灰狗长途汽车；特快海轮

**Virginia** [vəˈdʒinjə] *n.* 弗吉尼亚( 美国州 )

**Roanoke** [ˈrəuənəuk] *n.* 罗阿诺克( 美国城市 )

**Winchester** [ˈwintʃistə] *n.* 温彻斯特( 美国城市 )

**Richmond** [ˌritʃmənd] *n.* 里士满( 美国城市 )

**Harrisburg** [ˈhærisbə:g] *n.* 哈里斯堡( 美国城市 )

**Baltimore** [ˈbɔ:ltimɔ:] *n.* 巴尔的摩( 美国城市 )

**Philadelphia** [ˌfiləˈdelfiə] *n.* 费城 ( 美国城市 )

**institute** [ˈinsti,tju:t] *vt.* 开始；制定

**toll** [təul] *n.* ( 道路、港 口的 )通行费，过路税

## Phrases and Expressions

Washington Dulles International Airport 华盛顿达拉斯国际机场

Washington Flyer Services （弗来尔）华盛顿机场交通服务

Discover Card 美国主要的信用卡之一

New York 纽约

## Notes

**1** ...provide transportation at metered rates...

本句中，meter 本来意思是 "计量表"，在此用作动词，是过去分词作定语，修饰 rates，意思是通过打表来计费。

**2** To meet the hotel shuttle, proceed from the Baggage Claim level down a ramp and out the building to curbside.

本句中，to meet the hotel shuttle 是目的状语。本句主语应为旅客，被省略。

## Exercises

**EX. 1** **Answer the following questions.**

1. What transportation alternatives can Washington Dulles International Airport offer?

2. Can you rent cars at the airport? And how?

3. How can the disabled ask for help at the airport?

**EX. 2** Write out the English words according to the definitions given below.

| definitions | words |
|---|---|
| a chair with large wheels which can be turned by the user, used esp. by people who are unable to walk | |
| anything that is smaller than others of its kind | |
| of a chief city or the capital city of a country | |
| (a vehicle used for) a regular journey from one place to another and back by air, railway, bus, etc., usu. over a short distance | |
| the business center of a town or city | |
| a big expensive comfortable car | |
| a tax paid for the right to use a road | |
| of an area on the edge of a large town or city | |
| seller (esp. of small wares) | |
| offering the use of sth. for money | |

**EX. 3** Complete the following sentences with appropriate words or expressions from the text.

1. Wheelchair mini buses only _____ one chaired or disabled passenger and three additional non-chaired passengers.
2. SuperShuttle stops are clearly _____ on the Ground Transportation Level roadway outside the Main Terminal at Washington Dulles.
3. Metrorail farecards may be purchased from _____ located at the rail station.
4. Rental car _____ are transported to the rental car agencies via shuttle buses.
5. Stretch _____ and executive-class _____ are available with advance reservations through private vendors.
6. _____ connects the airport to multiple locations in Virginia.

**EX. 4** Translate the following sentences into Chinese.

1. Wheelchair mini buses only accommodate one chaired or disabled passenger and three additional non-chaired passengers. Smoking and non-smoking vehicles are available by request.
2. Operated by the Metropolitan Washington Airports Authority, the Washington Flyer Coach Service provides a convenient link between Washington Dulles and the West Falls Church Metrorail station. All coaches are disabled-accessible.

3. Stretch limousine and executive-class sedans are available with advance reservations through private vendors.

4. Greyhound has instituted a new toll-free number for travelers using its airport service.

## Part Three  Text B

# Train Travel

Imagine chugging along scenic routes in some of the best trains of the world, for nothing quite beats the romanticism of train travel. The gentle sway of the train, fleeting glimpses of landscapes as they come and go rapidly, the moving home-away-from-home has an unmatched old world charm. For sheer relaxation and self-indulgence train travel is the last word for those who enjoy the finer things in life. This passage will help you have a general understanding of the train service in the world.

### US & Canada General Info

In the United States, Amtrak, the national passenger rail service, runs a number of transcontinental routes. The northeast coast from Boston to Washington, D.C., is generally well served, and Chicago is a major rail terminus as well. Some trains travel overnight; you can sleep in your seat or book a bedroom, some with private bath, at additional cost. Most trains have dining cars with acceptable food, but you may prefer to bring your own. Excursion fares, when available, may save nearly half the round-trip fare.

Amtrak's service into Canada connects New York with Montreal, New York and Buffalo with Toronto, Chicago with Toronto, and Seattle with Vancouver.

VIA Rail Canada trains travel all over Canada, but the bulk of service is in a corridor from Québec City west to Windsor, Ontario, including Toronto, Montreal, Ottawa, and other cities. A western transcontinental route connects Toronto with Vancouver on the Pacific coast; an eastern transcontinental route connects Québec City and Montreal with Halifax, Moncton, and Gaspé on the east coast. Northern trains travel to remote regions: from Winnipeg to Churchill on the Hudson Bay, from Jasper to Prince Rupert on the Pacific coast, from Montreal to Jonquière and Senneterre in northern Québec.

### Europe General Info

Some national high-speed train systems have begun to link up to form the nucleus of a pan-European system. On a long journey, you still have to change trains a couple of times as the national railways jealously guard their prerogatives. French TGVs (Trains à Grande Vitesse), which serve most major cities in France, have been extended to Geneva, Lausanne, Bern, Zurich, Turin, and Milan. They connect with the latest generation of Italy's tilting Pendolino trains, also called Eurostar Italia. Italy's service extends beyond the country's borders with a service from

Turin to Lyon and, in a joint venture with the Swiss Railways, from Milan to Geneva and Zurich. Express Thalys trains operate from Brussels to Paris on high-speed tracks and from Brussels to Amsterdam and Cologne on conventional track. Germany's equally fast ICE trains connect Hamburg and points in between with Basel, and Mannheim with Munich.

High-speed trains travel at speeds of up to 190 mph on dedicated track and over 150 mph on old track, covering the distance from Paris to Marseilles in just over four hours, Hamburg to Munich in less than six. They have made both expensive sleeper compartments and budget couchettes (seats that convert into bunks) all but obsolete. Their other attraction is the comfort of a super-smooth ride. The flip side is the reservations requirement; rather than just hopping on the next train, you need to reserve in advance or allow enough time to make a reservation at the station.

Virtually all European systems, including the high-speed ones, operate a two-class system. First class costs substantially more and is usually a luxury rather than a necessity. Some of the poorer European countries retain a third class, but avoid it unless you're an adventure-minded budget traveler.

*Important Lines*

Eurostar: High-speed Eurostar trains, which use the Channel Tunnel ("Chunnel") to link London with Paris or Brussels in about three hours.

## Southeast Asia

Trains are an option in most Southeast Asian countries; there's even luxury service between Bangkok and Singapore. Travel by train is comfortable and efficient in Thailand, Malaysia, and Singapore; in Indonesia and the Philippines, you're better off traveling by boat. Except for those in Singapore and Thailand, most trains don't have class designations. You can buy tickets, get schedule and fare information, and, in Thailand and Malaysia, purchase discount passes through hotels, travel agents, and ticket counters at train stations. Expect to pay cash at counters; travel agents and hotels generally accept traveler's checks and credit cards. Make reservations at least a day or two in advance.

## Australia & Pacific General Info

Australia has a network of interstate, country, and urban trains offering first-and economy-class service. The major interstate trains are the *Indian-Pacific* from Sydney to Perth via Adelaide (26 hours Sydney—Adelaide, 38 hours Adelaide—Perth); the *Ghan* from Adelaide to Alice Springs (20[1/2] hours); the *Overland* (night service) and *Daylink* from Melbourne to Adelaide (12 hours); and the *XPT* (Express Passenger Train) from Sydney to Brisbane (15 hours). Service between Melbourne and Sydney is on the daytime or overnight *XPT* (10[1/2] hours).

Book early whenever possible, especially for the *Indian-Pacific* and the *Ghan* during peak times (from August to October and during Christmas holidays).

Except on long-distance trains such as the *Ghan* or the *Indian-Pacific*, dining amenities are minimal. Train travel is moderately priced. Trains are used most by the elderly and by the socially disadvantaged, who travel at a considerable discount. First class costs approximately 50% more than economy.

### *Latin America*

In most South American countries, trains do not play an important role in the transportation system.

One country to see at least in part by rail is *Paraguay*, where some lines are operated with steam locomotives dating from the 19th century. In *Peru*, take the three-hour run to Machu Picchu from Cuzco and the all-day ride from Cuzco to Puno on Lake Titicaca. In *Ecuador*, a worthwhile trip is the dawn-to-dusk running through the Andes down the Avenue of the Volcanoes between Quito and Riobamba. *Chile* has a good rail system that runs south from the capital through the Lake District; take the overnight trip from Santiago to Puerto Montt. In *Argentina*, where the rail system was built by the British, the most popular routes are all from Buenos Aires—the all-day or all-night ride to Bariloche is recommended.

Ticket prices are low, and there are usually two classes of travel. Chile and Argentina have sleeping and dining cars, the others have few facilities at all. Plan to buy tickets three days ahead (two weeks in summer), and arrive at the station well before departure time. Seats cannot be reserved before you leave. There are no rail passes except in Argentina.

To sum up, there is a unique attraction in train travel, the relaxing rhythmical sounds of the train on the tracks; the picturesque scenery unfolding before your eyes, as the train slowly winds its way through the ever changing landscape. Train travel is certainly faster and more hi-tech today than at any other point in history, however the great train journeys of the world still epitomize undivided attention and flawless service.

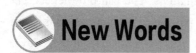

# New Words

**chug** [tʃʌg] *vi.* （发动机等）发出突突声

**scenic** [ˈsiːnik] *a.* 景色优美的

**romanticism** [rəuˈmænti,sizəm] *n.* 浪漫精神，浪漫主义

**sway** [swei] *n.* 摆动，摇动

**fleeting** [ˈfliːtiŋ] *a.* 快速的，敏捷的

**glimpse** [glimps] *n.* 一瞥，一睹

**unmatched** [ʌnˈmætʃt] *a.* 无比的，无匹敌的

**sheer** [ʃiə] *a.* 全然的，彻底的

**self-indulgence** [,selfinˈdʌldʒəns] *n.* 自我放任，自我沉溺

**info** [ˈinfəu] *n.* 信息，资料

**Amtrak** [ˈæmtræk] *n.* 美国铁路公司

**transcontinental** [,trænzkɔntiˈnentəl] *a.* 横贯大陆的

**Boston** [ˈbɔstən] *n.* 波士顿（美国马萨诸塞州首府）

**Chicago** [ʃiˈkɑːgəu] *n.* 芝加哥（美国中西部城市）

**terminus** [ˈtəːminəs] *n.* 终点站

**round-trip** [ˈraundtrip] *a.* 来回旅程的

**Montreal** [,mɔntriˈɔːl] *n.* 蒙特利尔（加拿大城市）

**Buffalo** [ˈbʌfələu] *n.* 布法罗（美国纽约州西部城市），水牛城

**Toronto** [təˈrɔntəu] *n.* 多伦多（加拿大城市）

**Seattle** [siˈætl] *n.* 西雅图（美国城市）

**Vancouver** [vænˈkuːvə] *n.* 温哥华（加拿大城市）

**bulk** [bʌlk] *n.* 大部分，大半

**Windsor** [ˈwinzə] *n.* 温莎（加拿大城市）

**Ontario** [ɔnˈteəriəu] *n.* 安大略省

**Ottawa** [ˈɔtəwə] *n.* 渥太华（加拿大城市）

**Halifax** [ˈhælifæks] *n.* 哈利法克斯市（加拿大城市）；哈利法克斯港

**Moncton** [ˈmʌŋktən] *n.* 蒙克顿（加拿大城市）

**Gaspé** [gæsˈpei] *n.* 加斯佩半岛（加）

**remote** [riˈməut] *a.* 遥远的，偏僻的

**Winnipeg** [ˈwinipeg] *n.* 温尼伯（加拿大城市）

**Churchill** [ˈtʃəːtʃil] *n.* 丘吉尔镇（加拿大马尼托巴省之一小城镇）

**Jasper** [ˈdʒæspə] *n.* 杰士伯（加拿大城市）

**Senneterre** [ˈsenitə] *n.* 圣尼特雷（加拿大城市）

**nucleus** [ˈnjuːkliəs] *n.* 核心，中心

**pan-** [pæn]（前缀）表示"全,总,泛"之意

**prerogative** [priˈrɔgətiv] *n.* 特权

**Geneva** [dʒiˈniːvə] *n.* 日内瓦（瑞士城市）

**Lausanne** [ləuˈzæn] *n.* 洛桑（瑞士西部城市）

**Bern** [bəːn] *n.* 伯尔尼（瑞士首都）

**Zurich** [ˈzuərik] *n.* 苏黎世（瑞士城市）

**Turin** [ˈtjuərin] *n.* 都灵（意大利西北部城市）

**Milan** [miˈlæn] *n.* 米兰（意大利北部城市）

**Brussels** [ˈbrʌslz] *n.* 布鲁塞尔（比利时首都）

**Amsterdam** [ˈæmstəˈdæm] *n.* 阿姆斯特丹（荷兰首都）

**Cologne** [kəˈləun] *n.* 科隆（德国城市）

**Hamburg** [ˈhæmbəːg] *n.* 汉堡（德国城市）

**Basel** [ˈbɑːzl] *n.* 巴塞尔（瑞士西北部城市），在莱茵河畔

**Mannheim** [ˈmænhaim] *n.* 曼海姆（德国西南部城市）

**Munich** [ˈmjuːnik] *n.* 慕尼黑（德国城市，巴伐利亚州首府）

**dedicated** [ˈdediˌkeitid] *a.* 专用的

**Marseilles** [mɑːˈsei] *n.* 马赛（法国城市）

**couchette** [kuːˈʃet] *n.* 睡铺，有卧铺的车厢

**bunk** [bʌŋk] *n.*（轮船，火车等的）铺位

**obsolete** [ˌɔbsəˈliːt] *a.* 荒废的，陈旧的

**substantially** [səbˈstænʃəli] *ad.* 实质上，充分地

**Chunnel** [ˈtʃʌnəl] *n.* 英吉利海峡隧道（铁路）

**Bangkok** [bæŋˈkɔk] *n.* 曼谷（泰国首都）

**Thailand** [ˈtailænd] *n.* 泰国

**designation** [ˌdezigˈneiʃən] *n.* 规定；名称

**interstate** [ˌintəˈsteit] *a.* 州际的

**urban** [ˈəːbən] *a.* 城市的，市内的

**Sydney** [ˈsidni] *n.* 悉尼（澳大利亚城市）

**Perth** [pəːθ] *n.* 珀斯（澳大利亚城市）

**Adelaide** [ˈædəleid] *n.* 阿德雷德（澳大利亚城市）

**Melbourne** [ˈmelbən] *n.* 墨尔本（澳大利亚城市）

**Brisbane** [ˈbrizbən] *n.* 布里斯班（澳大利亚东部城市）

**amenities** [əˈmiːnitiz] *n.* 令人愉快之事物

**minimal** [ˈminiməl] *a.* 最小的，最小限度的

**Paraguay** ['pærəgwai] *n.* 巴拉圭

**locomotive** [,ləukə'məutiv] *n.* 机车，火车头

**Peru** [pə'ru] *n.* 秘鲁

**Titicaca** [ti:ti'kɑ:kɑ:] *n.* 的的喀喀湖（在秘鲁和玻利维亚之间）

**Ecuador** ['ekwədɔ:] *n.* 厄瓜多尔

**dawn** [dɔ:n] *n.* 黎明，拂晓，破晓

**dusk** [dʌsk] *n.* 薄暮，黄昏

**Andes** ['ændi:z] *n.* 安第斯山脉

**avenue** ['ævə,nju:] *n.* 林荫道；大街

**volcano** [vɔl'keinəu] *n.* 火山

**Quito** ['ki:təu] *n.* 基多（厄瓜多尔首都）

**Chile** ['tʃili] *n.* 智利

**Santiago** [,sænti'ɑ:gəu] *n.* 圣地亚哥（智利首都）

**Argentina** [,ɑ:dʒən'ti:nə] *n.* 阿根廷

**rhythmical** ['riðmikl] *a.* 有节奏的，有韵律的

**picturesque** [,piktʃə'resk] *a.* 优美的；逼真的

**unfold** [ʌn'fəuld] *vi.* 伸展，打开

**hi-tech** ['hai'tek] *a.* 高科技的

**epitomize** [i'pitəmaiz] *vt.* 代表，成为……的典范

**undivided** [,ʌndi'vaidid] *a.* 不可分割的，完整的

**flawless** ['flɔ:ləs] *a.* 无瑕疵的，无缺点的

# Phrases and Expressions

Québec City  魁北克市
Hudson Bay  哈得逊湾
Prince Rup  鲁伯特王子市
Alice Springs  艾丽斯泉
VIA Rail Canada  加拿大国铁
a couple of  两个，几个

convert into  变成，转化成
all but  几乎，差不多
Latin America  拉丁美洲，南美洲
Puerto Montt  蒙特港市（智利）
wind its way  蜿蜒前进

# Notes

**1** ...train travel is the last word for those who enjoy the finer things in life.

本句中，last word 意为"好得无以复加的事物"。last word 还有其他意思，如"最后一句话；定论；最新形式"等。又如：

the last word in cars 最新型的轿车

**2** The flip side is the reservations requirement; rather than just hopping on the next train.

flip 的意思是"无理的，冒失的"。本句中，flip side 应理解为"不利的方面或不方便的方面"。rather than 可理解为"而不是"之意。

又如：

These shoes are comfortable rather than pretty.

这双鞋不好看，但是舒服。

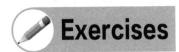 **Exercises**

**EX. 5** **Answer the following questions.**

1. What are the beautiful things of traveling by train?

2. What is the general condition of train travel in Europe?

3. Please compare the advantages and disadvantages of traveling by train, by ship and by plane.

**EX. 6** **Decide whether the following statements are *true* or *false*.**

1. Amtrak is the national passenger rail service in the United States.

2. Virtually all European systems, including the high-speed ones, operate a three-class system.

3. There's no luxury train service between Bangkok and Singapore.

4. Australia has a network of interstate, country, and urban trains offering first-and economy-class service.

5. Trains play an important role in the transportation system in most South American countries.

## Part Four Skill Training

**Forms**

The following is a Car Rental Form of Insider's Guide to Travel Services in Rio De Janeiro, Brazil.

**CAR RENTAL FORM**

**PLEASE FILL OUT ALL MANDATORY RED FIELDS.**

NAME:

E-MAIL:

CITY:

STATE:

COUNTRY:

PHONE:

FAX:

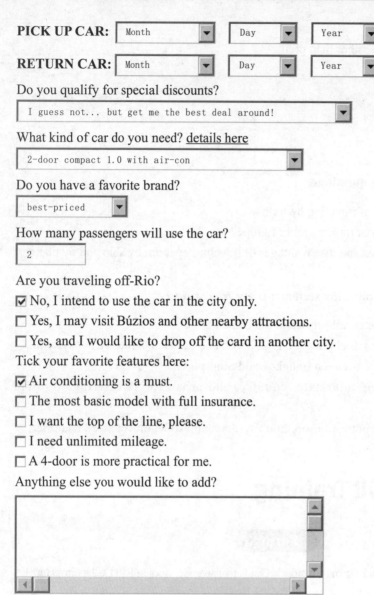

| PICK UP CAR: | Month ▾ | Day ▾ | Year ▾ |
| RETURN CAR: | Month ▾ | Day ▾ | Year ▾ |

Do you qualify for special discounts?

    I guess not... but get me the best deal around!    ▾

What kind of car do you need? <u>details here</u>

    2-door compact 1.0 with air-con    ▾

Do you have a favorite brand?

    best-priced    ▾

How many passengers will use the car?

    2

Are you traveling off-Rio?

☑ No, I intend to use the car in the city only.

☐ Yes, I may visit Búzios and other nearby attractions.

☐ Yes, and I would like to drop off the card in another city.

Tick your favorite features here:

☑ Air conditioning is a must.

☐ The most basic model with full insurance.

☐ I want the top of the line, please.

☐ I need unlimited mileage.

☐ A 4-door is more practical for me.

Anything else you would like to add?

[ Plea<u>s</u>e Process my Request ]    [ <u>R</u>eset this form ]

## Practical Writing

### How To Write Promotion Announcements

#### Ⅰ. Useful Expressions

1. How to create headlines to capture the reader's attention?

   Name your favorite Granny cookie and win a $30 gift certificate!

   Act now and get a $50 rebate!

   Act now and win a free Alpha ISDN modem of your choice!

2. How to use questions to provoke the reader's interest?

Dread cleaning up the dirty windows of your house? We will do it for you at a price you can't afford to pass up!

How to become a Citizen of the World without leaving the comfort of your home? We'll make it possible for you!

3. How to emphasize the user benefits?

The large memory of our handheld PC will allow you to run the latest, most sophisticated software.

No more need for a separate fax machine. Our high-speed modem provides hassle-free online access.

With our DX200 Digital Phone, you'll get the whole world at your fingertips!

4. How to offer details about your special offer?

To celebrate the opening of our new store, we'll take 10% off any item you purchase before May 31.

We'll offer you a limited number to be sold at 15% below list prices.

On these sales we shall allow you a special discount of 10%.

You will receive a special discount of 15%, an offer to be maintained until May 31.

This offer is good through May 31.

The program will run from May 15 to May 31.

5. How to encourage the reader to take immediate action?

To take advantage of this special offer, CALL NOW!

To order, call today 1-800-000-0000.

Go ahead and win a most stylish Eleganza Watch of your choice!

Hurry! The contest ends May 31.

Act now! This offer ends May 31.

This offer ends May 31 and will not be repeated.

For more information, call 000-0000.

## Ⅱ. Sample

Act Now and Get $400 or Win a FREE Trip to Las Vegas!

Imagine sending large files in seconds and without errors. Imagine communicating with clients, vendors, and distributors abroad at near LAN speeds. Imagine going to your favorite web sites and accessing their information in seconds instead of dozing off waiting for the words and graphics to crawl onto your screen.

You can stop imagining. It's possible now with Alpha ISDN Solutions for your home and office. Check the Alpha Special Offer below to locate the product that's just right for you and then go to the next page for details about this contest.

AlphaSuper ISDN, External or Internal
The best choice for businesses that need both high speed and seamless connections.
AlphaOffice ISDN, External or Internal
The best way to share Internet Access in a small office.
AlphaSX ISDN, Internal
The perfect choice for users who conduct business at home.
Act Now! This offer ends April 30, 1998!
To Order, Call today 1-800-0000000!

👤 **Simulate and create** ▶ You are a salesman of a company producing shampoo. Write a Promotion Announcement for your potential customers.

# Part Five  Related Information

| Text | Notes |
|---|---|
| **China Travel Briefing—Transportation** | |

*Civil Aviation*[1]

    The Civil Aviation Administration of China (CAAC)[2] provides safe and quality service. A network of 750 domestic[3] airlines is in operation in China, reaching 136 cities across the country with Beijing in the center. There are also 100 international airlines and 21 regional airlines, radiating[4] to 58 cities in 39 countries. The aircraft in service are at advanced world levels in terms of type and specification[5], and all the major airports are equipped with the world's best facilities. Air China is one of the safest air companies in the world.

*Land Transport*

    Rail transport is an important mode[6] of long-distance transportation in China. As of 2014, the country has 120,000 kilometers of railways, the second longest network in the world, including 16,000 kilometers of high-speed rail (HSR), the longest HSR[7] network in the world.

    China's railways are among the busiest in the world. In 2014, railways in China delivered 2.357 billion passenger trips, generating[8] 1,160.48 billion passenger-kilometers and carried 3.813 billion tons of freight[9], generating 2.753 billion cargo ton-kilometers.

    Since high-speed rail service in China was introduced[10] on April 18, 2007, daily ridership[11] has grown from 237,000 in 2007 to 2.49 million in 2014, making the Chinese HSR network the most heavily used in the world. Cumulative[12] ridership had reached 2.9 billion by October 2014.

    Driven by the increasing need of freight capacity[13], the railway network has expanded with the country budgeting[14] $130.4 billion for railway investment[15] in 2014, and plan to expand the network to 270,000 km by 2050.

    Highways China has built a total of 1.18 million kilometers of highways, which include 70-odd[16] state highways and 1,600-plus[17] provincial highways. Passenger service is excellent on China's expressways, featuring frequent dispatches[18] of high-grade, fast-running vehicles, and simplified check-ins. Buses, which generally run along through lines at an average speed of 100 kilometers per hours, are dispatched in a streamlined[19] fashion.

**Notes:**

[1] 民航
[2] 中国民用航空总局
[3] 国内的
[4] 辐射
[5] 技术规格
[6] 模式
[7] 高铁
[8] 产生
[9] 货运，货物
[10] 引进
[11] 客运量
[12] 累计的
[13] 能力
[14] 预算
[15] 投资
[16] 70 多
[17] 超过 1 600
[18] 分派，派遣
[19] 最新型的

*Getting around in a City Taxi* is a convenient means of transportation in large and medium-sized tourist cities in China, with fares ranging from one to two yuan per kilometer. Simply raise your hand, and the taxi stops immediately for hotels in Beijing and other tourist cities. Riding old-fashioned pedicabs[20] through Beijing's hutongs and back alleys is a fascinating tourist experience.

*Waterways*

*Maritime[21] Shipping Lines* The new Jianzhen, a luxury passenger and cargo liner operated by the Sino-Japanese[22] International Ferry[23] Company, sails once a week from Shanghai to Japan's Kobe[24], Osaka[25] and Yokohama[26] and a one-way trip along the route takes about 45 hours. The Yanjing is a passenger liner run by the Jinshen Steamboat Company, which shuttles once a week between Tianjin and Kobe. The Daren passenger and cargo liner, owned by the Dalian Steamboat Company, sails twice a week between Dalian and Inchon[27] in South Korea, with a one-way trip taking 15 hours. Operated by the Weihaiwei Eastern Shipping Company, the two luxury passenger liners, the Xinjinqiao and Xiangxuelan, sail three times a week from Weihai and Qingdao respectively to Inchon, with a one-way trip lasting for 14 hours.

*Domestic Ocean Liners* China's port cities are covered by a labyrinth[28] of maritime shipping lines. The most important of these are the Shanghai-Dalian, Dalian-Tianjin, Dalian-Yantai, Shanghai-Qingdao, Shanghai-Guangzhou, Beihai-Guangzhou, Shenzhen-Zhuhai, and Zhuhai-Hong Kong lines. Tracing these well-arranged domestic maritime shipping lines are many luxury pleasure boats and passenger liners.

*Inland Waterways* The mainland of China is crisscrossed[29] by a total of 226,800 kilometers of rivers, including 136,000 kilometers of inland waterways. The Shanghai-Chongqing line along the Yangtze River extends for 2,399 kilometers. On a given day the Three Gorges[30] of the Yangtze River are being plied by more than 50 luxury tourist boats.

| | |
|---|---|
| | [20] 三轮车 |
| | [21] 海上的 |
| | [22] 中日 |
| | [23] 渡船 |
| | [24] 神户 |
| | [25] 大阪 |
| | [26] 横滨 |
| | [27] 仁川 |
| | [28] 迷宫 |
| | [29] 互相交叉的 |
| | [30] 三峡 |

## Part Six  Guide to World Famous Sight

| Text | Notes |
|---|---|
| **The Statue of Liberty** | |

The Statue of Liberty was a gift to the United States from the people of France, conceived[1] and designed as a monument[2] to a great international friendship. But its significance has broadened and for many people throughout the world it has become the recognized[3] symbol of liberty.

[1] 构思，设想
[2] 纪念碑
[3] 公认的

*Historical Notes*

Construction of the Statue began in France in the year 1875, by sculptor[4] Auguste Bartholdi. The final completion date of the individual sections was in June of 1884, and it stood in Paris until it was dismantled[5] in early 1885 for shipping to the US. Engineering of the structure's assembly was done by Gustave Eiffel.

[4] 雕刻家
[5] 拆除

The French frigate[6] "Isere" transported the Statue from France to the United States. In transit[7] the Statue was reduced to 350 individual pieces and packed in 214 crates[8].

[6] 护卫舰
[7] 运输
[8] 柳条箱

The pedestal[9] was designed by architect Richard M. Hunt in 1877. Construction of the pedestal began in 1883 and was completed in 1884, and final assembly of the statue & pedestal was completed in 1886.

[9] 底座，基架

On October 28, 1886 President Grover Cleveland accepted The Statue on behalf of[10] the United States and said in part: "we will not forget that liberty here made her home; nor shall her chosen altar be neglected."

[10] 代表

There are 25 windows in the crown which comprise the jewels beneath the seven rays of the diadem[11]. The tablet which the Statue holds in her left hand reads, in Roman numerals, "July 4, 1776" the day of America's independence from Britain.

[11] 王冠

*The New Colossus*[12]

Not like the brazen[13] giant of Greek fame, with conquering limbs astride[14] from land to land; Here at our sea-washed, sunset gates shall stand a mighty[15] woman with a torch[16] whose flame is imprisoned lightning, and her name Mother of Exiles[17]. From her beacon[18]-hand glows[19] world-wide welcome; her mild[20] eyes command the air-bridged harbor that twin cities frame. "Keep ancient lands your storied pomp!" cries she with silent lips. "Give me your tired your poor, your huddled masses yearning[21] to breathe free, the wretched refuse of your teeming shore. Send these, the homeless, tempest-tossed[22] to me, I lift my lamp beside the golden door!"

[12] 巨像，巨人
[13] 黄铜制的
[14] 跨着
[15] 伟大的，非凡的
[16] 火炬，火把
[17] 流放，放逐
[18] 灯塔，照亮
[19] 放出光芒
[20] 温柔的
[21] 怀念，向往
[22] 飘摇不定的

# Unit 8

## Cruise

---

**Dialogues**

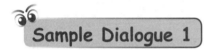

**Sample Dialogue 1**

👤 **Situation** ▶ Barbara and Ted are planning their holiday.

> ○ **Barbara**: Where shall we go for our holiday this year, Ted?
> ○ **Ted**:    How about Majorca? It's cheap, and good weather is guaranteed.
> ○ **Barbara**: I'd rather do something more exciting this year. Have you seen this ad for
> ○         adventure holidays in Scotland?
> ○ **Ted**:    I prefer lying on a beach to hang-gliding and canoeing.
> ○ **Barbara**: But we do that every year. I'd prefer to do something different this time. I'd
> ○         rather not go anywhere so crowded.
> ○ **Ted**:    Well, you have a point. Majorca was very crowded last time. I'd prefer
> ○         somewhere a little quieter too, but I don't fancy anything too active.
> ○ **Barbara**: How about Torquay? The weather's usually good and there are some lovely
> ○         walks around the coast.
> ○ **Ted**:    Sounds OK to me. Would you prefer to stay in a hotel or rent a cottage?

**Sample Dialogue 2**

> ○     A very common way to start a conversation is to talk about the weather. When you're
> ○ traveling, remember that there is considerable variation in climate in the United States.
> ○ *Conversation 1*
> ○ **A**: Beautiful day, isn't it?

**B**: Yes. It's not like what the radio said at all.

**A**: I wish it would stay this way for the weekend.

**B**: As long as it doesn't snow!

*Conversation 2*

**A**: It seems to be clearing up.

**B**: It's such a nice change.

**A**: I really don't think this weather will last.

**B**: Let's just hope it doesn't get cold again.

## Useful Expressions

1. When will it be convenient for you?
   什么时候对你来说比较方便？

2. How about going to...?
   去……怎么样？

3. Yeah, that sounds good.
   听起来不错。

4. It looks it's going to be sunny.
   看来天要晴了。

5. It's certainly a big improvement over yesterday.
   今天的天气比昨天肯定是好多了。

6. It's supposed to get cloudy and windy this afternoon.
   今天下午应该是多云有风。

## Task Dialogue 1

**Situation** ▶ Colin wants to go on an excursion this weekend. He is asking his friend, Jennifer, for advice.

## Task Dialogue 2

**Situation** ▶ You are traveling abroad and want to find someone to talk with. Try to open a conversation with a native.

# Part Two  Text A

## Cruising Industry

### Introduction to the Industry

A cruise offers all the things most people want in a vacation—romance, excitement, relaxation, adventure, escape, discovery, luxury, value and more—without the hassles nobody wants. It's no surprise, then, that most people who have taken a cruise rate cruising above any other vacation choice.

The groundwork for the modern day cruise industry was laid down as far as the early 1950's. Following the arrival of air transportation service between Europe and North America, large transatlantic liner companies were forced to seek alternate usage for their ships. Shipping lines took advantage of the traveling public's immense desire for exotic travel and exploration, and thus slowly refitted their large transatlantic liners for leisure cruising and repositioned them to warmer climates, gentler seas and exotic ports of call.

In an effort to tap into a broader spectrum of the vacation market, the 1960's saw shipping lines offering shorter (7-10 days) and more moderately priced Caribbean cruises from new homeports in South Florida. The proximity of the Port of Miami and Port Everglades to the Caribbean islands proved the key for US-based cruise travel.

The early 1970's saw the creation of companies such as Carnival Cruise Lines, Royal Caribbean, Norwegian Cruise Lines and the arrival of European based companies such as Peninsular and Oriental (future Princess Cruises), Cunard and Chandris (future Celebrity). As Caribbean cruising became main-stream, cruise lines embarked on a ship-building race that would help them secure market share and establish their ships as the largest and most modern vessels afloat.

The 1980's saw the industry mature and become a solid participant on the leisure and hospitality industries. As companies grew, so did their ships. As competition within the cruise industry grew, prices were reduced in order to attract a broader mix of passengers. As expected, cruise lines sought out means to reduce their operational expenses and started designing larger ships to maximize the benefits of economies of scale. Lesser operational expenses and an increase in cruise and on-board revenues fueled the drive for bigger, more efficient and more appealing ships.

## Economies of Scale

As port and itinerary differentiation became minimal among the major cruise lines, the attraction of the ship as a destination in itself became the main marketing focus for the cruise lines. The "Fun Ship" concept coined by Carnival Cruise Lines exemplifies this new trend as it became more about the ship than its destinations. New ships began to incorporate a variety of entertainment venues (bar, lounges, libraries, spas, workout facilities, business centers) in order to appeal to wider audiences. As more facilities were incorporated, ship sizes increased accordingly. The late 1990's saw the arrival of several ships in the 110,000-to 145,000-ton size with cabin capacities ranging between 2,500 and 3,000 passengers.

New ship construction, while the primary drive for new business, is just one of many factors that have contributed to the industry's rapid expansion. Better product positioning, changing demographics, a healthy economy, a wider range of cruise lengths and departure points, and the addition of innovative amenities and onboard facilities, have all played a role in the industry's rapid growth. Cruise ships have become "floating resorts" offering all the amenities and conveniences of modern day land facilities. The areas of dining, entertainment, shore excursion and on-board activities have changed dramatically in the last 20 years and now compete with the best facilities ashore.

### *Cruising Companies and Lines*

While there are several cruise lines serving the North American market, competition is dominated by the "Big Three" cruise groups. The Carnival Corporation (parent company of Carnival Cruise Lines, Holland America Line, Cunard/Seabourn Line and Costa Cruises), Royal Caribbean International (owner of Celebrity Cruises), the newly independent Princess Cruises and the recently acquired Norwegian Cruise Line (a wholly owned subsidiary of Malaysia-based Star Cruises) enjoy a combined market share of over 85%. The remainder of the industry is shared amongst smaller operators such as Disney Cruise Lines and the ultra-luxury operators such as Crystal Cruises, Silverseas Cruises and Radisson Seven Seas Cruises.

The Carnival Corporation, Royal Caribbean, Princess Cruises and Norwegian Cruise Lines are by far the most visible in the industry and their moves tend to determine industry direction and the nature of the competition. The larger lines tend to have a much broader line of service and market segmentation, while the smaller lines tend to be more specialized by serving niche markets and special itineraries catering to specific market segments. Historically this industry has been highly lucrative with high profit margins, below average competition, steadily rising sales and solid financial performances.

The worldwide cruise industry is now valued at $15bn. At the start of 2003, over 30 new ships costing a combined $12bn were on order for delivery over the next four years. Despite a recent slowdown in ship orders, worldwide cruise passengers are still projected to increase 60% from 10m in 2000 to more than 16m in 2009.

North America, the number one source market, has increased passenger numbers annually by 7% for the last 12 years and topped 7m in 2002.

The number two source market, the UK, has quadrupled its passenger numbers in the last 12 years to 800,000.

Continental Europe is now being targeted as the next major source market with the under-performing German and Spanish markets now expected to double over the next five years.

Asia, which was the fastest growing source market in the 1990s before regional economic problems stalled it, is expected to grow again from 2003.

By its nature, cruising is an enterprise that links the world. Cruise ships call at ports on every continent; their passengers and crews comprise people from every part of the world; and the industry benefits hundreds of countries and their citizens. One of the traditional appeals of a cruise is the opportunity it provides to visit several destinations in one excellent vacation experience. Frequent cruisers especially applaud cruises as a way to try out a vacation area to which they might want to return.

# New Words

**cruise** [kru:z] *n.* 乘船游览

**romance** [rəu'mæns] *n.* 浪漫

**relaxation** [ˌri:læk'seiʃən] *n.* 放松；松弛

**adventure** [əd'ventʃə] *n.* 冒险，历险

**luxury** ['lʌkʃəri] *n.* 奢侈；豪华

**hassle** ['hæsl] *n.* 困难，麻烦

**groundwork** ['graund,wə:k] *n.* 基础；根基

**transatlantic** [ˌtrænzət'læntik] *a.* 横跨大西洋的

**liner** ['lainə] *n.* 邮轮

**alternate** ['ɔ:ltəneit] *n.* 替换，备用

**immense** [i'mens] *a.* 极大的

**exotic** [ig'zɔtik] *a.* 异国情调的

**exploration** [ˌeksplɔ'reiʃən] *n.* 探索，探险

**refit** [ri:'fit] *vt.* 整修，改装

**reposition** [ˌri:pə'ziʃən] *vt.* 重新定位，再定位

**tap** [tæp] *vt.* 开发；利用

**spectrum** ['spektrəm] *n.* 领域，范围

**moderately** ['mɔdərətli] *ad.* 适度地

**Caribbean** [ˌkæri'biən] *a.* 加勒比海的

**proximity** [prɔk'siməti] *n.* 接近，临近

**embark** [im'ba:k] *vi.* 着手，从事

**vessel** ['vesl] *n.* 船

**afloat** [ə'fləut] *ad.* 在海上

**mature** [mə'tjuə] *a.* 成熟的

**participant** [pa:'tisipənt] *n.* 参与者，共享者

**maximize** ['mæksimaiz] *vt.* 取……最大值，最佳化

**appealing** [ə'pi:liŋ] *a.* 吸引人的，引起兴趣的

**itinerary** [ai'tinərəri] *n.* 旅程，旅行路线

**differentiation** [ˌdifəˌrenʃi'eiʃn] *n.* 区别

**exemplify** [ig'zemplifai] *vt.* 例证，例示

**trend** [trend] *n.* 倾向，趋势

**venue** ['venju:] *n.* 聚会地点

**spa** [spa:] *n.* 水疗

**workout** ['wə:kaut] *n.* 体育锻炼

**accordingly** [ə'kɔ:diŋli] *ad.* 因此；相应地

**capacity** [kə'pæsəti] *n.* 容量

**expansion** [ik'spænʃən] *n.* 扩大，扩张，发展

**demographics** [ˌdemə'græfiks] *n.* 人口统计学

**dominate** ['dɔmineit] *vt.* 统治，支配，控制

**subsidiary** [səb'sidiəri] *n.* 分公司，分支机构

**combined** [kəm'baind] *a.* 组合的，结合的

**remainder** [ri'meində] *n.* 残余，剩余部分

**ultra-luxury** ['ʌltrə'lʌkʃəri] *a.* 极其豪华的

**visible** ['vizəbl] *a.* 引人注目的

**move** [mu:v] *n.* 采取的行动，步骤

**segmentation** [ˌsegmən'teiʃən] *n.* 份额

**niche** [ni:ʃ] *n.* 适当的位置

**lucrative** ['lu:krətiv] *a.* 有利的，赚钱的

**margin** ['ma:dʒin] *n.* 余地；盈余，利润

**steadily** ['stedili] *ad.* 稳定地，稳固地

**slowdown** ['sləu,daun] *n.* 降低速度，减速

**project** [prə'dʒekt] *vt.* 预计，计划；设计

**quadruple** [kwɔ'dru:pl] *vt.* 使成四倍，翻两番

**stall** [stɔːl] *vt.* 使停转，使停止，迟延
**comprise** [kəmˈpraɪz] *vt.* 包含，由……组成

**applaud** [əˈplɔːd] *vt.* 赞同，称赞

## Phrases and Expressions

take advantage of  利用
port of call  停靠港
Port of Miami  迈阿密港（美国佛罗里达州东南部）
Port Everglades  美东港口
Carnival Corporation  嘉年华公司
Carnival Cruise Lines  嘉年华游轮公司
Holland America Line  荷美公司
Cunard/Seabourn Line  冠达 / 世鹏游轮
Costa Cruises  科斯塔游轮
Royal Caribbean International  皇家加勒比海游轮集团
Celebrity Cruises  名声游轮
Princess Cruises  公主游轮公司

Norwegian Cruise Lines  挪威游轮公司
Star Cruises  丽星游轮
Disney Cruise Lines  迪斯尼游轮
Crystal Cruises  水晶游轮
Silverseas Cruises  银海游轮
Radisson Seven Seas Cruises  瑞迪生七海游轮
economy of scale  规模经济
appeal to  引起兴趣，吸引
play a role in  起作用，扮演角色
by far  到目前为止
tend to  趋于
try out  试验，考验

## Notes

1　The early 1970's saw the creation of companies such as Carnival Cruise Lines, Royal Caribbean, Norwegian Cruise Lines and the arrival of European based companies such as Peninsular and Oriental (future Princess Cruises), Cunard and Chandris (future Celebrity).

　　本句中，The early 1970's 是句子的主语，saw 是谓语，宾语由两个并列部分 the creation of companies 和 the arrival of European based companies 组成，其后的 such as... 是对它们的举例说明。
本句中 saw 的意思是"经历，见证"。

2　The groundwork for the modern day cruise industry was laid down as far as the early 1950's.

　　本句中，lay down 意为"打下基础"；as far as 意为"远到，远在"。全句意为：现代巡游业早在 19 世纪 50 年代就打下了基础。又如：
They got married as far as 1995.
他们早在 1995 年就结婚了。

**3** New ship construction, while the primary drive for new business, is just one of many factors...

本句中，while the primary drive for new business 是一个时间状语从句，while 表示动作的"同时"进行。本句可理解为：新船的建造，同时也是促使这个新兴产业发展的首要动力，只是……的众多因素之一。又如：

While he was eating, I asked him to lend me 2 pounds.

当他正在吃饭时，我请他借给我两英镑。

# Exercises

**EX. 1** **Answer the following questions.**

1. How was cruising industry developed?

2. What are the main big cruising companies?

3. What is the main marketing focus for the cruise lines?

4. What are the main source markets of cruising?

**EX. 2** **Write out the English words according to the definitions given below.**

| definitions | words |
|---|---|
| sail about for pleasure | |
| risk, danger, e.g. in travel and exploration | |
| ship or aircraft of a line of ships or aircraft | |
| plan for, details of, records of a journey route | |
| comfortable sitting room, esp. in a club of hotel | |
| spring of mineral water having medicinal properties | |
| short journey, esp. by a number of people together for pleasure | |
| to say that you admire or agree with (a person's action or decision) | |
| a company which is owned by a larger company | |
| introducing changes and new ideas | |

**EX. 3** **Complete the following sentences with appropriate words or expressions from the text.**

1. The _____ for the modern day cruise industry was laid down as far as the early 1950's.

2. As competition within the cruise industry grew, _____ were reduced in order to attract a broader mix of passengers.

3. _____, the number one source market, has increased passenger numbers annually by 7% for the last 12 years and topped 7m in 2002.

4. The number two source market, _____, has quadrupled its passenger numbers in the last 12 years to 800,000.

5. The "_____" concept coined by Carnival Cruise Lines exemplifies this new trend as it became more about the ship than its destinations.

6. Cruise ships have become "_____" offering all the amenities and conveniences of modern day land facilities.

**EX. 4** **Translate the following sentences into Chinese.**

1. A cruise offers all the things most people want in a vacation—romance, excitement, relaxation, adventure, escape, discovery, luxury, value and more—without the hassles nobody wants.

2. Following the arrival of air transportation service between Europe and North America, large transatlantic liner companies were forced to seek alternate usage for their ships.

3. The 1980's saw the industry mature and become a solid participant on the leisure and hospitality industries.

4. As port and itinerary differentiation became minimal between the major cruise lines, the attraction of the ship as a destination in itself became the main marketing focus for the cruise lines.

## Part Three   Text B

## Cruise Industry Catering to Families

### Big ships, theme trips, home ports in the offerings

Improve your golf swing. Take a yoga class. Bring grandma and the kids. Marvel at a mega-ship.

And start your trip at a home port near you.

Such are the latest trends in the cruise industry. There are theme trips, activities for all ages, and classes in everything from cooking to financial management. Travel by extended families is growing. A slew of mammoth vessels—including the largest ocean liner in history, the Queen Mary 2, and five more ships with room for even more passengers—are due to be launched in 2004. And local departure ports, from Philadelphia to Mobile, Ala., are growing in popularity.

The trends reflect larger cultural swings: Travelers want more options, more time with loved ones, and fewer hassles in getting to their destinations.

"Vacationers don't want to spend five hours flying to get to their destination, and then get on a cruise," said Vicki Freed, marketing executive for Carnival Cruise Lines. "With close-to-home ports throughout North America, people can drive to their embarkation ports."

Ports in Florida and California hosted the most cruise passengers last year, but Hawaii, New York, New Orleans, Galveston, Seattle and Boston each served as departure points for hundreds of thousands more. Meanwhile smaller ports like Baltimore and Charleston, S.C., are increasingly busy.

Home ports are not the only example of how the industry is trying to accommodate travelers who'd rather not have to fly to get on a ship. Norwegian Cruise Lines has just launched the first Caribbean cruise to sail from New York City during the cold-weather months. Trips began leaving Manhattan on Sunday afternoons in November; they arrive in Orlando at eight a.m. Tuesday, then head for the islands. So far, New Yorkers' appetite for the ease of stepping on a boat without flying to Florida outweighs the discomfort of 24 hours bundled up on deck in winter coats; Norwegian says the ships are sailing at capacity.

An old adage about cruises painted the typical passenger as "newlywed, overfed or nearly dead," but demographics for cruises are changing. A million children took cruises in 2002, double the number from 1998, according to the Cruise Lines International Association, which represents 21 cruise lines. And with a five-day, $500 (or less) trip to a warm place (meals included), available in many markets, prices are affordable for middle-class families.

"Since Sept. 11, vacationing has been about being with people you care about," said Amanda Bliss, spokeswoman for Disney Cruises. More than half of Disney's passengers book more than one room at a time; parents and kids go with grandparents and sometimes even neighboring families.

Radisson Seven Seas, a luxury line that tends to attract an older, wealthier clientele than Disney, has seen grandparents booking cruises with their children and grandchildren. " They want to go together as a group," said spokeswoman Lauren Kaufman. "We're seeing a lot of anniversaries."

Once on board, families can dine and do some activities together, then separate to pursue individual interests. The old cruise model—eat a big meal, then sit in a deck chair until you dock somewhere interesting—has been replaced by parties for teenagers, games for kids, play spaces for toddlers, and spas, gyms and seminars for adults.

Larger vessels provide the space for this ever-growing choice of activities. The Queen Mary 2—as tall as a 21-story building, with a capacity of 2,620 people—has a planetarium and the world's largest floating library. Royal Caribbean's Voyager of the Seas, which carries 3,114 people, has an ice rink and a rock-climbing wall.

"Talk to 50 people getting off a ship and they'll describe 50 different vacations," said Bob Sharak, CLIA's executive director.

While the large ships provide economies of scale for the industry and many options for passengers, some travelers are repulsed by the idea of a seaborne mini-city bustling with thousands of people. After all, aren't vacations about escaping busy crowds for a little serenity? For these travelers, more intimate trips—like a 186-passenger cruise on China's Yangtze River, sponsored by Viking River Cruises—are more appealing.

Some cruises use themes to attract passengers. The 900-person Regal Princess will be crawling with twenty the mes when it features "jam bands" and their marathon concerts on January cruises. All-kosher luxury cruises are offered out of San Juan. A D-Day anniversary cruise will cross the English Channel to Normandy. And, as a result of the recent Massachusetts court ruling on same-sex marriage, a weeklong "honeymoon cruise" for 1,200 women departs Boston for Montreal on July 4th. The cruise is sponsored by Olivia Cruises, which specializes in travel for women.

But the industry's happy mantra that "There's a cruise for everyone!" was dampened by a series of public relations nightmares. Fifteen people died when the gangplank to the Queen Mary 2 collapsed in France as workers and their families boarded for a pre-launch tour. Environmental advocates complain that cruise ships pollute the water—a claim the industry disputes, citing the local and national regulations ships must comply with. And every time an outbreak of Norovirus—a common gastrointestinal illness—is reported aboard a cruise ship, many would-be passengers change their plans.

Despite the bad news, the number of passengers who take cruises each year keeps going up, with a record-breaking 8.3 million North Americans expected to cruise in 2003.

Of course that number pales next to the 40 million people who go to Orlando each year; only 15 percent of Americans have ever been on a cruise, according to CLIA. Yet the cruise industry doesn't see that as bad news. "We have," said Freed, of Carnival. "an opportunity to grow."

# New Words

**theme** [θiːm] *n.* 主题

**yoga** ['jəugə] *n.* 瑜珈，瑜珈术

**marvel** ['mɑːvəl] *vi.* 大为惊异，觉得惊奇

**slew** [sluː] *n.* 船头左右摇荡

**mammoth** ['mæməθ] *a.* 巨大的

**due** [djuː] *a.* 预期的

**launch** [lɔːntʃ] *vt.* 使（船）下水

**swing** [swiŋ] *n.* 巨大的改变

**executive** [ig'zekjutiv] *n.* 经理主管人员

**Florida** ['flɔridə] *n.* 佛罗里达（美国州名）

**California** [,kæli'fɔːnjə] *n.* 加利福尼亚（美国州名）

**Hawaii** [hə'wɑːiː] *n.* 夏威夷（美国州名）

**Galveston** ['gælvəstən] *n.* 加尔维斯敦（美国得克萨斯州南部港口城市）

**Charleston** ['tʃɑːlstən] *n.* 查尔斯顿（美国西弗吉尼亚州首府）

**Manhattan** [mæn'hætən] *n.* 曼哈顿岛（美国纽约一区）

**appetite** ['æpətait] *n.* 胃口，食欲

**ease** [iːz] *n.* 舒适，悠闲

**outweigh** [,aut'wei] *vt.* 比……更重

要，胜过

**bundle** ['bʌndl] vt. 捆扎

**adage** ['ædidʒ] n. 格言；谚语

**spokeswoman** ['spəuks,wumən] n. 女发言人，女代言人

**clientele** [,kli:ɔn'teil] n. 客户

**anniversary** [,æni'və:səri] n. 周年纪念日

**pursue** [pə'sju:] vt. 追求；寻求

**model** ['mɔdl] n. 模式

**toddler** ['tɔdlə] n. 刚学步的小孩

**seminar** ['semi,nɑ:] n. 研究会，讨论发表会

**planetarium** [,plænə'teəriəm] n. 天文馆，天象馆

**rink** [riŋk] n. 溜冰场，冰球场

**repulse** [ri'pʌls] vt. 拒绝，排斥

**serenity** [sə'renəti] n. 平静

**intimate** ['intimət] a. 亲密的，熟悉的

**sponsor** ['spɔnsə] vt. 发起，主办

**crawl** [krɔ:l] vi. 徐徐行进

**marathon** ['mærəθən] n. 马拉松赛跑，耐力的考验

**band** [bænd] n. 乐队

**kosher** ['kəuʃə] a. 正当的；合适的

**Normandy** ['nɔ:mən'di] n. 诺曼底（法国西北部一地区，北临英吉利海峡）

**Massachusetts** [,mæsə'tʃu:sits] n. 马萨诸塞（美国州名）

**dampen** ['dæmpən] vt. 使沮丧

**nightmare** ['nait,mɛə] n. 噩梦，可怕的事物

**gangplank** ['gæŋ,plæŋk] n. （上下船的）跳板

**collapse** [kə'læps] n. 倒塌，塌陷

**dispute** [di'spju:t] vt. 反驳，驳斥

**cite** [sait] vt. 引用，引证

**outbreak** ['aut,breik] n. （战争的）爆发；（疾病的）发作

**gastrointestinal** [gæstrəuin'testinl] n. 胃肠，肠胃

**pale** [peil] vi. 显得逊色，相形见绌

 # Phrases and Expressions

Yangtze River　长江

D-Day　（第二次世界大战中）盟国在西欧登陆日

New Orleans　新奥尔良（美国港口城市）

public relations　公共关系，公关

## Notes

**1** Travel by extended families is growing.

　　本句中，extended family 是指扩大的家庭（如数代同堂的家庭）。与其相对应的是 nuclear family，核心家庭（只包括父母和子女的家庭）及 DINK（double income, no kids），丁克家庭（夫妇都有工作，无孩子）。

**2** "Vacationers don't want to spend five hours flying to get to their destination, and then get on a cruise," said Vicki Freed, marketing executive for Carnival Cruise Lines.

本句中 marketing executive for Carnival Cruise Lines 是 Vicki Freed 的同位语。本句所用的句型是：spend some time (in) doing something，介词 in 可省略。请看下例：

I spent an hour reading.

我花了一小时读书。

**3** ...travelers who'd rather not have to fly to get on a ship.

本句中，who'd rather 是 who would rather。would rather 的意思是 "宁愿"，否定式是 would rather not，意思是 "不愿"。也可与 than 搭配使用，"would rather ...than..." 的意思是 "宁可……也不"。请看下例：

Which would you rather do, go to the cinema or stay at home?

你愿意去看电影还是待在家里？

He would rather die than surrender.

他宁死不屈。

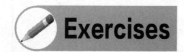

# Exercises

**EX. 5** **Answer the following questions.**

1. What are the latest trends in the cruise industry?

2. What activities are organized to cater to the interest of people of different age?

3. What is theme cruising?

4. Are there any bad effects of this industry? If yes, what are they?

**EX. 6** **Decide whether the following statements are *true* or *false*.**

1. The cruising trends reflect larger cultural swings: Travelers want more options, more time with loved ones, and fewer hassles in getting to their destinations.

2. "Newlywed, overfed or nearly dead" is a picture of today's cruising industry.

3. Once on board, families can dine and do some activities together, then separate to pursue individual interests.

4. Some cruises use themes to attract passengers.

5. Because of some bad news, the number of passengers who take cruises each year is declining.

# **Part Four** **Skill Training**

## Forms

*The following is a travel reservation form for Star Travel, Inc.*

Send reservations to:

Star Travel, Inc.

13899 Biscayne Blvd. Ste. 102 N

Miami, FL 33141

For additional Information, Please Call:

**Dade:** (305) 865-0357

**Broward:** (954) 523-5371

**Toll Free:** (800) 366-6298

### **Traveler Information Form**

Please print out this form, fill in the information, Print or Type, and send in to Star Travel.

All information MUST be completed for your application to be processed and accepted. No initials, please.

---

☐ Mr.    ☐ Mrs.    ☐ Miss    ☐ Ms    ☐ Dr.

| | | | |
|---|---|---|---|
| [ ] | [ ] | [ ] | [ ] |
| Last name **as it appears on passport** | First name **as it appears on passport** | Middle name | Nickname |

| | | | |
|---|---|---|---|
| [ ] | [ ] | [ ] | [ ] |
| Street Address | City | State | Zip |

| | |
|---|---|
| [ ] | [ ] |
| (Area Code) Home Phone | (Area Code) Office Phone |

☐ Single (1 Bed)          ☐ Twin (2 Beds)          ☐ Double (1 bed for 2 people)

☐ Triple (3 beds for 3 people)     ☐ Non-smoker          ☐ Smoker

I desire twin occupancy; my roommate's name is: [                    ]

(if not included on this reservation form)

Emergency contact person [        ] [        ] [            ]

MUST BE FILLED OUT!    Name          Relationship    Phone (Day) (Night)

### **ACCOMPANYING FAMILY MEMBER OR COMPANION**

☐ Mr.    ☐ Mrs.    ☐ Miss    ☐ Ms    ☐ Dr.

| | | | |
|---|---|---|---|
| [ ] | [ ] | [ ] | [ ] |
| Last name as it appears on passport | First name as it appears on passport | Middle name | Nickname |

| | | | |
|---|---|---|---|
| [ ] | [ ] | [ ] | [ ] |
| Street Address | City | State | Zip |

| | |
|---|---|
| [ ] | [ ] |
| (Area Code) Home Phone | (Area Code) Office Phone |

```
[                                                    ]
```
Name of Tour

```
[                        ]          [                        ]
```
Departure Date                          Departure City

## TOUR INFORMATION

### (Please print or type information below)

Check one:

☐ Master Card     ☐ Visa

☐ Discover        ☐ Am Ex

Account Number: [                        ]

Expiration Date: [                        ]

```
[                        ]
```
**Signature**

Tour Cost $ [            ] p.p

X [ # of People ] = $ [            ]

Single Supplement (If applicable):

$ [            ]

Applicable Taxes $ [            ] p.p

X [ # of People ] = $ [            ]

**Total Cost: $** [            ]

**IMPORTANT NOTE:**

We must receive a copy of the photo page of your passport (this is the page with your photo, passport number and other personal details). Please provide this copy with your deposit or final payment.

AIRLINE TICKETS AND DOCUMENTS CAN NOT BE ISSUED UNTIL WE RECEIVE THIS

COPY. Enclosed is a deposit/payment in full of **$** [            ] made payable to **Star Travel, Inc**.

I have read and do understand the *Terms and Conditions* and accept them on behalf of myself and my party.

```
[                        ]
```
Signature

```
[                        ]
```
Signature of traveling companion

```
[                        ]
```
Date

This form may be submitted electronically via the Internet. Star Travel will then contact you.

[ Reset ]    [ Submit ]

## Practical Writing

Signing a tour contract can safeguard the rights and interests of both the tourists and the agency. It serves as an attestation when dissension occurs. The following is a tour contract concerning skiing.

### Tour Contract

(Use the print function of your browser to print the contract for signature)

**Name** _____

**Address** _____

The tours described in this brochure are operated by Buckles & Boards Ski Shop, Inc., "Tour Operator" located at 2148 Ocean St., Marshfield, Ma. 02050.

This agreement sets forth the terms and conditions pursuant to which in return for payment by the tour participant, "Participant", of the amount specified as the price and a signed Participant's Application, Tour Operator agrees to provide the subject tour.

**DEPOSIT AND PAYMENT**: Deposit of $400.00 per person for land arrangements is required at time of booking. No reservation will be processed without deposit. Full and final is due 60 days before departure date. For bookings made within 30 days departure, add $20.00 per person. For final payments received later than date specified on contract or invoice add $20.00 per person.

**CANCELLATION OF AIRLINE TICKETS**: NON-REFUNDABLE. No travel date changes are allowed.

**ALTERATION OF LAND ARRANGEMENTS**: Due to frequent difficulties of changing reservations, and due to the amount of work involved therein, the operator is compelled to charge $25.00 per person for each change of itinerary.

**BAGGAGE**: One pair of skis with poles and ski boots are usually defined as one piece of baggage measuring 55 inches. If you have only one suitcase (not exceeding 62 inches) to be checked in, then one pair of skis, poles, and boots will usually be accepted as the remaining part of your free allowance. Check with the airlines for restrictions.

**AIR TRANSPORTATION**: The airfares are based on current tariff and are subject to change. Departure tax is additional. Air transportation includes round trip transatlantic jet economy class via regularly scheduled airlines. All prices are based GIT, APEX, or other group fares and regulations from the Departure City to the Destination City shown for each vacation as specified in the itinerary. Transatlantic transportation in Business class or First class may be arranged at additional cost.

**CANCELLATION AND REFUND POLICY**: The Tour Participant has the right to cancel reservations and receive a refund as set forth in the following schedule. All cancellations must be made in writing to Buckles & Boards Ski Shop, Inc., 2148 Ocean St., Marshfield, Ma 02050, 121 days prior to scheduled departure full refund, 90-120 days a charge of $200 per person 89 days prior to departure.

**NO REFUND** No refunds will be given on any unused portion of the tour package after departing from the United States. We reserve the right to cancel any individual participation in its entirety or any part thereof, by refunding a proportionate balance for the unused portion of the tour. For your protection, we urge you to consider travel insurance.

**NOT INCLUDED IN TOUR PRICE**: Transportation between your home and the airport of origin and termination; meals other than those specified; tips or gratuities; telephone charges; laundry; passport; health certificates and visa expenses; airport taxes; excess baggage charges; health and accident insurance; all items of a personal nature including wine, liquor, food and extra meals not included in the tour package.

**RESPONSIBILITY**: The TOUR OPERATOR and/or its agent act only in the capacity of agent for the passengers in all matters pertaining to travel whether by plane, rail, bus, steamer or any other means of conveyance. They shall assume no liability for injury, damage, loss, accident, delay or irregularity which may be occasioned either by reason of defect in any vehicle or through the acts or default of any company or person engaged in conveying the passengers or carrying out the arrangements of the tour. The tour operator can accept no responsibility for loss or additional expenses due to delay or changes in schedule or other causes. Baggage is carried at owner's risk and baggage insurance is recommended. The issuance of tickets and vouchers shall be deemed to be consent to the above conditions. The Tour Operator is not to be held responsible for the lack of snow or non-operation of the lifts at the ski resorts, or for the closure of access routes to or from the resorts due to snow or weather conditions; nor are they to be held liable for any additional expenses or consequences arriving there from. Similarly, they are not to be held responsible for the late arrival of passengers at airports or at resorts due to bad weather or road conditions, or for any other reasons beyond their control; nor are they to be held liable for payment of any refund for unused hotel accommodations or meals occasioned by such late arrivals at the hotels holding rooms as per confirmed itineraries.

**RESPONSIBILITY PARTICIPATING CARRIERS**: The sole responsibility of any airline used in any tour is limited to that set out in the passenger contract evidenced by the ticket. Airlines are not responsible for any act, omission or event during the time the passengers are not on board their aircraft. Persons missing a flight or tour must, at their own expense, transport themselves to the next point of the trip.

**Print name** _____

**Signature** _____

**Email Order Number** (*from receipt provided by on line checkout*) _____

**Phone:**_____

*Use the print button (or file/print) of your browser to print a copy of this document for signature. This form may be faxed to (781) 834-0311, or mailed to: Buckles and Boards Ski Shop, Inc., 2148 Ocean St., Marshfield, MA 02050*

👤 **Simulate and create** ▶ Draft a contract concerning cruising, simulating the above model.

# Part Five Related Information

| Text | Notes |
|---|---|
| **Tips for Cruising** | |
| *First time cruiser* | |
| Although you may have visions of a cruise being your all-time dream holiday—its best not to book a long cruise as your virgin[1] voyage. A long cruise can seem like an eternity[2] when you know there's no escape and it turns out not to be your sort of thing. Also, although you may never have suffered from sea-sickness before and the ships are becoming much more advanced, you may find the motion becomes a problem for you if you're on a ship for more than a few hours. | [1] 初次<br>[2] 永远 |
| A three or four days cruise is really recommended[3] as a taster[4] for travelers new to cruises. Just think—it's an excuse to have another (longer) cruise if you do find you love it! | [3] 推荐<br>[4] 尝试 |
| *Benefits of arriving early* | |
| Find out when you can board the ship—and aim to get there a bit earlier! This will give you a few advantages as you will avoid the crowds and you will have first shot[5] at the popular amenities[6] that will fill up quickly, e.g. spa, babysitting[7] services, salons[8] etc. You will be able to use the extra time to confirm everything is as you booked and check that the seating arrangements for dining meet your approval. Speak to the maitre d'hotel[9] as soon as possible. The earlier you do this, the more likely it is something can be changed to your liking. | [5] 机会<br>[6] 令人愉快的事物<br>[7] 照顾婴儿<br>[8] 沙龙<br>[9] 餐厅领班 |
| You will be able to sign up for any shore[10] excursions you fancy that you aren't already booked on—before they fill up! | [10] 海滨 |
| *Choose cabin[11]* | [11] 船舱 |
| A lot of the features of your cabin will depend on what feel you are trying to create on your cruise, or on how tight your budget[12] is. But with any cabin, you'll want to know what it's close to (both horizontally[13] and vertically[14])! | [12] 预算<br>[13] 水平地<br>[14] 垂直地 |
| If you suspect[15] you may suffer from seasickness, the smoothest areas to rest are in the lower, mid-ship—you may also wish to avoid those cabins with a view in this area as it is generally of a rolling[16] sea! The cabins to the front and rear[17] of the ship will be subject to the largest movements. | [15] 猜想；怀疑<br>[16] 起伏的<br>[17] 后部 |
| Rooms with windows will have a feeling of greater space than a windowless cabin of the same size— of course, you pay for this luxury[18]. Beware though, not all the rooms "with a view" have | [18] 奢侈；豪华 |

pleasant scenery through the window—it may just be of busy decks or lifeboats. Check the ships layout[19] before deciding if your view is worth the money!

*Tipping*[20]

As in a hotel, tipping is an important proportion of the wage that cruise line employees earn. In fact, some cruise lines even give you envelopes specifically[21] for handing out tips! You can usually request a guide to tipping from your cruise line, but the information below is a useful approximation[22] in the mean time!

Baggage handlers/porters[23] are generally tipped £0.50-£1.00 (approximately $1-$1.5) per bag they move to your cabin, for you.

Cabin Stewards[24] are usually given £2.00-£2.50 (about $3.00-$3.50) per passenger, per day.

The maitre d'hotel will receive a wide range of tips depending on the efforts they have made for you—some people hardly even encounter[25] them on a trip! Tip accordingly, between £2.00-£6.50 ($3.00-$10) for the whole cruise.

Waiting-on staff are normally rewarded with £1.00-£2.50 ($1.50-$3.50) per person, per day.

When you are in the bar or lounge, you will often find a 15% service charge added to your bill automatically—check if this is the case before handing out individual tips!

As with any tipping system, the amount given should be altered[26] according to the level of service shown!

**Contact with the outside world**

A number (for the ships satellite communications telephone) will be provided in the information pack[27] you receive from the cruise line when you book. This number should be left with someone at home to contact you with in the case of an emergency. It is not to be used for a chat—a member of the ships crew will have to try to locate you in order for you to receive the call.

The ships have radiophones and satellite communications available for use—the latter is much clearer but obviously you pay more for the privilege[28].

Calls home can be made at a cheaper rate and with better reception, while in port.

| | |
|---|---|
| [19] 布局 | |
| [20] 给小费 | |
| [21] 明确地 | |
| [22] 近似值 | |
| [23] 行李搬运工 | |
| [24] 服务员，乘务员 | |
| [25] 遇到 | |
| [26] 改变 | |
| [27] 组合件 | |
| [28] 特权，特许 | |

# Part Six Guide to World Famous Sight

| Text | Notes |
|------|-------|

### About Taj Mahal[1]

*Lovers die, but love shall not and death shall have no dominion[2]...*

In the year 1607 when a prince of the royal Mughal household[3] strolled down[4] the Meena Bazaar, accompanied by a string of fawning[5] courtiers[6], he caught a glimpse of a girl hawking[7] silk and glass beads. Five years and a wife later (in those days princes did not marry for love alone) the regal[8] 20-yr-old went to wed his 19-yr-old bride. It was a fairytale[9] union from the start, one that withstood court intrigues[10], battles for succession[11] and finally, the grand coronation[12]. And when she died on the 19th year of their marriage,he etched[13] her story in stone. The Taj Mahal is the living symbol of the monumental passion of Shah Jahan and Arjumand Banu. Which other love story has so grand a memorial?

### Agra, The Chosen City for Taj Mahal

Agra was the chosen city of the Mughal emperors during the early years. It was here that the founder of the dynasty, Babur, laid out the first formal Persian garden on the banks of the River Yamuna. Here, Akbar, his grandson, raised the towering ramparts[14] of the great Red Fort[15]. Within its walls, Jehangir built rose-red palaces, courts and gardens. Shahjahan embellished it with marbled[16] mosques[17], palaces and pavilions of gem-inlaid[18] white marble. Agra is globally renown[19] as the city of the Taj Mahal, a monument of love and imagination, that represents[20] India to the world.

### History of Taj Mahal India

The origin of the name the "Taj Mahal" is not clear. Court histories from Shah Jehan's reign only call it the rauza (tomb) of Mumtaz Mahal. It is generally believed that "Taj Mahal" (usually translated as either "Crown Palace" or "Crown of the Palace") is an abbreviated[21] version of her name, Mumtaz Mahal.

Notes:

[1] 泰姬陵
[2] 统治权
[3] 王室，家族
[4] 漫步，闲逛
[5] 奉承的
[6] 朝臣
[7] 兜售
[8] 豪华的
[9] 童话式的
[10] 迷人的
[11] 继续
[12] 加冕礼
[13] 蚀刻

[14] 壁垒，城墙
[15] 堡垒
[16] 大理石的
[17] 清真寺
[18] 宝石镶嵌的
[19] 使有声望
[20] 象征

[21] 简短的

The Taj Mahal is a deserving resting palace for an Emperor's Empress. It stands on the banks of the river Yamuna, which otherwise serves as a wide moat[22] defending the Great Red Fort of Agra, the center of the Mughal emperors until they moved their capital to Delhi in 1637. It was built by the fifth Mughal emperor, Shah Jahan in 1631 in memory of[23] his second wife, Mumtaz Mahal, a Muslim Persian princess[24]. She died while accompanying her husband in Burhanpur in a campaign[25] to crush[26] a rebellion[27] after giving birth to their 14th child.

| | |
|---|---|
| | [22] 护城河，城壕 |
| | [23] 为了纪念 |
| | [24] 穆斯林波斯公主 |
| | [25] 战役 |
| | [26] 镇压 |
| | [27] 叛乱，谋反 |

### Mumtaz Mahal—"Build me a Taj"

As Mumtaz Mahal lay dying, she asked four promises from the emperor: first, that he build the Taj; second, that he should marry again; third, that he be kind to their children; and fourth, that he visit the tomb on her death anniversary. He kept the first and second promises. Construction began in 1631 and was completed in 22 years. Twenty thousand people were deployed[28] to work on it. The principal architect was the Iranian architect Istad Usa; it is possible that the pietra dura work was coordinated by an Italian artist.

[28] 展开

### Taj Mahal—Wonder of the World

To people the world over, the Taj Mahal, mausoleum[29] of Mughal Emperor shah Jana's chief wife, Mumtaz Mahal, is synonymous[30] with India. Its curving, gently swelling[31] dome and the square base upon which it rests so lightly is a familiar image from hundreds of brochures[32] and travel books. The Taj is undoubtedly one of the most spectacular[33] buildings of the world. Renowned for its architectural magnificence and aesthetic beauty, it counts among man's proudest creations and is invariably[34] included in the list of the world's foremost[35] wonders. As a tomb, it has no match upon earth, for mortal remains have never been housed in greater grandeur[36].

[29] 陵墓
[30] 同义的
[31] 鼓起的
[32] 小册子
[33] 壮观的，引人入
　　胜的
[34] 总是
[35] 最重要的
[36] 庄严

# Unit 9

## Hotel

# Part One  Dialogues

### Sample Dialogue 1

👤 **Situation** ▶ Mr. Wang Liang is going to U.S.A. from Shanghai, China. Now he is making his reservation on the phone.

| | | |
|---|---|---|
| **Reservationist**: | Las Vegas MGM Grand Hotel. May I help you? |
| **Wang**: | Yes. I am calling from Shanghai, China. I'd like to book a double room with bath. |
| **Reservationist**: | When for, Sir? |
| **Wang**: | I plan to arrive at Las Vegas on July 10th and leave on July 18th. |
| **Reservationist**: | From July 10th to 18th. Just a moment, Sir... Yes, we have a vacancy for that period. What's your name, please? |
| **Wang**: | Wang Liang. Wang is my surname and Liang is my given name. |
| **Reservationist**: | Could you spell that, please? |
| **Wang**: | Wang—W-A-N-G, Liang—L-I-A-N-G. |
| **Reservationist**: | That's OK, Mr. Wang. You mean a double room with bath from the tenth of July to the eighteenth? |
| **Wang**: | That's right. |
| **Reservationist**: | By the way, how do you like to pay for it? This hotel prefers Visa and MasterCard. |
| **Wang**: | I see. I'll pay by MasterCard. When can I receive your confirmation? |
| **Reservationist**: | Not until you have paid 10 percent margin. You can get some detailed information about us on the line. Or you can receive a pamphlet if you tell us your address. |
| **Wang**: | I'll log on to the internet to know about you. I know your address. Thank you. Bye. |
| **Reservationist**: | Bye. |

## Sample Dialogue 2

**Situation** ▶ Mr. Wang is now checking in at the Reception Desk of Las Vegas MGM Grand Hotel.

**Reservationist**: Good afternoon, sir. Can I help you?

**Wang**: Good afternoon, I have booked a double room a week ago. I am Wang Liang.

**Reservationist**: Just a moment, please. I'll check the arrival list... Sorry to have kept you waiting, Mr. Wang. Yes, you have booked a double room from today to 18th.

**Wang**: That's right.

**Reservationist**: May I see your passport?

**Wang**: Here you are.

**Reservationist**: Thank you. Could you fill in the registration form, please?

**Wang**: OK. Is it all right?

**Reservationist**: Yes, thank you. How are you going to pay, in cash or by credit?

**Wang**: By MasterCard.

**Reservationist**: That's fine. Here is the key to Room 1120. The key card is printed with some information about our hotel services and regulation. Please keep it.

**Wang**: I'll do it.

**Reservationist**: The bellman will show you up. Have a nice day and enjoy your stay here.

**Wang**: Thank you.

## Useful Expressions

1. I'd like to book a room in your hotel.
   我想在你们旅馆订个房间。

2. Could I book a double room with bath?
   我想订个带浴室的双人间，可以吗？

3. I'm phoning to make a reservation for a single room for five nights beginning tomorrow.
   我来电话是想订个单人间，从明晚起住 5 个晚上。

4. My reservation is for the nights of October 8th to October 18th. I'll be leaving on October 19th.
   我想订个房间，从 10 月 8 日晚到 10 月 18 日晚，我准备 10 月 19 日离开。

5. I'll prefer a quiet room.
   我想要个安静点的房间。

6. We have a single room available on these days.
   这段时间，我们有个单人间。

7. Have you got a room overlooking the sea?
   你们有没有可以眺望大海的房间？

8. Do you prefer a room facing the sea or a room facing the mountains?

您喜欢面向大海的还是面向群山的房间？

9. I want to cancel my booking for a single room in the name of Wang Fan.

我想取消预订的单人间，我叫王帆。

10. What a pity! We have no vacancies for these nights.

太遗憾了，这几天晚上已经预订满了。

11. Would you like us to put you on our waiting list and call you back in case we have a cancellation?

需不需要把您列入我们的等待名单？一有取消预订的，我们就通知您。

## Task Dialogue 1

**Situation** ▶ Mr. Blunt wants to make a reservation for five days at Boston Hotel.

## Task Dialogue 2

**Situation** ▶ Mr. Blunt is checking in.

# Part Two    Text A

## Hotels

Stately country houses, luxurious castles, intimate old-world inns and modern premises are all included in this category. All hotels comply with statutory registration regulations, which cover physical requirements and the level of service provided. Most hotels welcome children. Hotels carrying the Family friendly symbol meet the particular needs of children, providing playgrounds, playroom, special menus, mealtimes, etc. Meals and refreshments must be available to non-residents.

### Hotel Classification

Irish hotels and guesthouses are classified under the star classification. Devised by Irish Tourist Board and the Irish Hotels Federation, the classification system makes it easier for visitors to evaluate and choose the hotel and guesthouse of their choice. Each hotel and guesthouse has a distinct character and range of facilities. Details on the style and services unique to each premise are listed in the accommodation listings.

## Hotel Classification Descriptions

### Five Star

These include Ireland the most luxurious hotels, all of which are of high international standards. They range from elegant, stately castles to prestigious country clubs and top class city hotels catering for both the business and tourist. All guest accommodation is luxurious and spacious suites are available. These fine hotels boast some of the country the best restaurants and offer a la carte lunch and dinner menus. Exceptional service and a personalized welcome are the norm in these hotels.

### Four Star

These include contemporary hotels of excellent quality and charming period houses renovated to a very high standard complete with all modern comforts. All guest accommodation is of high standard and half suites are usually available. Restaurant facilities provide excellent cuisine and service for the discerning diner. Table and/or a la carte lunch and dinner menus are available.

### Three Star

These range from small, family-operated premises to larger, modern hotels. Guest rooms are well decorated with the emphasis on comfort and all have private bathrooms with a bath and/or shower.

Restaurants offer high standards of cuisine in relaxed and hospitable surroundings. Table and/or a la carte dinner menus are available. These hotels offer a range of services making them ideal for the cost-conscious traveler seeking comfort.

### Two Star

These are more likely to be family-operated premises, selected for their charm and their comfortable facilities. All guest rooms have a telephone and most have a private bathroom with a bath and/or shower. Full dining facilities are available, representing excellent value and good wholesome food.

### One Star

Here you can enjoy the comforts of a pleasantly simple hotel where a warm welcome prevails. These premises offer all the mandatory services and facilities to a satisfactory standard, necessary for a most enjoyable and relaxed visit. Some great rooms have a private bathroom with a bath and/or shower.

### Guesthouses

Guesthouses vary from five-bedroom family houses, Georgian and Victorian residences to larger professionally-serviced modern premises. The informal atmosphere and personal attention are of features of this category. The availability of meals to non-residents is not a requirement; however, some provide this service. All guesthouses comply with statutory regulations which cover physical requirements and the level of service provided. Restaurant facilities are available in some guesthouses.

### Farmhouses

The premises in this category include old-style, period type, and modern farmhouses; the type of farming varies—mixed, tillage, dairy, sheep and poultry—all of interest to visitors, particularly if they come from the city. Evening meals are provided in some houses if notice is given before 12:00 noon each day. A new concept called Green Tourism, i.e. a holiday experience on a working farm, is also included in this category of accommodation.

### Town and Country Homes

This category of accommodation covers a variety of house in urban and rural areas, ranging from the modern bungalow of semi-detached, 2-storey house to the large period-style residence. Their main attraction is their homely atmosphere and the opportunity they provide to meet people in their own homes. Some premises provide evening meals if notice is given before 12:00 noon each day.

### Youth Hostels

Irish Youth Hostel Association (IYHA) has a chain of 37 registered Youth Hostels situated in most of the scenic areas of Ireland. These hostels provide simple multi-bedded rooms with comfortable beds and facilities for cooking one of own meals. Members of IYHA or other youth organizations affiliated to the International Youth Hostel Federation may use the hostels on production of their membership cards and non-members may buy stamps at the hostels entitling them to use the hostels.

The cost of membership per person resident in the Republic of Ireland is IR7.50 for senior (over 18 years) and IR4.00 for junior. For person resident outside Republic of Ireland, the cost is IR7.50.

### Holiday Hostels

Holiday Hostels provide clean, simple accommodation at a budget price, several with family rooms. They are ideally suited to the holiday-maker seeking a real alternative to conventional accommodation. The kitchen and common room often provide an international setting for socializing and meeting other hostellers from all over the world.

### Caravan and Camping Parks

Caravan and camping parks are categorized as following:

- four star parks offer an extensive range of facilities and good management
- three star parks offer a good range of facilities and good management
- two star parks offer limited facilities and good management
- one star parks offer minimum facilities required for registration

Those that meet the minimum requirements are identified by a special sign and listed in the guide which shows the facilities at each park (showers, telephone, shop, communal lounge rooms, indoor recreational facilities, children of play center, café, restaurant, laundry room, field game facilities). Firms offering touring caravans, motor-homes, tents and camping equipment may be included in the listing.

There are caravan and camping parks in twenty-two of the twenty-six counties. The majority are open from May to the end of September. Some are open throughout the year.

Mobile homes are hired fully equipped with crockery, bed-covering and kitchen utensils for the specified number of people.

*Self-Catering Accommodation*

This category of Accommodation covers a variety of premises in urban and rural areas, ranging from modern bungalows, old converted houses, semi-detached, two-storey houses to group schemes of purpose-designed units. The Irish Cottages and Holiday Homes Association is an organization whose members all manage a minimum of eight purpose-designed units of self-catering holiday accommodation.

# New Words

**premise** ['premis] *n.* 经营地址

**statutory** ['stætʃutəri] *a.* 法令的，法定的

**refreshment** [ri'freʃmənt] *n.* 点心，饮料

**classification** [ˌklæsifi'keiʃən] *n.* 分类，分级

**guesthouse** ['gesthaus] *n.* 上等旅社，宾馆

**evaluate** [i'væljueit] *vt.* 评价，估计

**distinct** [di'stiŋkt] *a.* 清楚的，明显的；截然不同的，独特的

**luxurious** [lʌg'zjuəriəs] *a.* 奢侈的，豪华的

**elegant** ['eligənt] *a.* 第一流的

**prestigious** [pre'stidʒəs] *a.* 享有声望的，声望很高的

**exceptional** [ik'sepʃnəl] *a.* 特别的，异常的

**norm** [nɔ:m] *n.* 标准，规范

**personalized** ['pə:sənəlaizd] *a.* 个性化的

**renovate** ['renəveit] *vt.* 革新，刷新，修复

**discerning** [di'sə:niŋ] *a.* 有辨识能力的

**hospitable** [hɔ'spitəbl] *a.* 好客的，招待周到的

**wholesome** ['həulsəm] *a.* 卫生的，有益的，健康的

**prevail** [pri'veil] *vi.* 流行，盛行；获胜，成功

**farmhouse** ['fɑ:mˌhaus] *n.* 农场里的住房，农舍，农家

**tillage** ['tilidʒ] *n.* 耕地

**poultry** ['pəultri] *n.* 家禽

**bungalow** ['bʌŋgəˌləu] *n.* 平房，小屋

**affiliated** [ə'filiətid] *a.* 附属的，有关联的

**conventional** [kən'venʃnəl] *a.* 惯例的，常规的，习俗的，传统的

**hosteller** ['hɔstələ] *n.* 旅馆主人

**caravan** ['kærəvæn] *n.* 旅行队，大篷车

**camping** ['kæmpiŋ] *n.* 露营，野营

**communal** [kɔ'mjuːnl] *a.* 公共的，公社的
**lounge** [laundʒ] *n.* 闲逛，休闲室
**recreational** [ˌrekri'eiʃənəl] *a.* 消遣的，娱乐的
**rockery** ['rɔkəri] *n.* 假山，假山庭院

**utensil** [juː'tensl] *n.* 器具
**cater** ['keitə] *vi.* 备办食物
**scheme** [skiːm] *n.* 安排，计划
**Irish** ['airiʃ] *n.* 爱尔兰人；爱尔兰语；爱尔兰 *a.* 爱尔兰的

 ## Phrases and Expressions

comply with　遵照，遵守
meet the needs of　满足需要
range from... to...　在……之间
cater for/to　顾及，迎合
decorated with　用……装饰，布置
a variety of　种种，各种各样
on production of　出示

be suited to/for　适合
Irish Tourist Board　爱尔兰旅游者委员会
Irish Hotels Federation　爱尔兰旅馆联盟
International Youth Hostel Federation　国际青年旅馆联盟
Irish Cottages and Holiday Homes Association　爱尔兰别墅及度假屋协会

 ## Abbreviations

IYHA (Irish Youth Hostel Association)　爱尔兰青年旅馆协会

## Notes

**1** Hotels carrying the friendly symbol meet the particular needs of children, providing playgrounds, playroom, special menus, mealtimes, etc.

　　本句中，carrying the friendly symbol 是一个现在分词短语作定语，修饰和限定 hotels；而另一个现在分词短语 providing playgrounds, playroom, special menus, mealtimes etc. 作结果状语，修饰谓语 meet the particular needs of。

**2** Devised by Irish Tourist Board and the Irish Hotels Federation, the classification system makes it easier for visitors to evaluate and choose the hotel and guesthouse of their choice.

　　本句中，devised by Irish Tourist Board and the Irish Hotels Federation 是一个过去分

词短语作原因状语，主句的主语是 the classification system，谓语是 makes，it 是形式宾语，真正的宾语是动词不定式短语 to evaluate and choose the hotel and guesthouse of their choice，easier 是宾语补足语。

**3** These include Ireland the most luxurious hotels, all of which are of high international standards.

本句 all of which are of high international standards 是一个非限定性的定语从句，修饰 hotels, be of high international standards 是 "be of + n." 结构，这种结构表示某种特点或性质。请看下例：

His speech is of importance.

他的讲话很重要。

**4** Members of IYHA or other youth organizations affiliated to the International Youth Hostel Federation may use the hostels on production of their membership cards and non-members may buy stamps at the hostels entitling them to use the hostels.

本句中，affiliated to the international Youth Hostel Federation 是一个过去分词短语作定语，修饰和限定 other youth organizations。entitling them to use the hostels 是一个现在分词短语作定语，修饰和限定 the hostels。on production of 的意思是 "出示"。请看下例：

Entrance is permitted only on production of a ticket.

只有出示入场券才能进入。

**5** Those that meet the minimum requirements are identified by a special sign and listed in the guide which shows the facilities at each park.

本句中，that meet the minimum requirements 是一个定语从句，修饰和限定 those，该从句中的 that 不能省略，因为它在从句中作主语。如果在从句中作宾语，that 常省略。请看下例：

Those that love us are our parents and our friends.

那些爱我们的人是我们的父母和朋友。（that 不能省略）

This is the book (that) I bought yesterday.

这是我昨天买的那本书。（that 可以省略）

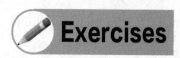 **Exercises**

**EX. 1** **Answer the following questions.**

1. Why are hotels and guesthouses classified?

2. Can you make a description of a five star hotel?

3. What is the Youth Hostel? And how much does a membership person pay for in the Republic of Ireland?

4. What are the caravan and camping parks?

**EX. 2** Write out the English words according to the definitions given below.

| definitions | words |
|---|---|
| very fine and costly; very comfortable | |
| showing attention to the needs of others, esp. by asking them into one's home | |
| a house which is all on level | |
| following accepted customs and standards, sometimes too closely | |
| a group of people with animals or vehicles traveling together for protection through unfriendly esp. desert areas | |
| a place where people live in tents or huts for a short time usu. for pleasure | |
| a small house or cottage adjacent to a main house, used for lodging guests | |
| domestic fowls, such as chickens, turkeys, ducks, or geese, raised for meat or eggs | |
| an instrument, an implement, or a container used domestically, especially in a kitchen | |
| to ascertain or fix the value or worth of | |

**EX. 3** Complete the following sentences with appropriate words or expressions from the text.

1. When we play the computer games, we have to _____ the rules.
2. We haven't yet been able to find a house that _____ our _____.
3. The children's ages _____ 5 _____ 15.
4. Our newspapers and magazines try to _____ all opinions of the public.
5. They _____ the wedding car _____ ribbons and flowers.
6. High stress levels are a _____ life for business executives.
7. That farmer is always looking for _____ wheat.

**EX. 4** Translate the following sentences into Chinese.

1. Hotels carrying the Family friendly symbol meet the particular needs of children, providing playgrounds, playroom, special menus, mealtimes, etc.

2. Devised by Irish Tourist Board and the Irish Hotels Federation, the classification system makes it easier for visitors to evaluate and choose the hotel and guesthouse of their choice.

3. They range from elegant, stately castles to prestigious country clubs and top class city hotels catering for both the business and tourist.

4. The premises in this category include old-style, period type, and modern farmhouses; the type of farming varies—mixed, tillage, dairy, sheep and poultry—all of interest to visitors, particularly if they come from the city.

5. Members of IYHA or other youth organizations affiliated to the International Youth Hostel Federation may use the hostels on production of their membership cards and non-members may buy stamps at the hostels entitling them to use the hostels.

## Part Three   Text B

## Finding Hotel Bargains

It's family vacation season. But rising gas prices and expensive airfares can really put a damper on what should otherwise be a relaxing family event. Where can you save a buck or two in order to make that dream vacation more affordable? Read on and you'll find some great resources for saving money on hotels, and a few lodging alternatives, too.

### *Online Booking Services*

I picked three favorite U.S. vacation destinations, and used the Web to find the most economical rooms possible. Pile the kids in the car—we're headed to Washington, D.C., Disney World, and Yellowstone National Park!

Since most vacation spots have dozens of hotels nearby, I tried to level the playing field as much as possible. I shopped for an average family for seven nights. When possible I requested a pool and a non-smoking room. Additionally, I tried to find hotels within five miles of the town's main attraction.

One thing I discovered is that prices vary quite a bit, so it is worthwhile to try several sites before settling on one place. Also, several of the booking services are more than happy to give you a room in a city, but it is much harder to find accommodations in more rural areas.

Another caveat: Some websites will do a bait and switch. They will claim that they have rooms for "$29 and up! " but the "and up" prices are all that you can find. Depending on how dedicated you are, you can always try calling the website's support line and get their customer service to help you to find the lowest rate. Sometimes this works.

One final suggestion: Always check the website of the hotel you may be staying at. For instance, when I stayed in Las Vegas over Mother's Day I found several low-cost hotels through booking agencies, but the lowest price I found was a special linked directly from a resort's home page.

### *Cheaper Alternatives—Hostels and B&Bs*

You may have noticed that the last entry has incredibly low rates. That is because they are quotes for local hostels. For those of you who aren't familiar with hostels, they're a wonderful low-cost alternative to traditional hotels. Hostels usually provide dormitory-style accommodations with separate quarters for males and females, but many have private/family rooms that can be reserved in advance.

Many people who have heard about hostels believe that they are only for students or are not the sort of place any self-respecting traveler would want to stay. Not true. I often stay at hostels and usually meet interesting folks and the inhabitants often have great budget tips for the local area!

Another alternative to the hotel is the bed and breakfast (B&B). There you're provided a room in a host's home and breakfast the next day. In some B&Bs you have to share the bathroom with other guests, or pay extra for a private bath. There are usually a few B&Bs in any area that you might want to vacation. Many B&B's welcome children (and pets!) and are often less expensive than a hotel chain.

The only drawback to B&Bs is that there is no central directory for them on the Internet. The easiest way to find them is to use a search engine such as Yahoo or Google and enter the name of the city and the words "bed and breakfast". Another resource (though not comprehensive) is www.bbonline.com. You can also check published directories available at most bookshops and on Amazon.com.

### Discounts from Other Sources

Most everyone knows that AAA will pick you up if you get a flat tire, but did you know they offer travel discounts? Some of them are quite substantial. In addition, they have their own online booking services. Most major hotel chains offer discounts through AAA.

Another favorite acronym in the travel world is AARP. The American Association of Retired Persons is a powerhouse for discounts of all sorts. In the hotel arena, you can earn 10% to 50% off the published rates when you stay at most major chains. The only bummer about this one is you have to be over 50 (or married someone who is).

A final source for travel discounts is to wait until the last minute. I certainly don't suggest this approach for a two-week family vacation, but if you are looking for a weekend away from home, some sites specialize in last-minute accommodations that often turn out to be great bargains.

This article is by no means exhaustive, and you may know of other websites or discounts. If you want to share them, please post them here. Happy travels!

 **New Words**

| | |
|---|---|
| **airfare** [ˈeəˌfeə(r)] *n.* 飞机票价 | **addition** [əˈdiʃən] *n.* 增加物；增加；加法，加 |
| **damper** [ˈdæmpə] *n.* 使人扫兴的人或事 | **worthwhile** [ˌwəːθˈwail] *a.* 值得做的，值得出力的 |
| **relax** [riˈlæks] *vi.* 放松，休息，休养 | **caveat** [ˈkeiviˌæt] *n.* 警告，告诫 |
| **buck** [bʌk] *n.* (美口) 元 | **bait** [beit] *n.* 饵，诱惑物 |
| **pile** [pail] *vt.* 堆起，堆积；挤 | |

**quote** [kwəut] *vt.* 引用，引证；提供，提出；报（价）

**traditional** [trə'diʃənəl] *a.* 传统的，惯例的

**dormitory** ['dɔ:mitri] *n.* 宿舍

**reserved** [ri'zə:vd] *a.* 保留的

**inhabitant** [in'hæbitənt] *n.* 居民，居住者

**drawback** ['drɔ:ˌbæk] *n.* 缺点；障碍

**directory** [dai'rektəri] *n.* 姓名地址录，目录

**comprehensive** [ˌkɔmpri'hensiv] *a.* 全面的，广泛的

**acronym** ['ækrənim] *n.* 只取首字母的缩写词

**powerhouse** ['pauəˌhaus] *n.* 发电站

**bummer** ['bʌmə] *n.* 无赖，游民，游荡者，乞讨者

**approach** [ə'prəutʃ] *n.* 接近，逼近，走近；方法

**resource** [ri'zɔ:s] *n.* 资源，财力；办法，智谋

**bit** [bit] *n.* 小块，少量

**Website** ['websait] *n.* 网站

**agency** ['eidʒənsi] *n.* 代理处，经销机构

**resort** [ri'zɔ:t] *n.* 胜地；诉诸

**dormitory-style** ['dɔ:mitri stail] *a.* 宿舍式的

**arena** [ə'ri:nə] *n.* 领域

**self-respecting** [ˌself ris'pektiŋ] *a.* 自尊的

**Yahoo** [jə'hu:] 美国雅虎公司

**Google** ['gu:gl] 美国谷歌公司

## Phrases and Expressions

put a damper on 使……扫兴；抑制
be headed to 向某处移动，朝某处行驶
Washington D.C. 华盛顿特区
Disney World 迪斯尼乐园
Yellowstone National Park 黄石国家公园
home page 主页
settle on 决定；解决
Las Vegas 拉斯维加斯

hear about 得知，听说
be familiar with 熟悉，通晓
share...with 与某人共享，分享
search engine 搜索引擎
Amazon.com 亚马逊网站
by no means 决不，一点也不
know of 听说，知道

## Abbreviations

B&Bs 包早餐旅馆
AAA (American Automobile Association) 美国汽车协会

AARP (American Association of Retired Persons) 美国退休者协会

## Notes

**1** But rising gas prices and expensive airfares can really put a damper on what should otherwise be a relaxing family event.

本句中，rising gas prices and expensive airfares 是一个动名词短语，作句子的主语。put a damper on 是谓语，意思是 "使……扫兴；抑制"。what should otherwise be a relaxing family event 作宾语。

**2** One thing I discovered is that prices vary quite a bit, so it is worth while to try several sites before settling on one place.

本句中，that prices vary quite a bit 是一个表语从句。it 是形式主语，而真正的主语是动词不定式短语 to try several sites before settling on one place。worth while 意为 "值得"，在句中作表语。

在 It is worth while... 句型中，worth while 后可接动名词或不定式。请看下例：

It is worth while making the decision.

It is worth while to make the decision.

**3** In the hotel arena, you can earn 10% to 50% off the published rates when you stay at most major chains.

本句中，you can earn 10% to 50% off the published rates 的意思是 "你可以赚得公布价格的百分之十到百分之五十"，off 的意思是 "从……下来"。请看下例：

Can you take something off the price?

你能减点价格吗？

**4** I certainly don't suggest this approach for a two-week family vacation, but if you are looking for a weekend away from home, some sites specialize in last-minute accommodations that often turn out to be great bargains.

本句中，if you are looking for a weekend away from home 是一个条件状语从句，that often turn out to be great bargains 是一个定语从句，修饰和限定 last-minute accommodations。look for 的意思是 "寻找"，specialize in 的意思是 "专攻，专门研究；专营"。请看下例：

You are looking for a fight if you say things like that to me.

如果你再这样跟我说话，你就要挨揍。

Jim is a doctor who specializes in heart diseases.

吉姆是一个专攻心脏病的医生。

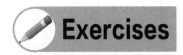 **Exercises**

**EX. 5** **Answer the following questions.**

1. What did the narrator do when he wanted to spend his holidays with his family?

2. What did the narrator find out at first?

3. What is the narrator suggestion and warning?

4. What is B&B?

5. What is AAA? And what does it do besides picking somebody up when he or she gets a flat tire?

**EX. 6** **Decide whether the following statements are *true* or *false*.**

1. The narrator picked three favorite U.S. vacation destinations, and used the Web to find the most economical rooms possible.

2. Now that most vacation spots have dozens of hotels nearby, the narrator tried to level the playing field as much as possible, shopped for an average family and requested a pool and a non-smoking room.

3. One thing the narrator discovered is that prices are almost the same, so it is not worthwhile to try several sites before settling on one place.

4. The bed and breakfast (B&B) hotel is a hotel where you're provided a room in a host's home and breakfast the next day. In some B&Bs you have to share the bathroom with other guests, or pay extra for a private bath.

5. The final source for travel discounts the narrator suggests is to wait until the last minute. If you are looking for a weekend away from home, some sites specialize in last-minute accommodations that often turn out to be great bargains.

# Part Four  Skill Training

## Forms

### *Hotel/Villa Reservation Form*

Nowadays making a reservation through the Internet is becoming more and more popular. For example you can make a reservation to one of the Hotels by logging on the Internet. All you have to do is to fill out the form and the rest will be taken care of by others.

### *Reserve me a room:*

Select a Hotel or a Villa:

○ Limor Hotel (details and price)     ○ Miruna Hotel (details and price)

○ Ruia Hotel (details and price)      ○ Alpin Hotel (details and price)

○ Zorile Villa (details and price)     ○ Ciucas Hotel (details and price)

○ EuroHotel (details and price)       ○ Tirol Hotel (details and price)

○ Andrei Villa (details and price)

○ Any available option (Give me more choices and I will decide based on the current rates)

The prices are FINAL. NO hidden taxes!

Kind of rooms:

| single | ▼ |

Check in

(Start date):

| 1 | ▼ | January | ▼ | 2003 | ▼ |

Number of nights to reserve

| |

Pay method (pay an advance and/or pay when arriving in Romania)

Choose one payment method:

○ Traveller Cheque/Bank Transfer

○ Credit Card

○ Cash (suitable only when arriving in Romania)

The reservation will be confirmed to you by E-mail with further informations.

OR Send me more informations.

Informations will be send by mail and are FREE !

☐ Poiana Brasov informations

E-mail:

| |

Full Name:

| |

Country:

| [please select a country] | ▼ |

Address:

| |

City/State/ZIP:

| | | |

Phone Number:

| |

Please verify your mail address and press Submit Order button.

[ SUBMIT ORDER ]

You will receive very soon an E-mail to let you know we have received your request.

In step 2 you may pay an advance using a Credit Card (VISA, Euro Card/Master Card or AMEX).

A travel agent will contact you shortly.

The payment must be made only after you receive the confirmation details from one of our Travel Agents.

Other option is to pay when you arrive in Romania.

We are one of the best travel agencies from Romania.

For any questions or for more information, don't hesitate to contact us at:

Romania_Reservations@RomaniaX.com

Alto Travel Agency will reserve for you the room.

"ALTO TOUR" one of the best rated Travel Agencies

## Practical Writing

### A Typical Registration Form

The form below is a typical registration form of temporary residence. Notice all the key facts and try to fill it out.

| The Great Wall Sheraton Hotel Beijing | 临时住宿登记表 REGISTRATION FORM OF TEMPORARY RESIDENCE | | |
|---|---|---|---|
| 房号 Room No. | 姓 Surname | 名 First name | 性别 Sex |
| 中文姓名 Name in Chinese | 国籍 Nationality | | 出生年月 Date of birth |
| 护照或证件号码 Passport or Certificate No. | | 签证种类及号码 Visa No. and Category | |
| 公司名称及本人地址 Company Name&Residential Address | | | |
| 抵达日期 Date of arrival | | 离店日期 Date of departure | |
| 接待单位 Received by | | 宾客签名 Guest Signature | |
| 离店时我的账目结算将由：ON CHECKING OUT MY ACCOUNT WILL BE SETTLED BY | | | |
| 现金 CASH | 旅行社凭单 TA VCHR | 美国运通 AMER EXP | 大来 DINERS    维萨 VISA |
| 日财卡 JCB | 万事达卡 MASTCARD | 联邦公司 FEDERAL COMPANY | |

## Part Five Related Information

| Text | Notes |
|---|---|
| **Safety Tips for Hotel Stays** | |
| Verify[1] all unexpected deliveries to the room with the front desk and always look through the peephole to see who is at the door before you open it. | [1] 检验，校验，查证 |
| Don't venture into large parking lots or darkened areas on hotel grounds. If you cannot avoid these areas, the hotel should be able to provide an escort[2]. Ask for one. | [2] 护卫（队），护送，陪同（人员） |
| Request a room that is not on the ground floor or accessible from the ground. | |
| Don't reveal[3] room numbers within earshot[4] of unfamiliar people. If a desk clerk mentions your room number out loud, request another room. Don't needlessly display your room key in public or carelessly leave it on the restaurant table, at the swimming pool, or other places where it can be easily stolen. | [3] 展现，显示，揭示，暴露<br>[4] 听力所及之范围 |
| Don't enter a room if the door is ajar[5]. When you check-in, request an escort to accompany you to your room and check it out. | [5]（门窗等）微开的 |
| Always use the deadbolts[6] or auxiliary locks provided on the door of your room. | [6]（门窗等的）插销 |
| Never sit in a room with the door left open. Never leave the door open when you leave the room, even to go for ice. | |
| Never display large amounts of cash in shops, taxis, hotel lobbies[7], or on the street. Don't call attention to yourself by wearing expensive jewelry. | [7] 大厅 |
| Carry a rubber doorstop with you and place it under the door of your room. Or carry a portable electronic safety device to use on the door or in the room itself. | |
| Avoid dimly[8] lit, out-of-the-way entryways when returning to your hotel or motel late in the evening. Use the main entrance of the facility. | [8] 微暗，朦胧 |
| Ask for a room near the office when checking into a motel. | |
| Avoid eating dinner alone at the same lodging establishment where you are staying whenever possible. | |

# Part Six Guide to World Famous Sight

| Text | Notes |
|------|-------|
| **The Egyptian Pyramid** | |
| The pyramids of Egypt fascinated[1] travelers and conquerors in ancient times and continue to inspire wonder in the tourists, mathematicians, and archeologists[2] who visit, explore, measure and describe them. | [1] 使着迷，使神魂颠倒<br><br>[2] 考古学家 |
| Tombs of early Egyptian kings were bench-shaped mounds[3] called mastabas[4]. Around 2780 B.C., King Djoser's architect, Imhotep, built the first pyramid by placing six mastabas, each smaller than the one beneath, in a stack to form a pyramid rising in steps. This Step Pyramid stands on the west bank of the Nile River at Sakkara[5] near Memphis[6]. Like later pyramids, it contains various rooms and passages, including the burial chamber of the king. | [3] 土墩，护堤<br>[4] 石室坟墓，斜纹坟墓<br><br><br><br>[5] 萨卡拉［埃］<br>[6] 孟斐斯（古埃及城市，废墟在今开罗之南） |
| The largest and most famous of all the pyramids, the Great Pyramid at Giza[7], was built by Snefru's son, Khufu, known also as Cheops[8], the later Greek form of his name. The pyramid's base covered over 13 acres and its sides rose at an angle of 51 degrees 52 minutes and were over 755 feet long. It originally stood over 481 feet high; today it is 450 feet high. Scientists estimate that its stone blocks average over two tons apiece, with the largest weighing as much as fifteen tons each. Two other major pyramids were built at Giza, for Khufu's son, King Khafre, and a successor of Khafre, Menkaure. Also located at Giza is the famous Sphinx[9], a massive statue of a lion with a human head, carved during the time of Khafre. | [7] 吉萨棉<br>[8] 基奥普斯<br><br><br><br><br><br><br><br><br>[9][希神]斯芬克司 |
| Pyramids did not stand alone but were part of a group of buildings which included temples, chapels, other tombs, and massive walls. Remnants[10] of funerary[11] boats have also been excavated; the best preserved is at Giza. On the walls of Fifth and Sixth Dynasty pyramids are inscriptions[12] known as the Pyramid Texts, an important source of information about Egyptian religion. The scarcity of ancient records, however, makes it difficult to be sure of the uses of all the buildings in the pyramid complex or the exact burial procedures. It is thought that the king's body was brought by boat up the Nile to the pyramid site and probably mummified[13] in the Valley Temple before being placed in the pyramid for burial. | [10] 残余，剩余，残迹<br>[11] 葬礼的，埋葬的<br>[12] 题字，碑铭<br><br><br><br><br><br><br><br>[13] 成木乃伊状，干瘪 |

There has been speculation[14] about pyramid construction. Egyptians had copper tools such as chisels[15], drills, and saws that may have been used to cut the relatively soft stone. The hard granite[16], used for burial chamber walls and some of the exterior casing, would have posed[17] a more difficult problem. Workmen may have used an abrasive[18] powder, such as sand, with the drills and saws. Knowledge of astronomy[19] was necessary to orient the pyramids to the cardinal[20] points, and water-filled trenches[21] probably were used to level the perimeter[22]. A tomb painting of a colossal[23] statue being moved shows how huge stone blocks were moved on sledges over ground first made slippery by liquid. The blocks were then brought up ramps[24] to their positions in the pyramid. Finally, the outer layer of casing stones was finished from the top down and the ramps dismantled[25] as the work was completed.

Most of the stone for the Giza pyramids was quarried[26] on the Giza plateau itself. Some of the limestone casing was brought from Tura[27], across the Nile, and a few of the rooms were cased with granite from Aswan. The Greek historian Herodius reported in the fifth century B.C. that his Egyptian guides told him 100,000 men were employed for three months a year for twenty years to build the Great Pyramid; modern estimates of the number of laborers tend to be much smaller.

Pyramid building was at its height from the Fourth through the Sixth Dynasties. Smaller pyramids continued to be built for more than one thousand years. Scores of them have been discovered, but the remains of others are probably still buried under the sand. As it became clear that the pyramids did not provide protection for the mummified bodies of the kings but were obvious targets for grave robbers, later kings were buried in hidden tombs cut into rock cliffs. Although the magnify[28] pyramids did not protect the bodies of the Egyptian kings who built them, the pyramids have served to keep the names and stories of those kings alive to this day.

| | |
|---|---|
| [14] 思索 | |
| [15] 凿子 | |
| [16] 花岗岩 | |
| [17] 形成，引起，造成 | |
| [18] 研磨的 | |
| [19] 天文学 | |
| [20] 主要的，最重要的 | |
| [21] 沟渠，堑壕 | |
| [22] 周界 | |
| [23] 巨大的，庞大的 | |
| [24] 斜坡，坡道 | |
| [25] 拆除 | |
| [26] 挖出，苦心找出；费力地找 | |
| [27] 图拉（印） | |
| [28] 宏伟的 | |

# Unit 10

## Restaurant

**Dialogues**

### Sample Dialogue 1

👤 **Situation** ▶ Mr. Thompson comes into a famous restaurant in Shanghai and the captain waiter greets him.

| | | |
|---|---|---|
| **Waiter**: | Hello, welcome to our restaurant. Take a seat, please. Here is the menu, sir. Which do you prefer, western food or Chinese food? |
| **Thompson**: | I'd like a real Chinese dinner, please. |
| **Waiter**: | Can you use chopsticks, sir? |
| **Thompson**: | Yes, but I can't use them skillfully. This is my first time to China. I'd like to take this opportunity to practice. |
| **Waiter**: | That's fine. |
| **Thompson**: | What kinds of Chinese cuisine do you serve? |
| **Waiter**: | We serve Shanghai food and Guangdong food. |
| **Thompson**: | I know they are quite different. I used to go to one restaurant in New York but I can't remember how exactly they are different. Could you tell me? |
| **Waiter**: | Shanghai food is oily and sweet and Guangdong food is light and fresh. |
| **Thompson**: | Oh, I see. I have already tasted Guangdong food. This time I'd like to try Shanghai food. |
| **Waiter**: | You can find some typical Shanghai food here. To make our western customers know better, the menu gives a brief description of each dish in English. |
| **Thompson**: | It's so thoughtful of you. I'm afraid it'll be some time before I make my decision. |
| **Waiter**: | It doesn't matter. Just take your time. |

**Thompson**: I can order now. Barbecue chicken, Plain sauté shrimps, and Green cabbage and dried mushroom.

**Waiter**: Do you want anything else?

**Thompson**: What is your recommendation?

**Waiter**: The soup is very nice tonight. Would you like to try a bit?

**Thompson**: Yes, please.

**Waiter**: Would you like some fruit?

**Thompson**: Yes, some grapes, please.

**Waiter**: Very well. I'll serve the dishes right away.

## Sample Dialogue 2

**Situation** ▶ Angeles and his friend Brake go to a western food restaurant in Shanghai, and a waiter is greeting them. They are ordering their dishes.

**Waiter**: Good evening. May I take your orders, sir?

**Angeles**: Yes. We would like to taste the roast beef this evening.

**Waiter**: Yes. Would you like it rare, medium or well-donc?

**Angeles**: I'd like mine well-done, please. How about you, Brake?

**Brake**: I like it medium.

**Waiter**: Yes, sir. Now there's a choice of vegetables, potatoes or fresh peas. What would you like to go with your beef?

**Brake**: I want to have mashed potatoes without gravy please.

**Angeles**: The same here.

**Waiter**: How about your dessert?

**Angeles**: No. Thank you. But I'd like to order some drink, please.

**Brake**: Me, too.

**Waiter**: The drink list is on the last page of the menu, sir.

**Brake**: A wine, please.

**Angeles**: I'd like a glass of white spirit, please.

**Waiter**: Yes, sir. I'll serve the dishes in a minute.

## Useful Expressions

1. Would you like to order now?

您现在点菜吗？

2. What do you recommend us to order?

你能为我们推荐什么菜吗？

3. I'd like to order a table for eight.

   我要订一张八人的桌子。

4. How do you like your fish?

   您觉得鱼好吃吗？

5. What kind of dressing would you like on your salad?

   您要的色拉加什么调料？

6. What soup do you like to recommend?

   请推荐一种汤。

7. We have got clear and cream soup at your choice.

   我们有清汤和奶油汤供您选择。

8. I'd like two ham sandwiches, two fried eggs and a pot of coffee.

   我要两个火腿三明治、两个煎鸡蛋和一杯咖啡。

9. Would you like your steak rare, under-done, medium or well-done?

   您喜欢牛肉做得生些、嫩些、适中还是老些？

10. Could you bring us our check, please?

    请把账单给我们拿来好吗？

## Part Two　Text A

## Chinese Food

A unique Chinese food is dim sum. Actually dim sum is more than just a category of dishes; it's an eating habit. Dim sums are small dishes taken for snacks or at tea time; they are served in restaurants on a trolley. Most of the dim sum dishes are steamed, but they may also be fried or braised. Common to all dim sums is that they are in small portions, bite size, and normally strongly flavored. Dim sum is of Cantonese origin and very popular not only in China but also in other asian countries.

Noodles occupy an important position in Chinese cuisine. Actually, the Chinese were the inventors of noodles and they were brought to the European noodle country, Italy, by Marco Polo only in the 13th century.

Unlike the Italians who can't explain why their spaghetti is impractically long, the Chinese do have a seemingly very logical reason why the longer the noodles are the better. To the ever superstitious Chinese, long noodles mean long life. Making noodles in the traditional Chinese way is an acrobatic art. The dough is pulled and whirled through the air in order to stretch it through centrifugal force; but today machines use other techniques.

In Chinese cuisine, noodles can be served in three ways: in a clear soup with meat and some vegetables, or mixed with meat and with a thickened sauce poured over or without sauce; whereas for noodles with sauce egg noodles are commonly used.

Egg noodle dishes with sauce appear on Chinese menus with English translations often specified as fried. This is grossly misleading as they are mostly just barely sautéd. There is nothing crisp in such a "fried" dish, and the rather tasteless cornstarch sauce gives the dish a porridge texture.

Those who want to eat dishes that are fried by Western standards must order deep-fried dishes in Chinese English terminology. Deep-fried dishes include spring rolls, shrimp, and prawns.

Except for the already mentioned clear soups with noodles, there also are many thickened soups in Chinese cuisine. The thickening is produced normally from cornstarch. Like clear soups, the thickened soups may contain meats, fish, seafood and vegetables. In contrast to Western cuisine, Chinese cooking commonly uses lettuce in soups but not in salads.

The two most famous Chinese soups, shark fin soup and bird's nest soup, appear to be thickened but the glutinous texture does, in neither case, result from the addition of cornstarch but from the two main ingredients, shark fin and bird's nests which are simmered for many hours.

As rice is processed into noodles, another common Chinese agricultural product, soy beans, is processed into bean curd. Bean curd didn't make it as far as Italy. It was, however, also integrated into other Asian cuisines. Bean curd accompanied original Chinese as commonly as potatoes accompany German dishes.

Bean curd, commonly known as tofu in the Western world, has the appearance and texture of soft cheese and is produced by milling soybeans and forming large cakes of it that can be stored for quite a while. It can be cut into slices, and as it is fairly tasteless by itself (just as noodles), it easily adopts the taste of sauces and the other ingredients of a dish.

A by-product of bean curd which has a less stable texture (like thickened milk) is commonly sold in Asia by ambulant vendors as a dessert or morning drink. They walk through the streets, equipped with two large aluminum baskets, the one containing the sweet bean curd milk, and the other some sauces, syrups, and other toppings.

Prominent as noodles may be in Chinese cuisine, the most basic staple food is rice. The Chinese word for rice is fan.

To serve food in portions for a single person is very untypical of Chinese dining habits. Usually, the side dishes to rice are not served individually but in a family style with large plates placed in the center of a table. This eating order is still strongly reflected in the way Chinese restaurants are furnished. Often there is inadequate space for people who come alone or in pairs. Mostly large round tables can be seen, with a round board in the middle that can be turned so everyone, using the chopsticks, can help himself or herself to a few bites from every plate.

It's commonly known that the Chinese invented chopsticks as a set of instruments to be used when eating but the reason behind that is not commonly known. Actually, the Chinese were taught to use chopsticks long before spoons and forks were invented in Europe. Chopsticks were strongly advocated by the great Chinese philosopher Confucius (551 BC–479 BC).

He reasoned that, as a matter of advancement in civilization, instruments used for killing must be banned from the dining table. Therefore, knives cannot be permitted, and that is why Chinese food is always chopped into bite size before it reaches the table.

Chinese cooking is not complicated in the manner that French cuisine is complicated. Much less depends on temperatures of ingredients and exact timing for frying, baking, or cooking. Most Chinese dishes are just cooked in water or oil. Of course, there are many delicacies but most of them do not require such an elaborate processing in the kitchen as does one of China's most famous dishes, Beijing duck.

China is a vast country and it is therefore no surprise that there are many regional variations in Chinese cuisine. In general, one can say that the Southern Chinese Cantonese cuisine puts more emphasis on fish and seafood and the Northern Chinese Beijing cuisine includes more meat. Of all meats, pork is most common in all Chinese cuisines.

The central Chinese regions of Sichuan and Hunan have the spiciest food in all of China. Garlic as well as chili is extensively used. In the case of exclusive dining, Chinese have a different orientation than Westerners. First, the ambience of a restaurant is much less important; even first-class Chinese restaurants tend to be simply and inexpensively furnished. Second, unlike European custom, a dish doesn't become much more expensive when prepared by a much better cook.

In Europe, a certain meal (for example baked duck) can cost many times as much in an exclusive restaurant than it does in an ordinary restaurant; in the case of Chinese restaurants it's less the particular preparations that make a restaurant first-class but more the use of fancy and more expensive foods. An exclusive Chinese restaurant for example will serve foods like abalone which can cost $50 and up per dish. But it's not the preparation that makes these foods so expensive, it's just the price of the raw material. Many more ordinary Chinese dishes do not cost much more in first-class Chinese restaurants than they do in plainer kinds.

Tea is preferred by the Chinese as a drink during all meals less for its own taste but to clear the palate of a former dish before proceeding to the next. And as proclaimed by the Hong Kong Tourist Association in their official guide, "The Chinese don't ruin the tea with such alien substances as milk, sugar or lemon."

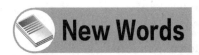

## New Words

| | |
|---|---|
| **category** [ˈkætəgəri] *n.* 种类 | **spaghetti** [spəˈgeti] *n.* 意大利式细面条 |
| **braise** [breiz] *vt.* 炖，蒸 | **impractically** [imˈpræktikəli] *ad.* 不切实际地 |
| **cuisine** [kwiˈziːn] *n.* 厨房烹调法，烹饪 | |

**superstitious** [ˌsuːpəˈstiʃəs] *a.* 迷信的

**acrobatic** [ˌækrəˈbætik] *a.* 杂技的，特技的

**dough** [dəu] *n.* 生面团

**whirl** [(h)wəːl] *vt.*（使）旋转

**grossly** [ˈgrəusli] *ad.* 严重地

**sauté** [ˈsəntei] *vt.* 炒

**crisp** [krisp] *a.* 脆的，易碎的

**cornstarch** [ˈkɔːnˌstɑːtʃ] *n.* 玉米淀粉

**porridge** [ˈpɔridʒ] *n.* 麦片粥，粥

**texture** [ˈtekstʃə] *n.* 质地

**prawn** [prɔːn] *n.* 对虾，明虾，大虾

**lettuce** [ˈletis] *n.* 莴苣，生菜

**fin** [fin] *n.* 鱼翅

**glutinous** [ˈgluːtinəs] *a.* 黏性的

**ingredient** [inˈgriːdiənt] *n.* 成分，因素

**simmer** [ˈsimə] *vt.* 慢煮

**milling** [ˈmiliŋ] *n.* 磨，制粉

**ambulant** [ˈæmbjələnt] *a.* 走动的

**aluminum** [əˈljuːminəm] *n.* 铝

**syrup** [ˈsirəp] *n.* 糖浆

**prominent** [ˈprɔminənt] *a.* 卓越的，显著的，突出的

**chopstick** [ˈtʃɔpˌstik] *n.* 筷子

**advocate** [ˈædvəkeit] *vt.* 提倡，鼓吹

**philosopher** [fiˈlɔsəfə] *n.* 哲学家，哲人

**Confucius** [kənˈfjuːʃəs] *n.* 孔子

**banned** [bænd] *a.* 被禁止的

**chop** [tʃɔp] *vt.* 斩碎

**fry** [frai] *vt.* 油炸，油煎

**elaborate** [iˈlæbəreit] *a.* 精心制作的

**spicy** [ˈspaisi] *a.* 辛辣的

**garlic** [ˈgɑːlik] *n.* 大蒜，蒜头

**chili** [ˈtʃili] *n.* 红辣椒

**exclusive** [ikˈskluːsiv] *a.* 高级的

**ambience** [ˈæmbiəns] *n.* 周围环境，气氛

**abalone** [ˌæbəˈləuni] *n.* 鲍鱼

**preferred** [priˈfəːd] *a.* 首选的

**palate** [ˈpælət] *n.* 味觉

**furnish** [ˈfəːniʃ] *vt.* 供应，提供，供给

**delicacy** [ˈdelikəsi] *n.* 精制食品

# Phrases and Expressions

dim sum　点心

more than　不仅仅，不止

in order to　为了

mix with　和……混合

pour over　浇注

appear on　出现，露面

except for　除了

result from　产生，发生

in contrast to　相反，大不相同

as far as　远到，直到

cut into　切小

equip with　装备

a set of　一组，一套

long before　很久以前

a matter of　作为一部分

put emphasis on　强调

help oneself to　自用

centrifugal force　地心引力

in the case of　就……说，至于……，论到，提到

Hong Kong Tourist Association　香港旅游者协会

# Notes

**1** Unlike the Italians, who can't explain why their spaghetti is impractically long, the Chinese do have a seemingly very logical reason why the longer the noodles are the better; to the ever superstitious Chinese, long noodles mean long life.

本句中，who can't explain why their spaghetti is impractically long 是一个非限定性定语从句，修饰 the Italians。在该从句中，why their spaghetti is impractically long 是一个宾语从句，作 explain 的宾语。do 在本句中起强调作用，一般译为"务必，一定，确实"等。why the longer the noodles are the better 是一个同位语从句，对 reason 做进一步补充说明。the more... the more... 表示"越……越……"，指两个事物在程度或数量上做等量减少或增加。

**2** Those who want to eat dishes that are fried by Western standards must order deep-fried dishes in Chinese English terminology.

本句中，who want to eat dishes that are fried by Western standards 是一个定语从句，修饰和限定 those。在该从句中，that are fried by Western standards 也是一个限定性定语从句，修饰 dishes，此处 that 在定语从句中作主语，不能省略。

**3** They walk through the streets, equipped with two large aluminum baskets, the one containing the sweet bean curd milk, and the other some sauces, syrups, and other toppings.

本句中 equipped with two large aluminum baskets 为过去分词短语作状语，表示伴随状况。注意：分词作伴随状况状语时不能用状语从句替换，但可改写成并列句。the one 是 containing the sweet bean curd milk 的逻辑主语，指 one large aluminum basket，and the other 后面省略了 containing。特指两个人或物中的另一个时，只能用 the other，不能用 other。请看下例：

He hurried to the hall, followed by two guards. (= He hurried to the hall and was followed by two guards.)

他匆匆忙忙走进大厅，身后跟着两个卫兵。

This one is red and the other is white.

这只是红的，另一只是白的。

**4** Of course, there are many delicacies but most of them do not require such an elaborate processing in the kitchen as does one of China's most famous dishes, Beijing duck.

本句中，such... as + 句子结构中的 as 用作连词，引导定语从句，表示"像……，诸如，像……这类"。请看下例：

It was such a fine day as they rarely saw in January.

这是一个他们在一月份很少能看到的好天气。

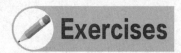

# Exercises

**EX. 1** **Answer the following questions.**

1. What is a unique of Chinese food?

2. In Chinese cuisine, how many ways are the noodles served and what are they?

3. What are the two famous Chinese soups?

4. What is the by-product of bean curd? How does it sold out?

5. What is the difference in serving food in Chinese restaurants or in Western restaurants?

**EX. 2** **Write out the English words according to the definitions given below.**

| definitions | words |
| --- | --- |
| to cook (meat) slowly in fat and little liquid in a covered dish | |
| a style of cooking | |
| a type of soft breakfast food made by boiling crushed grain (oatmeal) in milk or water | |
| either of a pair of narrow sticks held between the thumb and fingers and used in East Asian countries for lifting food to the mouth | |
| to speak in favor of; support (esp. an idea or plan) | |
| the character, quality, feeling, etc., of a place | |
| something pleasing and appealing, especially a choice food | |
| a soft, thick mixture of dry ingredients, such as flour or meal, and liquid, such as water, that is kneaded, shaped, and baked, especially as bread or pastry | |
| an element in a mixture or compound; a constituent | |

**EX. 3** **Complete the following sentences with appropriate words or expressions from the text.**

1. The courses aim to _____ people _____ the skills necessary for a job in this technological age.

2. _____ her lack of experience she would be the ideal person for the job.

3. Answering this question is just _____ using your intelligence.

4. Oil doesn't _____ water.

5. His English teacher _____ written work and grammar.

6. We _____ get cold winters and warm, dry summers in this part of the country.

**EX. 4** **Translate the following sentences into Chinese.**

1. Common to all dim sums is that they are in small portions, bite size, and normally strongly flavored. Dim sum is of Cantonese origin and very popular not only in China but also in other Asian countries.

2. The two most famous Chinese soups, shark fin soup and bird's nest soup appear to be thickened but the glutinous texture does, in neither case, result from the addition of cornstarch but from the two main ingredients, shark fin and bird's nests which are simmered for many hours.

3. A by-product of bean curd which has a less stable texture (like thickened milk) is commonly sold in Asia by ambulant vendors as a dessert or morning drink.

4. In general, one can say that the Southern Chinese Cantonese cuisine puts more emphasis on fish and seafood and the Northern Chinese Beijing cuisine includes more meat.

5. In Europe, a certain meal (for example baked duck) can cost many times as much in an exclusive restaurant than it does in an ordinary restaurant; in the case of Chinese restaurants it's less the particular preparations that make a restaurant first-class but more the use of fancy and more expensive foods.

## Part Three Text B

# Food in French Restaurant

Despite a common pan-gallic chauvinism, French cooking is not a monolith: it ranges from the olives and seafood of Provence to the butter and roasts of Tours, from the simple food of the bistro to the fanciful confections of the Tour d'Argent. However, it all shares seriousness about food. Throughout the country, French cooking involves a large number of techniques, some extremely complicated, that serve as basics. Any cook will tell you that French food will not tolerate shortcuts in regard to these fundamentals. Because mastery of sauces or pastry doughs is the center of the culinary arts, recipes themselves remain classic and constant. In a way similar to Japanese cuisine, it is expected that even the simplest preparation be undertaken in the most careful manner, which means disregarding the amount of time involved. This is one reason why French cooking has always seemed so daunting on the other side of the Atlantic. Americans love nothing more than combining innovation with time-saving; it is the particular genius of the United States and it couldn't be more at odds with the French aesthetic.

Not only do basic cooking techniques require great skill, but they also demand a deep understanding of the ingredients themselves. Just as the vintner knows that the finest Bordeaux comes from the grapes grown on that side of the hill and not this, so too the chef knows not only from which region come the finest petits pois (small, young green peas), but from which town—the same goes for asparagus, and even cauliflower. If there is something worth eating, and cooking, there is a best representative of such. Many foods are known by the town that made them famous, such as Pessac for strawberries, the peas of Saint-Germaine, Macau artichokes, the Charolais steer, butter of Isigny.

The French and English adapted service à la russe, in which courses are served separately, in the middle of the 19th century. A French meal might begin with a hot hors d'oeuvre (or for luncheon, a cold hors d'oeuvre) followed by soup, main course, salad, cheese, and finally dessert. The French operate with a strong sense that there is an appropriate beverage for every food and occasion. Wine is drunk with the meal, but rarely without food. An aperitif (a light alcoholic beverage such as Lillet) precedes the meal and a digestif may follow. This close relationship between food and wine may, in part, closely parallel the evolution of great cooking and great wine making. It is probably not coincidental that some of the best cooking in France happens in some of her finest wine-growing regions. In Burgundy, Bordeaux, Provence, and Touraine, wine is as prevalent in the cooking process as it is in the glass. Champagne as a beverage doesn't accompany food gracefully, likewise, as a region it is not well known for its food. One notable exception to this rule is Normandy, who, from her fantastic butter, cream, cheese, apples and the riches of the sea, has produced a marvelous local cuisine without the help of wine. However, the local Calvados, an apple-based eau-de-vie, may also explain the phenomenon.

The French are predominantly Catholic and thus have no eating prohibitions, though many dishes have a Lenten variation. Moreover, the Gauls are not afraid to eat anything. Kidney, brain, sweetbreads, tripe, blood sauces and sausages, sheep's foot, tongue, and intestines are all common in French cooking and hold equal standing with the meat of lamb, beef, pork, poultry, and game. Quite the opposite of being exotic, these foods are at the heart of the bourgeois menu, with seafood inevitably being the soul, and vegetables, the flesh.

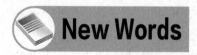

# New Words

**pan-gallic** [ˈpænˈgælik] *a.* 泛法国的
**Provence** [prɔˈvɔŋs] *n.* 普罗旺斯（法国东南部一地区）
**chauvinism** [ˈʃəuvəˌnizəm] *n.* 盲目的爱国心，沙文主义
**monolith** [ˈmɔnəliθ] *n.* 独石柱，独石碑，独块巨石

**olive** [ˈɔliv] *n.* 橄榄树，橄榄叶，橄榄枝
**bistro** [ˈbiːstrəu] *n.* 小酒馆，小咖啡店
**fanciful** [ˈfænsifl] *a.* 空想的；奇怪的，稀奇的
**confection** [kənˈfekʃən] *n.* 甜点
**seriousness** [ˈsiəriəsnəs] *n.* 严肃，

认真

**despite** [di'spait] *prep.* 不管，尽管，不论

**involve** [in'vɔlv] *vt.* 包括

**tolerate** ['tɔləreit] *vt.* 忍受，容忍

**shortcut** ['ʃɔ:t,kʌt] *n.* 捷径

**fundamental** [,fʌndə'mentl] *n.* 基本原则，基本原理

**mastery** ['mɑ:stəri] *n.* 掌握

**sauce** [sɔ:s] *n.* 酱汁，调味料

**pastry** ['peistri] *n.* 面粉糕饼，馅饼皮

**culinary** ['kʌlinəri] *a.* 厨房的，烹调用的

**classic** ['klæsik] *a.* 第一流的

**manner** ['mænə] *n.* 风格，方式，样式

**disregard** [,disri'gɑ:d] *vt.* 不理，漠视

**daunting** [,dɔ:ntiŋ] *a.* 使人畏缩的

**Atlantic** [æt'læntik] *n.* 大西洋

**innovation** [,inəu'veiʃən] *n.* 改革，创新

**odds** [ɔdz] *n.* 可能的机会，成败的可能性

**aesthetic** [i:s'θetik] *a.* 美学的，审美的，有审美感的

**vintner** ['vintnə] *n.* 葡萄酒商

**Bordeaux** [,bɔ:'dəu] *n.* 波尔多葡萄酒

**chef** [ʃef] *n.* 厨师

**petit** ['peti] *a.* 次要的，没价值的

**poi** [pɔi] *n.* 山芋食物

**asparagus** [ə'spærəgəs] *n.* 芦笋

**cauliflower** ['kɔli,flauə] *n.* 花椰菜

**strawberry** ['strɔ:bəri] *n.* 草莓

**pea** [pi:] *n.* 豌豆

**Charolais** ['ʃærəlei] *n.* 夏洛来牛（原产于法国）

**luncheon** ['lʌntʃən] *n.* 午宴，正式的午餐

**beverage** ['bevəridʒ] *n.* 饮料

**occasion** [ə'keiʒən] *n.* 场合，时机，机会

**aperitif** [ɑ'perətif] *n.* 开胃酒

**Burgundy** ['bə:gəndi] *n.* 勃艮第（法国东南部地名，该地产的红葡萄酒也名勃艮第）

**Touraine** [tu:'ren] *n.* 都兰（法国西部一地区）

**Gaul** [gɔ:l] *n.* 高卢（欧洲西部一地区）

**precede** [pri'si:d] *vt.* 领先（于），在……之前，先于

**digestif** [dai'dʒestif] *n.*（饭前或饭后喝的）助消化饮料

**cognac** ['kɔn,jæk] *n.* 干邑（白兰地酒的一种）

**parallel** ['pærəlel] *a.* 平行的，相同的

**coincidental** [kəu,insi'dentl] *a.* 一致的，符合的；巧合的

**prevalent** ['prevələnt] *a.* 普遍的，流行的

**champagne** [,ʃæm'pein] *n.* 香槟酒

**calvados** ['kælvədɔs] *n.* 苹果白兰地酒

**predominantly** [pri'dɔminəntli] *ad.* 主要地，突出地

**Catholic** ['kæθəlik] *n.* 天主教徒

**Lenten** ['lentn] *a.* 大斋戒的，大斋戒期间的

**kidney** ['kidni] *n.*（动物可食用的）腰子

**sweetbread** ['swi:t,bred] *n.* 杂碎

**tripe** [traip] *n.* 肚子，内脏

**intestine** [in'testin] *n.* 肠

**bourgeois** ['buəʒwɑ:] *n.* 中产阶级；商人

**inevitably** [in'evitəbli] *ad.* 不可避免，必定

**flesh** [fleʃ] *n.* 肉

**recipe** ['resəpi] *n.* 烹饪法，食谱，菜谱

**Phrases and Expressions**

Tour d'Argent　法国著名大酒店
a large number of　许多
in regard to　关于，有关
in a way　在某种程度上，从某一点上看
just as　正如，正好，恰恰是

be known by　认出，识别，出名
be not afraid to　不怕做某事
service à la russe　（法）俄罗斯式的服务
hors d'oeuvre　主菜前的小吃

## Notes

**1** Despite a common pan-gallic chauvinism, French cooking is not a monolith: it ranges from the olives and seafood of Provence to the butter and roasts of Tours, from the simple food of the bistro to the fanciful confections of the Tour d'Argent.

　　本句中，despite 是表示让步的介词，相当于 in spite of，意思是"尽管；不管"。其结构为 despite sth.。despite 在文体色彩上比 in spite of 更为正式。请看下例：
He came to the meeting despite his illness.
尽管有病，他还是来开会了。

**2** In a way similar to Japanese cuisine, it is expected that even the simplest preparation be undertaken in the most careful manner, which means disregarding the amount of time involved.

　　本句中，it 作形式主语，把主语从句置于句尾，主要是为了平衡句子结构（特别是谓语较短时），that 引导的主语从句可用 it 代替，但 that 不可以省略。which 在本句中引导的是非限定性定语从句，修饰 manner。in a way 表示"在某种程度上，从某一点上看"。

**3** Just as the vintner knows that the finest Bordeaux comes from the grapes grown on that side of the hill and not this, so too the chef knows not only from which region come the finest petits pois (small, young green peas), but from which town—the same goes for asparagus, and even cauliflower.

　　本句为 just as..., so... 结构；意思是"正如……，……也，犹如……一样"，表示的是比拟关系。as 引导的是含有比拟意义的方式状语从句，so 相当于"in the same way, in the same proportion"，引导主句。as 前加 just 表示强调。

　　本句中 not only... but (also) 意思是"不但……而且"用来连接平行的词或词组，主要强调的是后者。

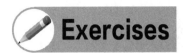

## Exercises

**EX. 5** **Answer the following questions.**

1. What is French cooking like?

2. Why has French cooking always seemed so daunting to Americans?

3. Can you name some famous foods which are known by the name of the town?

4. What is the typical French meal?

5. Introduce briefly on drinking in a French meal.

**EX. 6** **Decide whether the following statements are *true* or *false*.**

1. Throughout the country, French cooking involves a large number of techniques, some extremely complicated, that serve as basics.

2. Any cook can tell you that French food will have shortcuts in regard to these fundamentals. Because mastery of sauces or pastry doughs is the basis of the culinary arts.

3. One reason why French cooking has always seemed so daunting on the other side of the Atlantic is that it is much similar to Japanese cuisine, it is expected that even the simplest preparation be undertaken in the most careful manner.

4. Champagne as a beverage does accompany food gracefully, likewise, as a region it is not well known for its food.

5. Moreover, the Gauls are not afraid to eat anything. Kidney, brain, sweetbreads, tripe, blood sauces and sausages, sheep's foot, tongue, and intestines are all common in French cooking and hold equal standing with the meat of lamb, beef, pork, poultry, and game.

## Part Four Skill Training

### Forms

Because there are so many different nationalities and visitors in America, they can find almost any kind of restaurant in the most of the larger cities. Here is the form of dining guide in Hawaii, U.S.A. If you want to find a restaurant, you can first look through it and then make your decision.

## Your Handy DINING GUIDE

KEY: $$$$ - ($18 & over)
$$$ - ($13-$17)
$$ - ($8-$12)
$ - ($7-& under)
Based on average dinner entree'
*on menu or upon request

| | RESERVATIONS | ENTERTAINMENT | BREAKFAST | LUNCH | DINNER | PARKING |
|---|:---:|:---:|:---:|:---:|:---:|:---:|
| **CONTINENTAL cont.** | | | | | | |
| $$$$ **Oceanarium** (Map H #33) Pacific Beach Hotel / 921-6111 2490 Kalakaua Ave. / 922-1233 | • | | • | • | • | • |
| $$$$ **Pagoda Restaurant** 1525 Rycroft / 941-6611 | • | | • | • | • | • |
| $$$ **Pikake Terrace** (Map H #38) Princess Kaiulani Hotel 120 Kaiulani Ave. / 922-5811 | | • | • | • | • | • |
| $$$$ **Scott's Seafood Grill & Bar** Aloha Tower Marketplace 537-6800   (Map C:C3) | • | | | • | • | • |
| $$ **Surf Room** (Map H #42) Royal Hawaiian Hotel 2259 Kalakaua Ave. / 931-7194 | • | | • | • | • | • |
| $$ **Top of Waikiki** (Map H #21) Waikiki Business Plaza 2270 Kalakaua Ave. / 923-3877 | • | | | • | • | • |
| $$$ **W.C. Peacock & Co. Ltd.** (Map H #36) Sheraton Moana Surfrider Hotel 2353 Kalakaua Ave. / 922-3111 | • | | | | • | • |
| **DINNER CRUISE** | | | | | | |
| $$$ **Dream Cruises** / 592-5200 | • | | | • | • | • |
| $$$$ **Navatek I** / 848-6360 | • | • | | | • | • |
| **FAST FOOD** | | | | | | |
| $ **Jack-in-the Box** / Six Locations | | | • | • | • | |
| $ **McDonald's** / 4 Waikiki Locations Ala Moana Ctr. / Discovery Bay | | | • | • | • | |
| **GREEK** | | | | | | |
| $$ **Cafe Athena** (Map A:F10) Restaurant Row 500 Ala Moana Blvd. / 533-0665 | • | • | | • | • | |

## Practical Writing

Western menus are unfamiliar to the Chinese in general, as the eating habits are quite different. We give one sample western menu below, which from MORTON'S restaurant in San Francisco—the steakhouse.

| | Market Price |
|---|---|
| *APPETIZERS* | |
| Gulf Shrimp Cocktail | 9.95 |
| Blue Point Oysters on the Half Shell | 8.95 |
| Smoked Pacific Salmon | 9.95 |
| Black Bean Soup | 4.95 |
| *SALADS* | |
| Morton's Salad or Spinach Salad | 5.5 |
| Caesar Salad | 5.5 |
| Sliced Beefsteak Tomato & Purple Onion or Blue Cheese | 5.5 |
| *ENTREES* | |
| Porterhouse Steak | 29.95 |
| New York Strip Sirloin | 29.95 |
| Ribeye Steak | 23.95 |
| Domestic Rib Lamb Chops | 28.95 |
| Lemon Oregano Chicken | 17.95 |
| Fresh Fish of the Day | 19.95 |
| Whole Baked Maine Lobster | 32.95 |
| *VEGETABLES* | |
| Sauteed Fresh Spinach & Mushrooms | 4.25 |
| Sauteed Mushrooms | 4.25 |
| Steamed Fresh Broccoli | 4.25 |
| Steamed Fresh Asparagus | 6.95 |
| Baked Potato, Hashbrown Potatoes, | |
| Potato Skins, Lyonnaise Potatoes | 4.25 |
| *DESSERTS* | |
| Chocolate Hazelnut Cake with Mocha Sauce | 5.00 |
| Blueberry Compote with Lemon Semifreddo | 5.00 |
| Gravenstein Apple Tarte Tatin | 5.00 |

**Simulate and create** ▶ Suppose you are going to invite two foreign guests to a western food restaurant this weekend. Please order a western dinner meal for them according to the menu given above.

# Part Five    Related Information

| Text | Notes |
|---|---|
| **Tips on How to Enjoy Cheap Eats at the Restaurant** | |
| 1. If a restaurant is empty at a peak[1] meal time, ask yourself why. | [1] 最高峰，最高的 |
| 2. Always read the menu posted[2] outside before going in. This avoids[3] you being seated and finding you don't like anything on the menu, or worse yet, that the prices are too high. If the menu is not posted (which by law it should be), ask to see one before deciding to stay. All menus must clearly state[4] the prices, including VAT[5] (value-added-tax is the British equivalent of sales tax); whether a service charge is included and if so, how much; the cover charge; and the minimum if there is one. | [2] 公告<br>[3] 避免，消除<br><br><br><br>[4] 声明，陈述，规定<br>[5] 销售税 |
| 3. Watch the fine print. A cover charge is per person; a minimum charge is also per person. A steep[6] cover along with a hefty[7] 12 percent service charge on top of a three-course meal with wine, dessert[8], and coffee could be hard to swallow[9]. | [6] 不合理的<br>[7] 丰盛的一餐<br>[8] 餐后甜点<br>[9] 吞下，咽下 |
| 4. The service charge[10], whether discretionary[11] or added automatically, is the tip[12]. You are not expected to pay a single extra pence[13], unless the service has been out of this world. Beware[14] of the double service-charge trick[15]. | [10] 费用，收费<br>[11] 任意的，自由决定的<br>[12] 小费<br>[13] 额外的<br>[14] 小心，谨慎<br>[15] 诡计 |
| 5. While the set-price two-or three-course meal may have limited choices, it will represent the best value for money on the menu. | |

# Part Six    Guide to World Famous Sight

| Text | Notes |
|---|---|
| **The Eiffel Tower** | |
| ***History*** | [1]（法国巴黎的）埃菲尔铁塔 |
| In 1889, when the Tower Eiffel[1] was completed, it was the tallest building in the world at 300m. The Tower Eiffel was originally built as a temporary[2] structure to commemorate[3] the centenary[4] of the Revolution. And since, the Eiffel Tower has | [2] 暂时的，临时的<br>[3] 纪念<br>[4] 一百年 |

become an enduring[5] symbol[6] of the city of Paris. The Tower was originally built for the 1889 Exposition[7]. This steel construction defied[8] all traditional rules in architecture[9]. It is now the television transmitter[10] for the greater Paris region.

The Tower selected by a competition which was won by Gustave Eiffel, an engineer who had experience of constructing high level railway viaducts[11]. In the public eye, the tower had many mixed opinions, celebrated and loathed[12] in equal measure. Throughout its construction, the residents became convinced that it would collapse[13], and Eiffel had to personally assure them. The author Guy de Maupassant left Paris permanently to avoid looking at it's metallic[14] carcass, but others who espoused[15] more self-consciously modern views championed[16] the tower: Seurat and Douanier Rousseau were among the first to paint it, in 1889 and 1890 respectively. On a clear day, it is possible to see Chartres Cathedral[17] from the high level viewing platform.

### The "Tower"

There are three floors. The first is at 57m, the second at 115m, and the third at 276 m. The top of the aerial[18] is 320m above the ground. And on a nice day, you can see from the top of the platform, the whole of Paris and even the distant suburbs.

The 12,000 steel girder[19] are held together by 2,500,000 rivets[20] to produce a smooth, curving profile[21]. Its functional elegance[22] heralded[23] the dawn of Industrial Art, and has met with much sarcastic[24] comment from more conservative[25] observers ever since it was finished in 1889.

And in 1986 the external night-time floodlighting was replaced by a system of illumination[26] from within the tower's superstructure[27], so that it now looks at its magical best after dark.

| | |
|---|---|
| [5] 持久的 |
| [6] 标志 |
| [7] 博览会，展览会 |
| [8] 挑战；违抗 |
| [9] 建筑，建筑学 |
| [10] 发射机 |
| [11] 高架桥，高架铁路 |
| [12] 厌恶，憎恶 |
| [13] 倒塌，崩溃 |
| [14] 金属（性）的 |
| [15] 支持，赞成 |
| [16] 拥护，支持 |
| [17] 大教堂 |
| [18] 高耸的 |
| [19] 梁，钢桁的支架 |
| [20] 铆钉 |
| [21] 剖面，轮廓 |
| [22] 典雅，雅致 |
| [23] 预报 |
| [24] 讽刺的 |
| [25] 保守的，守旧的 |
| [26] 灯彩 |
| [27]（建筑物）上部构造 |

# Unit 11

# Sightseeing

## Part One — Dialogues

### Sample Dialogue 1

👤 **Situation** ▶ One guide is showing Tommy around Beijing. They are talking about some famous historical spots in Beijing.

**Guide**: Have you been to Beijing before?

**Tommy**: No. This is my first time to visit China. Will you recommend me some places of historical interest and scenic beauty?

**Guide**: Yes. I'd like to. Could you tell me how long would you like to stay in Beijing?

**Tommy**: Two or three days.

**Guide**: Well. Among the most famous are the Tian'anmen Square, the Palace Museum, the Summer Palace, the Temple of Heaven and the Great Wall.

**Tommy**: Please locate the Tian'anmen Square for me on the map. I can go there on my own.

**Guide**: It's here. Tian'anmen Square is one of the largest squares in the world. Many great historical events happened there. It is not far from your hotel. You can get there by taxi.

**Tommy**: Where is the Palace Museum?

**Guide**: It is located in the north of Tian'anmen. Until 1911 the palace was off-limits to ordinary citizens, so it is also known as the Forbidden City. It was constructed in a fourteen-year period during the 15th century. Twenty-four emperors lived and ruled there for almost 500 years. You can get there just by taking a walk from Tian'anmen Square.

**Tommy:** You mean it can tell me 500 years of Chinese history?

**Guide:** You're quite right. Another place well worth visiting is the Summer Palace. It is a grand park of historic importance. You can also learn something about the Chinese history there.

**Tommy:** What about the Great Wall?

**Guide:** The Great Wall is a place appealing to both Chinese and foreigners.

**Tommy:** Good idea! I'll try to find my time to visit it!

## Sample Dialogue 2

**Situation** ▶ Sightseeing in North America. It is Tonghui's first time to visit New York. The guide is suggesting him visiting some famous spots in New York.

**Tonghui:** I'd like to take a half-day tour around New York City. What do you have available?

**Guide:** Well. We have two half-day tours daily—one in the morning from 8:00 to 12:00 and another is in the afternoon, starting at 2:00.

**Tonghui:** I'd like to see the Statue of Liberty. Maybe it is the most famous single monument in the USA.

**Guide:** It is. It has become a symbol of New York and of the USA. For millions of immigrants, it was a symbol of the American dream. It was a gift from the French people. Its designer also designed the world famous Eiffel Tower.

**Tonghui:** Really? That must have been very spectacular.

**Guide:** It was. It has stood against the harsh sea air for more than 200 years. In 1986 it was renovated at the cost of 70 million dollar.

**Tonghui:** By the way, are visitors allowed to climb up the statue?

**Guide:** Yes. An elevator takes visitors to the top pedestal.

**Tonghui:** OK. That's the first thing I'd like to do.

**Guide:** I suggest you include Ellis Island in your trip. Ellis Island is a small island only a mile away from the Statue of Liberty. There you could know more about the American immigration. It was looked upon with dread by the immigrants.

**Tonghui:** Why was it?

**Guide:** Most immigrants could not speak English. They had to wait their turn to be examined by doctors and officials. They were afraid to be refused admission.

**Tonghui:** Well I guess I'll sign up for the tour of tomorrow morning anyway.

**Guide:** OK. Here is your ticket and some information about the tour.

**Tonghui:** Thank you very much. See you tomorrow.

**Guide:** See you tomorrow.

## Useful Expressions

1. It's a man-made wonder.

   这是一个人造的奇迹。

2. These exquisite scenes are a feast for the eye.

   旖旎的风光会让您一饱眼福。

3. The beauty of Shanghai is overwhelming.

   上海的美景真让人叹为观止。

4. We are proud of its architectural, cultural and culinary charms.

   我们为其建筑艺术、文化传统以及烹饪饮食感到自豪。

5. It is a city that never sleeps.

   这是一个不夜城。

6. The city seduces visitors with its natural beauty.

   这个城市以其自然美吸引着游客。

7. It offers visitors a cornucopia of cross-culture attractions.

   这里为游客们提供了许多跨文化的旅游场所。

8. The building is a landmark and a symbol of the city.

   这栋楼是这个城市的标志性建筑，也是这个城市的象征。

9. I was told that Hawaii beach is very famous all over the world.

   我听说夏威夷海滩是世界闻名的。

10. Could you tell me what to see here?

   你能告诉我这有什么可看的地方吗？

## Task Dialogue 1

**Situation** ▶ A tourist group has just arrived in Xi'an. You are sending them to the Hotel. Tell them the next day's itinerary and give them a brief introduction of the landscape they are going to see.

## Task Dialogue 2

**Situation** ▶ You have a whole day for sightseeing in London. Ask for some information on visiting famous London spots.

# Part Two  Text A

## Leisurely Sightseeing in Hong Kong

Most people think of Hong Kong as an island in China, whereas it is actually made up of two hundred and thirty six islands plus a chunk of mainland China bordering the Chinese province of Guangdong. Much of the area is uninhabited while other areas are among the most densely populated in the world. At the heart of it all is the seventy-eight-square-kilometer Hong Kong Island itself. The center of Hong Kong Island is the Business District where today, as the name suggests, the old business life goes on in some of the most expensive buildings in the world.

From Central, it is a seven-minute ferry ride across one of the world's great harbors to the Kowloon peninsula on the mainland. At the tip is the shopper's paradise of Tsimshatsui and beyond that are the high-rise business and commercial estates. Beyond Kowloon is the New Territories, which includes not only the border area with China, but also the other two hundred and thirty-five islands that make up Hong Kong and covers nine hundred and eighty square kilometers in total.

After spending a leisurely morning with Ken and Freddie, they took us for a very traditional meal at what looked to be a rather nice restaurant. The meal was Dim Sum which is a traditionally Cantonese meal served only for breakfast or in this instance lunch, but never dinner. The term Dim Sum means a snack and is often referred to as Yum Cha, which literally means of drink tea, since this is always served with Dim Sum meals. Eating Dim Sum is a social event, and today there is no exception as we met with some friends of Ken and Freddie that were at the party last night. We all sat around a huge circular table and the Dim Sum delicacies were served in a small bamboo basket in which they are normally steamed. All the time there were waitresses and waiters walking around pushing large trolleys with various steaming basket. Thank God that I was dining with experts as they were able to ask in Cantonese what each basket contained and then request the thing they liked. Each of the baskets contained four identical pieces and each basket was priced the same, so that at the end of the meal, the waiter simply added up the amount of baskets and that was the price that we were charged, which I thought was a great idea. It is estimated that there are around one thousand Dim Sum dishes to choose from and each of the trolleys being pushed around has a variation to all the others, so the overall choice is incredible. After lunch at 3:00 p.m., I went off to do a spot of sightseeing and also to do some shopping. Hong Kong is renowned for the choice available in the department stores as well as the numerous side streets in and around Tsimshatsui. I really wanted to buy Michelle some nice presents to take back with me, and the first thing that I purchased was a pair of Ray-Ban sunglasses which were $300. I found the shops packed from floor to ceiling with bargains and it was very hard to control just how much money I spent. Everywhere I went there were shops selling all the latest Hi-Fi and camera equipment, all at a fraction of the cost in England.

Hong Kong is the financial center of China, or even of Asia, therefore there was never a problem when it came to cashing traveler's cheques or paying with a Visa Card, the only problem is agreeing a price! You have to bargain with them over everything which really gets on one's nerves after a while. It is impossible to try and match a price up between one store and another, as the price is never displayed on the goods and so you have to ask an assistant for the price. I am convinced they say the first number that comes into their heads! Then comes the laborious task of trying to ascertain a reasonable price for the goods so that you can find out if you can afford it, let alone buy the thing!

Needless to say this can really start to wear one down, as once you have managed to find out the true price and you then say you will think about it, they throw their arms up with horror and try to make you feel guilty about wasting their time. If they displayed the price in the first place it would not happen. Anyway, I was successful in knocking them down to what I thought was a good price on a Sony Walkman tape/radio. Well I thought it was a good price and the guy took my money, so I don't suppose he lost anything on the deal. It cost me about 800¥ and when I returned to England and priced it up at a local shop, it was 250.00 pounds. So on that basis I think I obtained a bargain. It was a pity that I did not have lots of spare money as there was just about everything electrical that I had ever wanted to own all in one street!

I headed down to the harbor to get the Star Ferry across to Hong Kong Island to see what is described as one of the most breathtaking views in the world as the ferry crosses from Tsimshatsui to Central on Hong Kong Island. They weren't wrong! The ferry service runs 7 days a week from 6:00 a.m. to 11:30 p.m. and is continuous. You never have to wait more than a few minutes to take the seven-minute trip across the water and, assuming the weather is good, it beats the Mass Transit Railway hands down. There are two prices for the journey, lower deck was HK$1.00 and upper deck is HK$1.20 per trip. All the ferries have names like: Morning Star, Evening Star, Celestial Star, Shining Star etc.

Once on the Island I headed straight for Hong Kong central post office where I intended to post home all the extra warm-weather clothes that I still had with me. I knew for a fact that the weather both here and in Thailand was going to be very hot and so the more things that I had in my back-pack, the hotter I was going to be when walking around. I have to say that I was fairly ruthless in what I had decided to post home and sent most things from my Timberland boots to all my long legged trousers, except for the one pair I would need when I arrived back into the U.K. The post office was very efficient as was everything in Hong Kong. There were boxes on sale for me to select the size required and then fill it with my belongings. There was a supply of sticky tape to seal the boxes and sticky labels to write on. Why cannot the U.K. post offices be as helpful and efficient as the ones that we have developed in Hong Kong? The cost of posting the things home was HK$243, a cheap price for a bit of comfort.

Once I had unloaded my clothes and books I headed off to explore Hong Kong Island and see some of the world's most expensive buildings, one of which was the Hong Kong and Shanghai Bank Building, which is the headquarters of the Bank. As well as being one of the most expensive buildings in the world, it is also one of the strangest, hence the name that the locals have given it, "The Robot Building". This is because lots of the buildings are all visible from the outside. The escalators and lifts are made of clear plastic so that all the gears and other moving parts can be seen. The entire inside is walled with glass which gives the workers inside dizzy views if they get too close to the walls. Another building that I visited was the Bond Building, yet another strang-looking building that is typically found in Hong Kong.

I had planned to spend the rest of the day on the island so that I could see The Peak both at daylight and also during the evening when it would be dark thus giving me good views of Hong Kong in both types of light. Every guide book quotes: "If you haven't been to The Peak, then you have not been to Hong Kong", so I definitely was not going to miss the views that the books talked of. If nothing else it was a good chance to get Hong Kong into perspective as the views over the harbor, with the aircraft landing at the airport in the distance, were truly breathtaking.

Victoria Peak, or just, "The Peak" as it is known, has been the place to live ever since the British moved in, and today the price of real estate is astronomical. There is a tram to transport the visitors to the top where they will find the Peak Tower which is a type of scenic shopping mall. There were high-powered binoculars on the balcony which, for HK$1.00 for a few minutes, were worth every cent. By around 6:30 p.m. it started to get dark and slowly the whole city started to illuminate against the crisp clear skies making the visibility excellent. I have to say that Hong Kong by night is staggering! It was the only way to see the country properly, first the view by sunlight and then shortly after by moonlight. The entire skyline was alight with neon lights allowing me to see for miles and miles. Surprisingly there were only one or two other people up there with me and I had to drag myself away at around 10:00 p.m., not because I was bored, but because I had to go and get the ferry back to Kowloon and then the train back to the New Territories, to return to Ken & Freddie where I was staying. I did some shopping on the way and bought Michelle a silk kimono from a silk shop at The Peak.

Once I was back in Kowloon, I went to a typically British pub in Tsimshatsui where there were many English. Then I headed home and I arrived at around 12:00 midnight feeling absolutely exhausted, this was due to the fact that I had missed the last bus from the train station, up the hill to Ken & Freddie and the walk was a killer.

Next day, I just had a leisurely day walking around the streets of Hong Kong, taking in the sight and sounds of the place. I had tried to get out of the tourist areas and find the places where the Hong Kong Chinese do their shopping which, Ken had told me, was Mongkok. I found the prices in Mongkok a little cheaper than those in Kowloon but there was still the problem of having to bargain for a price, just to see if you might be interested or not.

I was very grateful to Ken and Freddie for putting me up at their apartment as there was very little cheap accommodation available in Hong Kong, probably due to the very high price for land.

The day actually shot by and after a great Chinese meal in Tsimshatsui I rang Michelle at 8:40 p.m. which was good as always. After chatting to her I went back to the New Territories to Ken and Freddie and watched a film on the television, which incidentally, was just as good the U.K. with English speaking channels (as well as Chinese), showing the latest films that have been released.

# New Words

**whereas** [wɛər'æz] *conj.* 然而，尽管，但是；鉴于

**uninhabited** [ˌʌnin'hæbitid] *a.* 无人居住的，杳无人迹的

**densely** [densli] *ad.* 浓密地，浓厚地

**Kowloon** ['kau'lu:n] *n.* 九龙（香港对面的半岛），九龙港埠

**Cantonese** [ˌkæntə'ni:z] *n.* 广东人，广东话

**ferry** ['feri] *n.* 摆渡，渡船，渡口

**peninsula** [pə'ninsjulə] *n.* 半岛

**paradise** ['pærədaiz] *n.* 天堂

**commercial** [kə'mə:ʃəl] *a.* 商业的，贸易的

**estate** [i'steit] *n.* 不动产，财产

**literally** ['litərəli] *ad.* 照字面意义，逐字地

**bamboo** [ˌbæm'bu:] *n.* 竹子

**waitress** ['weitrəs] *n.* 女服务生

**request** [ri'kwest] *vt.* 请求，要求

**identical** [ai'dentikəl] *a.* 同一的，同样的

**variation** [ˌveəri'eiʃən] *n.* 变更，变化

**overall** ['əuvər,ɔ:l] *a.* 全部的，全面的

**incredible** [in'kredəbl] *a.* 难以置信的

**numerous** ['nju:mərəs] *a.* 众多的，许多的，无数的

**bargain** ['bɑ:gin] *n.* 讨价还价；便宜货

**ascertain** [ˌæsə'tein] *vt.* 确定，弄清

**display** [di'splei] *vt.* 陈列，展览；显示

**laborious** [lə'bɔ:riəs] *a.* 艰苦的，费力的

**reasonable** ['ri:znəbl] *a.* 合理的，有道理的

**needless** ['ni:dləs] *a.* 不需要的，不必要的

**guilty** ['gilti] *a.* 犯罪的，有罪的，心虚的

**guy** [gai] *n.* 家伙，人

**breathtaking** ['breθ,teikiŋ] *a.* 惊人的，惊险的

**beat** [bi:t] *vt.* 打，打败

**back-pack** [bæk pæk] *n.* 背包

**ruthless** ['ru:θləs] *a.* 无情的，残忍的

**Timberland** ['timbəlænd] *n.* 美国户外品牌

**efficient** [i'fiʃənt] *a.* 有效率的

**sticky** ['stiki] *a.* 黏的，黏性的

**label** ['leibl] *n.* 标签，签条，商标，标志

**seal** [si:l] *vt.* 封，密封

**headquarters** [hed'kwɔ:təz] *n.* 总部

**hence** [hens] *ad.* 因此，从此

**escalator** ['eskə,leitə] *n.* 电动扶梯，自动扶梯

**gear** [giə] *n.* 传动装置

**dizzy** ['dizi] *a.* 晕眩的，昏乱的，使头晕目眩的，令人头昏眼花的

**definitely** ['defənətli] *ad.* 明确地，干脆地

**tram** [træm] *n.* 有轨电车

**binoculars** [bi'nɔkjuləz] *n.* 双眼望远镜

**balcony** ['bælkəni] *n.* 阳台

**illuminate** [i'lu:mineit] *vt.* 照明，照亮；使灿烂，以灯火装饰

**staggering** ['stægəriŋ] *a.* 令人惊愕的

**kimono** [ki'məunəu] *n.* 和服

**incidentally** [ˌinsi'dentəli] *ad.* 附带地，顺便提及地

**Mongkok** ['mɔŋkɔk] *n.* 旺角

**Phrases and Expressions**

think of... as  把……看作是，以为……是
be made up of  由……组成，由……构成
a chunk of  一大块
at the heart of  在……中心
Hong Kong Island  香港岛
the Business District  商业区，商贸区
New Territories  新界
in total  整个地
Dim Sum  点心
Yum Cha  饮茶
refer to as  把……称作，把……当作
at the end of  在……末端，在……的结尾
add up  加起来
go off  离去，走掉
be renowned for  以……有名，以……著名
as well as  也，又

wear sb. down  使……挫败
throw up one's arms  举起双手
knock down  杀价，降价
head for  走向，向……方向前进
Star Ferry  天星小轮
the Mass Transit Railway  大众铁路运输
Celestial Star  天星
Sony Walkman  索尼随身听
on/for sale  出售（的）
a bit of  一点儿，少量的
let alone/leave alone  不加干涉，让他去
Victoria Peak  维多利亚山顶
the Bond Building  债券大楼
get out of  使离开，使逃脱
be grateful to sb. for sth.  因某事而感谢某人

## Notes

**1** Most people think of Hong Kong as an island, whereas it is actually made up of two hundred and thirty six islands plus a chunk of mainland China bordering the Chinese province of Guangdong.

　　本句中，whereas 是一个连词，表示相反的情况，意思是"但是，可是，而……，却……"，等于"but，although"。bordering the Chinese province of Guangdong 是一个现在分词短语作定语，修饰和限定 mainland China。分词短语作定语时一般放在被修饰词之后，往往可以用定语从句代替。think of ... as 的意思是"把……看作是，以为是……"，bordering 可译为"与……接壤"。

**2** The center of Hong Kong Island is the Business District where today, as the name suggests, the old business life goes on in some of the most expensive buildings in the world.

　　本句中，where 引导的是一个定语从句，修饰 the business district。as the name suggests 是插入语，as 为连词，引导方式状语从句，表示"如同，像"。请看下例：

He speaks English just as Englishmen do.

他讲英语就像英国人一样。

**3** Beyond Kowloon is the New Territories, which includes not only the border area with China, but also the other two hundred and thirty five islands that make up Hong Kong and covers nine hundred and eighty square kilometers in total.

本句是一个表语提前的倒装句，为了保持句子平衡，将主语与宾语倒置。本句中有两个定语从句，一个是非限定性定语从句 which includes not only the border area with China, but also the other two hundred and thirty five islands，修饰 the New Territories，另一个是限定性定语从句 that make up Hong Kong and covers nine hundreds and eighty square kilometers in total，修饰和限定 islands。

④ You have to bargain with them over everything, which really gets on one's nerves after a while.

本句中，which really gets on one's nerves after a while 是一个非限定性定语从句，是对前面句子的补充说明。over 在本句中是介词，意思是"关于，对于"。请看下例：

There is no point in arguing over something that's as unimportant as that.

就这样无关紧要的事情进行争论毫无意义。

⑤ Surprisingly there were only one or two other people up there with me and I had to drag myself away at around 10:00 p.m., not because I was bored, but because I had to go and get the ferry back to Kowloon and then the train back to the New Territories, to return to Ken & Freddie where I was staying.

本句中，not because... but because 这种结构意为"不是因为……，而是因为……"，引导的是原因状语从句。请看下例：

I can't go to the cinema with you, not because I don't like the film, but because I have no time for it.

我不能跟你去看电影，不是因为我不喜欢这部电影，而是我没有时间。

⑥ I found the prices in Mongkok to be a little cheaper than those in Kowloon but there was still the problem of having to bargain for a price, just to see if you might be interested or not.

本句使用的句型是 find + 宾语 + 动词不定式。

find 的常用结构还有：（1）find + oneself；（2）find + 宾语 + 现在分词；（3）find + it + 形容词 + 动词不定式。请看下例：

You'll soon find yourself without any friends at all if you keep on being so rude to everyone.

如果你继续对大家如此无礼，你很快就会发现你没有朋友。

I eventually found her reading a newspaper at home.

我最后发现她在家看报纸。

I find it difficult to explain this sentence.

我发现这句话很难解释。

# Exercises

**EX. 1** **Answer the following questions.**

1. What is Hong Kong actually made up of and what is the area of Hong Kong Island itself?

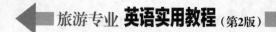

2. How were the Dim Sum delicacies severed?

3. When you want to go shopping in Hong Kong, what do you have to do?

4. What is the Star Ferry?

5. What scenic spots does the author suggest to visit?

**EX. 2** **Write out the English words according to the definitions given below.**

| definitions | words |
|---|---|
| not inhabited; unfit to be lived in | |
| a piece of land almost completely surrounded by water | |
| (in the Bible) the Garden of Eden, home of Adam and Eve; a place of perfect happiness | |
| something that can be or was bought cheaply | |
| to fasten or close with a seal or a tight cover of band of something | |
| a piece of paper, cloth, etc., fixed to something, on which is written what it is, who owns it, etc. | |
| to discover with certainty, as through examination or experimentation | |
| apart from the main subject; parenthetically | |
| to provide or brighten with light or to decorate or hang with lights | |
| marked by or requiring long, hard work | |

**EX. 3** **Complete the following sentences with appropriate words or expressions from the text.**

1. He always _____ his wife _____ "the old woman".

2. I'm going to Berlin next week, please come and start work _____ of May.

3. The region _____ its outstanding natural beauty.

4. Prices of video recorders have come down—we paid $250 for ours and now it is _____ for only $150.

5. He felt that he should be treated with the respect _____ his senior position.

6. I am informed that you have finished that report by weekend. I'm _____ you _____ all that you've done.

**EX. 4** **Translate the following sentences into Chinese.**

1. Much of the area is uninhabited while other areas are among the most densely populated in the world.

2. After spending a leisurely morning with Ken and Freddie, they took us for a very traditional meal at what looked to be a rather nice restaurant.

3. Hong Kong is renowned for the choice available in the department stores as well as the numerous side streets in and around Tsimshatsui.

4. You never have to wait more than a few minutes to take the seven minute trip across the water and, assuming the weather is good, it beats the Mass Transit Railway hands down.

5. By around 6:30 p.m. it started to get dark and slowly the whole city started to illuminate against the crisp clear skies making the visibility excellent.

## Part Three  Text B

## How to Make Your Itinerary

If you would like to start from scratch, these are the first pieces of information necessary to start the process:

Do you expect a group of students, adults, or will it be mixed?

The minimum and the maximum number of travelers expected.

Prorate: One free trip per how many paying travelers? (The standard prorate is 1:6.)

Departure City

Departure Date

Return Date

Type of Accommodations: Triples/Quads for Students, and Twins/Doubles for Adults; or all Twins/Doubles for everyone?

Hotel Quality: 2-star; 3-and 4-star; 4-star only; or 5-star.

Meal Plan: Breakfast only; Breakfast and Dinner; or Breakfast/Lunch/Dinner. (The standard is Breakfast and Dinner.) You may vary this on certain days or request meal vouchers.

Do you want a full-time Journey Director, or are there cities in which you would like to be on your own?

The next step is designing a day-by-day itinerary. What are the overnight cities? What the morning, afternoon and evening activities you would like to plan for each day? You also need to pay attention not only to dates, but days of the week, since some attractions are closed on particular days of the week.

First of all, ask yourself what you'd like to see for the trip. Let's say, someone likes suburb scenes of natural formations. Another may want to see magnificent architectural buildings with their histories. Even going to beach paradise, someone likes to have more time to relax but the others like to do a variety of water sports. If you know the favorites, it will be easier to decide how long to stay in different places.

The second thing to consider is the length of your vacation. It is no good to fly far away for a week holiday. Long transport time will shorten your chance to see more. The air ticket is relatively expensive in proportion to the number of days you stay there.

Budget is also a constraint on itinerary planning. A sum of 17,000¥ saving can be enough for two-month trip to travel around in Africa, but definitely inadequate for European trip.

After considering the above, decide your destination and gather some information about the places. You need to read travel books, know the transport time from one city to another and briefly know what to see in those places. The following may help you as a reference.

*7-day trip*

Stop at one or two places in a country. For most Asian countries, the air ticket prices are cheap and involve less flying time from Hong Kong, China. However, do not attempt to travel all around the country nor to cover several countries. Let's say, only visit an island in Thailand instead of Thailand + Singapore + Malaysia all together (like what the travel tours offer). In fact, you can visit them next time as the ticket price is not expensive.

*14-day trip*

We still suggest you to visit Southeast Asian countries. You can see more or travel to different towns within one country. More flying only wastes your time and adds up your costs. Forget Europe if you can!

*30-day trip*

It is worth to go farther like Europe, Africa, America, South America, the Middle East or New Zealand, etc. Time allows you to cross countries. A trip to France, the Netherlands, Germany, Switzerland is very enough but not too many. Greece and Turkey are far away from Western European countries. Boat trips between Greek islands take time. Concentrate on some parts rather than choosing isolated ones or extreme ends. For instance, traveling 3-4 countries like Israel, Jordan and Egypt in the Middle East is good enough. For some very large/long countries like Indonesia, Nepal, you may need a month to look around.

*60-day trip*

Says for 60 days in the Middle East, I can go to Israel, Jordan, Egypt, Turkey plus Greece. If in Europe, I can make use of my European Pass to travel around up to 7-8 countries including Italy which stretches long at south or go to southeast to Spain.

Here is a typical example of classic Europe tour itinerary:

### Day 1   London-Ferry-Calais-Brussels

This morning, at check-in point you will meet your tour guide and join the coach for a leisurely drive from London to Dover port, to board the ferry for the short channel crossing to Calais. Upon arrival, we clear the necessary customs and immigration and proceed through

Belgium. Late afternoon we check in, for our two-night stay. In the evening enjoy a night tour of Brussels, which will include Grand Place, European Parliament buildings. Evening at leisure.

### Day 2    Amsterdam-Brussels

Today we visit the Madurodam Model Village to see miniature Holland. Later we drive north through the flat landscape of Holland passing windmills from a bygone era, to Amsterdam for a canal cruise through the city's complex system of waterways and to visit a diamond house and to see cutters at work. Late evening return to our hotel.

### Day 3    Brussels-Cologne-Mannheim

Proceed east across Belgium and into Germany. Joining the Autobahn, we arrive at the famous city of Cologne where you can marvel Europe's largest Gothic twin spire cathedral. Continuing our drive into the Rhine valley we board a cruise ship for an unforgettable trip along the River Rhine. Admire the majestic views, mountain top fairy tale castles and fortresses of a bygone era. Late evening check into our hotel for overnight stop.

### Day 4    Mannheim-Zurich area

Depart this morning for Switzerland. Enter into the enchanting Black Forest region, where you will marvel at the timeless serenity and unparalleled scenery around you. Our first stop is at scenic Lake Titisee where you have time to admire the scenery. Continuing our drive, we cross the Swiss border and stop at Schaffhausen to visit the majestic Rhine Falls. Later we check into our hotel.

### Day 5    Zurich-Engelberg- Lucerne-Zurich

Driving through the Swiss alpine region and the winding mountain roads to the valley of Engelberg, where we start our ascent to board the world's only revolving cable car reaching the peak of 10,000 feet and the highest viewpoint in central Switzerland. In the afternoon we begin our descent and visit the town of Lucerne where you have to shop for superb Swiss watches and chocolates. Later we join our boat for a cruise on Lake Lucerne and to see the Swiss folklore program of costumes and dances.

### Day 6    Zurich-Vaduz-Innsbruck-Mestre area

Early morning we depart for Austria. On route we enter the small principality of Liechtenstein and to Vaduz. Continuing our journey we pass the spectacular Austrian alpine region and drive through the Arlberg Tunnel to Innsbruck. Later we visit the Swarovski crystal museum. Early evening we cross Europe's highest bridge and the Italian border, winding our way through the Brenner pass, late evening we check into our hotel.

### Day 7    Venice-Florence

Your tour starts with a boat ride on a Vaporetto to one of the most romantic cities of the world. Later we visit the most elegant square in the world—St. Marks Square. Early afternoon we depart across the Appennines and the gentle hilly countryside of Tuscany to Florence. On arrival in the city of the Medicis, we will visit Piazzale Michelangelo to enjoy one of the best views of this Renaissance city across the River Arno.

### Day 8　Florence-Rome-Florence

Passing sunlit valleys of the Chianti wine country and ancient fortresses perched high on the hills to reach the "Eternal City". On arrival, we meet our expert local guide who will show us the splendors of the Vatican and St. Peters a renaissance masterpiece. In the afternoon we take in other ancient sights—the Coliseum, the Roman Forum, which was the political center of the Roman Empire and the spectacular fountain where you may make a wish. Late evening return to our hotel.

### Day 9　Florence-Pisa-Zurich area

Joining the Autostrada we first visit Pisa where you can marvel at one of the wonders of the world, the legendary Leaning Tower and also the Square of Miracles. Continuing our journey north, we enter into Switzerland. Late evening check into our hotel.

### Day 10　Zurich-Interlaken-Jungfrau- Zurich

We first drive to the town of Interlaken, where we start our ascent to visit Trummelbach falls. Later board the train for the scenic journey to the top of Europe—Jungfrau and the highest railway station in Europe. In the afternoon we begin our descent. Late evening we return to our hotel.

### Day 11　Zurich-Paris

Early morning we leave the Swiss Alps behind us. Once into France, we join the super fast highways driving past vineyards and mustard fields. Early evening we arrive in Paris and visit the top floor of the Eiffel Tower to witness a spectacular panoramic view of the city. Later we check into our hotel and have the evening at leisure.

### Day 12　Paris

We meet our expert local guide to visit the Palace of Versailles, the former residence of the famous "Sun King". Later on the city tour our guide will introduce us to the main sights: Champs Elysees, Place de Concorde, Arc de Triomphe and the Louvre museum. This evening enjoy a romantic dinner cruise on the River Seine, admire the spectacular facades from your boat and enjoy the entertainment on board. Finally join us for an exciting optional Lido cabaret show.

### Day 13　Paris-Calais-Ferry-London

This morning we visit a French perfumery for some last minute shopping. Early afternoon we depart and journey north for Calais to board the ferry for the return channel crossing. On arrival at Dover we board our local coach and arrive London late evening where the tour ends and time to say farewell to all the friends you have made on tour.

*Tour Cost*

|  | Tour Cost | London Package-*Free*-Hurry ! Limited Offer | Lido Option |
|---|---|---|---|
| **Adult** | $ 1,999.00 | *Free* | $ 140.00 |
| **Child 2-11 yrs** | $ 1,599.00 | *Free* | $ 140.00 |
| **Single Person** | $ 2,499.00 | *Free* | $ 140.00 |

*Above rates are based on Adult (aged 12 years+) Based on Twin/Triple Share Rooms and Child Sharing parents room (age 02-11 yrs).*

*For details on our London Package please contact our reservation team.*

| **YOUR TOUR INCLUDES** |
|---|
| 12 nights in first class Hotel shown or similar with private facilities. |
| 12 Vegetarian buffet breakfasts and 12 Indian Lunches & 11 Dinners & 1 Dinner cruise Meal plan is indicated at the bottom of your daily itinerary. B = Breakfast, D = Indian dinner, L = Indian lunch |
| All coach transportation by executive cruise liners from departure to tour termination points. |
| All sightseeing, entrances and excursions as mentioned by the itinerary. Services of Bi-lingual Taj Tours Manager throughout the tour. |

# New Words

**prorate** [prəuˈreit] *vt.* 按比例分配，分派

**triple** [ˈtripl] *n.* 三个一组

**quad** [kwɔd] *n.* 四个一组

**voucher** [ˈvautʃə] *n.* 凭证，凭单

**particular** [pəˈtikjulə] *a.* 特殊的，特别的，独特的

**suburb** [ˈsʌbə:b] *n.* 市郊，郊区

**formation** [fɔ:ˈmeiʃən] *n.* 形成，构成

**magnificent** [mæɡˈnifisnt] *a.* 华丽的，宏伟的

**constraint** [kənˈstreint] *n.* 约束，强制

**inadequate** [inˈædikwət] *a.* 不充分的，不适当的

**Netherlands** [ˈneðələndz] *n.* 荷兰（西欧国家）

**Switzerland** [ˈswitsələnd] *n.* 瑞士（中欧国家）

**Nepal** [nəˈpɔ:l] *n.* 尼泊尔（南亚国家）

**Israel** [ˈizreil] *n.* 以色列（西南亚国家）

**Jordan** [ˈdʒɔ:dn] *n.* 约旦（西南亚国家）

**briefly** [ˈbri:fli] *ad.* 暂时地，简要地

**reference** [ˈrefərəns] *n.* 提及，涉及，参考

**attempt** [əˈtempt] *vt.* 尝试，企图

**Dover** [ˈdəuvə] *n.* 多佛（英国东南部港市）

**Calais** ['kælei] *n.* 加来（法国北部港市）

**Belgium** ['beldʒəm] *n.* 比利时（西欧国家）

**miniature** ['minətʃə] *n.* 缩小的模型

**windmill** ['wind,mil] *n.* 风车，风车房

**bygone** ['baigɔn] *a.* 过去的

**waterway** ['wɔːtə,wei] *n.* 水路

**autobahn** ['ɔtəubɑːn] *n.*（德国的）高速公路

**Gothic** ['gɔθik] *a.* 哥特式的

**spire** ['spaiə] *n.* 尖顶

**cathedral** [kə'θiːdrəl] *n.* 大教堂

**castle** ['kɑːsl] *n.* 城堡

**fortress** ['fɔːtrəs] *n.* 堡垒，要塞

**enchanting** [in'tʃɑːntiŋ] *a.* 讨人喜欢的，迷人的

**Schaffhausen** ['ʃɑːfhausən] *n.* 沙夫豪森（瑞士北部城市）

**unparalleled** [ʌn'pærəleld] *a.* 无比的，无双的，空前的

**Lucerne** [luː'səːn] *n.* 卢塞恩（瑞士中部城市）

**alpine** ['ælpain] *n.* 阿尔卑斯山

**ascent** [ə'sent] *n.* 攀登；上坡路

**revolving** [ri'vɔlviŋ] *a.* 旋转的

**superb** [suː'pəːb] *a.* 庄重的，堂堂的，华丽的；极好的

**costume** ['kɔstjuːm] *n.* 装束，服装

**folklore** ['fəuk,lɔː(r)] *n.* 民间传说

**Vaduz** [vɑː'duːts] *n.* 瓦杜兹（列支敦士登首都）

**Innsbruck** ['inzbruk] *n.* 因斯布鲁克（奥地利西部城市）

**principality** [,prinsə'pæləti] *n.* 公国，侯国

**Liechtenstein** ['liktənstain] *n.* 列支敦士登（中欧国家）

**Venice** ['venis] *n.* 威尼斯（意大利东北部港市）

**Florence** ['flɔːrəns] *n.* 佛罗伦萨（意大利中部城市）

**vaporetto** [,væpə'retəu] *n.*（运河中载客的）交通汽艇

**renaissance** [ri'neisəns] *n.* 文艺复兴，文艺复兴时期

**Rome** [rəum] *n.* 罗马（意大利首都）

**chianti** [ki'ænti] *n.* 意大利基安蒂葡萄酒

**perch** [pəːtʃ] *vt.* 栖息；位于

**coliseum** [,kɔli'siəm] *n.* 大剧场

**fountain** ['fauntin] *n.* 喷泉

**Pisa** ['piːzə] *n.* 比萨（意大利西北部城市）

**autostrada** [ɔ'təustrɑːda] *n.* 意大利的高速公路

**descent** [di'sent] *n.* 降下，降落

**mustard** ['mʌstəd] *n.* 芥菜

**panoramic** [,pænə'ræmik] *a.* 全景的

**cabaret** ['kæbərei] *n.* 酒店或夜总会的卡巴莱歌舞表演

**perfumery** [pə'fjuːməri] *n.* 香料店

 # Phrases and Expressions

start from scratch　从零开始，从头做起
pay attention to　关心，注意
first of all　首先

in proportion to　与……成比例，与……相称
instead of　代替
in fact　事实上

concentrate on　集中，全神贯注于

rather than　而不

check in　入住酒店

European Pass　欧洲通票

the River Rhine　莱茵河（源出瑞士境内的阿尔卑斯山，贯穿西欧多国）

Black Forest　黑林山（在德国西南部）

Rhine Falls　莱茵河瀑布

Lake Lucerne　卢塞恩湖

Swarovski crystal museum　施华洛世奇水晶博物馆

St. Marks Square　圣马可广场（意大利威尼斯市）

River Arno　亚诺河（意大利中部河流）

St. Peters　圣彼得大教堂

the Roman Formum　古罗马广场

Jungfrau　少女峰（瑞士）

Trummebach falls　特鲁蒙巴奇瀑布（意大利）

the Swiss Alps　瑞士阿尔卑斯山脉

Eiffel Tower　埃菲尔铁塔（法国巴黎）

Palace of Versailles　凡尔赛宫（法国）

Champs Elysees　爱丽舍宫（法国巴黎的总统官邸）

the Appennines　亚平宁山脉

Place de Concorde　协和广场(法国巴黎）

Arc de Triomphe　凯旋门（法国巴黎）

Louvre museum　罗浮宫国立艺术博物馆（法国巴黎）

the River Seine　塞纳河（法国北部河流）

# Notes

**1** You also need to pay attention not only to dates, but days of the week, since some attractions are closed on particular days of the week.

本句中 since some attractions are closed on particular days of the week 是一个表示原因的状语从句，修饰谓语 need。since 表示一种附带的原因，或者表示已知的、显然的理由，意思是"既然"。请看下例：

Since you say so, I suppose it is true.

既然你这么说，我想这是真的。

**2** However, do not attempt to travel all around the country nor to cover several countries.

本句中，nor 的意思是"也不，不"，语气比 neither 强。请看下例：

"I can't swim." "Nor can she."

"我不会游泳。""她也不会。"

**3** Concentrate on some parts rather than choosing isolated ones or extreme ends.

本句中 rather than 用作连词，意为"宁肯…… 而不"、"不是……而是"，其后面的成分表示否定概念，所连接的可以是名词、名词短语、代词、动词不定式、副词、形容词等，被连接的成分应在词性上保持一致。请看下例：

He is a writer rather than a teacher.

与其说他是个教师，不如说他是个作家。

We are to blame rather than they.

该受责备的是我们，而不是他们。

She wrote rather than telephoned.

她写了信，而不是打了电话。

## Exercises

**EX. 5** **Answer the following questions.**

1. If you would like to start from scratch, what do you think of first?
2. As you make an itinerary, what are you advised to do first?
3. What are some other things you should consider while making an itinerary?
4. What would you like to do last?
5. If I have 60 days in the Middle East, where does the author advice me to go?

**EX. 6** **Decide whether the following statements are *true* or *false*.**

1. You also need to pay attention not only to dates, but days of the week, since some attractions are closed on particular days of the week.
2. The air ticket is relatively cheap in proportion to the number of days you stay there.
3. A sum of 17,000¥ saving can be enough for three months trip to travel around in Africa, but definitely inadequate for European trip.
4. However, do not attempt to travel all around the country nor to cover several countries.
5. If you have 30 days, it is worth to go farther like Europe, Africa, America, South America, the Middle East or New Zealand, etc.

## Part Four    Skill Training

### Forms

A good itinerary must have a few factors: (1) Be knowledgeable about the destination and clients. (2) Make it as interesting as possible. (3) Be concise and informative. (4) Streamline your draft several times and improve it through actual use. Here is a form from the Internet. It may help you to make a good itinerary.

**Request form for itinerary by post or E-mail**

**I would like to receive itineraries by** | E-mail ▼ |

(please use the "tab" button to move through details below)

**First name**

**Last name**

**E-mail**

(details below are only necessary if you want info via post)

**Street address**

206

Address (cont.) [                                    ]

City [                                    ]

State/Province [                              ]

Zip/Postal code [        ]

Country [                            ]

**Please select from the following tours available for 2016 and we will send detailed itineraries.**

### Australia and New Zealand

**Queensland**
- ☐ South East Queensland
- ☐ Carnarvon Girraween
- ☐ Western QLD & Gulf
- ☐ North Queensland Coast

**Northern Territory**
- ☐ Alice to Uluru
- ☐ Top End

**Western Australia**
- ☐ The Kimberley
- ☐ WA Wildflowers

### Europe

- Southern Italian Sojourn
- ☐ Goreme-Gallipoli (Turkey)
- ☐ Northern Spain

- ☐ Hiking UK/Ireland
- ☐ Berlin to Blumau

- ☐ Heart of Italy
- ☐ Swiss Sojourn

### North America

- ☐ Yosemite to Utah
- ☐ Yellowstone to Yoho

- ☐ Seascapes & lava lands
- ☐ Yukon to Alaska

- ☐ Canadian Rockies

### Would you like to be on our postal mailing list?

You will receive our full tour program in November each year + quarterly newsletters by post
○ Yes   ○ No
(please make sure you have completed address details above)

### Would you like to receive our E-mail newsletter?

You will receive our regular "walking & adventure travel" E-mail newsletter (currently being sent every 3 months)
○ Yes   ○ No
(please make sure you have completed E-mail details above)

Newsletter Format: [ html ▼ ]

Do you have any comments or questions?

[                                                        ]

[ Submit Form ] [ Reset Form ]

## Practical Writing

### The Best of China Tourv

14 DAYS/13 NIGHTS—Beijing/Xi'an/Shanghai/Suzhou/Hangzhou/Guilin/Guangzhou

### Day 1　Arrive in Beijing

Welcome to Beijing, capital of China. On arrival, you will be met by our CITS guide and transferred to your hotel.

### Day 2　Beijing

Morning tour to Tian'anmen Square, located in the heart of the capital, and the Forbidden City—one of the greatest feats of ancient Chinese architecture. Afternoon sightseeing includes Summer Palace—a former summer resort area of the royal family, or a visit to the Temple of Heaven where the emperors prayed for good harvests. Enjoy the famous Beijing roast dinner in the evening.

### Day 3　Beijing

Full day excursion to the Great Wall—the landmark of China. It is one of the most amazing feats of manmade construction on earth visible from outer space. After lunch, a drive to the Ming Tombs along the sacred way with giant marble figures and animals guarding the tomb area for deceased emperors of Ming Dynasty. Beijing Opera or acrobatic performance will be attended in the evening.

### Day 4　Beijing-Xi'an by air

Take a 1.5 hour flight to Xi'an, the great ancient capital and the eastern end of the Silk Road. City tour begins with a visit to the Big Wild Goose Pagoda which was built in 652 A.D. It contains a large volume of Buddhist scripture which were obtained from India by the eminent monk Xuanzang.

### Day 5　Xi'an

A full day visit includes the unparalleled highlight of an excursion to the incredible Terra-Cotta Warriors and Horses at the Tomb of Qin Shi Huang, the first emperor of unified China. Added highlights are visits to the Huaqing Hot Spring—a former resort area especially for the emperor and royal family and a visit to the Banpo Village—the remains of a neolithic village dating back 6,000 years. Primitive tools and household utensils are displayed in the Banpo Museum. Tonight enjoy Tang Dynasty Dinner & Show.

### Day 6　Xi'an-Shanghai by air

Depart Xi'an for Shanghai, the bustling commercial heart of China. City tour begins with a stroll along the lively waterfront "The Bund". An acrobatic is shown for your evening entertainment.

### Day 7　Shanghai

Sightseeing the classical Yu Yuan, the Jade Buddha Temple where two rare jade statues of

Shikyamuni Buddha are treasured, and the Children's Palace.

### Day 8 Shanghai-Suzhou by train

A morning train ride takes you to Suzhou, the famous garden city. City tour begins with visiting the Garden of Master of Fishing Nets and the Silk Reeling Factory.

### Day 9 Suzhou-Hangzhou by train

Morning tour the Lingering Garden, the ancient Water Gate and the famous Silk Embroidery Research Institute. Proceed to Hangzhou, the "Paradise on Earth" by train in the afternoon. Transfer to your hotel.

### Day 10 Hangzhou

Today's tours starts with a cruise on the scenic West Lake, the highlight in the city, followed by trip to Lingyin Monastery and a Tea Production Village.

### Day 11 Hangzhou-Guilin by air

Fly to Guilin—a charming city with magnificent peaks and rivers, beautiful rocks and fantastic caves. Sightseeing begins with visits to the most famous Reed Flute Caves, Elephant Trunk Hill and Fubo Hill up where you can climb for the panoramic view of the city.

### Day 12 Guilin

Enjoy a morning cruise down the winding Li River to Yangshuo, viewing the spectacular scenery as it reflects in the crystal clear water. You can explore Yangshuo a small town with many stalls selling traditional Chinese articles. Return to Guilin by coach for dinner.

### Day 13 Guilin-Guangzhou by air

Fly to Guangzhou, the Southern gateway to China. City tour features the Memorial Hall of Dr. Sun Yatsen, the Six Banyan Pogada and Temple and the Five-Ram Statue.

### Day 14 Your journey comes to an end this morning as you board an express train for Hong Kong.

👤 **Simulate and create** ▶ Look at the sample carefully and try to make a 14-day tour itinerary: Beijing-Xi'an-Chengdu-Yangtze River Cruise-Shanghai.


## Part Five  Related Information

| Text | Notes |
|---|---|
| **Sightseeing** | |
| When possible, travel with another person when sightseeing or shopping, particularly[1] at night. | [1] 特别是，尤其是 |
| Be aware of your surroundings and trust your instincts[2]. Do not feel embarrassed[3] to leave an uncomfortable situation. | [2] 本能 [3] 使难堪，使为难 |

| | |
|---|---|
| Walk with purpose and project an assertive[4] and business-like image[5]. Criminals[6] will be discouraged[7] if you do not appear vulnerable[8] or easily intimidated[9]. | [4] 自信的<br>[5] 形象<br>[6] 罪犯<br>[7] 气馁 |
| Select sightseeing companies and guides carefully. Make sure they are legitimate[10]. Check with your hotel staff for recommendations[11]. | [8] 易受攻击的<br>[9] 威胁的，恫吓的<br>[10] 合法的<br>[11] 建议，劝告 |
| When asking for directions, first look for a police officer or another public employee (i.e., bus driver), or go into a nearby business. | |
| Do not carry large amounts of cash. Use traveler's checks and debit ATM[12] cards. Keep a record of traveler's check numbers, Credit Card numbers, photocopy[13] of passport and other valuable documents separate from originals[14]. | [12] 自动取款机<br>[13] 影印件<br>[14] 原件 |
| If you must carry a large amount of cash, separate it from your purse or wallet and carry it inside clothing. | |
| Be careful and alert when cashing traveler's checks, or using a cash machine. Never let someone see how much money you have in your wallet, or where you keep your money. | |
| Don't wear expensive jewelry[15] and watches when out sightseeing. If you must wear it, wear it inside your clothing. | [15] 珠宝首饰 |
| Pickpockets[16] are often attracted to crowded places. They often work in teams of two or three; one may create a distraction[17] while the other one lifts your wallet. Be aware of someone who bumps[18], shoves[19] or gets too close. | [16] 扒手<br>[17] 分心<br>[18] 碰（伤),撞（破）<br>[19] 推挤，猛推 |
| Don't tempt[20] a thief by leaving your purse or wallet unattended[21]. It only takes a second to grab[22] it. | [20] 诱惑，引诱<br>[21] 没人照顾<br>[22] 抢夺，攫取 |
| Learn to carry your purse or wallet safely. Purses should be closed, held in front of your body, with your arm across it. Wallets should be carried a front pants pocket or in an interior jacket pocket. | |
| Aggressive[23] panhandling[24] is illegal in Seattle. If someone obstructs[25] or intimidates you, and aggressively begs for money, you do not have to give them money, and you can report this offense[26] to the police department. Please do not encourage or reward panhandling. | [23] 好斗的<br>[24] 街头乞讨<br>[25] 阻挠，妨碍<br>[26] 进攻，冒犯 |

# Part Six  Guide to World Famous Sight

| Text | Notes |
|---|---|
| **Spain Culture—Bullfighting** | |
| ***Origins and History of Bullfighting***[1] | [1] 斗牛 |
| Bullfighting is certainly one of the best-known—although at the same time most controversial[2]—Spanish popular customs. This Fiesta[3] could not exist without the toro bravo, a species of bull of an | [2] 有争议的<br>[3] 祭奠，圣日 |

ancient race that is only conserved[4] in Spain. Formerly this bull's forebears[5], the primitive urus[6], were spread out over wide areas of the world. Many civilizations revered[7] them, the bull cults[8] on the Greek island of Crete are very well known. The Bible tells of sacrifices[9] of bulls in honor of divine[10] justice.

[4] 保存
[5] 祖先
[6] 野牛
[7] 尊敬，崇敬
[8] 祭仪，礼拜式
[9] 祭品
[10] 神圣的

Bulls also played an important role in the religious ceremonies of the Iberian tribes[11] living in Spain in prehistoric[12] times. The origins of the plaza de toros (bullring) are probably not the Roman amphitheatres[13] but rather the Celtic-Iberian temples where those ceremonies were held. Near Numancia in the province of Soria one of them has survived, and it is supposed that bulls were sacrificed to the gods there.

[11] 伊比利亚部落
[12] 史前的
[13] 圆形剧场

While religious bull cults[14] go back to Iberians, it was Greek and Roman influences that converted it into a spectacle[15]. In the 18th century this tradition was more or less abandoned and the poorer population invented bullfighting on foot. Francisco Romero was a key figure in laying down the rules for the new sport.

[14]（牛）崇拜
[15] 奇观，景象

### What a Corrida[16] is about

[16] 斗牛

If you are not familiar with corridas de toreros (bullfights), here is what happens in order, so that you can decide by yourself whether you want to see one when you are in Spain. A corrida starts with the paseillo, when everybody involved in the bullfight enters the ring and presents themselves to the president and public.

Two persons on horseback look up to the president's box and symbolically ask for the keys. Behind that door the bulls are waiting. When the door opens and the first bull enters the spectacle starts for real. It consists of three parts, called tercios ("thirds"), the separation of which is signaled with a bugle[17] call. There are three toreros—bullfighters[18] (the better-known word "toreador" is actually never used in modern Spanish) in each corrida, each being allotted[19] two bulls. In the first tercio the bullfighter uses the capote[20], a rather large cape[21] that is a pinkish-mauve[22] color on one side and yellow on the other.

[17] 喇叭
[18] 斗牛士
[19] 分配
[20] 斗篷
[21] 披肩
[22] 紫红色

Now the two picadors[23] enter on horseback, armed with a sort of lance[24]. The second tercio is la suerte de banderillas. Three banderilleros must stick a pair of banderillas[25] into the charging bull's back. In the final suerte suprema the bullfighter uses the muleta[26], a small red cloth draped from a stick. He has to show his mastery to dominate the bull, and to establish an artistic symbiosis between man and beast. The corrida ends with the torero using his sword to kill the bull.

[23] 骑马斗牛士
[24] 标枪，长矛器具
[25] 斗牛用的短标枪
[26] 斗牛士用的红布

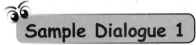

# Unit 12

## Shopping

**Part One** **Dialogues**

### Sample Dialogue 1

👤 **Situation** ▶ Teller is going shopping in a department store in Beijing and a shop assistant is serving him.

| | |
|---|---|
| **Shop Assistant**: | Good morning. May I help you, sir? |
| **Teller**: | I'm just looking around right now; thank you... May I see this sweater? |
| **Shop Assistant**: | Yes, certainly. Here is a nice-looking one. |
| **Teller**: | Yes. It is attractive. I like the design, but I think the color is... I am quite conservative. Let me see that gray and blue one. |
| **Shop Assistant**: | This one? |
| **Teller**: | Yes. How much does it cost? |
| **Shop Assistant**: | 1,480 yuan. |
| **Teller**: | 1,480? It is nice, but that's too expensive for a sweater. |
| **Shop Assistant**: | Well. Touch it and you will know it is pure wool. The price is fair, sir! It's a famous brand. It stands wear and will never lose shape. |
| **Teller**: | It's well beyond the range I can accept. Do you have discount? |
| **Shop Assistant**: | I'm afraid I don't. You see it's the latest fashion and it sells like hot cakes. |
| **Teller**: | OK. I'll take it. By the way, will this be cash or charge? |
| **Shop Assistant**: | Both cash and charge are acceptable. |
| **Teller**: | Yes. That'll be fine. Here is the money. |
| **Shop Assistant**: | Thank you. Goodbye, Sir. |
| **Teller**: | Goodbye. |

## Sample Dialogue 2

**Situation** ▶ Teller is going to finish his tour of China. He will go back home. Now he wants to buy his wife a present.

**Shop Assistant**: Good morning, sir. Anything I can do for you?

**Teller**: I'm trying to find a gift for my wife.

**Shop Assistant**: How do you like the blouse? Here are some latest styles. Are you interested?

**Teller**: I like this one. But I found it difficult to decide on the right design.

**Shop Assistant**: I recommend this simple design to you. I bet your wife will like it.

**Teller**: That is a good idea.

**Shop Assistant**: Do you think it OK?

**Teller**: Everything except the color. Do you have a lighter red? The dark blue doesn't fit my wife's complexion.

**Shop Assistant**: Yes. Here are two red ones in different shades.

**Teller**: This color is just what I've been expecting. I'll take this one, medium size?

**Shop Assistant**: Yes, please wait a minute.

**Teller**: How much is it?

**Shop Assistant**: 360 yuan. I'm pleased that you like it.

**Teller**: Have you got a nice case to go with it?

**Shop Assistant**: Yes. I'll get one for you. Bye-bye.

**Teller**: Bye-bye.

## Useful Expressions

1. How much in all, please?
   请问总共是多少钱？

2. How many dollars do I owe you?
   我该付您多少美元？

3. It's nice, but it's too expensive for a hat.
   帽子倒是挺好的，但就是太贵了。

4. Can you allow a higher discount?
   折扣能再大些吗？

5. Ten percent discount is the farthest we can do.
   我们最多只能打9折。

6. Does the price include the sales tax?
   这个价格包括销售税吗？

7. I don't think it's the rock-bottom price. Can you lower it any more?
   我想这可能不是最低价吧，能降低些吗？

8. May I ask what size you wear?

请问您穿多大尺码的？

9. I want one pair of large size, two pairs of medium size and three pairs of small size.

我想买 1 双大号的、2 双中号的、3 双小号的。

10. Unfortunately，the size you want is not available.

非常遗憾，我们没有您要的尺码。

11. It's marvelous that the dress suits me.

这套衣服很合身，真是太棒了。

## Task Dialogue 1

**Situation ▶** You are shopping in a department store in New York. You want to buy yourself a jacket. A shop assistant is serving you.

## Task Dialogue 2

**Situation ▶** You will finish your tour of New York and you are going to buy your parents gifts. Now you are asking the information from a shop assistant.

## Part Two  Text A

### Shopping in China

Shopping is probably one of the best reasons for visiting China. This bargain-hunters paradise offers a tremendous selection of high-quality arts and crafts, including porcelain, ceramics, cloisonné, silks, embroideries, antiques and much more. The low cost of labor in China makes for incredible bargains by western standards.

If you're traveling with a tour group, your guide will no doubt take you to the factory gift shops or "Friendship Stores" at the end of each tour. In fact, he or she will generally discourage you from buying souvenirs from street hawkers, by saying that the products are of inferior quality. While this is true, if you're just looking for some token souvenirs, you can get some real bargains, at a fraction of the cost from that of the official stores. In some cases, items offered by the street vendors cannot be found anywhere else. But remember—there are no warranties, all sales are final, and they do not accept American Express!

The Friendship Stores were originally opened only to foreigners and used special Chinese money. Nowadays, they are just a chain of department stores that offer a wide variety of over-priced goods. The advantage of shopping in the Friendship Stores is that the prices are clearly marked and there will generally be someone who speaks English there. They will accept cash, traveler's check and major charge cards and will arrange for overseas shipping on heavy items. However, shopping in the street markets are a lot more fun, particularly if you enjoy haggling and saving money.

### What to Buy

China offers a wide range of local products that are found nowhere else in the world. They include silk, embroidery works, tea, cloisonné, jade, carvings, pottery, jewelry, carpets, papercuts, herbal medicines, cultural relics, antiques, calligraphy, paintings and more. What you buy will probably depend on where you go and what products are available in the region.

### Art, Calligraphy & Paintings

Traditional paintings, calligraphy and scrolls can be purchased from the Friendship Stores. The selection is surprisingly good and the quality is usually quite good, although the prices are generally higher than the markets and shops.

Regional art produced by young local artists is becoming increasingly popular with tourists. Brightly colored paintings depicting rural scenes are known as "Farmers Paintings" and can be purchased in Xi'an. Kunming, Dali and Lijiang are also known for their local art. The prices for original art are quite reasonable and make good souvenirs or gifts for family and friends.

Shanghai and Beijing are probably the best places to look for contemporary paintings.

### Antiques

Popular antiques in China range from Qing Dynasty artifacts (such as jade, porcelain, snuff bottles and opium boxes) to relics of the colonial era. Shanghai street markets are the best places to look for colonial souvenirs, which include such items as old telephones, cameras, watches, radios, photo albums, books, toys, typewriters, cigarette cases, desk lamps, posters, suitcases and more.

However, be aware that while many antiques in China are genuine, some are simply reproductions. Traditional furniture may be made from old wood and sold to unsuspecting tourists as the real thing. Chinese law will only allow certain antiques to be taken out of the country—those dated after 1797 (during the reign of Emperor Jiaqing of the Qing dynasty). Genuine antiques should carry a red wax seal indicating that it is authentic and can be exported from China. Make sure that you have the required receipts to show customs officials on your departure; otherwise, your antiques may be confiscated.

### Textile

China is the place to purchase genuine pure silk. Suzhou, located near Shanghai, produces some of the best silk embroidery in China. The factory stores and Friendship Stores in Suzhou offer an impressive range of good quality clothes, sheets, pillowcases and Chinese embroidery. However, the price of silk has increased considerably in recent years due to higher quality and the strong interest from tourists.

Cashmere scarves and sweaters are mainly produced in Mongolia, so are best purchased in the Inner Mongolian capital of Hohhot or in Beijing.

Many of the best textiles are made by national minorities from such areas as Yunnan and Guangxi. Hand-woven shawls are available in the street markets or shops of Kunming, Dali or Lijiang.

## Tea & Teapots

Chinese tea and teapot sets make excellent gifts to take home. Hangzhou Longjing (Dragon Well) green tea is considered the best green tea in China. Pu Erh is a fine red tea from Yunnan Province. Every city has their own small teashops and teahouses where many varieties of teas can be purchased.

## Clothing

Modern clothing can be found in the larger cities such as Beijing, Shanghai, Guangzhou and Hong Kong. Designer-label clothing, either genuine or fakes, are available everywhere. The street markets and shops have just about every major designer-label you may want. Just be aware that the imitations are definitely inferior in quality, but they may be good for a laugh as long as you don't overpay for them. There is saying that clothing is probably one of the "best buys" in China because of the low labor costs.

## Where to Buy

You should definitely check out the local department stores, rather than just rely on the Friendship Stores. The prices will generally be lower than the "tourist" stores and you will get a dose of real life in China. Just remember that the clothing may only be available in Chinese sizes, which are much smaller than western sizes.

If you're on a tour, check out the merchandise at the factory stores, where the prices are often less than at the Friendship Stores. Bear in mind that most stores offer commissions to the tour guides, so don't be surprised if your guide encourages you to shop there. Unless you're a true shopaholic, you will soon be numbed by all the merchandise available.

With arrival of the new entrepreneur in China, you will see many small shops and street hawkers at all the major tourist spots, trying to separate you from your hard-earned dollar. If you're willing to haggle with them, you can often come away with some real bargains. The trick is to determine what you're willing to pay, and even then, it will probably be too much. Never pay the asking price!

Hong Kong is a story unto itself. This used to be a favorite shopping Mecca for tourists from around the world, but it is no longer a "bargain center". Prices of cameras and electronic goods are roughly the same as those in most western countries. The big advantage is in the variety of goods available here. It is said that "If you can't find it here, then you don't need it." Pick up a free copy of Shopping in Hong Kong, from the Hong Kong Tourist Association, and head for the markets.

## Things to Shop for in Beijing

Antiques, books, furs, suede, cashmere, hand-embroidered linen, rugs, carpets, jade, jewelry, name chops, porcelain, clothing, and regional arts and crafts.

### Things to Shop for in Shanghai

Silk products (handkerchiefs, shirts, dresses, jackets, pajamas), silk embroidery, cloisonné, porcelain, vases, tea, and scroll paintings.

### Things to Shop for in Southwest China

Precious and semi-precious stones, marble, tea, arts and crafts by ethnic minorities.

### Things to Shop for in Hong Kong

Camera, computers, CDs, DVDs, electronic gadgets, herbal medicine, suits and clothing.

# New Words

**bargain-hunter** ['bɑːgin 'hʌntə] *n.* 到处找便宜货的人

**paradise** ['pærədais] *n.* 天堂

**tremendous** [trə'mendəs] *a.* 极大的，巨大的

**craft** [krɑːft] *n.* 工艺，手艺

**porcelain** ['pɔːslin] *n.* 瓷器，瓷

**ceramics** [sə'ræmiks] *n.* 制陶术，制陶业

**cloisonné** [klwɑːzɔŋ'nei] *n.* 景泰蓝

**embroidery** [im'brɔidəri] *n.* 刺绣品，刺绣

**antique** [æn'tiːk] *n.* 古物，古董

**discourage** [dis'kʌridʒ] *vt.* 使气馁；阻碍

**souvenir** [ˌsuːvə'niə] *n.* 纪念品

**hawker** ['hɔːkə] *n.* 叫卖小贩

**inferior** [in'fiəriə] *a.* 下等的，下级的；差的，次的

**token** ['təukən] *a.* 象征的，表意的

**warranty** ['wɔrənti] *n.*（正当）理由，（合理）根据

**over-priced** ['əuvəpraist] *a.* 定价过高的

**haggle** ['hægl] *vi.* 讨价还价

**carving** ['kɑːviŋ] *n.* 雕刻品，雕刻

**pottery** ['pɔtəri] *n.* 陶器，陶器制品

**papercut** ['peipəkʌt] *n.* 剪纸

**calligraphy** [kə'ligrəfi] *n.* 书法

**scroll** [skrəul] *n.* 卷轴，卷形物

**surprisingly** [sə'praiziŋli] *ad.* 令人惊讶地

**depict** [di'pikt] *vt.* 描述，描写

**reasonable** ['riːznəbl] *a.* 合理的，有道理的

**contemporary** [kən'tempərəri] *a.* 当代的，同时代的

**opium** ['əupiəm] *n.* 鸦片

**colonial** [kə'ləuniəl] *a.* 殖民的，殖民地的

**album** ['ælbəm] *n.* 集邮本，照相簿，签名纪念册

**reproduction** [ˌriːprə'dʌkʃən] *n.* 再现；复制品

**reign** [rein] *n.* 统治，朝代

**genuine** ['dʒenjuin] *a.* 真实的，真正的

**authentic** [ɔː'θentik] *a.* 可信的

**confiscate** ['kɔnfiˌskeit] *vt.* 没收，充公，查抄

**textile** ['tekˌstail] *n.* 纺织品

**purchase** ['pəːtʃəs] *vt.* 买，购买

**pillowcase** ['piləuˌkeis] *n.* 枕头套

**cashmere** ['kæʃˌmiə] *n.* 开司米，山羊绒

**minority** [mai'nɔrəti] *n.* 少数；少数民族

**hand-woven** [hænd 'wəuvən] *n.* 手工织物

**shawl** [ʃɔːl] *n.* 披肩，围巾

**fake** [feik] *n.* 假货

**imitation** [ˌimi'teiʃən] *n.* 模仿，效法；赝品，仿造物

**overpay** [ˌəuvə'pei] *vt.* 付款过多

**miscellaneous** [misə'leiniəs] *a.* 各种各样混在一起的，混杂的

**memorabilia** [ˌmemərə'biliə] *n.* 值得记忆的事物，纪念品

**badge** [bædʒ] *n.* 徽章，证章

**mug** [mʌg] *n.* 大杯子

**merchandise** ['məːtʃəndaiz] *n.* 商品，货物

**numb** [nʌm] *vt.* 使麻木

**commission** [kə'miʃən] *n.* 佣金，回扣

**shopaholic** [ʃɔpə'hɔlik] *n.* 购物狂

**entrepreneur** [ˌɔntrəprə'nəː] *n.* 企业家；主办人

**unto** ['ʌntuː] *prep.* 到，向，直到

**mecca** ['mekə] *n.* 发祥地，圣地

**suede** [sweid] *n.* 绒面革

 ## Phrases and Expressions

make for  有利于，对……有益，支持

Friendship Stores  友谊商场

discourage sb. from doing sth.  劝止某人做某事

a fraction of  一小部分

a wide range of  范围广的，大范围的

depend on  依靠，取决于，因……而定

be popular with  受……欢迎，在……间名声好

be known for  因……而著名

look for  寻找

be made from  由……制成

be taken out of  带出

be made by  由……制造

check out  核实，最后检查

rely on  依赖，依靠，信赖

a dose of  一回，一次，一番

bear in mind  牢记

pick up  拾起，崛起

snuff bottle  鼻烟壶

electronic gadget  小家电

## Notes

**1** This bargain-hunters paradise offers a tremendous selection of high-quality arts and crafts, including porcelain, ceramics, cloisonné, silks, embroideries, antiques and much more.

　　本句中，including 是介词，意思是"包括……，包含……"。反义词是 excluding。请看下例：

There are six people, including three women.

有六个人，包括三个妇女。

**2** While this is true, if you're just looking for some token souvenirs, you can get some real bargains, at a fraction of the cost from that of the official stores.

　　本句中，while 引导的是条件状语从句，突出对比主句和从句所表示的两种差异情况。that 指代 the cost。

**3** Shanghai street markets are the best places to look for colonial souvenirs, which include such items as old telephones, cameras, watches, radios, photo albums, books, toys, typewriters, cigarette cases, desk lamps, posters, suitcases and more.

　　本句中 which 引导的是非限定性定语从句，修饰 souvenirs。such as 是介词短语，可分开，意为"诸如，像……这类"，后跟名词。请看下例：

I have never seen such a bright student as she.

我从来都没见过像她这么聪明的学生。

**4** Genuine antiques should carry a red wax seal indicating that it is authentic and can be exported from China.

　　本句中，indicating that it is authentic and can be exported from China 是现在分词短语，作定语，修饰和限定 a red wax seal。that it is authentic and can be exported from China 作现在分词 indicating 的宾语。

**5** Cashmere scarves and sweaters are mainly produced in Mongolia, so are best purchased in the Inner Mongolian capital of Hohhot or in Beijing.

　　本句中"so + be 动词"是一种常用的倒装结构，表示前面肯定句中所说的情况也适用于其他某人或某物，表示肯定意义。so 后面也可以跟情态动词或助动词。请看下例：

They will travel to England. So will we.

他们要去英国旅行，我们也要去。

He can swim. So can his brother.

他会游泳，他弟弟也会。

I work in this company. So does he.

我在这家公司工作，他也在。

**6** Unless you're a true shopaholic, you will soon be numbed by all the merchandise available.

　　本句中，unless 是从属连词，用于引导条件状语从句，意思是"除非，如果……不"，unless 本身具有否定意义，因此所引导的从句谓语动词用肯定式，相当于 if…not。请看下例：

Don't come to my office unless I telephone you.

如果我不给你打电话就不要到我办公室来。

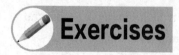 **Exercises**

**EX. 1** **Answer the following questions.**

1. Why do visitors like to do shopping in China?

2. What are the advantages of shopping in the Friendship Stores?

3. If the visitors want to buy paintings, calligraphy and scrolls, where they should go?

4. Do you know the Chinese law about taking antiques out of China?

5. If you plan to travel in southwest China and Tibet, what would you like to buy?

**EX. 2** **Write out the English words according to the definitions given below.**

| definitions | words |
|---|---|
| people looking for things at a low price | |
| (cups, dishes, etc., made of ) thin shiny material of very fine quality, which is produced by baking a clay mixture | |
| (a piece of furniture, jewelry, etc., that is) old and therefore becoming rare valuable | |
| to try to prevent (an action, or someone from doing something) esp. by showing disfavor | |
| to seize (private property) officially and without payment, esp. as a punishment | |
| (an amount of ) money, usu. related to the value of goods sold, paid to the salesman who sold them | |
| goods bought and sold in business; commercial wares | |
| made up of a variety of parts or ingredients | |
| to deprive of confidence, hope, or spirit | |
| something reproduced, especially in the faithfulness of its resemblance to the form and elements of the original | |
| a token of remembrance; a memento | |

**EX. 3** **Complete the following sentences with appropriate words or expressions from the text.**

1. The company has hired dozen of academic consultants on _____ matters.

2. Having faster computers would _____ a more efficient system.

3. The North African coast _____ increasingly _____ British holidaymakers.

4. Please _____ your fruit and vegetables' weight at the local supermarket.

5. _____ wet leaves on the line, this train will arrive an hour late.

6. He didn't do the jog very well, but _____ that he was ill at the time.

7. He _____ straight _____ home after he finished his work.

**EX. 4** **Translate the following sentences into Chinese.**

1. The low cost of labor in China makes for incredible bargains by western standards.

2. In fact, he or she will generally discourage you from buying souvenirs from street hawkers, by saying that the products are of inferior quality.

3. What you buy will probably depend on where you go and what products are available in the region.

4. Just be aware that the imitations are definitely inferior in quality, but they may be good for a laugh as long as you don't overpay for them.

5. If you're willing to haggle with them, you can often come away with some real bargains.

## Part Three    Text B

## Shopping in the USA

Most people visiting the USA enjoy shopping for bargains. Some of the most popular items for shoppers from other countries are American whiskey, children's clothing, trendy jeans, superior bed linens and lush bath towels. You could find many shopping bargains provided you know where to shop and how to take advantage of competitive sales.

### Department Stores

Department stores are large shopping malls which offer a wide range of merchandise including fashion clothing, house ware, appliances, luggage and jewelry. Usually the merchandise offered by these stores is branded, good quality and is of the latest fashion.

Department stores do not offer merchandise at bargain prices. However they frequently feature seasonal sales with attractive discounts. During these periods you could buy a high quality product at bargain prices.

Big Christmas sales are held from December 26th to mid-January. Winter merchandise goes on sale during February. Additionally they have special promotions and clearance sales all through the year.

Most of the big department stores are a part of national wide chain and can be found in many cities. Some well-known national department stores are: Lord & Taylor, Hecht's, Strawbridge's, Kaufman's, Filene's, Macy's, Bloomingdale's, Burdine's, Lazarus, Rich's, Nordstrom's, Sak's, Dayton-Hudson's, Marshall's and Bergdorf-Goodman.

### General Merchandise Stores

Sears and JC Penny are the two large national chains with stores all over USA. Though these stores are similar to the department stores, they do not offer high fashion or prestige merchandise. Instead they offer good quality merchandise at affordable prices. They are well known for their children's clothing, home appliances, house wares and domestic appliances. Sears is famous for its selection of tools and lawn and garden merchandise.

### *Discount Stores*

Discount stores are very popular places for shopping. They sell good quality merchandise at affordable prices and lower quality merchandise at very low prices. You may find inexpensive merchandise at a discount store provided you are not looking for latest fashions and best brands.

Some national discount chains with stores across the USA are: K-Mart, Wal-Mart, Target and Caldor.

### *Outlet Malls*

Outlet malls, also known as factory outlets, are the stores where high quality and branded merchandise are offered at discount rates ranging from 20% to 40%. The merchandise offered by these outlet malls has minor manufacturing flaws or last season/previous year remainders.

Many of the top brands like Levi's, Ralph Lauren, Timberland, and Pioneer can be found in most outlet malls and are often a bargain hunter's paradise.

### *New York City-Shopping*

There's something for everyone in every price range in New York. Do you have a sudden yearning for bootleg Velvet Underground tracks? Head to Other Music. Looking for vintage? Resurrection can set you up nicely. How about a poster from Woody Allen's *Manhattan*? Movie Star News is your destination.

The city whets acquisitive appetites with widely various shopping experiences. For every bursting department store, there's a minimalist boutique; for every nationally familiar brand, there's a local favorite. National chains often make their New York stores something special, with unique sales environments and merchandise.

One of Manhattan's biggest shopping lures is the bargain—a temptation fueled by Loehmann's, H&M, and other discount. Hawkers of not-so-real Rolex watches and Kate Spade bags are stationed at street corners, even on Madison Avenue, and Canal Street is lined with counterfeit Gucci logos and Burberry plaid. There are uptown thrift shops where socialites send their castoffs, and downtown spots where the fashion crowd turns in last week's super trendy must-haves. And of course, thousands of eyes train on the cycles of sales.

Antiquing is fine art in Manhattan. Goods include everything from rarefied museum-quality to wacky and affordable. Premier shopping areas are on Madison Avenue North of 57th Street, and East 60th Street between 2nd and 3rd Avenues, where more than 20 shops, dealing in everything from 18th-century French furniture to art deco lighting fixtures, cluster on one block. Around West 11th and 12th Streets, between University Place and Broadway, a tantalizing array of settees, bedsteads, and rocking chairs can be seen in the windows of about two dozen dealers, many of whom have trade-only signs on their doors; a card from your architect or decorator, however, may get you inside. Finally, for 20th-century furniture and fixtures, head south of

Houston Street, especially along Lafayette Street. Most dealers are closed on Sunday. Many small dealers cluster in three antiques "malls".

New York is one of the world's major auctioning centers, where royal antiques, ancient art, and pop-culture memorabilia all have their moment on the block. Look for announcements in the *New York Times*, or in the weekly magazines *Time Out New York* and *New York*. If you plan to raise a paddle, be sure to attend the sale preview and review the catalog for price estimates.

 **New Words**

**whiskey** ['wiski] *n.* 威士忌酒

**trendy** ['trendi] *a.* 流行的

**jeans** [dʒi:nz] *n.* 牛仔裤

**linen** ['linin] *n.* 亚麻布，亚麻制品

**lush** [lʌʃ] *a.* 豪华的

**mall** [mɔ:l] *n.* 购物商场，商业街

**ware** [wɛə] *n.* 陶器，器皿

**appliance** [ə'plaiəns] *n.* 用具，器具

**Christmas** ['krisməs] *n.* 圣诞节（纪念耶稣基督诞生的节日，12 月 25 日）

**additionally** [ə'diʃənəli] *ad.* 加之，又

**promotion** [prə'məuʃən] *n.* 促销

**clearance** ['kliərəns] *n.* 清除，清理

**well-known** [wel nəun] *a.* 知名的，大家知道的

**prestige** [pre'sti:ʒ] *n.* 声望，威望，威信

**lawn** [lɔ:n] *n.* 草地，草坪

**manufacturing** [,mænju'fæktʃəriŋ] *a.* 制造业的

**flaw** [flɔ:] *n.* 缺点；裂纹，瑕疵

**yearning** ['jə:niŋ] *n.* 向往

**bootleg** ['bu:t,leg] *a.* 非法制造贩卖的

**velvet** ['velvit] *a.* 天鹅绒的；柔软的，光滑的

**vintage** ['vintidʒ] *n.* 制造年期，葡萄收获期

**resurrection** [,rezə'rekʃən] *n.* 复苏

**poster** ['pəustə] *n.* 海报，招贴

**whet** [wet] *vt.* 磨，磨快；使兴奋

**acquisitive** [ə'kwizətiv] *a.* 想获得的，可学到的

**minimalist** ['miniməlist] *n.* 最低限要求者

**boutique** [bu:'ti:k] *n.* 专卖流行衣服的小商店

**lure** [ljuə] *vt.* 引诱

**temptation** [temp'teiʃən] *n.* 诱惑，诱惑物

**Burberry** ['bə:bəri] *n.* 巴宝莉（英国奢侈品牌）

**plaid** [plæd] *n.* 格子花呢披肩，格子花呢

**thrift** [θrift] *n.* 节俭，节约

**castoff** ['kɑ:stɔ:f] *n.* 废弃物

**wacky** ['wæki] *a.* 古怪的

**cluster** ['klʌstə] *vi.* 丛生，成群

**tantalizing** ['tæntə,laiziŋ] *a.* 非常着急的

**deco** [dei'kəu] *n.* 装饰，装潢（decoration）

**premier** ['premiə] *a.* 第一的，首要的

**array** [ə'rei] *n.* 衣服，大批

**bedstead** ['bed,sted] *n.* 床架

dealer ['di:lə] *n.* 经销商，商人

architect ['ɑːkiˌtekt] *n.* 建筑师

decorator ['dekəˌreitə] *n.* 裱糊匠

auction ['ɔːkʃən] *vt.* 拍卖

catalog ['kætəlɔg] *n.* 目录，目录册

estimate ['estimeit] *vt.* 估计，估价，评估

Hecht's [hekts] *n.* 赫克特百货公司

Strawbridge's ['strɔːbridʒiz] *n.* 斯特劳布里奇百货公司

Sak's [sæks] *n.* 萨克百货公司

Marshall's ['mɑːʃəlz] *n.* 马歇尔百货公司

Sears [siəz] *n.* 西尔斯百货公司

Levi's ['liːvaiz] *n.* 李维斯（美国牛仔裤品牌）

Pioneer [ˌpaiə'niə] *n.* 先锋（日本影音设备品牌）

Loehmann's ['ləumənz] *n.* 洛曼百货公司

Broadway ['brɔːdˌwei] *n.* 纵贯纽约市的大街道，百老汇

K-Mart ['keimɑːt] *n.* K-玛特折扣店

Wal-Mart ['wɔlmɑːt] *n.* 沃尔玛折扣店

 ## Phrases and Expressions

Lord & Taylor  罗德与泰勒百货公司

Dayton-Hudson's  戴顿–赫德森百货公司

Bergdorf-Goodman  伯格多弗–古德曼百货公司

JC Penny  JC 潘尼百货公司

be similar to  与……相似

Target and Caldor  塔格特和考尔德折扣店

Ralph Lauren  拉尔夫·劳伦（美国服装品牌）

Woody Allen's  伍迪·艾伦（美国导演）

H&M  英国服装品牌

Rolex  劳力士（瑞士手表品牌）

Kate Spade  美国时尚品牌

madison avenue  麦迪逊大街

dealing in  做买卖，经营

Houston Street  休斯敦大街

Lafayette Street  拉菲尔大街

*New York Times*  《纽约时报》

*Time Out New York*  《纽约休闲》

*New York*  《纽约周刊》

raise a paddle  提高赌注，叫价

## Notes

**1** You could find many shopping bargains provided you know where to shop and how to take advantage of competitive sales.

本句中，provided you know where to shop and how to take advantage of competitive sales 是一个条件状语从句，provided 是连词，意为"倘若……，只要，在……条件下"。

where to shop and how to take advantage of competitive sales 是一个宾语从句，作 know 的宾语。

**2** Premier shopping areas are on Madison Avenue North of 57th Street, and East 60th Street between 2nd and 3rd Avenues, where more than 20 shops, dealing in everything from 18th-century French furniture to art deco lighting fixtures, cluster on one block.

本 句 中，where more than 20 shops, dealing in everything from 18th-century French furniture to art deco lighting fixtures, cluster on one block 引导的是非限定性定语从句，修饰 avenues。dealing in everything from 18th-century French furniture to art deco lighting fixtures 为现在分词短语作定语，修饰 20 shops。

**3** Around West 11th and 12th Streets, between University Place and Broadway, a tantalizing array of settees, bedsteads, and rocking chairs can be seen in the windows of about two dozen dealers, many of whom have trade-only signs on their doors; a card from your architect or decorator, however, may get you inside.

本句中，many of whom have trade-only signs on their doors 是一个非限定性定语从句，修饰 dealers。

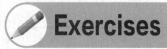 **Exercises**

**EX. 5** **Answer the following questions.**

1. What items do the visitors from the other countries want to buy when they come to the USA?

2. What are the department stores like in the USA?

3. Say something about the discount stores, what are they like?

4. How about the outlet malls? Is it popular in the USA?

5. If you want to buy some antiques, ancient art and etc. in New York City, what should you do?

**EX. 6** **Decide whether the following statements are *true* or *false*.**

1. A lot people from other countries like to buy American whiskey, children's clothing, trendy jeans, superior bed linens and lush bath towels.

2. Department stores always offer merchandise at bargain prices. They feature seasonal sales with attractive discounts. During these periods people could buy a high quality product at high prices.

3. Most of the big department stores are a part of nation wide chain and can be found in many cities. Some well-known national department stores are: Lord & Taylor, Hecht's etc.

4. Sears and JC Penny offer good quality merchandise at affordable prices and they are well known for their children's clothing, home appliances, house wares and domestic appliances.

5. Discount stores sell good quality merchandise at affordable prices and lower quality merchandise at very high prices. You can find expensive merchandise at a discount store provided you are not looking for latest fashions and best brands.

6. New York is one of the world's major auctioning centers, where royal antiques, ancient art, and pop-culture memorabilia all have their moment on the block.

## Part Four  Skill Training

**Forms**

Nowadays, shopping from the Internet is becoming more and more popular, especially for the youth. They like to buy everything through the Internet. There are many famous shopping websites. Here is a form from the Internet. You can try to fill out the form and submit it. Then you make it.

| Amount* | Order* | | ISBN / ISSN* | Author/Title* |
|---|---|---|---|---|
| | Book | ▼ | | |
| | Book | ▼ | | |

Shipping charges are not included.
Back Issues: Subject to availability.

**Personal Data**

| Last name | * | |
|---|---|---|
| First name | * | |
| E-mail address | * | |
| Customer number | | |

**If you fill in your customer number, the remaining fields marked with * are not mandatory.**

| Type of order | * | Private order | ▼ |
|---|---|---|---|
| Phone (optional) | | | |
| Fax (optional) | | | |

## Delivery Address

Institution

**Street** *

**Zip** *

**City** *

**Country** *

## Billing Address

☐ same as the delivery address Institution

**Street** *

**Zip** *

**City** *

**Country** *

## Payment

**Method of payment** * ⦿ Invoice   ○ Credit Card

VAT (optional)

**Customers in EU countries**, please state your VAT identification number if applicable.

**Credit Card** *    Please select a Credit Card

If you order by Credit Card, please note that all data will be sent **without any encryption**.

**Credit Card no.** *          **Expiry date***

## Comments

Submit    **General Conditions of Delivery and Payment**

**Practical Writing**

### How to Write an Information

An information includes notice and announcement. It is a kind of simple style and is usually used to arrange the activities and organize work. While writing the information, please pay much attention to:

1) At the beginning, "Notice or Announcement" must be written.

2) The body part should be simple and understandable. It may include the time, place, main content and the informant.

3) The person whom is informed is usually used in general reference. e.g. Dear guests, Dear travelers etc.

Here are two samples of information.

---

**Notice**

Tourists are requested to note that The Great Wall originally scheduled for tomorrow, June 5th is now put off until June 7th. We shall visit the Forbidden City (Zijin Cheng) instead.

June 4th, 2004 China International Travel Service

**Announcement**

Passengers from New York to Shanghai flight the US Air 028 is leaving in 15 minutes. Please have your boarding cards ready and go through Gate 5. We wish you a pleasant journey. Good-bye.

---

**Simulate and create** ► According to the samples, write one notice on a lecture on Chinese Folk Culture by Mr. Wang and write an announcement on the plane landing.

## Part Five   Related Information

| Text | Notes |
|---|---|
| **Tax-Free Shopping in Europe** | |
| In Europe, most prices include a value-added tax or VAT[1] that can be as high as 25 percent. This is like a sales tax, except that it's built into the price you pay instead of being added at the cash register[2]. | [1] 增值税 |
| | [2] 收银机 |
| If you're a tourist from another country, you may be able to claim a VAT refund[3]. You can do this in several ways: | [3] 退还，退款 |

1. Use the store's refund affiliate[4], which can be identified by a decal[5] such as "Tax-Free Shopping" or "CashBack" in the store window.

[4] 加入，接受为会员
[5] 贴花纸

This is the easiest and most reliable[6] method by far. The store gives you a "tax-free shopping cheque" that you present to customs when you leave the country or the European Union. You then take your stamped cheques to the refund service's airport desk or border kiosk[7] for an immediate[8] refund, drop them in a special box, or mail them to the refund service's nearest office after you get home. You can have refunds credited to your Visa, MasterCard, or other credit card in your own currency.

[6] 可靠的，可信赖的

[7] 亭子
[8] 直接的，立即的

Global Refund is the biggest VAT refund service; it represents more than 210,000 merchants in 34 countries. CashBack is another popular service in Europe. Important: You don't decide which service to use. The retailer[9] does, so you'll need to process each "tax-free shopping cheque" with the company indicated on the cheque.

[9] 零售商人

2. Get a refund directly from the shop where you make your purchase.

Request a VAT refund form, have it stamped by a customs official when you leave the country or the European Union, then mail the stamped form back to the store (assuming[10] that the shop is willing to handle refunds this way).

[10] 假定，设想

Note: For smaller transactions[11], the cost of cashing a foreign-currency[12] check may exceed[13] the amount of the refund. However, it's worth considering for large purchases or if the merchant will credit the refund to your credit-card account instead of mailing you a check. In the latter case, your credit-card company will automatically convert[14] the refund to your local currency.

[11] 交易
[12] 外汇
[13] 超越，胜过

[14] 使转变，转换

3. Charge your purchase with a credit card and ask the shop to make two charge slips: one for the amount of the sale after deduction[15] of the VAT, and the other for the amount of the VAT.

[15] 减除，扣除

The store will post the larger transaction but set the VAT charge slip aside. After you've had your VAT refund form stamped by customs, mail it back to the store, and the merchant will destroy the VAT charge slip without submitting[16] it. (Not all merchants will go along with this method, and it works best in stores that handle credit-card transactions manually.)

[16] 提交

Important: Don't wait until you get home to think about VAT refunds. Learn how tax-free shopping works, request tax-free shopping cheques or VAT refund forms when you make your purchases, and have the cheques or forms stamped by a local customs official before you leave for home.

# Part Six  Guide to World Famous Sight

| Text | Notes |
|---|---|
| **Hawaii** | |

The Hawaiian Islands are located in the middle of the Pacific Ocean[1] approximately[2] 2,400 miles (4,000km) southwest of California[3]. You can go there only by airplane or boat. There are six major islands: Oahu[4], Maui[5], the Big Island of Hawaii[6] Kauai[7], Molokai[8] and Lanai[9]. Each island is unique and may feature live volcanoes[10], lava[11] flows, tropical[12] rain forests, beautiful beaches, sugar cane[13] fields, pineapple plantations or historic sites. These tropical paradises attract about 7 million tourists each year, but most visitors only see one or two of the islands.

You can easily travel between the islands by using one of the two domestic airlines: Aloha[14] or Hawaiian. Flights are frequent and inexpensive. When landing at each airport, be sure to look for the racks of free coupon[15] magazines. Each island has its own coupon book with lots of discounts.

The climate is consistent[16] and enjoyable. Temperatures seldom fall below 65 degrees or rise above 80 throughout the year. A pleasant breeze[17] frequently cools the day. Don't forget your sunscreen[18], or sun block! In such pleasant conditions, you can easily forget that the tropical sun causes severe sunburn[19] to anyone not accustomed to it. Rainfall varies by location but can be an almost daily occurrence in the rain forests.

Visitors are warmly welcomed and quickly enveloped by the "Aloha" spirit of Hawaii. Life is very informal on the islands and the dress is casual[20]. Take lots of casual warm weather clothing and don't forget your swimwear! Men visiting the islands usually buy and wear "Aloha shirts" made of bright colorful fabrics. Women usually buy colorful muumuus[21] (loose fitting comfortable dresses that can be worn anywhere in Hawaii).

Accommodations on the islands include plenty of hotels and motels in various price ranges. If you stay longer than a few days, there are also lots of condominiums[22] and apartments for rent. Car rentals are readily available and are the best way to see all of the spectacular scenery on most of the islands. When visiting Oahu, long-term car rentals are not a good choice as parking is very limited in Honolulu[23]. Tour buses and daily car rentals are much better options[24] on Oahu.

**Notes:**

[1] 太平洋
[2] 近似地，大约
[3] 加利福尼亚，加州
[4] 瓦胡岛
[5] 毛伊岛
[6] 夏威夷大岛
[7] 考艾岛
[8] 莫洛凯岛
[9] 拉来岛
[10] 火山
[11] 火山岩
[12] 热带的
[13] 甘蔗
[14] 欢迎（问候语）
[15] 商家的优待券
[16] 一致的，协调的
[17] 微风
[18] 防晒油
[19] 晒斑
[20] 随便的，非正式的
[21] 穆穆袍
[22] 共管
[23] 火奴鲁鲁（即"檀香山"）
[24] 选择

| Hawaii enforces[25] a strict quarantine[26] inspection upon arrival. You will not be allowed to take any fresh fruit, flowers, plants and certain meats into the state. Small sniffer[27] dogs very efficiently search all luggage and passengers on arrival. | [25] 执行<br>[26] 检疫，隔离<br>[27] 嗅探器 |
| --- | --- |

# Unit 13

## Leaving

**Part One** **Dialogues**

### Sample Dialogue 1

👤 **Situation** ▶ Tommy has finished his travel in China and is going to return home. Now one guide is seeing him off at the airport.

**Tommy**: When does the plane take off?

**Guide**: At ten thirty. There's still one hour to go.

**Tommy**: Mr. Wang, during my trip in the past month or so, you've shown your concern for me in every respect. I really don't know how to express my gratitude.

**Guide**: It's very nice of you to say so.

**Tommy**: I've had a very enjoyable stay in China. I've been to many tourist attractions and places of historical interest. What's more, I've learned some Chinese from you.

**Guide**: I'm so happy that you've had a good time.

**Tommy**: Thanks to the trip, I've made acquaintances with so many Chinese friends here. Before I came here, I only had an understanding of China from books and papers. Now I've seen China with my own eyes.

**Guide**: It's more important to learn from real life.

**Tommy**: It's a pity I haven't got enough time for many other places.

**Guide**: Come to China again. You're always welcome!

**Tommy**: I certainly shall, thank you.

**Guide**: Then, I'll be pleased to be your guide again.

**Tommy**: Wonderful. I hope we'll keep in touch.

**Guide**: So do I.

**Tommy**: I'll write to you when I'm back. Goodbye, Mr. Wang.

**Guide**: Goodbye. Good journey!

## Sample Dialogue 2

**Situation** ▶ Mr. Tedder is coming back from China. Albert from a Travel agency is calling him and asking him something about his travel.

**Albert**: Did you have a good trip, Mr. Tedder?

**Tedder**: Yes. It was marvelous! We had a wonderful time.

**Albert**: How was the service on the flight?

**Tedder**: Quite good. It was a very pleasant flight and not too crowded.

**Albert**: How was the hotel?

**Tedder**: It was very comfortable. I liked the location, It was easy to get to many tourist attractions from the hotel.

**Albert**: How was the food?

**Tedder**: Just great. Really, the food in the hotel restaurant was delicious, and I found many little eating places that were excellent and had very reasonable price.

**Albert**: I'm so glad you enjoyed your vacation.

**Tedder**: I certainly did and I want to thank you for all your help in arranging it.

## Useful Expressions

1. Did you have a good trip?
   旅行愉快吗？

2. We had a wonderful time.
   我们玩得非常痛快。

3. How is the service in the hotel？
   酒店的服务怎么样？

4. By the way, what do you think has impressed you most in Beijing?
   顺便问一下，北京给你最深的印象是什么？

5. Are you accustomed to traveling by air?
   你习惯乘飞机旅行吗？

6. Can you sleep well in the plane?
   你在飞机上能睡得好吗？

7. I have got my ticket. I just need a seat confirmation.
   我已经买了机票了。我只是要确认一下座位。

8. I want to cancel my flight reservation.
   我想取消我预定的航班。

## Task Dialogue 1

**Situation** ▶ Tommy has just traveled to China, and he is talking with his best friend Korn about his experience.

## Task Dialogue 2

**Situation** ▶ You are the manager of Butterfield Travel Agency, and you are talking with Tommy who has just come back from China.

## Part Two  Text A

## Things to Do Before Leaving

Departure is relatively much simpler. As mentioned above, you have to take out the things that you had declared with the copy of your Customs Luggage Declaration Form which you filled in on your arrival. If any item is missing, a certificate by the relevant department is required (for instance, a certificate from the police is required if something is stolen); otherwise, you have to pay import duty according to the Custom regulations.

- Pre-flight, check with your airline for: flight status; any special travel needs; airport arrival time and traveling with pets.
- Before leaving for the airport, make sure you have your ticket and proper identification (one photo ID or two pieces of identification—one must be issued by a government authority). For electronic ticketing, airlines accept a valid driver's license, passport or a birth certificate with a photo ID.
- Plan ahead and allocate additional time for potential traffic delays.
- Remember to let the person meeting you (if applicable) know your airline, flight number and arrival and departure times. Designate a meeting place.
- Ensure that you have an ID label outside of each piece of luggage. In addition, always place your name, address and phone number inside each piece of luggage in case of loss. ID labels can be obtained at airline ticket counters. You can also attach a piece of yarn or tape to your luggage for easier identification. Check your luggage in advance for rips and tears since airlines will not be responsible for lost items if your bags are in poor condition.
- You will be limited to one piece of carry-on baggage and one personal item (handbag, laptop computer, briefcase, etc.). Backpacks must be checked. Keep to the essentials; prescriptions, valuables (camera & jewelry) and important documents. Although small amounts (up to 16 oz.) of personal care items (deodorant, perfume, shaving cream, etc.)

are allowed, it is recommended that you pack these items in your checked luggage.

- Prohibited carry-on items include: any item with a folding or retractable blade; box cutters and spare blades; carpet knives and spare blades; corkscrews; cutting instruments; ice picks; knives of any length; mace/pepper spray; martial arts devices; metal scissors with pointed tips; replica weapons; straight razors; tools; toy transformed robots; and toy weapons.

- Airline fares are highly competitive so research and compare fares for airlines serving Worcester Regional Airport. Use the web to find the cheapest airfares by inputting key words or phrases such as "lowest air fares" or "bargain air fares" to your search engine. Be sure to specify Worcester Regional Airport as your choice for arrival and/or departure. You can also stipulate Worcester as your designated airport when reviewing websites for individual airlines, which provide additional ticket opportunities for air travelers. A travel agent can also assist you in finding the best fares via Worcester Regional Airport.

- Be aware that several factors can sometimes help to lower the cost of your ticket. Discount fares are restricted and are usually limited to a certain number of seats per flight and are often non-refundable. Carefully check all details to ensure that they meet your travel needs before making final arrangements.

- Remember when you compare fares that travel costs consist of more than just the fee for your airline ticket. Factor in the price of ground transportation, parking, restrictions and even delays to determine your total cost of travel. Consider the time of year when you are traveling, as certain periods such as school holiday weeks involve heavier passenger loads, more traffic and tightened parking situations at larger airports like Logan International Airport. The best bargains are the ones, like flying through Worcester Regional Airport, that offer you the easiest, most convenient and dependable experiences overall.

- Please be advised that extra time may be required at the airport due to heightened FAA security regulations. It is recommended that you arrive at least one and a half hours prior to your scheduled flight, but be sure to check with your travel professional since wait time change frequently. Be prepared to show ID as requested. To pass security checkpoints, you must have a ticket, a travel agency itinerary, and/or a confirmation letter of an airline ticket.

- For wheelchair assistance, medical conditions or special dietary needs, contact your ticketed airline at least twenty-four hours in advance.

- In the case of unaccompanied minors, please check with your airline for travel clearing security check points and boarding requirements.

- To get information about flight cancellations and delays, contact your airline for information or consult their websites for any updates.

The following is the procedure of departure at Narita International Airport.

- Passengers must present their check-in baggage for security inspection before proceeding to the check-in counter. Please present tickets and passports at the airline check-in counter and hand over all the luggage to be checked in (not carry-on luggage).

- Check-in staff will return tickets and passports along with boarding passes and baggage claim receipts.

- Passengers on travel agency group tours should then complete departure and boarding procedures as instructed by the group leader.

- All passengers are subject to a security check for aircraft security and must submit carry-on baggage and personal effects for scanning.

- Please show your boarding pass to the security officer and place your carry-on baggage on the scanner conveyor belt.

- Passengers must then pass through the metal detector.

- Passengers carrying cash or monetary instruments in excess of the specified limit should submit a Customs declaration form.

- Present your passport, boarding pass, and embarkation card at the Passport Control counter.

- At the boarding gate, please follow the directions of the airline staff and present your boarding pass.

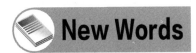 **New Words**

**relatively** [ˈrelətivli] *ad.* 相关地，相对地

**declare** [diˈklɛə] *vt.* 申报（纳税品）

**relevant** [ˈreləvənt] *a.* 有关的，相应的

**duty** [ˈdjuːti] *n.* 税

**electronic** [elekˈtrɔnik] *a.* 电子的

**potential** [pəˈtenʃəl] *a.* 潜在的，可能的

**delay** [diˈlei] *n.* 耽搁，延迟

**applicable** [əˈplikəbl] *a.* 可适用的，可应用的

**designate** [ˈdezigneit] *vt.* 指定，指派

**yarn** [jɑːn] *n.* 纱，纱线，绳子

**tape** [teip] *n.* 带子，带

**rip** [rip] *n.* 裂口，裂缝

**carry-on** [ˈkæriɔn] *n.* 随身行李

**briefcase** [ˈbriːfˌkeis] *n.* 公文包

**backpack** [ˈbækˌpæk] *n.* 背包

**prescription** [priˈskripʃən] *n.* 指示，规定，命令

**deodorant** [diːˈəudərənt] *n.* 除臭剂

**perfume** [ˈpəːfjuːm] *n.* 香味，芳香，香水

**folding** [ˈfəuldiŋ] *a.* 可折叠的

**retractable** [riˈtræktəbl] *a.* 可收回的

**blade** [bleid] *n.* 刀刃，刀片

**corkscrew** [ˈkɔːkskruː] *n.* 开塞钻，螺丝锥

**instrument** [ˈinstrumənt] *n.* 工具，器械，器具

**martial** [ˈmɑːʃəl] *a.* 战争的，军事的

**scissors** [ˈsizəz] *n.* 剪刀

**replica** [ˈreplikə] *n.* 复制品

**razor** [ˈreizə] *n.* 剃刀

**fare** [feə] *n.* 费用

**competitive** [kəm'petətiv] *a.* 竞争的

**stipulate** ['stipjuleit] *vt.* 规定，保证

**agent** ['eidʒənt] *n.* 代理，代理商

**via** ['viːə] *prep.* 经，通过，经由

**restricted** [ri'striktid] *a.* 受限制的，有限的

**non-refundable** [nɔŋri'fʌndəbl] *a.* 不可退款的

**arrangement** [ə'reindʒmənt] *n.* 排列，安排

**restriction** [ri'strikʃən] *n.* 限制，约束

**dietary** ['daiətəri] *n.* 规定的食物

**minor** ['mainə] *n.* 未成年人

**cancellation** [ˌkænsə'leiʃən] *n.* 取消

**consult** [kən'sʌlt] *vt.* 请教，咨询，查询

**update** [ʌp'deit] *n.* 更新

**check-in** [tʃekin] *n.*（机场）登记，报到

**inspection** [in'spekʃən] *n.* 检查，视察

**effects** [i'fekts] *n.* 动产，家庭财物

**Scan** [skæn] *vt.* 扫描

**conveyor** [kən'veiə] *n.* 传送机，传送带

 # Phrases and Expressions

take out 取出；带到

Customs Luggage Declaration Form 海关行李报关单

fill in 填写

make sure 尽力做到，保证

in addition 另外，加之

in case of 假如，如果发生

a piece of 一片，一段，一块

be responsible for 负责任

be in good/poor condition （物件）无 / 有破损

laptop computer 膝上型计算机

keep to 遵守，信守

Worcester Regional Airport 伍斯特地区机场（美）

be aware 知道，觉得

meet one's needs 满足某人需要

consist of 由……组成

such as 例如，诸如

Logan International Airport 洛根国际机场（美）

be prepared to do/for 准备着

hand over 移交，交出

along with 与……一道，与……一起

pass through 经过，通过，穿过

in excess of 超过

 # Abbreviations

FAA (Federal Aviation Administration) 联邦航空局

# Notes

**1** Check your luggage in advance for rips and tears since airlines will not be responsible for lost items if your bags are in poor condition.

本 句 中，since airlines will not be responsible for lost items if your bags are in poor condition 是原因状语从句，修饰 Check。since 表示一种附带的原因，或者表示已知的、显然的理由。意思是"既然"。在该状语从句中，if your bags are in poor condition 是条件状语从句，修饰从句的谓语 will not be responsible for。

**2** Although small amounts (up to 16 oz.) of personal care items (deodorant, perfume, shaving cream, etc.) are allowed, it is recommended that you pack these items in your checked luggage.

本句中，although 引导的是让步状语从句，表示"虽然，即使，尽管"的意思。although 比较正式。让步状语从句可以放在主句前或主句后。

注意：在 although 引导的让步状语从句中，主句前不能有 but。请看下例：

I had very good time although I didn't know anybody at the party.

尽管晚会上的人我都不认识，但我还是很开心。

Although you don't like wine, just try a glass of this.

虽然你不喜欢喝酒，还是尝一杯吧。

本句中，It is recommended that you pack these items in your checked luggage 是一个虚拟语气的句子。英语中，recommend 后面的宾语从句的谓语动词要用动词原形或 should + 动词原形。请看下例：

I recommend that you inquire about the job.

我建议你了解一下这项工作的情况。

It is recommended that you arrive at least one and a half hours prior to your scheduled flight.

建议你至少在航班起飞前一个半小时到达机场。

**3** You can also stipulate Worcester as your designated airport when reviewing websites for individual airlines, which provide additional ticket opportunities for air travelers.

本句中，as 用作介词，表示"作为，充当"。在句子当中作宾语补足语。which provide additional ticket opportunities for air travelers 是非限定性定语从句，修饰 websites。

**4** Consider the time of year when you are traveling, as certain periods such as school holiday weeks involve heavier passenger loads, more traffic and tightened parking situations at larger airports like Logan International Airport.

本句中，as 用作连词，引导原因状语从句，表示"因为"。such as 的意思是"诸如，像……这类"，后跟名词。

**5** In addition, always place your name, address and phone number inside each piece of luggage in case of loss.

本句中，in case of 后面接名词或动名词短语，与 in case（后面接句子）的意义相同，相当于 lest 或 if，意思是"以防，假使"。in the case of 意为"就某人或某事而言"。请看下例：

Take the umbrella in case of rain.

带把伞以防下雨。

Poverty depresses most people; in the case of my father, it was otherwise.

贫穷使大部分人沮丧，但对我父亲来说，不尽然。

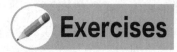
# Exercises

**EX. 1**  **Answer the following questions.**

1. What would you do when you prepare to leave?

2. What would you do before leaving for the airport?

3. What would you do with your luggage?

4. What are the prohibited carry-on items?

5. How can we buy the cheapest airfares?

6. What factors should you consider?

**EX. 2**  **Write out the English words according to the definitions given below.**

| definitions | words |
|---|---|
| to make a full statement of (property for which tax may be owed to the government) | |
| something (such as an official paper) which proves who one is | |
| an official paper, card etc., showing that permission was given to do something, usu. for a payment | |
| a close copy e.g. of a painting or other work of art. | |
| a person who acts for another, esp. one who represents the business affairs of a firm | |
| without someone or something else going with one | |
| to go to (a person, book, etc.) for information, advice, etc. | |
| belongings; personal property | |
| flat leather or plastic case for carrying documents | |
| person under the age of full legal responsibility | |

**EX. 3**  **Complete the following sentences with appropriate words or expressions from the text.**

1. Never spend _____ your income.

2. You draw the trees and I'll _____ the sky.

3. _____ fire, ring the bell.

4. Who _____ breaking the mirror?

5. Michael _____ because he always takes his exercise.

6. _____ wet leaves on the line, this train will arrive an hour late.

7. The thief _____ to the police.

**EX. 4** **Translate the following sentences into Chinese.**

1. As mentioned above, you have to take out the things that you had declared with the copy of your Customs Luggage Declaration Form which you filled in on your arrival.

2. Check your luggage in advance for rips and tears since airlines will not be responsible for lost items if your bags are in poor condition.

3. Airline fares are highly competitive so research and compare fares for airlines serving Worcester Regional Airport.

4. Carefully check all details to ensure that they meet your travel needs before making final arrangements.

5. Please be advised that extra time may be required at the airport due to heightened FAA security regulations.

## Part Three   Text B

## Returning Home After Traveling Abroad May Be Problematic

Traveling to Europe is a great experience. Unfortunately, getting home isn't always the joyful celebration that one expects. After a long time in a country, packing everything up is a frustrating exercise. The flight back to the United States makes for a long day, as the six-hour time difference on top of a 10-hour flight returns one home only four hours after the departure time. This also makes for a bad case of jet lag. Just to make things really interesting, the day is capped off by a trip through U.S. Customs.

The Second Law of Thermodynamics guarantees that entropy will always increase in a closed system. This has been rigorously proven by millions of travelers who never manage to pack their luggage for the trip home into the same suitcases used to bring it overseas. It seems that travelers always bring back far more than they take.

There are a few ways to make the packing easier. First, many items can be safely discarded to make room for souvenirs. Second, several companies make either expandable luggage or bags that fold up small enough to carry over just to hold the extra stuff. Finally, there are services in many European towns that will ship excess luggage back to the States.

Before heading home, take stock of what needs to go along. If space is at all an issue, leave the travel guides in Europe. Although this seems like a waste of money and paper, they aren't worth the weight or the space. Travel books are updated every year, and with good reason. This year, many buildings are closed for renovation getting ready for the new millennium. Half of Rome is under scaffolding in preparation for the Jubilee that the Pope has declared for 2000. Next year, several special events will happen all over the Continent. The information in this year's guidebooks will be quite out of date soon. Also consider throwing out toiletries, clothes that have become damaged, or anything that will sit on the back of the shelf if it makes it to the States.

If nothing else can be thrown out, and there is still not enough room, extra luggage is another answer. Tote is one of the many companies that make small bags that fold up into a pocket and store fairly flat. These can be acquired at Macy's, Rich's, or a luggage store before going to Europe, or they can be purchased abroad. They also make good pillows and laundry bags along the way. Many people carry a day pack for short side trips; this can be pressed into service for extra items on the return trip. These do not fold down as well, but they are more useful while in Europe.

The third option is to ship excess items home. This can get expensive, as everything has to travel by air. Many cities have an excess baggage service that will provide packing materials and handle all shipping arrangements, including Customs. This is really only a good option if one's luggage will exceed the allowable limit otherwise, or if one is going from northern to southern Europe and the warm clothes are no longer needed.

Customs provides the final trial to the traveler returning home. There is a lot of misinformation about what can and cannot be brought into the United States. The simple answer is that it differs depending on where one is coming from. Generally, the common denominator is a total value of no more than $400 in goods, including no more than one liter of alcohol for those over 21, and up to 100 cigars or 200 cigarettes (one carton) in tobacco products. Alcohol and tobacco may be subject to taxes in the city where they enter the United States. Despite rumors to the contrary, Cuban cigars are still illegal.

The Customs Service provides a brochure called *Know Before You Go*, which explains the current regulations. This brochure is available on the international concourse of most airports.

## New Words

**problematic** [ˌprɔbləˈmætik] *a.* 产生问题的，造成困难的

**experience** [ikˈspiəriəns] *n.* 经验，阅历，经历

**unfortunately** [ʌnˈfɔːtjnətli] *ad.* 不幸地

**joyful** [ˈdʒɔifl] *a.* 快乐的，令人欢欣的

**celebration** [ˌseləˈbreiʃən] *n.* 庆祝，庆典

**expect** [ikˈspekt] *vt.* 期待，盼望，指望，料想

**frustrate** [frʌˈstreit] *vt.* 挫败，阻挠，使感到灰心

**lag** [læg] *n.* 迟延，滞后

**thermodynamics** [ˌθəːməudaiˈnæmiks] *n.* 热力学

**guarantee** [ˌgærənˈtiː] *vt.* 保证，允诺，确保

**entropy** [ˈentrəpi] *n.* 熵，平均信息量

**rigorous** [ˈrigərəs] *a.* 严格的，严厉的

**discard** [disˈkɑːd] *vt.* 丢弃，抛弃

**expandable** [ikˈspændəbl] *a.* 可张开的，可扩大的

**renovation** [ˌrenəˈveiʃən] *n.* 革新

**scaffolding** [ˈskæfəuldiŋ] *n.* 脚手架

**jubilee** [ˈdʒuːbiliː] *n.* 周年大庆

**Pope** [pəup] *n.* 罗马教皇

**continent** [ˈkɔntinənt] *n.* 大陆

**toiletry** [ˈtɔilitri] *n.* 化妆品，化妆用具

**tote** [təut] *vt.* 手提，背负，携带

**fairly** [ˈfɛəli] *ad.* 相当地，还算

**acquire** [əˈkwaiə] *vt.* 获得，取得

**Macy's** [ˈmeisiz] *n.* 梅西百货

**Rich's** [ˈritʃiz] *n.* 里奇百货

**laundry** [ˈlɔːndri] *n.* 洗熨

**pack** [pæk] *vt.* 包装，收拾（行李）

**allowable** [əˈlauəbl] *a.* 可容许的，可承认的

**trial** [ˈtraiəl] *n.* 试验，考验

**misinformation** [ˌmisinfəˈmeiʃən] *n.* 误报，误传

**denominator** [diˈnɔmiˌneitə] *n.* 标准，共同特性

**cigar** [siˈgɑː] *n.* 雪茄

**cigarette** [ˌsigəˈret] *n.* 香烟，纸烟

**carton** [ˈkɑːtən] *n.* 硬纸盒，纸板箱

**tobacco** [təˈbækəu] *n.* 烟草，烟草制品

**rumor** [ˈruːmə] *n.* 流言，谣言，传闻

**contrary** [ˈkɔntrəri] *n.* 反面，相反

**Cuban** [ˈkjuːbən] *a.* 古巴（人）的

**concourse** [ˈkɔŋkɔːs] *n.* 中央大厅，广场

## Phrases and Expressions

pack sth. up 把……收起来放好

on top of 除……之外，此外

US Customs 美国海关

bring back 拿回来，带回来

make room 腾出地方

fold up 折起

at all （用于否定句）丝毫，一点

out of date 过时

throw out 扔掉

make it 办成功

as well 同样，也

depending on/upon 视……而定

up to 一直到，多达

subject to 需要……的，可有……的

# Notes

**1** The flight back to the United States makes for a long day, as the six-hour time difference on top of a 10-hour flight returns one home only four hours after the departure time.

本句中，as 用作连词，用于引导原因状语从句，表示"因为"，相当于 because。另外，only 作副词，意思是"仅仅，只是"，可以修饰形容词、副词或动词。

**2** This is really only a good option if one's luggage will exceed the allowable limit otherwise, or if one is going from northern to southern Europe and the warm clothes are no longer needed.

本句中，otherwise 是副词，表示"除此之外；在一切其他方面"。no longer 为短语，表示"不再"，多用于肯定句和书面语，放在行为动词前，但要放在 be 动词后。请看下例：

She no longer works here.

她不再在这里工作了。

We are no longer poor.

我们再也不穷了。

**3** Generally, the common denominator is a total value of no more than $400 in goods, including no more than one liter of alcohol for those over 21, and up to 100 cigars or 200 cigarettes (one carton) in tobacco products.

本句中，no more than 表示数量时，意为"只有，仅仅"，相当于 only，含有少的意思。请看下例：

I have no more than 20 dollars.

我只有 20 美元。

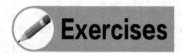

# Exercises

**EX. 5** **Answer the following questions.**

1. What is the narrator's feeling on traveling to Europe?

2. How many hours time difference for the flight from Europe to back the USA?

3. Why does the narrator suggest leaving the guidebook?

4. What is the narrator's third suggestion?

5. What kind of services does the Customs service provide?

**EX. 6** **Decide whether the following statements are *true* or *false*.**

1. In the narrator's opinion traveling to Europe is a great experience, and getting home is also always the joyful celebration that one expects.

2. This has been rigorously proven by millions of travelers who never manage to pack their luggage for the trip home into the same suitcases used to bring it overseas.

3. There are three ways to make the packing easier. First, throw away something and make room for souvenirs. Second, make either expandable luggage or bags and fold them up small enough

to carry over. Third, ship the excess luggage back to the States.

4. Generally, the common denominator is a total value of no more than $500 in goods, including no more than one liter of alcohol for those over 18, and up to 200 cigars or 400 cigarettes (one carton) in tobacco products.

5. Travelers can find a brochure called *Know Before You Go*, which explains the current regulations on the international concourse of most airports.

## Part Four  Skill Training

**Forms**

### The Evaluation Online

After returning from your trip, you will receive an evaluation form. Look this over and fill it out. Ask your team leader about any questions you may have. We welcome your thoughts on the overall trip, what impressed you the most and any suggestions you have for future team trips.

**Name:**

**Address:**

**City, State, Country, Zip:**

**E-mail Address:**

**Phone:**

**Country Visited:**

**Trip Dates:**

**What did you enjoy the most about your trip?**

**What was your least favorite part of the trip?**

**Would you like to come on a team again sometime?**
○Yes          ○No

**Would you like to be the leader of a team sometime in the future?**

○Yes          ○No

**Do you think the information provided to you beforehand adequately prepared you for this trip?**

○Yes          ○No

**If not, please explain how you could have been better prepared.**

```
┌──────────────────────────────────────────────┬──┐
│                                              │▲│
│                                              ├──┤
│                                              │▼│
├──┬──────────────────────────────────────┬───┼──┤
│◄│                                      │►│  │
└──┴──────────────────────────────────────┴───┴──┘
```

**Do you have any constructive suggestions or observations to make concerning improving future mission trips?**

```
┌──────────────────────────────────────────────┬──┐
│                                              │▲│
│                                              ├──┤
│                                              │▼│
├──┬──────────────────────────────────────┬───┼──┤
│◄│                                      │►│  │
└──┴──────────────────────────────────────┴───┴──┘
```

**Would you be willing to commit to some ongoing work of Missionary Ventures and join with us in "Carrying the WORD to the world"?**

○Yes          ○No

## Practical Writing

Please try to fill in this baggage declaration form carefully and learn about everything mentioned in the form.

**Baggage Declaration Form**

NAME _____

NATIONALITY_____    PASSPORT NO. _____

FROM/TO _____

NUMBER OF ACCOMPANYING CHILDREN UNDER 16 _____

HAND BAGGAGE _____ Pcs. CHECKED BAGGAGE _____ Pcs.

| ITEM | ENTRY | EXIT |
|---|---|---|
| CHINESE & FOREIGN CURRENCIES | Description & Amount | |
| | | |
| GOLD & SILVER ORNAMENTS | | |

| TRIP NECESSITIES | BRAND | PIECE | BRAND | PIECE |
|---|---|---|---|---|
| CAMERA | | | | |
| TAPE RECORDER | | | | |
| VIDEO & MOVIE CAMERA | | | | |
| OTHER ARTICLES DUE TO CUSTOM PROCEDURES | | | | |
| GOODS & SAMPLES | Yes/No | | Yes/No | |
| RECORDED VIDEO TAPE | Yes/No | | Yes/No | |
| PRINTED MATTER | Yes/No | | Yes/No | |
| ANTIQUES | Yes/No | | Yes/No | |

| DURABLE CONSUMER GOODS (PRICE=>RMB 50.00) AND GIFTS (TOTAL PRICE=>RMB50.00) | | | |
|---|---|---|---|
| DESCRIPTION | BRAND | PIECE | CUSTOMS REMARKS |
| | | | |
| | | | |

IN ADDITION. _____ PIECES OF UNACCOMPANIED BAGGAGE ARE TO BE IMPORTED THROUGH _____ WITHIN 3 MONTHS.

SIGNATURE: _____ DATE:_____

CUSTOMS REMARKS:

CUSTOMS ENDORSEMENT: _____

# Part Five  Related Information

| Text | Notes |
|---|---|
| **Home Security**<br><br>    Notify family members and/or neighbors as to how long you will be away from home. Place valuables[1] in the bank. Suspend[2] all deliveries, including your newspaper subscription[3]. Have the post office hold your mail. Leave a house key with a neighbor and set up | [1] 贵重物品<br>[2] 延缓<br>[3] 订阅 |

automatic timers[4] to activate lights and play the TV or radio at set times. Turn the thermostat[5] down to 55-63 degrees (if you generally keep it set at a higher temperature); turn the thermostat up to 76-78 degrees (if you live in a hot and humid[6] climate). Disconnect electrical appliances[7] and turn off the hot-water heater. Empty and defrost[8] the refrigerator[9]; keep the refrigerator door propped open in order to avoid mildew[10]. Secure all window and door locks.

| | |
|---|---|
| | [4] 定时器 |
| | [5] 温度调节装置 |
| | [6] 湿润的 |
| | [7] 电器，器具 |
| | [8] 除霜，解冻 |
| | [9] 电冰箱 |
| | [10] 发霉，生霉 |

Arrange for the care of your house, lawn, garden, plants, and pets. Well-kept grounds give the impression that the house continues to be lived in. Arrange for the in-home care or boarding of your pets. Ask a family member, friend, or neighbor to make periodic[11] checks of your home or consider employing a house-sitting service.

[11] 定期的

### Leaving for the Airport

Always reconfirm[12] your airline reservations[13] before leaving home, preferably[14] 72 hours in advance of your departure. When making or reconfirming any arrangements, be sure to obtain[15] the name of the person with whom you have spoken as well as a confirmation number.

[12] 再次确认

[13] 预定

[14] 更适宜

[15] 得到，获得

Arrive for your flight a little early. Airlines suggest that passengers on international flights arrive a minimum of two hours before take-off. Give yourself extra time to avoid getting frazzled[16] should you be slowed down by heavy traffic or inclement[17] weather on your way to the airport.

[16] 疲惫的

[17] 险恶的，恶劣的

Leave an itinerary with hotel telephone and fax numbers as well as the contact number with someone. Let one or two people know where to reach you.

### Keep an Open Mind

When you leave your home, you are embarking[18] on a journey that will take you to places that are very different from your usual way of life. Try to be flexible[19] and enjoy the unexpected. Embrace[20] new sights, sounds, people, and the culture around you. Sample[21] the food, try to speak the language, ask questions, and smile; you will return home a more knowledgeable[22] person with happy memories. Many travelers have told us that Chinese people are the friendliest people in the world. Go and find out for yourself!

[18] 登上，从事

[19] 灵活的

[20] 接受，包含

[21] 尝试

[22] 有见识的，知识渊博的

# Part Six Guide to World Famous Sight

| Text | Notes |
|---|---|
| **Sydney Opera House**[1] | [1] 悉尼歌剧院 |
| The Sydney Opera House is a performing[2] arts center that sits at the edge of the harbor[3] of Sydney, Australia's[4] largest city and the capital of the state of New South Wales[5]. It includes a concert hall[6], an opera theater[7] (also used for ballet), a drama theater[8], and a playhouse[9]. | [2] 表演的<br>[3] 海港<br>[4] 澳大利亚<br>[5] 新南威尔士<br>[6] 音乐厅<br>[7] 歌剧院 |
| The Sydney Opera House took fourteen years and almost $90 million to complete. | [8] 戏剧院<br>[9] 剧场 |
| Jorn Utzon[10], a Danish[11] architect, designed the opera house. He won an international competition held in 1956. More than 230 entries were received from around the world. | [10] 乔恩·乌特佐<br>[11] 丹麦 |
| Utzon has described the opera house as being like a sculpture[12]. It seems to change shape depending upon the direction from which you look at it. | [12] 雕塑品<br>[13] 改革性的，全新的<br>[14] 特点 |
| The most revolutionary[13] feature[14] of the opera house is its roof, which is made of ribbed[15] shells of precast[16] concrete[17]. All the segments[18] were mass-produced. The design, based on the curve of a sphere[19], became a reality with the help of 1960s computer technology. | [15] 有棱纹的<br>[16] 预浇制的<br>[17] 混凝土<br>[18] 部分<br>[19] 球体 |
| For many years the Iora Australian Aborigines[20] lived in the Sydney area. Bennelong Point, where the opera house is located, was named for an Aboriginal man who lived there when the British arrived and established the first European settlement in 1788. | [20] 澳大利亚土著居民 |
| The opera house was built to look like part of Sydney Harbor[21]. The curved roofs look like the sails of boats in the harbor. | [21] 悉尼港 |
| Just as the Eiffel Tower is a symbol for Paris and the Statue of Liberty is a symbol for New York, the opera house has become a symbol for Sydney. | |

## 单词表

abalone [ˌæbəˈləuni] n. 鲍鱼（10A）[1]

absolutely [ˈæbsəluːtli] ad. 完全地，绝对地（6A）

access [ˈækses] n. 使用；接近（3A）

accessibility [əkˌsesəˈbiləti] n. 易接近，可到达（3A）

accessories [əkˈsesəriz] n. 辅助设备，附件（3B）

accommodate [əˈkɔmədeit] vt. 容纳（7A）

accommodation [əˌkɔməˈdeiʃən] n. 膳宿（1A）

accordingly [əˈkɔːdiŋli] ad. 因此；相应地（8A）

accredit [əˈkredit] vt. 信任；授权（3B）

accreditation [əˌkrediteiʃən] n. 委派；鉴定合格（3B）

acquire [əˈkwaiə] vt. 获得，取得（13B）

acquisitive [əˈkwizətiv] a. 想获得的，可学到的（12B）

acrobatic [ˌækrəˈbætik] a. 杂技的，特技的（10A）

acronym [ˈækrənim] n. 只取首字母的缩写词（9B）

adage [ˈædidʒ] n. 格言；谚语（8B）

adapter [əˈdæptə] n. 适配器（2B）

addition [əˈdiʃən] n. 增加物；增加；加法，加（9B）

additionally [əˈdiʃənəli] ad. 加之，又（12B）

Adelaide [ˈædəleid] n. 阿德雷德（澳大利亚城市）（7B）

adequate [ˈædikwət] a. 适当的；足够的（6B）

administration [ədˌminiˈstreiʃən] n. 管理，经营；行政部门（2B）

administrative [ədˈministrətiv] a. 管理的，行政的（5B）

advance [ədˈvɑːns] n. 预付，预支（2A）

advancement [ədˈvɑːnsmənt] n. 前进，提升（5B）

adventure [ədˈventʃə] n. 冒险，历险（8A）

adverse [ˈædvəːs] a. 不利的（6B）

advocate [ˈædvəkit] vt. 提倡，鼓吹（10A）

aesthetic [iːsˈθetik] a. 美学的，审美的，有审美感的（10B）

affiliated [əˈfiliətid] a. 附属的，有关联的（9A）

affiliation [əˌfiliˈeiʃən] n. 联系；从属关系（3B）

affix [əˈfiks] vt. 使固定；贴上，粘上（4A）

affordable [əˈfɔːdəbl] a. 能支付得起的（3A）

afloat [əˈfləut] ad. 在海上（8A）

agency [ˈeidʒənsi] n. 代理处，经销机构（9B）

agent [ˈeidʒənt] n. 代理，代理商（13A）

airfare [ˈiəˌfeə(r)] n. 飞机票价（9B）

airfield [ˈiəˌfiːld] n. 飞机场（6B）

airline [ˈɛəˌlain] n. 航空公司（5B）

airliner [ˈɛəˌlainə] n. 大型客机；班机（5A）

airside [ˈeəsaid] n. 对空面，机场控制区（6B）

aisle [ail] n. 走廊，过道（5A）

album [ˈælbəm] n. 集邮本，照相簿，签名纪念册（12A）

alcohol [ˈælkəˌhɔl] n. 酒精；酒（5A）

alerting [əˈləːtiŋ] n. 警戒，告警（6B）

alignment [əˈlainmənt] n. 队列（6B）

allocate [ˈæləkeit] vt. 分派，分配（4A）

allowable [əˈlauəbl] a. 可容许的，可承认的（13B）

allowance [əˈlauəns] n. 允许；容差（4A）

alpine [ˈælpain] n. 阿尔卑斯山（11B）

---

1 括号里的数字代表单元名，字母代表文章序号。10A代表本单词出自第10单元的Part A。

alternate ['ɔːltəneit] *n.* 替换，备用（8A）

alternative [ɔːl'təːnətiv] *n.* 可供选择的办法或事物（7A）

altitude ['ælti,tjuːd] *n.*（海拔）高度（5A）

aluminum [ə'ljuːminəm] *n.* 铝（10A）

ambience ['æmbiəns] *n.* 周围环境,气氛（10A）

ambulance ['æmbjuləns] *n.* 救护车（2B）

ambulant ['æmbjələnt] *a.* 走动的（10A）

amenities [ə'miːnitiz] *n.* 令人愉快之事物（7B）

amenity [ə'miːnəti] *n.* 宜人；礼仪（3A）

ample ['æmpl] *a.* 充足的；充分的（5B）

Amsterdam ['æmstə'dæm] *n.* 阿姆斯特丹（荷兰首都）（7B）

Amtrak ['æmtræk] *n.* 美国铁路公司（7B）

Andes ['ændiːz] *n.* 安第斯山脉（7B）

anniversary [,æni'vəːsəri] *n.* 周年纪念日（8B）

announcement [ə'naunsmənt] *n.* 广播，通告（4A）

annually ['ænjuəli] *ad.* 一年一次，每年（6B）

anticipate [æn'tisipeit] *vt.* 预期，期望（6B）

antique [æn'tiːk] *n.* 古物，古董（12A）

aperitif [ɑ'perətif] *n.* 开胃酒（10B）

appealing [ə'piːliŋ] *a.* 吸引人的，引起兴趣的（8A）

appetite ['æpətait] *n.* 胃口，食欲（8B）

applaud [ə'plɔːd] *vt.* 赞同，称赞（8A）

appliance [ə'plaiəns] *n.* 用具，器具（12B）

applicable [ə'plikəbl] *a.* 可适用的，可应用的（13A）

applicant ['æplikənt] *n.* 申请者（5B）

appraisal [ə'preizəl] *n.* 评估证明；鉴定书（2A）

approach [ə'prəutʃ] *n.* 接近，逼近，走近；方法（9B）

approximate [ə'prɔksimeit] *a.* 近似的，大约的（7A）

architect ['ɑːki,tekt] *n.* 建筑师（12B）

arena [ə'riːnə] *n.* 领域（9B）

Argentina [,ɑːdʒən'tiːnə] *n.* 阿根廷（7B）

arrangement [ə'reindʒmənt] *n.* 排列，安排（13A）

array [ə'rei] *n.* 衣服，大批（12A）

arrest [ə'rest] *n.* 逮捕，拘留（2A）

ascent [ə'sent] *n.* 攀登；上坡路（11B）

ascertain [,æsə'tein] *vt.* 确定，弄清（11A）

asparagus [ə'spærəgəs] *n.* 芦笋（10B）

asset ['æset] *n.* 资产，财产（3A）

assign [ə'sain] *vt.* 分配，指派（6A）

assist [ə'sist] *vt.* 援助，帮助（5B）

assistance [ə'sistəns] *n.* 帮助，协助（3B）

associated [ə'səuʃieitid] *a.* 关联的，相关的（3A）

assume [ə'sjuːm] *vt.* 假定；设想（3B）

Atlantic [æt'læntik] *n.* 大西洋（10B）

attach [ə'tætʃ] *vt.* 缚上，系上（7A）

attempt [ə'tempt] *vt.* 尝试，企图（11B）

attendant [ə'tendənt] *n.* 服务员（1A）

attendant [ə'tendənt] *n.* 服务员，乘务员（5A）

auction ['ɔːkʃən] *vt.* 拍卖（12B）

authentic [ɔː'θentik] *a.* 可信的（12A）

authority [ɔː'θɔrəti] *n.* 权力；管理机构（7A）

authorize ['ɔːθəraiz] *vt.* 批准；授权（2B）

autobahn ['ɔtəubɑːn] *n.*（德国的）高速公路（11B）

autostrada [ɔː'təustrɑːdɑ] *n.* 意大利的高速公路（11B）

availability [ə,veilə'biliti] *n.* 可用性；有效性；实用性（1A）

available [ə'veiləbl] *a.* 可得到的;可利用的(2B)

avenue ['ævə,njuː] *n.* 林荫道；大街（7B）

aviation [,eivi'eiʃən] *n.* 飞行，航空；航空学，航空术（6B）

backpack ['bæk,pæk] *n.* 背包（2B）

back-pack [bæk pæk] *n.* 背包（11A）

backpack ['bæk,pæk] *n.* 背包（13A）

badge [bædʒ] *n.* 徽章，证章（12B）

baggage ['bægidʒ] *n.* 行李（2B）

bait [beit] *n.* 饵，诱惑物（9B）

balcony ['bælkəni] *n.* 阳台（11A）

Baltimore ['bɔːltimɔː] *n.* 巴尔的摩（美国城市）（7A）

bamboo [,bæm'buː] *n.* 竹子（11A）

band [bænd] *n.* 乐队（8B）

Bangkok [bæŋ'kɔk] n. 曼谷（泰国首都）（7B）

banned [bænd] a. 被禁止的（10A）

bargain ['bɑ:gin] n. 讨价还价；便宜货（11A）

bargain-hunter ['bɑ:gin 'hʌntə] n. 到处找便宜货的人（12A）

Basel ['bɑ:zl] n. 巴塞尔（瑞士西北部城市），在莱茵河畔（7B）

beacon ['bi:kən] n. 信标，灯标（6B）

beat [bi:t] vt. 打，打败（11A）

bedstead ['bed,sted] n. 床架（12B）

Belgium ['beldʒəm] n. 比利时（西欧国家）（11B）

bellboy ['bel,bɔi] n. 行李服务员；侍者（2B）

belonging [bi'lɔŋiŋ] n. 所有物，财产；行李（6A）

benchmark ['bentʃ,mɑ:k] n. 基准（3A）

benefit ['benifit] vt. 有益于，有助于（1A）

Bern [bə:n] n. 伯尔尼（瑞士首都）（7B）

beverage ['bevəridʒ] n. 饮料（10B）

bin [bin] n. 箱柜（5A）

binoculars [bi'nɔkjuləz] n. 双眼望远镜（11A）

bistro ['bi:strəu] n. 小酒馆，小咖啡店（10B）

bit [bit] n. 小块，少量（9B）

blade [bleid] n. 刀刃，刀片（13A）

board [bɔ:d] vt. 让乘客登机（或上船等）（4A）

boom [bu:m] vi. 繁荣，兴隆（1B）

bootleg ['bu:t,leg] a. 非法制造贩卖的（12B）

Bordeaux [,bɔ:'dəu] n. 波尔多葡萄酒（10B）

Boston ['bɔstən] n. 波士顿（美国马萨诸塞州首府）（7B）

boundary ['baundəri] n. 边界，分界线（4B）

bourgeois ['buəʒwɑ:] n. 中产阶级；商人（10B）

boutique [bu:'ti:k] n. 专卖流行衣服的小商店（12B）

braise [breiz] vt. 炖，蒸（10A）

brand [brænd] n. 商标，牌子（1A）

breathtaking ['breθ,teikiŋ] a. 惊人的，惊险的（11A）

briefcase ['bri:f,keis] n. 公文包（13A）

briefing ['bri:fiŋ] n. 简令；飞行前指示（5A）

briefly ['bri:fli] ad. 暂时地，简要地（11B）

Brisbane ['brizbən] n. 布里斯班（澳大利亚东部城市）（7B）

Broadway ['brɔ:d,wei] n. 纵贯纽约市的大街道，百老汇（12B）

brochure ['brəuʃə] n. 小册子（2A）

Brussels ['brʌslz] n. 布鲁塞尔（比利时首都）（7B）

buck [bʌk] n. <美口> 元（9B）

budget ['bʌdʒit] n. 预算（3A）

Buffalo ['bʌfələu] n. 布法罗（美国纽约州西部城市），水牛城（7B）

bulk [bʌlk] n. 大部分，大半（7B）

bummer ['bʌmə] n. 无赖，游民，游荡者，乞讨者（9B）

bund [bʌnd] n. 堤岸；码头（1B）

bundle ['bʌndl] vt. 捆扎（8B）

bungalow ['bʌŋgə,ləu] n. 平房，小屋（9A）

bunk [bʌŋk] n. （轮船，火车等的）铺位（7B）

Burberry ['bə:bəri] n. 巴宝莉（英国奢侈品牌）（12B）

bureau ['bjuərəu] n. 局；办事处（2A）

burgeon ['bə:dʒən] vi. （迅速）成长，发展（1A）

Burgundy ['bə:gəndi] n. 勃艮第（法国东南部地名，该地产的红葡萄酒也名勃艮第）（10B）

bustling ['bʌsliŋ] a. 熙熙攘攘的；忙碌的（1B）

bygone ['baigɔn] a. 过去的（11B）

cabaret ['kæbərei] n. 酒店或夜总会的卡巴莱歌舞表演（11B）

cabin ['kæbin] n. 机舱，船舱（5A）

Calais ['kælei] n. 加来（法国北部港市）（11B）

calendar ['kælində] n. 日历，历法（5B）

California [,kæli'fɔ:njə] n. 加利福尼亚（美国州名）（8B）

calligraphy [kə'ligrəfi] n. 书法（12A）

calvados ['kælvədɔs] n. 苹果白兰地酒（10B）

camping ['kæmpiŋ] n. 露营，野营（9A）

cancellation [,kænsə'leiʃən] n. 取消（13A）

Cantonese [,kæntə'ni:z] n. 广东人，广东话（11A）

capability [,keipə'biləti] n. 能力；性能（6B）

capacity [kə'pæsəti] n. 容积，容量（6B）

capacity [kə'pæsəti] n. 容量（8A）

capital ['kæpitəl] *n.* 大写字母（6A）

caravan ['kærəvæn] *n.* 旅行队，大篷车（9A）

carbon ['ka:bən] *n.* 副本（2B）

cargo ['ka:gəu] *n.*（船、飞机所载的）货物（5B）

Caribbean [,kæri'biən] *a.* 加勒比海的（8A）

carousel [,kærə'sel] *n.* 传送带（6A）

carrier ['kæriə] *n.* 从事运输业的公司或企业；运载工具（5B）

carry-on ['kæriɔn] *n.* 随身行李（13A）

cart [ka:t] *n.* 大车，手推车（5B）

carton ['ka:tən] *n.* 硬纸盒，纸板箱（13B）

carving ['ka:viŋ] *n.* 雕刻品，雕刻（12A）

cashmere ['kæʃ,miə] *n.* 开司米，山羊绒（12A）

casino [kə'si:nəu] *n.* 娱乐场；赌场（1A）

castle ['ka:sl] *n.* 城堡（11B）

castoff ['ka:stɔ:f] *n.* 废弃物（12B）

catalog ['kætəlɔg] *n.* 目录，目录册（12B）

category ['kætəgəri] *n.* 种类（10A）

cater ['keitə] *vi.* 备办食物（9A）

catering ['keitəriŋ] *n.* 公共饮食业（1A）

cathedral [kə'θi:drəl] *n.* 大教堂（11B）

Catholic ['kæθəlik] *n.* 天主教徒（10B）

cauliflower ['kɔli,flauə] *n.* 花椰菜（10B）

caveat ['keivi,æt] *n.* 警告，告诫（9B）

ceiling ['si:liŋ] *n.* 升限，绝对升限（6B）

celebration [,selə'breiʃən] *n.* 庆祝，庆典（13B）

ceramics [sə'ræmiks] *n.* 制陶术,制陶业（12A）

certificate [sə'tifikət] *n.* 证书（2A）

certified ['sə:tifaid] *a.* 被鉴定的（5B）

champagne [ʃæm'pein] *n.* 香槟酒（10B）

characteristic [,kæriktə'ristik] *n.* 特 性，特 征（6B）

charge [tʃa:dʒ] *n.* 费用（4A）

Charleston ['tʃa:lstən] *n.* 查尔斯顿（美国西弗吉尼亚州首府）（8B）

Charolais ['ʃærəlei] *n.* 夏洛来牛（原产于法国）（10B）

chart [tʃa:t] *n.* 图表（7A）

charter ['tʃa:tə] *n.* 租，包（船、车、飞机等）（6B）

chauvinism ['ʃəuvə,nizəm] *n.* 盲目的爱国心，沙文主义（10B）

check-in [tʃekin] *n.*（机场）登记，报到（13A）

checkpoint ['tʃek,pɔint] *n.* 检查站（4B）

chef [ʃef] *n.* 厨师（10B）

chianti [ki'ænti] *n.* 意大利基安蒂葡萄酒（11B）

Chicago [ʃi'ka:gəu] *n.* 芝加哥（美国中西部城市）（7B）

Chile ['tʃili] *n.* 智利（7B）

chili ['tʃili] *n.* 红辣椒（10A）

cholera ['kɔlərə] *n.* 霍乱（2A）

chop [tʃɔp] *vt.* 斩碎（10A）

chopstick ['tʃɔp,stik] *n.* 筷子（10A）

Christmas ['krisməs] *n.* 圣诞节（纪念耶稣基督诞生的节日，12月25日）（12B）

chug [tʃʌg] *vi.*（发动机等）发出突突声（7B）

Chunnel ['tʃʌnəl] *n.* 英吉利海峡隧道（铁路）（7B）

Churchill ['tʃə:tʃil] *n.* 丘吉尔镇（加拿大马尼托巴省之一小城镇）（7B）

chute [ʃu:t] *n.* 滑道（5B）

cigar [si'ga:] *n.* 雪茄（13B）

cigarette [,sigə'ret] *n.* 香烟，纸烟（13B）

circulate ['sə:kjuleit] *vt.*（使）流通（2B）

cite [sait] *vt.* 引用，引证（8B）

Citibank ['sitibæŋk] *n.* 美国花旗银行（2B）

civilian [si'viljən] *a.* 民间的，民用的（5B）

claim [kleim] *n.* 认领（6A）

classic ['klæsik] *a.* 第一流的（10B）

classification [,klæsifi'keiʃən] *n.* 分类，分级（9A）

clearance ['kliərəns] *n.* 清除，清理（12B）

client ['klaiənt] *n.* 顾客，客户（3A）

clientele [,kli:ɔn'teil] *n.* 客户（8B）

climate ['klaimət] *n.* 气候（2B）

cloisonné [klwa:zɔŋ'nei] *n.* 景泰蓝（12A）

cluster ['klʌstə] *vi.* 丛生，成群（12B）

coach [kəutʃ] *n.* 长途汽车（3A）

coastal ['kəustl] *a.* 沿海的；海岸的（1B）

cockpit ['kɔk,pit] *n.* 驾驶员座舱（5B）

code [kəud] *n.* 代号；代码（4B）

coffer ['kɔfə] *n.* 保险箱（1A）

cognac ['kɔn,jæk] *n.* 干邑（白兰地酒的一种）（10B）

coin [kɔin] *n.* 硬币（6A）

coincidental [kəu,insi'dentl] *a.* 一致的，符合的；巧合的（10B）

coliseum [,kɔli'siəm] *n.* 大剧场（11B）

collapse [kə'læps] *n.* 倒塌，塌陷（8B）

collateral [kə'lætərəl] *n.* 抵押品，担保物（2A）

Cologne [kə'ləun] *n.* 科隆（德国城市）（7B）

colonial [kə'ləuniəl] *a.* 殖民的，殖民地的（12A）

combination [,kɔmbi'neiʃən] *n.* 结合，联合（5B）

combine [kəm'bain] *vt.* 联结；结合（1B）

combined [kəm'baind] *a.* 组合的，结合的（8A）

commercial [kə'mə:ʃəl] *a.* 商业的，贸易的（11A）

commission [kə'miʃən] *n.* 佣金，回扣（12A）

committed [kə'mitid] *a.* 承诺……的（3B）

communal [kɔ'mju:nl] *a.* 公共的，公社的（9A）

community [kə'mju:niti] *n.* 社区；团体（1A）

commuter [kə'mju:tə] *n.* （远距离）上下班往返的人（5B）

comparison [kəm'pærisn] *n.* 比较，对照（6B）

compartment [kəm'pɑ:tmənt] *n.* 行李柜（2B）

compatible [kəm'pætəbl] *a.* 协调的，一致的；兼容的（3B）

competitive [kəm'petətiv] *a.* 竞争的（13A）

complicated ['kɔmpli,keitid] *a.* 错综复杂的（2B）

component [kəm'pəunənt] *n.* 组成部分，成分（6B）

comprehensive [,kɔmpri'hensiv] *a.* 全面的，广泛的（9B）

comprise [kəm'praɪz] *vt.* 包含，由……组成（8A）

compulsory [kəm'pʌlsəri] *a.* 必须做的，强制的（3A）

concept ['kɔnsept] *n.* 观念；概念（1A）

concerning [kən'sə:niŋ] *prep.* 关于，涉及（2B）

concourse ['kɔŋkɔ:s] *n.* 中央大厅，广场（13B）

confection [kən'fekʃən] *n.* 甜点（10B）

confirm [kən'fə:m] *vt.* 确定，确认（2A）

confiscate ['kɔnfi,skeit] *vt.* 没收，充公，查抄（12A）

Confucius [kən'fju:ʃəs] *n.* 孔子（10A）

consent [kən'sent] *n.* 同意；赞成（2B）

conservation [,kɔnsə'veiʃən] *n.* 保护；保持；保存（1A）

consortium [kən'sɔ:tiəm] *n.* 国际财团（3B）

constitute ['kɔnsti,tju:t] *vt.* 构成（5B）

constraint [kən'streint] *n.* 约束，强制（11B）

consulate ['kɔnsjulət] *n.* 领事馆（2A）

consult [kən'sʌlt] *vt.* 请教，咨询，查询（13A）

consume [kən'sju:m] *vt.* 吃，喝；消耗（5A）

consumption [kən'sʌmpʃən] *n.* 消费（1A）

contemporary [kən'tempərəri] *a.* 当代的，同时代的（12A）

Continent ['kɔntinənt] *n.* 大陆（13B）

contrary ['kɔntrəri] *n.* 反面，相反（13B）

contribution [,kɔntri'bju:ʃn] *n.* 贡献；捐献（1A）

convenient [kən'vi:niənt] *a.* 便利的，方便的（7A）

conventional [kən'venʃnəl] *a.* 惯例的，常规的，习俗的，传统的（9A）

convergence [kən'və:dʒəns] *n.* 会聚，集中（1A）

convert ['kɔnvə:t] *vt.* 兑换；转变（2B）

conveyor [kən'veiə] *n.* 传送机，传送带（13A）

co-operate [kəu'ɔpəreit] *vi.* 合作（6A）

copilot ['kəu,pailət] *n.* （飞机的）副驾驶员（5B）

corkscrew ['kɔ:kskru:] *n.* 开塞钻，螺丝锥（13A）

cornerstone ['kɔ:nə,stəun] *n.* 基础，基石（1A）

cornstarch ['kɔ:n,stɑ:tʃ] *n.* 玉米淀粉（10A）

corridor ['kɔridɔ:] *n.* 通道，走廊（7A）

costume ['kɔstju:m] *n.* 装束，服装（11B）

couchette [ku:'ʃet] *n.* 睡铺，有卧铺的车厢（7B）

counterfeit ['kauntəfit] *a.* 伪造的，假冒的（2A）

courier ['kuriə] *n.* 信使，送急件的人；旅游服务员（5B）

courtesy ['kə:təsi] *n.* 谦恭，礼貌（7A）

coverage ['kʌvəridʒ] *n.* 覆盖范围（6B）

craft [krɑ:ft] *n.* 工艺，手艺（12A）

crash [kræʃ] *n.* 碰撞，坠落，坠毁（5A）

crawl [krɔ:l] *vi.* 徐徐行进（8B）

creativity [,kri:ei'tivəti] *n.* 创造力；创造性（1A）

credibility [,kredə'biləti] *n.* 可靠，可信（3A）

crescent-shaped ['kreznt ʃeipt] *a.* 新月形的（1B）

crew [kru:] *n.*（船上、飞机上的）工作人员；全体船员；全体乘务员（5A）

crisp [krisp] *a.* 脆的，易碎的（10A）

critical ['kritikəl] *a.* 关键的，决定性的（3A）

crosswind ['krɔs,wind] *n.* 横风，侧风（6B）

cruise [kru:z] *n.* 乘船游览（8A）

Cuban ['kju:bən] *a.* 古巴（人）的（13B）

cuisine [kwi'zi:n] *n.* 厨房烹调法，烹饪（10A）

culinary ['kʌlinəri] *a.* 厨房的，烹调用的（10B）

culture-based ['kʌltʃə beist] *a.* 基于文化的（1A）

curbside ['kə:bsaid] *n.* 街道边（4A）

currency ['kʌrənsi] *n.* 货币（2A）

custom ['kʌstəm] *n.* 风俗；习惯（1B）

customs ['kʌstəmz] *n.* 关税；海关（2A）

cut-off ['kʌtɔf] *n.* 截止点（4B）

cycle ['saikl] *n.* 周期，循环（5B）

dampen ['dæmpən] *vt.* 使沮丧（8B）

damper ['dæmpə] *n.* 使人扫兴的人或事（9B）

Danish ['deiniʃ] *a.* 丹麦的（2B）

database ['deitə,beis] *n.* 数据库，资料库（3A）

daunting [,dɔ:ntiŋ] *a.* 使人畏缩的（10B）

dawn [dɔ:n] *n.* 黎明，拂晓，破晓（7B）

dealer ['di:lə] *n.* 经销商，商人（12B）

declaration [,deklə'reiʃən] *n.* 申报；宣布（2B）

declare [di'klεə] *vt.* 申报（纳税品）（13A）

deco [dei'kəu] *n.* 装饰,装潢（decoration）（12B）

decorator ['dekə,reitə] *n.* 裱糊匠（12B）

dedicated ['dedi,keitid] *a.* 专用的（7B）

defer [di'fə:] *vt.* 推迟，延期（3A）

define [di'fain] *vt.* 定义，详细说明（6B）

definitely ['defənətli] *ad.* 明确地,干脆地（11A）

definition [,defi'niʃən] *n.* 定义；解说（3A）

degree [di'gri:] *n.* 学位（5B）

delay [di'lei] *n.* 耽搁，延迟（13A）

delicacy ['delikəsi] *n.* 精制食品（10A）

deliver [di'livə] *vt.* 递送（5B）

delta ['deltə] *n.* 三角洲（1B）

demanding [di'mɑ:ndiŋ] *a.* 过分要求的，苛求的（6B）

demographics [,demə'græfiks] *n.* 人口统计学（8A）

demonstration [,demən'streiʃən] *n.* 示范（5A）

denomination [di,nɔmi'neiʃən] *n.* 面额，票面金额（2A）

denominator [di'nɔmi,neitə] *n.* 标准，共同特性（13B）

densely [densli] *ad.* 浓密地，浓厚地（11A）

deodorant [di:'əudərənt] *n.* 除臭剂（13A）

departure [di'pɑ:tʃə] *n.* 启程，出发，离开（4A）

depict [di'pikt] *vt.* 描述，描写（12A）

descent [di'sent] *n.* 降下，降落（11B）

designate ['dezigneit] *vt.* 指定，指派（13A）

designation [,dezig'neiʃən] *n.* 规定；名称（7B）

despite [di'spait] *prep.* 不管,尽管,不论（10B）

destination [,desti'neiʃən] *n.* 目的地，终点（5A）

detector [di'tektə] *n.* 探测器（5A）

deter [di'tə:] *vt.* 阻止，防止（2A）

determine [di'tə:min] *vt. & vi.* 决定,确定（6A）

dietary ['daiətəri] *n.* 规定的食物（13A）

differentiation [,difə,renʃi'eiʃn] *n.* 区别（8A）

digestif [dai'dʒestif] *n.*（饭前或饭后喝的）助消化饮料（10B）

diphtheria [dip'θiəriə] *n.* 白喉（2A）

diploma [di'pləumə] *n.* 证书，文凭（3A）

directory [dai'rektəri] *n.* 姓名地址录，目录（9B）

dirt [də:t] *n.* 污垢，泥土（5B）

disabled-accessible [dis'eibld ək'sesəbl] *a.* 可供残疾人使用的（7A）

discard [dis'kɑ:d] *vt.* 丢弃，抛弃（13B）

discerning [di'sə:niŋ] *a.* 有辨识能力的（9A）

discount ['dis,kaunt] *n.* 折扣（3A）

discourage [dis'kʌridʒ] vt. 使气馁; 阻碍（12A）

disembark [,disim'bɑːk] vt. 使下（车、船、飞机等）（5B）

disorientation [dis,ɔːriən'teiʃən] n. 方向知觉的丧失; 迷惑（5B）

dispatcher [di'spætʃə] n. 调度员（7A）

display [di'splei] vt. 陈列，展览; 显示（11A）

dispute [di'spjuːt] vt. 反驳，驳斥（8B）

disregard [,disri'gɑːd] vt. 不理，漠视（10B）

disseminate [di'semineit] vt. 散布，传播（消息、观念等）（3A）

distinct [di'stiŋkt] a. 清楚的，明显的; 截然不同的，独特的（9A）

distinction [di'stiŋkʃən] n. 区别; 差别（3A）

distinctly [di'stiŋktli] ad. 清楚地; 明显地; 截然不同地; 独特地（1A）

distinguish [di'stiŋgwiʃ] vt. 区别，辨别（6B）

diversify [dai'vəːsifai] vt. 使多样化; 变化（1A）

dizzy ['dizi] a. 晕眩的，昏乱的，使头晕目眩的，令人头昏眼花的（11A）

documentation [,dɔkjumen'teiʃən] n. 证明文件的提供（3A）

domestic [də'mestik] a. 家庭的; 国内的（1A）

dominate ['dɔmineit] vt. 统治，支配，控制（8A）

dormitory ['dɔːmitri] n. 宿舍（9B）

dormitory-style ['dɔːmitri stail] a. 宿舍式的（9B）

double-digit ['dʌbl 'didʒit] a. 两位数的（1B）

dough [dəu] n. 生面团（10A）

Dover ['dəuvə] n. 多佛（英国东南部港市）（11B）

downtown [daun'taun] n. 市中心区，商业区（7A）

downturn ['daun,təːn] n. 低迷时期（3A）

drawback ['drɔː,bæk] n. 缺点; 障碍（9B）

drug [drʌg] n. 麻醉药品,麻醉剂; 瘾性毒品（6A）

due [djuː] a. 预期的（8B）

duration [dju'reiʃən] n. 持续时间; 期间（2B）

dusk [dʌsk] n. 薄暮，黄昏（7B）

dust [dʌst] vt. 撒（5B）

duty ['djuːti] n. 税（13A）

dynamic [dai'næmik] a. 有活力的，精力充沛的（1B）

ease [iːz] n. 舒适，悠闲（8B）

ecological [,iːkə'lɔdʒikl] a. 生态的（1B）

ecologically [,iːkə'lɔdʒikli] ad. 生态地（1A）

ecosystem ['iːkəu,sistəm] n. 生态系统（1A）

Ecuador ['ekwədɔː] n. 厄瓜多尔（7B）

effects [i'fekts] n. 动产，家庭财物（13A）

efficiency [i'fiʃənsi] n. 效率，功效（6B）

efficient [i'fiʃənt] a. 有效率的（11A）

elaborate [i'læbəreit] a. 精心制作的（10A）

electronic [elek'trɔnik] a. 电子的（13A）

elegant ['eligənt] a. 第一流的（9A）

embark [im'bɑːk] vi. 着手，从事（8A）

embassy ['embəsi] n. 大使馆; 使馆官员（2A）

embroidery [im'brɔidəri] n. 刺绣品，刺绣（12A）

emergence [i'məːdʒəns] n. 出现（1A）

emphasize ['emfəsaiz] vt. 强调，着重（5B）

employ [im'plɔi] vt. 雇用; 用，使用（1A）

employment [im'plɔimənt] n. 雇用; 工作; 职业（1A）

enchanting [in'tʃɑːntiŋ] a. 讨人喜欢的，迷人的（11B）

encounter [in'kauntə] n. 遭遇，遇到（5B）

endorsement [in'dɔːsmənt] n. 背书，签署文件; 认可（2A）

engine ['endʒin] n. 发动机; 机车，火车头（1A）

enhance [in'hɑːns] vt. 增加; 提高（1B）

ensure [in'ʃɔː] vt. 确保，保证（5A）

enter ['entə] vt. 进入（6A）

entertainment [,entə'teinmənt] n. 款待; 娱乐; 娱乐表演（1A）

entrepreneur [,ɔntrəprə'nəː] n. 企业家; 主办人（12A）

entropy ['entrəpi] n. 熵，平均信息量（13B）

entry ['entri] n. 进入（6A）

environment [in'vairənmənt] n. 环境; 外界（1A）

epitomize [i'pitəmaiz] vt. 代表，成为……的典范（7B）

equalize ['i:kwəlaiz] vt. 使相等；补偿（1A）

escalator ['eskə,leitə] n. 电动扶梯，自动扶梯（11A）

essential [i'senʃəl] a. 必要的，必不可少的（5B）

establishment [i'stæbliʃmənt] n. 建立，成立（1A）

estate [i'steit] n. 不动产，财产（11A）

estimate ['estimeit] vt. 估计，估价，评估（12B）

Euro ['juərəu] n. 欧元（2B）

evacuation [i,vækju'eiʃən] n. 撤退；疏散（5A）

evaluate [i'væljueit] vt. 评价，估计（9A）

excavate ['ekskəveit] vt. 挖掘（1B）

exceed [ik'si:d] vt. 超过，超出（2A）

exceptional [ik'sepʃnəl] a. 特别的，异常的（9A）

exclusive [ik'sklu:siv] a. 高级的（10A）

exclusively [ik'sklu:sivli] ad. 排外地，专有地（7A）

excursion [ik'skə:ʃən] n. 远足；短途旅行（3A）

execute ['eksi,kju:t] vt. 执行，实行（6B）

executive [ig'zekjutiv] n. 经理主管人员（8B）

exemplify [ig'zemplifai] vt. 例证，例示（8A）

exempt [ig'zempt] vt. 免除（2B）

exit ['eksit] n. 安全门；出口（5A）

exotic [ig'zɔtik] a. 异国情调的（8A）

expand [ik'spænd] vi. 扩大（1A）

expandable [ik'spændəbl] a. 可张开的，可扩大的（13B）

expansion [ik'spænʃən] n. 扩大，扩张，发展（8A）

expect [ik'spekt] vt. 期待，盼望，指望，料想（13B）

expedite ['ekspədait] vt. 促进，加速（2A）

experience [ik'spiəriəns] n. 经验，阅历，经历（13B）

expire [ik'spaiə] vi. 期满，终止（4A）

exploration [,eksplɔ'reiʃən] n. 探索，探险（8A）

express [ik'spres] a. 急速的（7A）

extensive [ik'stensiv] a. 广大的，广阔的，广泛的（5B）

extinguisher [ik'stiŋgwiʃə] n. 灭火器（6B）

facilitate [fə'siləteit] vt. 使容易，使便利（6B）

facility [fə'siliti] n.（常作 facilities）设施，设备（1A）

fairly ['fɛəli] ad. 相当地，还算（13B）

fake [feik] n. 假货（12A）

fanciful ['fænsifl] a. 空想的；奇怪的，稀奇的（10B）

fare [fɛə] n. 费用（13A）

farecard ['fɛəkɑ:d] n. 月票卡（7A）

farmhouse ['fɑ:m,haus] n. 农场里的住房，农舍，农家（9A）

fatigue [fə'ti:g] n. 疲乏；劳累（5B）

ferry ['feri] n. 摆渡，渡船，渡口（11A）

figure ['figə] n. 数字（6B）

fin [fin] n. 鱼翅（10A）

firm [fə:m] n. 公司，（合伙）商号（5B）

flaw [flɔ:] n. 缺点；裂纹，瑕疵（12B）

flawless ['flɔ:ləs] a. 无瑕疵的，无缺点的（7B）

fleeting ['fli:tiŋ] a. 快速的，敏捷的（7B）

flesh [fleʃ] n. 肉（10B）

flexibility [,fleksə'biləti] n. 灵活性（3B）

flip [flip] vi. 用指轻弹；翻（3B）

Florence ['flɔ:rəns] n. 佛罗伦萨（意大利中部城市）（11B）

Florida ['flɔridə] n. 佛罗里达（美国州名）（8B）

fluctuate ['flʌktjueit] vi. 波动，起伏（3A）

folding ['fəuldiŋ] a. 可折叠的（13A）

folklore ['fəuk,lɔ:(r)] n. 民间传说（11B）

forecast ['fɔ:kɑ:st] vt. 预测，预报（1B）

foremost ['fɔ:məust] a. 最重要的；主要的（1A）

formation [fɔ:'meiʃən] n. 形成，构成（11B）

fortress ['fɔ:trəs] n. 堡垒，要塞（11B）

foster ['fɔstə] vt. 养育，培植；促进 1A

fountain ['fauntin] n. 喷泉（11B）

franc [fræŋk] n. 法郎（2B）

franchise ['fræntʃaiz] n. 经销权，专卖权，特许（3B）

frequent ['fri:kwənt] a. 经常的，频繁的（4B）

frequently ['fri:kwəntli] ad. 常常，频繁地（3A）

frigid ['fridʒid] a. 寒冷的（2B）

frustrate [frʌ'streit] vt. 挫败，阻挠，使感到灰心（13B）

fry [frai] vt. 油炸，油煎（10A）

fulfill [ful'fil] vt. 履行；实现；完成（计划等）（1A）

function ['fʌŋkʃən] n. 功能，作用（5B）

fundamental [ˌfʌndə'mentl] n. 基本原则，基本原理（10B）

furnish ['fə:niʃ] vt. 供应，提供，供给（10A）

furnishings ['fə:niʃiŋz] n. 家具陈设（6B）

Galveston ['gælvəstən] n. 加尔维斯敦（美国得克萨斯州南部港口城市）（8B）

gaming ['geimiŋ] n. 赌博，赌胜负（1A）

gangplank ['gæŋˌplæŋk] n.（上下船的）跳板（8B）

garlic ['gɑ:lik] n. 大蒜，蒜头（10A）

Gaspé [gæs'pei] n. 加斯佩半岛（加）（7B）

gastrointestinal [gæstrəuin'testinl] n. 胃肠，肠胃（8B）

Gaul [gɔ:l] n. 高卢（欧洲西部一地区）（10B）

gear [giə] n. 传动装置（11A）

generate ['dʒenəreit] vt. 产生，创造（1A）

generic [dʒə'nerik] a. 普通的，一般的（3B）

Geneva [dʒi'ni:və] n. 日内瓦（瑞士城市）（7B）

genuine ['dʒenjuin] a. 真实的，真正的（12A）

glimpse [glimps] n. 一瞥，一睹（7B）

global ['gləubəl] a. 球形的；全球的，全世界的（1A）

glutinous ['glu:tinəs] a. 黏性的（10A）

Google ['gu:gl] 美国谷歌公司（9B）

Gothic ['gɔθik] a. 哥特式的（11B）

graft [grɑ:ft] n. 嫁接；移植（1A）

grant [grɑ:nt] vt. 同意，准予（6A）

grease [gri:s] n. 油脂（5B）

greyhound ['greiˌhaund] n. 美国灰狗长途汽车；特快海轮（7A）

grossly ['grəusli] ad. 严重地（10A）

ground [graund] n. 场所；基础，根据（3A）

groundwork ['graundˌwə:k] n. 基础；根基（8A）

guarantee [ˌgærən'ti:] vt. 保证，允诺，确保（13B）

guesthouse ['gesthaus] n. 上等旅社，宾馆（9A）

guidance ['gaidəns] n. 指导，领导（5B）

guilty ['gilti] a. 犯罪的，有罪的，心虚的（11A）

guy [gai] n. 家伙，人（11A）

haggle ['hægl] vi. 讨价还价（12A）

Halifax ['hælifæks] n. 哈利法克斯市（加拿大城市）；哈利法克斯港（7B）

halt [hɔ:lt] n. 停止，暂停（5A）

Hamburg ['hæmbə:g] n. 汉堡（德国城市）（7B）

handicapped ['hændiˌkæpt] a. 身体有缺陷的（4A）

handler ['hændlə] n. 管理人，操纵者（5B）

hand-woven [hænd 'wəuvən] n. 手工织物（12A）

handy ['hændi] a. 手边的，就近的，唾手可得的，便利的（6A）

Harrisburg ['hærisbə:g] n. 哈里斯堡（美国城市）（7A）

hassle ['hæsl] n. 困难，麻烦（8A）

Hawaii [hə'wɑ:i:] n. 夏威夷（美国州名）（8B）

hawker ['hɔ:kə] n. 叫卖小贩（12A）

headquarters [hed'kwɔ:təz] n. 总部（11A）

Hecht's [hekts] n. 赫克特百货公司（12B）

helicopter ['heliˌkɔptə] n. 直升机（5B）

hence [hens] ad. 因此，从此（11A）

heritage ['heritidʒ] n. 遗产；继承权；传统（1A）

hesitate ['heziteit] vi. 犹豫，踌躇（6A）

hi-tech ['hai'tek] a. 高科技的（7B）

holder ['həuldə] n. 持有者（6A）

horrendous [hɔ'rendəs] a. 可怕的（4B）

hospitable [hɔ'spitəbl] a. 好客的，招待周到的（9A）

hydraulic [hai'drɔ:lik] a. 水力的，水压的（5B）

identical [ai'dentikəl] a. 同一的，同样的（11A）

identification [aiˌdentifi'keiʃən] n. 身份证明（2A）

identify [ai'dentifai] vt. 鉴别，标识（4A）

illegal [i'li:gəl] a. 违法的，不合规定的（5B）

illuminate [i'lu:mineit] vt. 照明，照亮；使灿烂，以灯火装饰（11A）

imitation [ˌimi'teiʃən] n. 模仿，效法；赝品，仿造物（12A）

immense [i'mens] a. 极大的（8A）

immigration [ˌimiˈgreiʃən] *n.* 移居入境，移民入境（4A）

immunization [ˌimjunaiˈzeiʃən] *n.* 免疫（2A）

impose [imˈpəuz] *vt.* 征税（2B）

impractically [imˈpræktikəli] *ad.* 不切实际地（10A）

improve [imˈpruːv] *vt.* 改善，改进（1A）

improvement [imˈpruːvmənt] *n.* 改进，进步（5B）

inadequate [inˈædikwət] *a.* 不充分的，不适当的（11B）

incentivize [inˈsentivaiz] *vt.* 刺激，激励（3B）

incidentally [ˌinsiˈdentəli] *ad.* 附带地，顺便提及地（11A）

income [ˈinkʌm] *n.* 收入，收益（1A）

incorporate [inˈkɔːpəreit] *vt.* 合并；一体化（1A）

incredible [inˈkredəbl] *a.* 难以置信的（11A）

indicate [ˈindikeit] *vt.* 指出；表明（3B）

indicator [ˈindiˌkeitə] *n.* 指示器（6B）

individually [ˌindiˈvidʒuəli] *ad.* 个别地；单独地；个人地（5B）

Indonesia [ˌindəuˈniːzjə] *n.* 印度尼西亚（1B）

industry [ˈindəstri] *n.* 工业；企业（1A）

inevitably [inˈevitəbli] *ad.* 不可避免，必定（10B）

inexpensive [ˌinikˈspensiv] *a.* 便宜的，不贵的（1A）

inferior [inˈfiəriə] *a.* 下等的，下级的；差的，次的（12A）

infest [inˈfest] *vt.* 大量滋生（2B）

inflate [inˈfleit] *vt.* 使膨胀，使充气（5B）

influence [ˈinfluəns] *vt.* 影响（3A）

info [ˈinfəu] *n.* 信息，资料（7B）

infrastructure [ˈinfrəˌstrʌktʃə] *n.* 基础设施，基础建设（1A）

ingredient [inˈgriːdiənt] *n.* 成分，因素（10A）

inhabitant [inˈhæbitənt] *n.* 居民，居住者（9B）

initial [iˈniʃəl] *a.* 最初的；词首的（1A）

initiation [iˌniʃiˈeiʃən] *n.* 开始，启动（1B）

innovation [ˌinəuˈveiʃən] *n.* 改革，创新（10B）

Innsbruck [ˈinzbruk] *n.* 因斯布鲁克（奥地利西部城市）（11B）

inoculate [iˈnɔkjuleit] *vt.* 预防注射，接种疫苗（2B）

inspection [inˈspekʃən] *n.* 检查，视察（13A）

install [inˈstɔːl] *vt.* 安装（6B）

institute [ˈinstiˌtjuːt] *vt.* 开始；制定（7A）

instructor [inˈstrʌktə] *n.* 指导者（5B）

instrument [ˈinstrumənt] *n.* 工具，器械，器具（13A）

instrumentation [ˌinstrumenˈteiʃən] *n.* 检测仪表，仪表设备（6B）

insurance [inˈʃuərəns] *n.* 保险（3A）

integrate [ˈintiˌgreit] *vt.* 使成整体，使一体化（1B）

integrity [inˈtegrəti] *n.* 完整性；正直（3A）

intention [inˈtenʃən] *n.* 意图，目的（4A）

interact [ˌintərˈækt] *vi.* 相互作用，交互（5B）

interior [inˈtiəriə] *n.* 内部（5B）

intersection [ˈintəˌsekʃən] *n.* 十字路口，交叉点（6B）

interstate [ˌintəˈsteit] *a.* 州际的（7B）

intestine [inˈtestin] *n.* 肠（10B）

intimate [ˈintimət] *a.* 亲密的，熟悉的（8B）

invariably [inˈveəriəbli] *ad.* 不变地，总是（3B）

investment [inˈvestmənt] *n.* 投资（1A）

involve [inˈvɔlv] *vt.* 包括（10B）

Irish [ˈairiʃ] *n.* 爱尔兰人；爱尔兰语；爱尔兰 *a.* 爱尔兰的（9A）

irregular [iˈregjulə] *a.* 不规律的（5B）

Israel [ˈizreil] *n.* 以色列（西南亚国家）（11B）

issue [ˈisuː] *vt.* 发给（6A）

itinerant [aiˈtinərənt] *a.* 巡回的（6B）

itinerary [aiˈtinərəri] *n.* 旅程，旅行路线（8A）

Jacksonville [ˈdʒæksənvil] *n.* 杰克逊维尔（美国佛罗里达州东北部港市）（2B）

Jasper [ˈdʒæspə] *n.* 杰士伯（加拿大大城市）（7B）

jeans [dʒiːnz] *n.* 牛仔裤（12B）

Jordan [ˈdʒɔːdn] *n.* 约旦（西南亚国家）（11B）

joyful [ˈdʒɔifl] *a.* 快乐的，令人欢欣的（13B）

jubilee [ˈdʒuːbiliː] *n.* 周年大庆（13B）

keyboard ['ki:bɔ:d] *n.* 键盘（5B）

kidney ['kidni] *n.*（动物可食用的）腰子（10B）

kimono [ki'məunəu] *n.* 和服（11A）

K-Mart ['keɪmɑːt] *n.* K-玛特折扣店（12B）

knot [nɔt] *n.* 节，海里/小时（航速单位）（6B）

kosher ['kəuʃə] *a.* 正当的；合适的（8B）

Kowloon ['kau'lu:n] *n.* 九龙（香港对面的半岛），九龙港埠（11A）

Krone ['krəunə] *n.* 克朗（丹麦、挪威的货币单位）（2B）

label ['leibl] *n.* 标签，签条，商标，标志（11A）

laborious [lə'bɔ:riəs] *a.* 艰苦的，费力的（11A）

lag [læg] *n.* 迟延，滞后（13B）

landing ['lændiŋ] *n.* 降落（6B）

landscape ['lænd,skeip] *n.* 风景；山水画；地形（1B）

launch [lɔ:ntʃ] *vt.* 使（船）下水（8B）

laundry ['lɔ:ndri] *n.* 洗熨（13B）

Lausanne [ləu'zæn] *n.* 洛桑（瑞士西部城市）（7B）

lawn [lɔ:n] *n.* 草地，草坪（12B）

layover ['lei,əuvə] *n.* 中途的短暂停留，临时滞留，中途下车（5B）

Lenten ['lentn] *a.* 大斋戒的，大斋戒期间的（10B）

leprosy ['leprəsi] *n.* 麻风（2B）

lettuce ['letis] *n.* 莴苣，生菜（10A）

Levi's ['li:vaiz] *n.* 李维斯（美国牛仔裤品牌）（12B）

levy ['levi] *vt.* 征收，征税（4A）

license ['laisəns] *vt.* 准许；发给执照；批准（3A）

Liechtenstein ['liktənstain] *n.* 列支敦士登（中欧国家）（11B）

lighting ['laitiŋ] *n.* 照明，照明设备（6B）

limousine [,limə'zi:n] *n.* 豪华轿车（7A）

linen ['linin] *n.* 亚麻布，亚麻制品（12B）

liner ['lainə] *n.* 邮轮（8A）

lira ['liərə] *n.* 里拉（意大利的货币单位）（2B）

literally ['litərəli] *ad.* 照字面意义,逐字地（11A）

livelihood ['laivlihud] *n.* 生活，生计（1A）

load [ləud] *vt.* 装载，装填（5B）

localizer ['ləukəlaizə] *n.* 定位器，定位信标（6B）

locate [ləu'keit] *vt.* 找到……位置（5A）

locomotive [,ləukə'məutiv] *n.* 机车，火车头（7B）

lodging ['lɔdʒiŋ] *n.* 住宿（2A）

Loehmann's ['ləumənz] *n.* 洛曼百货公司（12B）

lot [lɔt] *n.* 一块地，地区（7A）

lounge [laundʒ] *n.* 闲逛，休闲室（9A）

Lucerne [lu:'sə:n] *n.* 卢塞恩（瑞士中部城市）（11B）

lucrative ['lu:krətiv] *a.* 有利的，赚钱的（8A）

luncheon ['lʌntʃən] *n.* 午宴，正式的午餐（10B）

lure [ljuə] *vt.* 引诱（12B）

lush [lʌʃ] *a.* 豪华的（12B）

luxurious [lʌg'zjuəriəs] *a.* 奢侈的，豪华的（9A）

luxury ['lʌkʃəri] *n.* 奢侈；豪华（8A）

Macy's ['meisiz] *n.* 梅西百货（13B）

magnificent [mæg'nifisnt] *a.* 华丽的，宏伟的（11B）

maintain [men'tein] *vt.* 保持，维持（6B）

maintenance ['meintənəns] *n.* 保养，维护，维修（5B）

malaria [mə'lɛəriə] *n.* 疟疾（2A）

Malaysia [mə'leizə] *n.* 马来西亚（1B）

mall [mɔ:l] *n.* 购物商场，商业街（12B）

mammoth ['mæməθ] *a.* 巨大的（8B）

mandatory ['mændətəri] *n.* 法定的；强制的（2A）

maneuver [mə'nu:və] *n.* 机动，调动（6B）

Manhattan [mæn'hætən] *n.* 曼哈顿岛（美国纽约一区）（8B）

manner ['mænə] *n.* 风格，方式，样式（10B）

Mannheim ['mænhaim] *n.* 曼海姆（德国西南部城市）（7B）

manufacturing [,mænju'fæktʃəriŋ] *a.* 制造业的（12B）

marathon ['mærəθən] *n.* 马拉松赛跑，耐力的考验（8B）

margin ['mɑ:dʒin] *n.* 余地；盈余，利润（8A）

marketing ['mɑ:kitiŋ] *n.* 销售，市场营销（3A）

marking ['mɑ:kiŋ] *n.* 记号，标识（2A）

markka ['mɑ:kɑ:] *n.* 马克（芬兰的货币单位）（2B）

Marseilles [mɑ:'sei] *n.* 马赛（法国城市）（7B）

Marshall's ['mɑ:ʃəlz] *n.* 马歇尔百货公司（12B）

martial ['mɑ:ʃəl] *a.* 战争的，军事的（13A）

marvel ['mɑ:vəl] *vi.* 大为惊异，觉得惊奇（8B）

Maryland ['mɛərilænd] *n.* 马里兰（美国州）（7A）

Massachusetts [,mæsə'tʃu:sits] *n.* 马萨诸塞（美国州名）（8B）

mastery ['mɑ:stəri] *n.* 掌握（10B）

match [mætʃ] *vt.* 匹配，相配（1A）

mature [mə'tjuə] *a.* 成熟的（8A）

mausoleum [,mɔ:sə'li:əm] *n.* 陵墓（1B）

maximize ['mæksimaiz] *vt.* 取……最大值，最佳化（8A）

maximum ['mæksiməm] *n.* 最大量，最大限度（4A）

measles ['mi:zlz] *n.* 麻疹（2A）

mecca ['mekə] *n.* 发祥地，圣地（12A）

mechanic [mi'kænik] *n.* 技工，机修工，机械工（5B）

media ['mi:diə] *n.* 大众传播媒介（3A）

medication [,medi'keiʃən] *n.* 药物治疗；药物（2A）

mega ['megə] *a.* 巨大的（3B）

Melbourne ['melbən] *n.* 墨尔本（澳大利亚城市）（7B）

memorabilia [,memərə'biliə] *n.* 值得记忆的事物，纪念品（12A）

merchandise ['mə:tʃəndaiz] *n.* 商品，货物（12A）

metropolitan [,metrə'pɔlitən] *a.* 大城市的（7A）

metrorail ['metrəureil] *n.* 地下铁道（7A）

microorganism [,maikrəu'ɔ:gənizm] *n.* 微生物（2B）

Milan [mi'læn] *n.* 米兰（意大利北部城市）（7B）

mileage ['mailidʒ] *n.* 英里数，英里里程（4B）

military ['militəri] *a.* 军队的；军人的（4A）

millennium [mi'leniəm] *n.* 一千年（1A）

milling ['miliŋ] *n.* 磨，制粉（10A）

mini ['mini] *n.* 迷你型，袖珍型；小型机（7A）

miniature ['minətʃə] *n.* 缩小的模型（11B）

minimal ['miniməl] *a.* 最小的，最小限度的（7B）

minimalist ['miniməlist] *n.* 最低限要求者（12B）

minimum ['miniməm] *n.* 最小量，最小数（4B）

minor ['mainə] *n.* 未成年人（13A）

minority [mai'nɔrəti] *n.* 少数；少数民族（12A）

misc [misk] *n.* 其他事宜，杂项（5A）

miscellaneous [misə'leiniəs] *a.* 各种各样混在一起的，混杂的（12A）

misinformation [,misinfə'meiʃən] *n.* 误报，误传（13B）

mobility [məu'biləti] *n.* 流动性（5B）

mode [məud] *n.* 方式，模式；样式（1A）

model ['mɔdl] *n.* 模式（8B）

moderately ['mɔdərətli] *ad.* 适度地（8A）

moderation [,mɔdə'reiʃən] *n.* 适度（5A）

Moncton ['mʌŋktən] *n.* 蒙克顿（加拿大城市）（7B）

Mongkok ['mɔŋkɔk] *n.* 旺角（11A）

Mongolia [mɔŋ'gəuliə] *n.* 蒙古（1B）

monitor ['mɔnitə] *n.* 监视器，显示器（5A）

monolith ['mɔnəliθ] *n.* 独石柱，独石碑，独块巨石（10B）

Montreal [,mɔntri'ɔ:l] *n.* 蒙特利尔（加拿大城市）（7B）

motel [məu'tel] *n.* 汽车旅馆（1A）

move [mu:v] *n.* 采取的行动，步骤（8A）

mug [mʌg] *n.* 大杯子（12A）

multi-faceted ['mʌlti 'fæsitid] *a.* 涉及多方面的（1A）

multiple ['mʌltipl] *a.* 多次的；多样的（6A）

mumps [mʌmps] *n.* 腮腺炎（2A）

Munich ['mju:nik] *n.* 慕尼黑（德国城市，巴伐利亚州首府）（7B）

municipality [mju:,nisi'pæləti] *n.* 市政当局（3A）

museum [mju:'zi:əm] *n.* 博物馆，博物院（1A）

mustard ['mʌstəd] n. 芥菜（11B）

nature ['neitʃə] n. 性质，特性；种类（5B）

navigational [.nævi'geiʃənl] a. 航行的，导航的（6B）

needless ['ni:dləs] a. 不需要的,不必要的(11A)

negotiate [ni'gəuʃieit] vt. 商定，达成（协议）（3B）

Nepal [nə'pɔ:l] n. 尼泊尔（南亚国家）（11B）

Netherlands ['neðələndz] n. 荷兰（西欧国家）（11B）

newsstand ['nju:z,stænd] n. 书报摊，书报亭（2B）

niche [ni:ʃ] n. 适当的位置（8A）

nightmare ['nait,mɛə] n. 噩梦，可怕的事物（8B）

non-refundable [nɔnri'fʌndəbl] a. 不可退款的（13A）

norm [nɔ:m] n. 标准，规范（9A）

Normandy ['nɔ:mən,di] n. 诺曼底（法国西北部一地区，北临英吉利海峡）(8B)

nucleus ['nju:kliəs] n. 核心，中心（7B）

numb [nʌm] vt. 使麻木（12A）

numerous ['nju:mərəs] a. 众多的，许多的，无数的（11A）

obsolete [.ɔbsə'li:t] a. 荒废的，陈旧的（7B）

obtain [əb'tein] vt. 得到，获得（2A）

occasion [ə'keiʒən] n. 场合,时机,机会（10B）

occupation [.ɔkju'peiʃən] n. 职业（5B）

odds [ɔdz] n. 可能的机会,成败的可能性(10B)

olive ['ɔliv] n. 橄榄树，橄榄叶，橄榄枝（10B）

Ontario [ɔn'tɛəriəu] n. 安大略省（7B）

onward ['ɔnwəd] a. 向前的，前进的（5A）

operational [.ɔpə'reiʃənl] a. 操作的，运作的（6B）

opium ['əupiəm] n. 鸦片（12A）

optimum ['ɔptiməm] a. 最适宜的（6B）

option ['ɔpʃən] n. 选择，选项；选择权（7A）

orientation [.ɔ:riən'teiʃən] n. 方向，方位（6B）

Ottawa ['ɔtəwə] n. 渥太华（加拿大城市）（7B）

outbreak ['aut,breik] n.（战争的）爆发；（疾病的）发作（8B）

outlet ['aut,let] n. 出路，销路（3B）

outweigh [,aut'wei] vt. 比……更重要，胜过（8B）

overall ['əuvər,ɔ:l] a. 全部的，全面的（11A）

overhead ['əuvə,hed] n. 日常开支（3B）

overpay [.əuvə'pei] vt. 付款过多（12A）

over-priced ['əuvəpraist] a. 定价过高的（12A）

overtake [.əuvə'teik] vt. 赶上；追上（1B）

pack [pæk] vt. 包装，收拾（行李）（13B）

package ['pækidʒ] n. 包裹，包（5B）

palate ['pælət] n. 味觉（10A）

pale [peil] vi. 显得逊色，相形见绌（8B）

pan- [pæn]（前缀）表示"全,总,泛"之意（7B）

pan-gallic ['pæn'gælik] a. 泛法国的（10B）

panoramic [,pænə'ræmik] a. 全景的（11B）

papercut ['peipəkʌt] n. 剪纸（12A）

paradise ['pærədais] n. 天堂（12A）

paradise ['pærədaiz] n. 天堂（11A）

Paraguay ['pærəgwai] n. 巴拉圭（7B）

parallel ['pærəlel] a. 平行的，相同的（10B）

parcel ['pɑ:sl] n. 小包，包裹（5B）

participant [pɑ:'tisipənt] n. 参与者，共享者（8A）

particular [pə'tikjulə] a. 特殊的，特别的，独特的（11B）

passport ['pɑ:spɔ:t] n. 护照（2A）

pastry ['peistri] n. 面粉糕饼，馅饼皮（10B）

patio ['pætiəu] n. 院子；室外就餐处（6B）

patron ['peitrən] n. 顾客，老主顾（7A）

pavement ['peivmənt] n. 人行道（6B）

pea [pi:] n. 豌豆（10B）

peninsula [pə'ninsjulə] n. 半岛（11A）

perch [pə:tʃ] vt. 栖息；位于（11B）

performance [pə'fɔ:məns] n. 性能，运行（6B）

perfume ['pə:fju:m] n. 香味,芳香,香水（13A）

perfumery [pə'fju:məri] n. 香料店（11B）

permanent ['pə:mənənt] a. 永久的，持久的（2A）

personality [,pə:sə'næləti] n. 个性,人格（5B）

personalized ['pə:sənəlaizd] a. 个性化的（9A）

personnel [,pə:sə'nel] n. 人员，职员（5B）

Perth [pə:θ] *n.* 珀斯（澳大利亚城市）（7B）

pertussis [pə'tʌsis] *n.* 百日咳（2A）

Peru [pə'ru] *n.* 秘鲁（7B）

petit ['peti] *a.* 次要的，没价值的（10B）

phenomenon [fə'nɔminən] *n.* 现象（1A）

Philadelphia [,filə'delfiə] *n.* 费城（美国城市）（7A）

Philippines [,filə'pi:nz] *n.* 菲律宾（1B）

philosopher [fi'lɔsəfə] *n.* 哲学家，哲人（10A）

picturesque [,piktʃə'resk] *a.* 优美的；逼真的（7B）

pile [pail] *vt.* 堆起，堆积；挤（9B）

pillar ['pilə] *n.* 支柱，柱子（1B）

pillow ['piləu] *n.* 枕头，枕垫（5B）

pillowcase ['piləu,keis] *n.* 枕头套（12A）

pilot ['pailət] *n.* 飞行员；飞机驾驶员（5B）

pin [pin] *n.* 个人识别号，个人身份码（4B）

Pioneer [,paiə'niə] *n.* 先锋（日本影音设备品牌）（12B）

Pisa ['pi:zə] *n.* 比萨（意大利西北部城市）（11B）

piston ['pistən] *n.* 活塞（6B）

plaid [plæd] *n.* 格子花呢披肩，格子花呢（12B）

planetarium [,plænə'teəriəm] *n.* 天文馆，天象馆（8B）

plug [plʌg] *n.*（电源）插座（2B）

poi [pɔi] *n.* 山芋食物（10B）

polio ['pəuliəu] *n.* 脊髓灰质炎；小儿麻痹症（2A）

Pope [pəup] *n.* 罗马教皇（13B）

porcelain ['pɔ:slin] *n.* 瓷器，瓷（12A）

porridge ['pɔridʒ] *n.* 麦片粥，粥（10A）

portion ['pɔ:ʃən] *n.* 部分；一份（6A）

poster ['pəustə] *n.* 海报，招贴（12B）

potential [pə'tenʃəl] *a.* 潜在的，可能的（13A）

potentially [pə'tenʃəli] *ad.* 潜在地（1B）

pottery ['pɔtəri] *n.* 陶器，陶器制品（12A）

poultry ['pəultri] *n.* 家禽（9A）

powerhouse ['pauə,haus] *n.* 发电站（9B）

prawn [prɔ:n] *n.* 对虾，明虾，大虾（10A）

precautionary [pri'kɔ:ʃənəri] *a.* 预防的（5A）

precede [pri'si:d] *vt.* 领先（于），在……之前，先于（10B）

precision [pri'siʒən] *n.* 精确，精密度，精度（6B）

predominantly [pri'dɔminəntli] *ad.* 主要地，突出地（10B）

preferred [pri'fə:d] *a.* 首选的（10A）

preflight ['pri:'flait] *a.* 飞行前的，为起飞做准备的（5A）

premier ['premiə] *a.* 第一的，首要的（12B）

premise ['premis] *n.* 经营地址（9A）

prerogative [pri'rɔgətiv] *n.* 特权（7B）

prescription [pri'skripʃən] *n.* 指示，规定，命令（13A）

preserve [pri'zə:v] *vt.* 保护，保持（6B）

pressurize ['preʃəraiz] *vt.* 增压；密封（5A）

prestige [pre'sti:ʒ] *n.* 声望，威望，威信（12B）

prestigious [pre'stidʒəs] *a.* 享有声望的，声望很高的（9A）

prevail [pri'veil] *vi.* 流行，盛行；获胜，成功（9A）

prevalent ['prevələnt] *a.* 普遍的，流行的（10B）

primarily [prai'merəli] *ad.* 首先，主要地（3B）

principal ['prinsəpəl] *a.* 主要的；首要的（6B）

principality [,prinsə'pæləti] *n.* 公国，侯国（11B）

prior ['praiə] *a.* 预先的；在前的（2A）

priority [prai'ɔrəti] *n.* 优先；优先权（1B）

problematic [,prɔblə'mætik] *a.* 产生问题的，造成困难的（13B）

procedure [prə'si:dʒə] *n.* 手续；程序（6A）

proceed [prə'si:d] *vi.* 进行，继续下去（4A）

procrastinator [prəu,kræsti'neitə] *n.* 拖延者，拖拉者（4B）

professional [prə'feʃnl] *a.* 专业的，职业的（5B）

profitable ['prɔfitəbl] *a.* 有利可图的，可赚钱的（3B）

progressively [prəu'gresivli] *ad.* 前进地，渐进地（6B）

project [prə'dʒekt] *vt.* 预计，计划；设计（8A）

projected ['prəudʒektid] *a.* 预计的，计划中的（3A）

projecting [prə'dʒektiŋ] *a.* 突出的，伸出的（6B）

prominent ['prɔminənt] *a.* 卓越的，显著的，突出的（10A）

promotion [prə'məuʃən] *n.* 促销（12B）

promotional [prə'məuʃənəl] *a.* 升职的（5B）

promptly ['prɔmptli] *ad.* 迅速地，敏捷地（3B）

proper ['prɔpə] *a.* 适当的；正确的（5B）

prorate [prəu'reit] *vt.* 按比例分配，分派（11B）

Provence [prɔ'vɔŋs] *n.* 普罗旺斯（法国东南部一地区）（10B）

proximity [prɔk'siməti] *n.* 接近，临近（8A）

publicity [pʌb'lisəti] *n.* 公开；宣传，广告（3A）

purchase ['pə·tʃəʃ] *vt.* 买，购买（12A）

pursue [pə'sju:] *vt.* 追求；寻求（8B）

quad [kwɔd] *n.* 四个一组（11B）

quadruple [kwɔ'dru:pl] *vt.* 使成四倍，翻两番（8A）

qualification [ˌkwɔlifi'keiʃən] *n.* 资格,条件（3A）

quarantine ['kwɔrənti:n] *n.* 检疫（2B）

Quito ['ki:təu] *n.* 基多（厄瓜多尔首都）（7B）

quote [kwəut] *vt.* 引用，引证；提供，提出；报（价）（9B）

ramp [ræmp] *n.* 坡道；客机梯子（6B）

range [reindʒ] *vi.* 在……范围内变化（3B）

rate [reit] *n.* 价格，费用（7A）

rating ['reitiŋ] *n.* 等级级别（5B）

razor ['reizə] *n.* 剃刀（13A）

reasonable ['ri:znəbl] *a.* 合理的，有道理的（12A）

reasonable ['ri:znəbl] *a.* 合理的，有道理的（11A）

reassure [ˌri:ə'ʃuə] *vt.* 安慰，使安心（3A）

receipt [ri'si:t] *n.* 收据，收条（2A）

recipe ['resəpi] *n.* 烹饪法，食谱，菜谱（10B）

recommendation [ˌrekəmen'deiʃən] *n.* 推荐；介绍（3B）

reconfirm [ˌri:kən'fə:m] *vt.* 再次证实，再次确认（4B）

recreation [ˌrekri'eiʃən] *n.* 消遣；娱乐（1A）

recreational [ˌrekri'eiʃənəl] *a.* 消遣的，娱乐的（9A）

recruit [ri'kru:t] *vt.* 招募（5B）

reference ['refərəns] *n.* 提及，涉及，参考（11B）

refit [ri:'fit] *vt.* 整修，改装（8A）

reforestation [ˌri:fɔri'steiʃən] *n.* 重新造林（5B）

refreshment [ri'freʃmənt] *n.* 点心，饮料（9A）

regarding [ri'gɑ:diŋ] *prep.* 关于（6A）

regional ['ri:dʒənl] *a.* 地区性的,地域性的（1A）

register ['redʒistə] *vt.* 登记，注册（3A）

registration [ˌredʒi'streiʃən] *n.* 注册；登记（2A）

regulation [ˌregju'leiʃən] *n.* 规则，规章（6B）

reign [rein] *n.* 统治，朝代（12A）

reject ['ri:dʒekt] *vt.* 拒绝；不接受（4A）

relatively ['relətivli] *ad.* 相关地，相对地（13A）

relax [ri'læks] *vi.* 放松，休息，休养（9B）

relaxation [ˌri:læk'seiʃən] *n.* 放松；松弛（8A）

relevant ['reləvənt] *a.* 有关的，相应（13A）

reliability [riˌlaiə'biliti] *n.* 可靠性（6B）

relic ['relik] *n.* 遗物，古物（2B）

remainder [ri'meində] *n.* 残余，剩余部分（8A）

remainder [ri'meində] *n.* 剩余物；其他的人（5B）

remote [ri'məut] *a.* 遥远的，偏僻的（7B）

renaissance [ri'neisəns] *n.* 文艺复兴，文艺复兴时期（11B）

renovate ['renəveit] *vt.* 革新，刷新，修复（9A）

renovation [ˌrenə'veiʃən] *n.* 革新（13B）

rental ['rentl] *n.* 租赁（7A）

repetitious [ˌrepi'tiʃəs] *a.* 反复的；重复的（5A）

replica ['replikə] *n.* 复制品（13A）

reposition [ˌri:pə'ziʃən] *vt.* 重新定位，再定位（8A）

representative [ˌrepri'zentətiv] *n.* 代表（2B）

reproduction [ˌri:prə'dʌkʃən] *n.* 再现；复制品（12A）

repulse [ri'pʌls] *vt.* 拒绝，排斥（8B）

request [ri'kwest] *vt.* 请求，要求（11A）

rescue ['reskju:] *vt.* 援救，营救（5B）

reservation [ˌrezə'veiʃən] *n.* 预订（2A）

reserved [ri'zə:vd] *a.* 保留的（9B）

resort [ri'zɔ:t] *n.* 胜地；诉诸（9B）

resource [ri'zɔ:s] *n.* 资源，财力；办法，智谋（9B）

responder [ri'spɔndə] *n.* 回应者；应答器（6B）

restricted [ri'striktid] *a.* 受限制的，有限的（13A）

restriction [ri'strikʃən] *n.* 限制，约束（13A）

resurrection [ˌrezə'rekʃən] *n.* 复苏（12B）

retain [ri'tein] *vt.* 保留；保持（2B）

retractable [ri'træktəbl] *a.* 可收回的（13A）

revenue ['revənju:] *n.* 国家的收入；税收（1A）

reverse [ri'və:s] *a.* 背面的，反面的（6A）

reversibly [ri'və:sibli] *ad.* 可逆地（1A）

revolving [ri'vɔlviŋ] *a.* 旋转的（11B）

rhythmical ['riðmikl] *a.* 有节奏的，有韵律的（7B）

Rich's ['ritʃiz] *n.* 里奇百货（13B）

Richmond [ˌritʃmənd] *n.* 里士满（美国城市）（7A）

rigorous ['rigərəs] *a.* 严格的，严厉的（13B）

ringgit ['riŋgit] *n.* 林吉特（马来西亚的货币单位）（2B）

rink [riŋk] *n.* 溜冰场，冰球场（8B）

rip [rip] *n.* 裂口，裂缝（13A）

Roanoke ['rəuənəuk] *n.* 罗阿诺克（美国城市）（7A）

rockery ['rɔkəri] *n.* 假山，假山庭院（9A）

romance [rəu'mæns] *n.* 浪漫（8A）

romanticism [rəu'mænti,sizəm] *n.* 浪漫精神，浪漫主义（7B）

Rome [rəum] *n.* 罗马（意大利首都）（11B）

round-trip ['raundtrip] *a.* 来回旅程的（7B）

routinely [ru:'ti:nli] *ad.* 例行公事地（5B）

rubella [ru:'belə] *n.* 风疹（2A）

rumor ['ru:mə] *n.* 流言，谣言，传闻（13B）

runway ['rʌnwei] *n.* 飞机跑道（6B）

ruthless ['ru:θləs] *a.* 无情的，残忍的（11A）

Sak's [sæks] *n.* 萨克百货公司（12B）

Santiago [ˌsænti'ɑ:gəu] *n.* 圣地亚哥（智利首都）（7B）

sauce [sɔ:s] *n.* 酱汁，调味料（10B）

scaffolding ['skæfəuldiŋ] *n.* 脚手架（13B）

scale [skeil] *n.* 范围；比例（1A）

Scan [skæn] *vt.* 扫描（13A）

scenic ['si:nik] *a.* 景色优美的（7B）

Schaffhausen ['ʃɑ:fhausən] *n.* 沙夫豪森（瑞士北部城市）（11B）

schedule ['ʃedju:l] *n.* 时间表；进度表（5B）

scheduled ['ʃedju:ld] *a.* 预定的（4B）

scheme [ski:m] *n.* 安排，计划（9A）

schilling ['ʃiliŋ] *n.* 先令（奥地利的货币单位）（2B）

scissors ['sizəz] *n.* 剪刀（13A）

scope [skəup] *n.* 范围；机会（5B）

screen [skri:n] *vt.* 筛选，审查（5B）

screener ['skri:nə] *n.* 扫描器（4A）

scroll [skrəul] *n.* 卷轴，卷形物（12A）

scrutiny ['skru:tini] *n.* 详细检查（4A）

seal [si:l] *vt.* 封，密封（11A）

Sears [siəz] *n.* 西尔斯百货公司（12B）

Seattle [si'ætl] *n.* 西雅图（美国城市）（7B）

secure [si'kjuə] *a.* 安全的（4A）

security [si'kjuərəti] *n.* 安全（5A）

sedan [si'dæn] *n.* 轿车（7A）

segmentation [ˌsegmən'teiʃən] *n.* 份额（8A）

self-indulgence [ˌselfin'dʌldʒəns] *n.* 自我放任，自我沉溺（7B）

self-respecting [ˌself ris'pektiŋ] *a.* 自尊的（9B）

seminar ['semi,nɑ:] *n.* 研究会，讨论发表会（8B）

Senneterre ['senitə] *n.* 圣尼特雷（加拿大城市）（7B）

sensitive ['sensətiv] *a.* 敏感的；灵敏的（1A）

serenity [sə'renəti] *n.* 平静（8B）

seriousness ['siəriəsnəs] *n.* 严肃，认真（10B）

shaver ['ʃeivə] *n.* 剃须刀（2B）

shawl [ʃɔ:l] *n.* 披肩，围巾（12A）

sheer [ʃiə] *a.* 全然的，彻底的（7B）

shipper ['ʃipə] *n.* 托运人，发货人（5B）

shopaholic [ˌʃɔpə'hɔlik] *n.* 购物狂（12A）

shortcut ['ʃɔ:t,kʌt] *n.* 捷径（10B）

shuttle ['ʃʌtl] *n.* 往返汽车（6A）

sign [sain] *vt. & vi.* 签名（于），署名（于）

*n.* 标记，符号，记号

signify ['signifai] *vt.* 表示；意味（1A）

simmer ['simə] *vt.* 慢煮（10A）

Singapore [ˌsiŋgə'pɔ:] *n.* 新加坡（1B）

single ['siŋgl] *a.* 单一的（6A）

slew [slu:] *n.* 船头左右摇荡（8B）

slowdown ['sləuˌdaun] *n.* 降低速度，减速（8A）

smallpox ['smɔ:lˌpɔks] *n.* 天花（2A）

souvenir [ˌsu:və'niə] *n.* 纪念品（12A）

spa [spɑ:] *n.* 水疗（8A）

spaghetti [spə'geti] *n.* 意大利式细面条（10A）

specific [spə'sifik] *a.* 明确的，具体的（4A）

spectacular [spek'tækjulə] *a.* 壮观的；引人注目的（1B）

spectrum ['spektrəm] *n.* 领域，范围（8A）

sphere [sfiə] *n.* 领域，范围（1A）

spicy ['spaisi] *a.* 辛辣的（10A）

spire ['spaiə] *n.* 尖顶（11B）

split [split] *vt.* 分开；分工（5B）

spokeswoman ['spəuksˌwumən] *n.* 女发言人，女代言人（8B）

sponsor ['spɔnsə] *vt.* 发起，主办（8B）

spot [spɔt] *vt.* 认出；发现（3B）

stack [stæk] *vt.* 堆叠（5B）

staggering ['stægəriŋ] *a.* 令人惊愕的（11A）

stall [stɔ:l] *vt.* 使停转，使停止，迟延（8A）

stamp [stæmp] *n.* 邮票；印花；印，图章 *vt. & vi.* 在……压印

standard ['stændəd] *n.* 标准，规格（6B）

staple ['steipl] *vt.* 用订书钉订住（6A）

status ['steitəs] *n.* 情况，状态（4B）

statutory ['stætʃutəri] *a.* 法令的，法定的（9A）

stay [stei] *n.* 逗留（6A）

steadily ['stedili] *ad.* 稳定地，稳固地（8A）

sterile ['sterail] *a.* 消过毒的，无菌的（6B）

sticky ['stiki] *a.* 黏的，黏性的（11A）

stimulate ['stimjuleit] *vt.* 刺激，激励（1A）

stipulate ['stipjuleit] *vt.* 规定，保证（13A）

strawberry ['strɔ:bəri] *n.* 草莓（10B）

Strawbridge's ['strɔ: bridʒiz] *n.* 斯特劳布里奇百货公司（12B）

stretch [stretʃ] *n.* 伸展，延伸（2B）

subjectively [səb'dʒektivli] *ad.* 主观地（3B）

submit [səb'mit] *vt.* 提交；递交（2B）

subsequent ['sʌbsikwənt] *a.* 随后的，后来的；继起的（1A）

subsidiary [səb'sidiəri] *n.* 分公司，分支机构（8A）

substantial [səb'stænʃəl] *a.* 大量的，可观的（3A）

substantially [səb'stænʃəli] *ad.* 实质上，充分地（7B）

subtropical [ˌsʌb'trɔpikəl] *a.* 亚热带的（2B）

suburb ['sʌbə:b] *n.* 市郊，郊区（11B）

suburban [sə'bə:bən] *a.* 郊外的，偏远的（7A）

suede [sweid] *n.* 绒面革（12A）

superb [su:'pə:b] *a.* 庄重的，堂堂的，华丽的；极好的（11B）

superior [su'piəriə] *a.* 较高的；较好的，出众的（1B）

supersonic [ˌsju:pə'sɔnik] *a.* 超音速的，超声的（6B）

superstitious [ˌsu:pə'stiʃəs] *a.* 迷信的（10A）

supervise ['su:pəvaiz] *vt.* 监督，管理，指导（5B）

surprisingly [sə'praiziŋli] *ad.* 令人惊讶地（12A）

surroundings [sə'raundiŋz] *n.* 环境（5B）

survivable [sə'vaivəbl] *a.* 可以存活的（5A）

suspicious [sə'spiʃəs] *a.* 可疑的；引起怀疑的（4A）

sustainable [sə'steinəbl] *a.* 可持续发展的（1A）

sustained [sə'steind] *a.* 持续不变的（1B）

sway [swei] *n.* 摆动，摇动（7B）

sweetbread ['swi:tˌbred] *n.* 杂碎（10B）

swindle ['swindl] *vt.* 诈骗（2A）

swing [swiŋ] *n.* 巨大的改变（8B）

Switzerland ['switsələnd] *n.* 瑞士（中欧国家）（11B）

Sydney ['sidni] *n.* 悉尼（澳大利亚城市）（7B）

sync [siŋk] *n.* 同时；同步（5A）

synergetic [sinə'dʒetik] *a.* 协同的，协作的；协同作用的（1A）

syrup ['sirəp] *n.* 糖浆（10A）

take-off ['teikɔf] *n.* 起飞（6B）

tantalizing ['tæntə,laiziŋ] *a.* 非常着急的（12B）

tap [tæp] *vt.* 开发；利用（8A）

tape [teip] *n.* 带子，带（13A）

taxiway ['tæksiwei] *n.* 滑行道（6B）

teamwork ['ti:m,wз:k] *n.* 联合作业，协力（5B）

temperate ['tempərət] *a.* （气候）温和的（2B）

temptation [temp'teiʃən] *n.* 诱惑，诱惑物（12B）

terminal ['tə:minl] *n.* 航站楼（5A）

terminus ['tə:minəs] *n.* 终点站（7B）

territory ['terətəri] *n.* 领土，版图（2B）

tetanus ['tetənəs] *n.* 破伤风（2A）

textile ['tek,stail] *n.* 纺织品（12A）

texture ['tekstʃə] *n.* 质地（10A）

Thailand ['tailænd] *n.* 泰国（1B）

Thailand ['tailænd] *n.* 泰国（7B）

theme [θi:m] *n.* 主题（8B）

thermodynamics [,θə:məudai'næmiks] *n.* 热力学（13B）

thrift [θrift] *n.* 节俭，节约（12B）

thrive [θraiv] *vi.* 兴旺，繁荣（1A）

thru [θru:] *prep.* 经过，通过（美 = through）（4B）

Tibet ['tibet] *n.* 西藏（2B）

tight [tait] *a.* 严厉的；紧的（4B）

tillage ['tilidʒ] *n.* 耕地（9A）

Timberland ['timbəlænd] *n.* 美国户外品牌（11A）

tip [tip] *n.* 小费（2A）

tip [tip] *n.* 小费（2B）

tissue ['tisju:] *n.*（人、动植物细胞的）组织（2B）

Titicaca [ti:ti'kɑ:kɑ:] *n.* 的的喀喀湖（在秘鲁和玻利维亚之间）（7B）

tobacco [tə'bækəu] *n.* 烟草，烟草制品（13B）

toddler ['tɔdlə] *n.* 刚学步的小孩（8B）

toiletry ['tɔilitri] *n.* 化妆品，化妆用具（13B）

token ['təukən] *a.* 象征的，表意的（12A）

tolerate ['tɔləreit] *vt.* 忍受，容忍（10B）

toll [təul] *n.*（道路、港口的）通行费，过路税（7A）

Toronto [tə'rɔntəu] *n.* 多伦多（加拿大城市）（7B）

tote [təut] *vt.* 手提，背负，携带（13B）

touch [tʌtʃ] *n.* 触地；碰（6B）

Touraine [tu:'ren] *n.* 都兰（法国西部一地区）（10B）

tourismtourism ['tuərizm] *n.* 旅行，旅游，观光（1A）

tourist ['tuərist] *n.* 旅行者，旅游者（1A）

track [træk] *vt.* 跟踪，追踪（5B）

traditional [trə'diʃənəl] *a.* 传统的，惯例的（9B）

tram [træm] *n.* 有轨电车（11A）

transaction [træn'zækʃən] *n.* 交易；办理（2A）

transatlantic [,trænzət'læntik] *a.* 横跨大西洋的（8A）

transcontinental [,trænzkɔnti'nentəl] *a.* 横贯大陆的（7B）

transformer [træns'fɔ:mə] *n.* 变压器（2B）

transmitter [trænz'mitə] *n.* 发射机，发送器（6B）

transportation [,trænspɔ:'teiʃən] *n.* 运输，运送（1A）

tremendous [trə'mendəs] *a.* 极大的，巨大的（12A）

trend [trend] *n.* 倾向，趋势（8A）

trendy ['trendi] *a.* 流行的（12B）

trial ['traiəl] *n.* 试验，考验（13B）

trigger ['trigə] *vt.* 引发，引起（4A）

tripe [traip] *n.* 肚子，内脏（10B）

triple ['tripl] *n.* 三个一组（11B）

trolley ['trɔli] *n.* 手推车；电车（6A）

tropical ['trɔpikl] *a.* 热带的（2B）

tuberculosis [tju:,bə:kju'ləusis] *n.* 结核病，肺结核（2B）

turbulence ['tə:bjuləns] *n.* 紊流，湍流（5A）

Turin ['tjuərin] *n.* 都灵（意大利西北部城市）（7B）

typhoid ['taifɔid] *n.* 伤寒症，伤寒（2A）

ultra-luxury ['ʌltrə'lʌkʃəri] *a.* 极其豪华的（8A）

unaccompanied [,ʌnə'kʌmpənid] *a.* 没有陪伴的（5B）

undivided [ˌʌndiˈvaidid] *a.* 不可分割的，完整的（7B）

unexpected [ˌʌnikˈspektid] *a.* 意外的，想不到的（5A）

unfold [ʌnˈfəuld] *vi.* 伸展，打开（7B）

unfortunately [ʌnˈfɔ:tjnətli] *ad.* 不幸地（13B）

uninhabited [ˌʌninˈhæbitid] *a.* 无人居住的，杳无人迹的（11A）

unload [ʌnˈləud] *vt.* 卸货；卸下（5B）

unmatched [ʌnˈmætʃt] *a.* 无比的，无匹敌的（7B）

unparalleled [ʌnˈpærəleld] *a.* 无比的，无双的，空前的（11B）

unto [ˈʌntu:] *prep.* 到，向，直到（12A）

update [ʌpˈdeit] *n.* 更新（13A）

upgrade [ˈʌpˌgreid] *vt.* 使升级；提升（1A）

urban [ˈə:bən] *a.* 城市的，市内的（7B）

utensil [ju:ˈtensl] *n.* 器具（9A）

utilization [ˌju:təlaiˈzeiʃən] *n.* 利用，应用（6B）

vaccination [ˌvæksiˈneiʃən] *n.* 接种疫苗（2A）

Vaduz [vɑ:ˈdu:ts] *n.* 瓦杜兹（列支敦士登首都）（11B）

valid [ˈvælid] *a.* 有效的（2B）

validity [vəˈlidəti] *n.* 有效性；合法性（2A）

Vancouver [vænˈku:və] *n.* 温哥华（加拿大城市）（7B）

vaporetto [ˌvæpəˈretəu] *n.*（运河中载客的）交通汽艇（11B）

variation [ˌveəriˈeiʃən] *n.* 变更，变化（11A）

vary [ˈveəri] *vi.* 变化；不同（2A）

vehicle [ˈvi:ikl] *n.* 交通工具；传达手段（6B）

velvet [ˈvelvit] *a.* 天鹅绒的；柔软的，光滑的（12B）

vendor [ˈvendə] *n.* 供应者，卖者（7A）

venereal [vəˈniəriəl] *a.* 性病的（2B）

Venice [ˈvenis] *n.* 威尼斯（意大利东北部港市）（11B）

venue [ˈvenju:] *n.* 聚会地点（8A）

verification [ˌverifiˈkeiʃən] *n.* 确认，查证（6A）

verify [ˈverifai] *vt.* 证实；核实（4A）

vessel [ˈvesl] *n.* 船（8A）

vestibule [ˈvestiˌbju:l] *n.* 门廊，前厅（7A）

via [ˈvi:ə] *prep.* 经，通过，经由（13A）

video [ˈvidiəu] *n.* 电视，录像，视频（5A）

vintage [ˈvintidʒ] *n.* 制造年期，葡萄收获期（12B）

vintner [ˈvintnə] *n.* 葡萄酒商（10B）

Virginia [vəˈdʒinjə] *n.* 弗吉尼亚（美国州）（7A）

visa [ˈvi:zə] *n.* 签证（2A）

visibility [ˌvizəˈbiləti] *n.* 能见度（6B）

visible [ˈvizəbl] *a.* 引人注目的（8A）

visual [ˈviʒuəl] *a.* 看的，视觉的（6B）

visually [ˈviʒuəli] *ad.* 在视觉上地；真实地（5A）

volcano [vɔlˈkoinou] *n.* 火山（7B）

volt [vəult] *n.* 伏特（电压单位）（2B）

voucher [ˈvautʃə] *n.* 凭证，凭单（11B）

vow [vau] *vi.* 发誓，立誓（1B）

wacky [ˈwæki] *a.* 古怪的（12B）

waitress [ˈweitrəs] *n.* 女服务生（11A）

walkman [ˈwɔ:kmən] *n.* 随身听（5A）

Wal-Mart [ˈwolmɑ:t] *n.* 沃尔玛折扣店（12B）

ware [weə] *n.* 陶器，器皿（12B）

warranty [ˈworənti] *n.*（正当）理由，（合理）根据（12A）

waterway [ˈwɔ:təˌwei] *n.* 水路（11B）

well-being [ˌwelˈbi:iŋ] *n.* 康乐，安宁；福利（1A）

well-known [wel nəun] *a.* 知名的，大家知道的（12B）

wheelchair [ˈwi:lˌtʃeə] *n.* 轮椅（7A）

whereas [weərˈæz] *conj.* 然而，尽管，但是；鉴于（11A）

whet [wet] *vt.* 磨，磨快；使兴奋（12B）

whirl [(h)wə:l] *vt.*（使）旋转（10A）

whiskey [ˈwiski] *n.* 威士忌酒（12B）

wholesome [ˈhəulsəm] *a.* 卫生的，有益的，健康的（9A）

Winchester [ˈwintʃistə] *n.* 温彻斯特（美国城市）（7A）

windmill [ˈwindˌmil] *n.* 风车，风车房（11B）

Windsor [ˈwinzə] *n.* 温莎（加拿大城市）（7B）

wingspan [ˈwiŋˌspæn] *n.* 翼展（6B）

Winnipeg ['winipeg] *n.* 温尼伯（加拿大城市）（7B）

win-win [win win] *a.* 双赢的（3B）

withdraw [wið'drɔ:] *vt.* 退出，离开（3B）

workout ['wə:kaut] *n.* 体育锻炼（8A）

worthwhile [,wə:θ'wail] *a.* 值得做的，值得出力的（9B）

Yahoo [jə'hu:] 美国雅虎公司（9B）

yarn [jɑ:n] *n.* 纱，纱线，绳子（13A）

yearning ['jə:niŋ] *n.* 向往（12B）

yoga ['jəugə] *n.* 瑜珈，瑜珈术（8B）

Zurich ['zuərik] *n.* 苏黎世（瑞士城市）（7B）

# 词组表

a bit of  一点儿，少量的（11A）

a chunk of  一大块（11A）

a couple of  两个，几个（7B）

a dose of  一回，一次，一番（12A）

a fraction of  一小部分（12A）

a host of  一大群，许多（1A）

a large number of  许多（10B）

a matter of  作为一部分（10A）

a piece of  一片，一段，一块（13A）

a set of  一组，一套（10A）

a variety of  种种，各种各样（9A）

a wide range of  范围广的，大范围的（12A）

according to  根据（6B）

account for  说明……的原因（1A）

add up  加起来（11A）

air carrier  运货飞机，运输机（4A）

air hostess  空中小姐（4A）

air taxi  短程小客机，出租飞机（5B）

airport construction fee  机场建设费（4A）

Alice Springs  艾丽斯泉（7B）

all but  几乎，差不多（7B）

along with  与……一道，与……一起（13A）

Amazon.com  亚马逊网站（9B）

American Express  美国运通公司（2B）

appeal to  引起兴趣，吸引（8A）

appear on  出现，露面（10A）

apply for  申请（2B）

Arc de Triomphe  凯旋门（法国巴黎）（11B）

arrange for  安排（5B）

as far as  远到，直到（10A）

as well as  也，又（11A）

as well  同样，也（13B）

at all  （用于否定句）丝毫，一点（13B）

at the end of  在……末端，在……的结尾（11A）

at the expense of  以……为代价，在损害……的情况下（1A）

at the heart of  在……中心（11A）

attempt to do sth.  企图做某事，尝试做某事（1A）

attribute... to...  归因于（1A）

balance of payments  贸易差额，国际收支，收支差额（1A）

bar code  条形码（4B）

base on  基于（6B）

be about to  将要，快要（5A）

be adjacent to  相邻的，邻近的（6B）

be aware  知道，觉得（13A）

be aware of  知道，明白；意识到（1A）

be determined by  由……决定（1A）

be established as  被确定为（1A）

be expected to  期待，盼望，指望；预期（1A）

be familiar with  熟悉，通晓（9B）

be grateful to sb. for sth.  因某事而感谢某人（11A）

be headed to  向某处移动，朝某处行驶（9B）

be in good/poor condition  （物件）无/有破损（13A）

be involved in  涉及（3A）

be keen on 喜爱，喜欢（3B）

be known by 认出，识别，出名（10B）

be known for 因……而著名（12A）

be made by 由……制造（12A）

be made from 由……制成（12A）

be made up of 由……组成，由……构成（11A）

be not afraid to 不怕做某事（10B）

be popular with 受……欢迎，在……间名声好（12A）

be prepared to do/for 准备着（13A）

be related to 与……相关的；与……有关系（1A）

be renowned for 以……有名,以……著名（11A）

be responsible for 负责任（13A）

be similar to 与……相似（12B）

be subject to 未独立的，受制于……的（2A）

be suited to/for 适合（9A）

be taken out of 带出（12A）

bear in mind 牢记（12A）

Bergdorf-Goodman 伯格多弗－古德曼百货公司（12B）

bill of sale 抵押证券（2A）

Black Forest 黑林山（在德国西南部）（11B）

Boarding Pass 登机卡（4A）

boarding pass 登机证（6A）

bring back 拿回来，带回来（13B）

by far 到目前为止（8A）

by no means 决不，一点也不（9B）

call for 要求（6A）

call up 打电话给（6A）

Carnival Corporation 嘉年华公司（8A）

Carnival Cruise Lines 嘉年华游轮公司（8A）

cater for/to 顾及，迎合（9A）

Celebrity Cruises 名声游轮（8A）

Celestial Star 天星（11A）

centrifugal force 地心引力（10A）

chamber of commerce 商会（3A）

Champs Elysees 爱丽舍宫（法国巴黎的总统官邸）（11B）

charter flights 包机（3A）

check in 入住酒店（11B）

check out 核实，最后检查（12A）

close corporation 封闭式公司（3A）

commercial airlines 商业航空公司（1A）

comply with 遵照，遵守（9A）

comprise of 由……组成（6B）

concentrate on 集中，全神贯注于（11B）

consist of 由……组成（13A）

contribute to 贡献（1A）

convert into 变成，转化成（7B）

Costa Cruises 科斯塔游轮（8A）

counter foil 存根（6A）

credit card 信用卡（2A）

Crystal Cruises 水晶游轮（8A）

cultural heritage resources 文化遗产资源（1A）

Cunard/Seabourn Line 冠达 / 世鹏游轮（8A）

customs clearance 报关，海关结关（6A）

Customs Luggage Declaration Form 海关行李报关单（13A）

cut into 切小（10A）

Dayton-Hudson's 戴顿－赫德森公司（12B）

D-Day （第二次世界大战中）盟国在西欧登陆日（8B）

deal with 处理，应付（3A）

dealing in 做买卖，经营（12B）

decorated with 用……装饰，布置（9A）

depend on 依靠，取决于，因……而定（12A）

depending on/upon 视……而定（13B）

dim sum 点心（10A）

Dim Sum 点心（11A）

Diners Card 大莱卡（2B）

discourage sb. from doing sth. 劝止某人做某事（12A）

Discover Card 美国主要的信用卡之一（7A）

Disney Cruise Lines 迪斯尼游轮（8A）

Disney World 迪斯尼乐园（9B）

domestic airline 国内航班（6A）

due to 因为；由……引起（1A）

economy of scale 规模经济（8A）

Eiffel Tower 埃菲尔铁塔（法国巴黎）（11B）

electronic gadget 小家电（12A）

equip with 装备（10A）

European Pass　欧洲通票（11B）

except for　除了（10A）

fall into　属于（6B）

fill in　填写（13A）

fill out　填写（2B）

first of all　首先（11B）

fold up　折起（13B）

Friendship Stores　友谊商场（12A）

gas station　加油站（1A）

get out of　使离开，使逃脱（11A）

go off　离去，走掉（11A）

Green Card　绿卡（6A）

gross domestic product　国内生产总值（1B）

Ground Transportation　地面交通（6A）

H&M　英国服装品牌（12B）

hair dryer　吹风机（2B）

hand over　移交，交出（13A）

have dependency on　依靠；信赖（1A）

head for　走向，向……方向前进（11A）

hear about　得知，听说（9B）

help oneself to　自用（10A）

holiday package　假日旅行整体计划（3A）

Holland America Line　荷美公司（8A）

home page　主页（9B）

Hong Kong Island　香港岛（11A）

Hong Kong Tourist Association　香港旅游者协会（10A）

hors d'oeuvre　主菜前的小吃（10B）

Houston Street　休斯敦大街（12B）

Hudson Bay　哈得逊湾（7B）

impact on　影响（1A）

Imperial Palace　故宫（1B）

in a way　在某种程度上，从某一点上看（10B）

in accordance with　与……一致，依照（3A）

in addition　另外，加之（13A）

in addition to　除了（3B）

in advance　提前（2A）

in case of　假如，如果发生（13A）

in contrast to　相反，大不相同（10A）

in excess of　超过（13A）

in fact　事实上（11B）

in order to　为了（10A）

in proportion to　与……成比例，与……相称（11B）

in regard to　关于，有关（10B）

in sync with　与……相一致（6A）

in terms of　在……方面；根据，按照（1A）

in the case of　就……说，至于……，论到，提到（10A）

in the event of　万一，如果（5B）

in total　整个地（11A）

instead of　代替（11B）

intercultural awareness　跨文化意识（1A）

International Youth Hostel Federation　国际青年旅馆联盟（9A）

Irish Cottages and Holiday Homes Association　爱尔兰别墅及度假屋协会（9A）

Irish Hotels Federation　爱尔兰旅馆联盟（9A）

Irish Tourist Board　爱尔兰旅游者委员会（9A）

JC Penny　JC 潘尼百货公司（12B）

jet aircraft　喷气式飞机（1A）

jet lag　时差，时差反应，时差综合征（5B）

Jungfrau　少女峰（瑞士）（11B）

just as　正如，正好，恰恰是（10B）

Kate Spade　美国时尚品牌（12B）

keep one's wits about　保持警惕，保持清醒头脑（5A）

keep to　遵守，信守（13A）

keep track of　保持联系；明了（2A）

knock down　杀价，降价（11A）

know of　听说，知道（9B）

Lafayette Street　拉菲尔大街（12B）

Lake Lucerne　卢塞恩湖（11B）

laptop computer　膝上型计算机（13A）

Las Vegas　拉斯维加斯（9B）

Latin America　拉丁美洲，南美洲（7B）

leisure time　空闲，空闲时间（1A）

let alone/leave alone　不加干涉，让他去（11A）

linear dimension　线性尺寸（4A）

local economy　地方经济（1A）

log in　进入（系统），注册，登录（4B）

Logan International Airport　洛根国际机场

（美）（13A）

long before  很久以前（10A）

look for  寻找（12A）

Lord & Taylor  罗德与泰勒百货公司（12B）

Los Angeles  洛杉矶（美国城市）（4B）

Louvre museum  罗浮宫国立艺术博物馆（法国巴黎）（11B）

madison avenue  麦迪逊大街（12B）

make for  有利于，对……有益，支持（12A）

make it  办成功（13B）

make room  腾出地方（13B）

make sense  合理（3B）

make sure  尽力做到，保证（13A）

make up  组成，构成（5B）

Master Card  万事达卡（2B）

meet one's needs  满足某人需要（13A）

meet the needs of  满足需要（9A）

mix with  和……混合（10A）

mom and pop store  夫妻店（3B）

more than  不仅仅，不止（10A）

multiplier effect  乘法效应，倍增效应（1A）

New Orleans  新奥尔良（美国港口城市）（8B）

New Territories  新界（11A）

New York Times  《纽约时报》（12B）

New York  《纽约周刊》（12B）

New York  纽约（7A）

non-immigrant visa  非移民签证（6A）

Norwegian Cruise Lines  挪威游轮公司（8A）

on/for sale  出售（的）（11A）

on behalf of  代表（3B）

on production of  出示（9A）

on top of  除……之外，此外（13B）

one way or the other  从某种意义上来说；以某种方式；无论如何（3B）

out of date  过时（13B）

pack sth. up  把……收起来放好（13B）

Palace of Versailles  凡尔赛宫（法国）（11B）

pass through  经过，通过，穿过（13A）

pay attention to  关心，注意（11B）

pick up  拾起，崛起（12A）

Place de Concorde  协和广场(法国巴黎)（11B）

play a role in  起作用，扮演角色（8A）

Port Everglades  美东港口（8A）

port of call  停靠港（8A）

Port of Miami  迈阿密港（美国佛罗里达州东南部）（8A）

pour over  浇注（10A）

Prince Rup  鲁伯特王子市（7B）

Princess Cruises  公主游轮公司（8A）

prior to  在……之前（6A）

propeller-driven airplane  螺旋桨飞机（5B）

Propriety Limited or (Pty) Ltd Company  有限责任公司（3A）

public relations  公共关系，公关（8B）

Puerto Montt  蒙特港市（智利）（7B）

put a damper on  使……扫兴；抑制（9B）

put emphasis on  强调（10A）

Québec City  魁北克市（7B）

Radisson Seven Seas Cruises  瑞迪生七海游轮（8A）

raise a paddle  提高赌注，叫价（12B）

Ralph Lauren  拉尔夫·劳伦（美国服装品牌）（12B）

range from... to...  在……之间（9A）

rate of exchange  兑换率（2A）

rather than  而不（11B）

refer to as  把……称作，把……当作（11A）

rely on  依赖，依靠，信赖（12A）

result from  产生，发生（10A）

result in  导致（3A）

Rhine Falls  莱茵河瀑布（11B）

River Arno  亚诺河（意大利中部河流）（11B）

Rolex  劳力士（瑞士手表品牌）（12B）

Royal Caribbean International  皇家加勒比海游轮集团（8A）

sales tax  销售税（1A）

scenic spot  风景点（1B）

search engine  搜索引擎（9B）

serve as  充当……（1A）

service à la russe  （法）俄罗斯式的服务（10B）

settle on  决定；解决（9B）

share...with  与某人共享，分享（9B）

Silverseas Cruises　银海游轮（8A）

snuff bottle　鼻烟壶（12A）

sole proprietor　个人业主（3A）

Sony Walkman　索尼随身听（11A）

specialize in　擅长于，专攻（3B）

St. Marks Square　圣马可广场（意大利威尼斯市）（11B）

St. Peters　圣彼得大教堂（11B）

Star Cruises　丽星游轮（8A）

Star Ferry　天星小轮（11A）

start from scratch　从零开始，从头做起（11B）

stem from　源于，基于，出于（3A）

subject to　需要……的，可有……的（13B）

subject... to...　使服从；使遭受（2B）

such as　例如，诸如（13A）

Sumitomo Bank of Japan　住友银行（2B）

Swarovski crystal museum　施华洛世奇水晶博物馆（11B）

take advantage of　利用（8A）

take out　取出；带到（13A）

Target and Caldor　塔格特和考尔德折扣店（12B）

tax revenue　税收（1A）

telephone booth　电话亭（2B）

Temple of Heaven　天坛（1B）

tend to　趋于（8A）

tertiary industry　第三产业（1B）

the Appennines　亚平宁山脉（11B）

the Bond Building　债券大楼（11A）

the Business District　商业区，商贸区（11A）

the Great Wild Goose Pagoda　大雁塔（1B）

the Mass Transit Railway　大众铁路运输（11A）

the River Rhine　莱茵河（源出瑞士境内的阿尔卑斯山，贯穿西欧多国）（11B）

the River Seine　塞纳河（法国北部河流）（11B）

the Roman Formum　古罗马广场（11B）

the Stele Forest　碑林（1B）

the Swiss Alps　瑞士阿尔卑斯山脉（11B）

the Terra Cotta Warriors and Horses　兵马俑（1B）

think of... as　把……看作是，以为……是（11A）

throw out　扔掉（13B）

throw up one's arms　举起双手（11A）

Tibet Autonomous Region　西藏自治区（2B）

time frame　时间范围，时间帧（6B）

Time Out New York　《纽约休闲》（12B）

time zone　时区（6A）

to the point　中肯，扼要（6A）

tote bag　手提包（2B）

Tour d'Argent　法国著名大酒店（10B）

transit card/transit visa　转机卡（5A）

travel agency　旅行社（3A）

traveler's check　旅行支票（2A）

Travelex　通济隆公司（2B）

trolley cart　手推车（6A）

Trummebach falls　特鲁蒙巴奇瀑布（意大利）（11B）

try out　试验，考验（8A）

US Customs　美国海关（13B）

up to　一直到，多达（13B）

up-to-date　最近的，最新的（2A）

VIA Rail Canada　加拿大国铁（7B）

Victoria Peak　维多利亚山顶（11A）

view as　认为；把……看作是（1A）

Visa Card　维萨卡（2B）

Washington D.C.　华盛顿特区（9B）

Washington Dulles International Airport　华盛顿达拉斯国际机场（7A）

Washington Flyer Services　（弗来尔）华盛顿机场交通服务（7A）

wear sb. down　使……挫败（11A）

weather forecast　天气预报（2B）

wind its way　蜿蜒前进（7B）

Woody Allen's　伍迪·艾伦（美国导演）（12B）

Worcester Regional Airport　伍斯特地区机场（美）（13A）

World Health Organization　世界卫生组织（2A）

Yangtze River　长江（8B）

yellow fever　黄热病（2A）

Yellowstone National Park　黄石国家公园（9B）

Yum Cha　饮茶（11A）

## 缩写表

AAA (American Automobile Association) 美国汽车协会（9B）

AARP (American Association of Retired Persons) 美国退休者协会（9B）

AC (alternating current) 交流电（2B）

AIDS (acquired immune deficiency syndrome) 艾滋病（获得性免疫缺损综合征）（2B）

ATM (Automated Teller Machine) 自动取款机（2A）

B&Bs 包早餐旅馆（9B）

CLIA (The Cruise Line International Association) 国际游船协会（3B）

FAA (Federal Aviation Administration) 联邦航空局（13A）

GPS (Global Positioning System) 全球定位系统（6B）

IATA (International Air Travel Association) 国际航空运输协会（3A）

ID (identification) 身份证明（4A）

IDD 国际直拨长途电话（2B）

ILS (Instrument Landing System) 仪表着陆系统（6B）

IT (Information Technology) 信息技术（1A）

IYHA (Irish Youth Hostel Association) 爱尔兰青年旅馆协会（9A）

JCB JCB 信用卡（JCB 为日本国际信用卡公司）（2B）

MLS (Microwave Landing System) 微波着陆系统（6B）

NAVAID (airport navigation aids) [ 航空 ] 助航系统（6B）

NDB (Non-Directional Beacon) 无方向性信标（归航台）（6B）

PRC (People's Republic of China) 中华人民共和国（2B）

VOR (Very-high-frequency Omnidirectional Range) 甚高频全向无线电信标（6B）

VORTAC (VHF Omni Range Tactical Communications) 甚高频全向无线电信标战术通信（6B）

WTTC (The World Travel and Tourism Council) 世界旅游业理事会（1A）

WWII (World War Two) 第二次世界大战　1A

## "导游资格考试旅游英语" 模拟试题 1

**I. Multiple-choice question. (20 points)**

Blacken the correct answer on the "Answer Sheet" .

1. I got 90 _____.

    A. scores          B. mark          C. points          D. score

2. We should _____ a good study habit of taking notes in class.

    A. develop          B. improve          C. make          D. remain

3. Is he _____ his girlfriend was once a thief?

    A. aware of          B. aware that          C. knowing that          D. aware of that

4. Some people have birthday cakes _____ noodles.

    A. instead          B. instead for          C. instead to          D. instead of

5. I try to _____ a few dollars each month in order to buy a new bike.

    A. set up          B. set out          C. set off          D. set aside

6. There are _____ areas offering a variety of meals and services all within a hotel.

    A. no many          B. difference          C. different          D. too much

7. Ruth finally _____ to find what she was looking for.

    A. tried          B. managed          C. succeeded          D. achieved

8. The plane is taking off. Please _____ your seat belt.

    A. loose          B. quicken          C. fasten          D. hasten

9. It was so noisy at night _____ I could hardly sleep.

    A. so          B. but          C. what          D. that

10. Paris is _____ that we can hardly visit all the beautiful parks in two or three days.

    A. such a large city                  B. so a large city

    C. such large a city                D. a such large city

11. Unlike most Europeans, many Americans _____ bacon and eggs for breakfast every day.

    A. used to eating                B. are used to eating

    C. are used to eat               D. used to eat

12. The _____ for driving too fast is at least ten dollars in this country.

    A. fine                     B. money

    C. tip                       D. pay

13. My friend suggests that Mr. Bellow _____ a taste of Sichuan dishes.

    A. has                B. have                C. had               D. would have

14. _____ the next days we will be studying English grammar.

    A. Whenever       B. Between         C. Within           D. At

15. If I were in your position, I would _____ another restaurant.

    A. have tried       B. have been tried     C. try              D. tried

16. Room service is _____ in the room.

    A. to clean up                        B. to do service

    C. to serve meals                    D. to take care of guests

17. It is necessary to greet the guest with a hearty smile _____ to create a pleasant atmosphere and make the guest feel at home.

    A. so that            B. in order         C. such as         D. because of

18. By the time he retires Mr. Smith _____ in this hotel for almost 40 years.

    A. will have worked                  B. will work

    C. have worked                     D. will has worked

19. The tourist industry _____ greatly to the economy of that country.

    A. supports         B. benefits          C. assists          D. contributes

20. If we _____ to deal with these problems now, things will get out of control.

    A. miss              B. delay            C. fail            D. deny

## II. Reading comprehension. (15 points)

**Passage 1**

    Each student at an engineering college in Canada gets a steel ring upon graduation as well as graduation certificate.

    There is a story behind the unusual ring. Several years ago, a graduate from this engineering college designed an iron-steel bridge. Unfortunately, because of the mistakes in his design, the bridge collapsed soon after it came into use.

    This event shook the engineering college. And the head of the college decided to take back the framework of the iron-steel bridge and use it as the material for making rings to give the students upon their graduation. The college wants the students to remember this lesson forever so as to avoid making such mistakes again.

1. Upon graduation each student is given a steel ring as a _____.

    A. gift from the college

    B. lesson to avoid making any mistakes in design

    C. model to make designs

    D. warning not to make iron-steel bridge

2. The wrongly-designed iron-steel bridge was finally _____.

    A. shipped away

    B. sold at a low price

    C. made into many rings

    D. used again after repairing

3. The ring is quite unusual because _____.

    A. its design is excellent

    B. it is very expensive

    C. it is different from others

    D. it had a sad story

4. The best title for the passage is _____.

    A. A Great Mistake

    B. A Shocking Event

    C. A Warning Ring

    D. A Wrongly-designed Bridge

5. Which of the following statements is true according to the passage? _____.

    A. The iron-steel bridge collapsed soon after it was built.

    B. The iron-steel bridge has been used ever since it was built.

    C. The iron-steel bridge didn't come into use until it collapsed.

    D. The bridge collapsed because it was designed by a poor student.

**Passage 2**

American cities are similar to other cities around the world. In every country, cities reflect the values of the culture. Cities contain the very best aspects of a society: opportunities for education, employment, and entertainment. They also contain the very worst parts of a society: violent crime, racial conflict, and poverty.

American cities are changing, just as American society is changing. After World War II, city residents became wealthier, more prosperous. They had more children. They needed more space. They move out of their apartments in the city to buy their own homes. They bought houses in the suburbs, areas near a city where people live. These are areas without many offices or factories. During the 1950s the American "dream" was to have a house in the suburbs.

Now things are changing. The children of the people who left the cities in 1950s are now adults. They, unlike their parents, want to live in the cities. Many young professionals, doctors, lawyers, and executives are moving back into the city. Many are single; others are married, but often without children. They prefer the city to the suburbs because their jobs are there; they are afraid of the fuel shortage; or they just enjoy the excitement and opportunities which the city offers. A new class is moving into the city—a wealthier, more mobile class.

Only a few years ago, people thought that the older American cities were dying. Some city residents now see a bright, new future. Others see only problems and conflicts. One thing is sure: many dying cities are alive again.

6. Paragraph 1 _____.

    A. explains why American cities are changing

    B. shows that American cities have many problems

C. is a description of cities

D. says American cities contain the very best aspects of a society

7. In the 1950s the American "dream" was _____.

   A. to have a house                       B. to buy a new house in the suburbs

   C. to have a big car                       D. to buy an apartment in the city

8. In paragraph 3, the author gives _____ reasons why people want to live in cities.

   A. two           B. four           C. five           D. three

9. According to the article, cities are _____.

   A. sick           B. living          C. alive again       D. dying

10. The movement of people to and from the city can explain _____.

   A. racial conflict                     B. social changes

   C. violent crime                     D. the best aspects of a society

**Passage 3**

During the early American colonial years, corn was more plentiful than wheat, so corn bread was more common than wheat bread. Friendly Indians showed colonists how to grow corn and how to prepare it for food and pioneer women then improved the Indian cooking techniques. When people traveled, they went on foot or horseback, sleeping and eating in the forests. They carried corn bread for sustenance; the corn bread came to be called journey cake. Later when roads and taverns were built and stagecoaches carried passengers, journey cake became johnnycake, a name many easterners still use for corn bread. The kinds of bread made with cornmeal were—and still are—almost without limit.

Every region has its specialties. From the start, southerners showed a preference for white cornmeal, northerners for yellow. And pioneers on the frontier, when they ran out of yeast, made salt-rising bread. They stirred together water, a little water-ground cornmeal, potatoes, and salt. They set the mixture, uncovered, in a warm place until it absorbed bacteria from the air and began to ferment. Then they removed the potatoes and used the liquid as leavening for their bread, made with white flour.

11. In colonial times, why was corn bread more common than wheat bread?

   A. The colonists preferred corn bread.

   B. Corn bread did not spoil as rapidly as wheat bread did.

   C. Corn was more abundant.

   D. The colonists did not know how to make wheat bread.

12. Which of the following can be inferred from the passage about the preference for a particular kind of corn bread?

   A. It tends to vary geographically.

   B. It corresponds an individual's social class.

C. It changes over a period of time.

D. It depends on whether or not the individual is a gourmet.

13. The bacteria necessary for the fermentation of salt-rising bread came form the _____.

    A. flour          B. potatoes          C. air          D. salt

14. In the making of salt-rising bread, cornmeal was _____.

    A. used to make the liquid that caused the bread to rise

    B. combined with white flour to make the bread

    C. the main kind of flour used

    D. used when potatoes were not available

15. The best title for this passage is _____.

    A. "Original American Breads"        B. "Life in Colonial American"

    C. "Cooking on the Frontier"        D. "Salt-rising Bread"

**III. Complete the following dialogue according to the Chinese version. (10 points)**

A: Excuse me? Could you change a room for me?

B: _____（发生了什么事，先生）？

A: There's something wrong with the bathroom tap. It was making noise all night _____（以至于我不能入睡）.

B: I'm sorry to hear that. _____（我马上叫人来修理）.

A: Thank you. But I hope _____（最好还是给我换个房间）.

B: We don't have a spare room at present. I'll _____（一有房间我就给你换）.

A: OK. Be sure not to forget.

B: Certainly, sir.

**IV. Answer the following questions. (10 points)**

1. What is the aim of a hotel?

2. What are the famous specialties of Cantonese food and Beijing food respectively?

3. Please list four ways to find out the guest's name.

4. Why do hotels encourage guests' complaints?

5. Please name four traditional Chinese souvenirs.

**V. Rewrite the sentences in a more courteous way. (5 points)**

1. "What's the name?"

2. "I really don't know anything about the shops around here."

3. "I need you to join me this evening in the Kara OK."

4. "Mr. Bellow isn't in at present."

5. "We don't have the dish you want."

## VI. Special terms. (20 points)

i. Translate the following into English. (10 points)

1. 报摊          2. 主菜          3. 游客          4. 标准间          5. 航空标志

6. 住处          7. 保险          8. 行李架          9. 郊区          10. 观光游

ii. Translate the following into Chinese. (10 points)

1. complimentary

2. appointment

3. normal

4. feast

5. banquet

6. assorted

7. seafood

8. shark's fin

9. pigeon

10. prawn

## VII. Translation. (20 points)

i. Translate the following sentences into English. (10 points)

1. 这个饭店有可能发展成为国际一流的饭店。

2. 如果一切顺利的话，我们可能提前完成任务。

3. 对不起，劳您久等了，但我只能依次为客人服务。

4. 餐厅经营是饭店系统中各个组成部分的综合活动。

5. 我想买点高级滋补品，因为人们说中药有神奇的效力。

ii. Translate the following into Chinese. (10 points)

For over 200 years, visitors to the United States have been trying to explain what makes Americans different from the people of other countries. Few have succeeded, because the United States is not like every other country in the world. It is a nation of nations.

But who were the earliest Americans? And how did the population come to be so mixed.

### 参考答案

**I. Multiple-choice question. (20 points)**

| 1 | 2 | 3 | 4 | 5 | 6 | 7 | 8 | 9 | 10 |
|---|---|---|---|---|---|---|---|---|----|
| C | A | B | D | D | C | B | C | D | A |
| 11 | 12 | 13 | 14 | 15 | 16 | 17 | 18 | 19 | 20 |
| B | A | B | C | C | A | B | A | D | C |

## II. Reading comprehension. (15 points)

| 1 | 2 | 3 | 4 | 5 | 6 | 7 | 8 | 9 | 10 | 11 | 12 | 13 | 14 | 15 |
|---|---|---|---|---|---|---|---|---|----|----|----|----|----|----|
| B | C | D | C | A | C | B | D | C | B  | C  | A  | C  | B  | A  |

## III. Complete the following dialogue according to the Chinese version. (10 points)

A: Excuse me? Could you change a room for me?

B: <u>What's happened, Sir?</u>

A: There's something wrong with the bathroom tap. It was making noise all night <u>that I could hardly fall asleep.</u>

B: I'm sorry to hear that. <u>I'll have it fixed at once.</u>

A: Thank you. <u>But I hope you could change the room for me.</u>

B: We don't have a spare room at present. I'll <u>do it as soon as there is one.</u>

A: OK. Be sure not to forget.

B: Certainly, sir.

## IV. Answer the following questions. (10 points)

1. The aim of a hotel is to create a home for all the traveling guests who need rest, food and drink.

2. The famous specialties of Cantonese food are Roast Suckling Pig, the Battle between the Dragon and the Tiger, Fried Milk, Salt-Baked Chicken and Dog Meat Casserole. The famous specialties of Beijing food are Roast Beijing Duck, Imperial Court Food, Instant-boiled Mutton, Peking Dumpling.

3. 1) What's your name, please?

   2) May I know your name, please?

   3) Could you tell me your name, please?

   4) Could I have your name, please?

4. First, it helps to better the service of the hotel. Through guests' complaints, the hotel managers can find out the problems in their management and service. Their service will be improved by solving these problems. Second, it offers the opportunity to win the guests to increase the hotel's income and market shares.

5. Hangzhou and Suzhou silk, fine china, Su Embroidery and Chinese tea.

## V. Rewrite the sentences in a more courteous way. (5 points)

1. "Would you please tell me the name?"

2. "I'm afraid I don't know anything about the shops around here."

3. "I'd like you to join me this evening in the Kara OK."

4. "Sorry. Mr. Bellow isn't in at the moment."

5. "We are terribly sorry we don't have the dish you want."

## VI. Special terms. (20 points)

i. Translate the following into English. (10 points)

1. newsstand    2. entree    3. tourist    4. standard room    5. airlines logo

6. accommodation    7. insurance    8. rack    9. suburbs    10. sightseeing tour

ii. Translate the following into Chinese. (10 points)

| 1 | 2 | 3 | 4 | 5 |
|---|---|---|---|---|
| 赞美的 | 预约 | 正常的 | 盛宴 | 宴会 |
| 6 | 7 | 8 | 9 | 10 |
| 各式各样的 | 海鲜 | 鱼翅 | 鸽子 | 对虾 |

**VII. Translation. (20 points)**

i. Translate the following sentences into English. (10 points)

1. This hotel is likely to develop into an international first-class hotel.

2. If everything goes well, we may fulfill the task ahead of time.

3. Sorry to have kept you waiting, but I have to serve the guests in turn.

4. Restaurant management is a comprehensive activity of all parts of the hotel system.

5. I'd like to buy some tonics, because people say that Chinese medicine has a magical effect.

ii. Translate the following into Chinese. (10 points)

在过去的 200 多年里，到过美国的游客一直试图解释是什么使美国人与其他国家的人不同。迄今很少有人成功做到，因为美国并不像世界上其他国家那样，它是一个多民族的国家。

但是，谁是最早的美国人？它的人口是如何变得这么混杂？

## "导游资格考试旅游英语"模拟试题 2

**I. Listening Comprehension (15')**

**Omitted**

**II. Grammar and Vocabulary (20')**

16. _____ at the station, he found the train gone.

    A. Arrived      B. Arriving      C. Having arrived      D. In arriving

17. He was charged with _____ driving.

    A. negligence      B. negligent      C. neglect      D. neglected

18. _____ by the climb, he sat down to rest.

    A. Exhausted      B. Exhaust      C. Exhausting      D. Having exhausted

19. He is _____ lazy to revise his work.

    A. so      B. very      C. too      D. much

20. He looked at me as if I _____ a monster.

    A. am      B. were      C. was      D. have been

21. The meat _____ bad if it is left in the sun.

    A. go      B. goes      C. went      D. will go

22. All that _____ is not gold.

    A. glitter           B. glitters           C. glittering           D. glittered

23. By the end of the year I _____ quite a lot of money.

    A. will save           B. will be saving           C. will have saved           D. save

24. The receptionist suggested that the guest _____ to the Summer Palace by taxi.

    A. went           B. was going           C. had to go           D. go

25. I am looking forward to _____ you soon.

    A. see           B. in seeing           C. be seeing           D. seeing

26. The river was _____ deep _____ we could not cross.

    A. too, that           B. so, that           C. very, that           D. so, and

27. Though this kind of bean curd does not smell _____, it tastes _____.

    A. well, well           B. well, good           C. good, well           D. good, good

28. The guest may _____ the key in his room.

    A. left           B. leave           C. to have left           D. have left

29. When the tourists _____ the Yuyuan Garden, they went back to the hotel.

    A. had visited           B. visited           C. have visited           D. having visited

30. In case a fire breaks out, you can leave the building by the fire _____.

    A. escape           B. ladder           C. stairs           D. steps

31. _____ worried about is his son's survival in the airplane crash on September 11, 2001.

    A. The old man is                    B. What is the old man

    C. That the old man is              D. What the old man is

32. How long _____ you _____ for us?

    A. have waited           B. will wait           C. have been waiting           D. had been waiting

33. Covers had been _____ for thirty guests.

    A. lay           B. laid           C. lain           D. laying

34. We shall _____ the flag when the sun _____.

    A. raise, rises           B. raise, rose           C. raise, rise           D. raise, will rise

35. He enjoyed the Dim Sum so much that he accepted a second _____ when it was offered.

    A. offer           B. helping           C. sharing           D. portion

## III. Reading Comprehension (15')

### A

Until the 1980s, the American homeless population comprised mainly older males. Today, homelessness strikes much younger part of society. In fact, a 25-city survey by the U.S. Conference of Mayors in 1987 found that families with children make up the fastest growing part of the homeless population. Many homeless children gather in inner cities; this transient and frequently frightened student population creates additional problems—both legal and educational—for already overburdened urban school administrators and teachers.

Estimates of the number of homeless Americans range from 350,000 to three million. Likewise, estimates of the number of homeless school children vary radically. A U.S. Department of Education report, based on state estimates, states that there are 220,000 homeless school-age children, about a third of whom do not attend school on a regular basis. But the National Coalition for the Homeless estimates that there are at least two times as many homeless children, and that less than half of them attend school regularly.

One part of the homeless population that is particularly difficult to count consists of the "throwaway" youths who have been cast of their homes. The Elementary School Center in New York City estimates that there are 1.5 million of them, many of whom are not counted as children because they do not stay in family shelters and tend to live by themselves on the streets.

Federal law, the Stewart B. McKinney Homeless Assistance Act of 1987, includes a section that addresses the educational needs of homeless children. The educational provisions of the McKinney Act are based on the belief that all homeless children have the right to a free, appropriate education.

36. It is implied in the first paragraph that _____.

    A) the writer himself is homeless, even in his eighties

    B) many older homeless residents are going on strike in 25 cities

    C) there is a serious shortage of academic facilities

    D) homeless children are denied the opportunity of receiving free education

37. The National Coalition for the Homeless believes that the number of homeless children is _____.

    A) 350,000        B) 1,500,000        C) 440,000        D) 110,000

38. One part of the homeless population is difficult to estimate. The reason might well be _____.

    A) the homeless children are too young to be counted as children

    B) the homeless population is growing rapidly

    C) the homeless children usually stay outside school

    D) some homeless children are deserted by their families

39. The McKinney Act is mentioned in this passage in order to show that _____.

    A) the educational problems of homeless children are being recognized

    B) the estimates on homeless children are hard to determine

    C) the address of grade-school children should be located

    D) all homeless people are entitled to free education

40. The passage mainly deals with _____.

    A) the legal problems of the homeless children

    B) the educational problems of homeless children

    C) the social status of older males

    D) estimates on the homeless population

**B**

Being in a different place from one's usual residence is an essential feature of tourism. This means that transportation companies are one vital aspect in the tourist industry.

For many years, railroads have formed the first successful system of mass transportation, carrying crowds of tourists from one place to another. However, the automobile has replaced the railroad for most local travel. The automobile offers convenience. The traveler can depart from his own home and arrive at his destination without transferring luggage or having to cope with any other difficulties. Nowadays, motor buses have partly replaced railroad passenger service on many local routes in a number of cities. However, railroad transportation is still very popular in many Asian countries for internal travels.

The airplane has become very commonplace for long distance travel. Now more and more people would like to take planes on their trips. Traveling by plane is faster and quite safe.

Ships still play an important part of tourism. A cruise is a voyage by ship that is made for pleasure rather than for a fixed destination. The cruise ship serves as the hotel for the passengers as well as their transportation. When the tourists reach a port, they are usually conducted on a one-day excursion, but they return to the ship to eat and sleep.

Without the modern high-speed forms of transportation available to large numbers of tourists, tourism would not have become such a successful industry.

41. Why has the automobile now replaced the railroad for most local travels?

    A. Because it is cheaper.

    B. Because it is faster.

    C. Because many people own cars.

    D. Because the traveler can depart from his own home and arrive at his destination without transferring luggage.

42. The best advantage of air travel to tourists is that _____.

    A. it is cheaper than railroad travel

    B. it is faster and safer than railroad travel

    C. it leaves more time for sightseeing for the traveler

    D. it is easier to get air tickets than train tickets

43. What conveniences does a cruise ship offer?

    A. It serves as a hotel for the passengers as well as their transportation.

    B. It reaches many ports.

    C. It offers good food.

    D. It can arrive at any port the travelers wish.

44. A cruise is a voyage by ship made for _____.

    A. a fixed destination               B. travel

    C. pleasure                      D. relaxation

45. If there were no modern high-speed forms of transportation available to tourists, _____.

    A. tourists would have to go on foot from one place to another

    B. tourism would not be so successful

    C. nobody would like to travel

    D. it would be impossible for people to travel

## C

Cultural norms so completely surround people, so permeate thought and action that we never recognize the assumptions on which their lives and their sanity rest. As one observer put it, if birds were suddenly endowed with scientific curiosity they might examine many things, but the sky itself would be overlooked as a suitable subject; if fish were to become curious about the world, it would never occur to them to begin by investigating water. For birds and fish would take the sky and sea for granted, unaware of their profound influence because they comprise the medium for every fact. Human beings, in a similar way, occupy a symbolic universe governed by codes that are unconsciously acquired and automatically employed. So much so that they rarely notice that the ways they interpret and talk about events are distinctively different from the ways people conduct their affairs in other cultures.

As long as people remain blind to the sources of their meanings, they are imprisoned within them. These cultural frames of reference are no less confining simply because they cannot be seen or touched. Whether it is an individual neurosis that keeps an individual out of contact with his neighbors, or a collective neurosis that separates neighbors of different cultures, both are forms of blindness that limit what can be experienced and what can be learned from others.

It would seem that everywhere people would desire to break out of the boundaries of their own experiential worlds. Their ability to react sensitively to a wider spectrum of events and peoples requires an overcoming of such cultural parochialism. But, in fact, few attain this broader vision. Some, of course, have little opportunity for wider cultural experience, though this condition should change as the movement of people accelerates. Others do not try to widen their experience because they prefer the old and familiar, seek from their affairs only further confirmation of the correctness of their own values. Still others recoil from such experiences because they feel it dangerous to probe too deeply into the personal or cultural unconscious. Exposure may reveal how tenuous and arbitrary many cultural norms are; such exposure might force people to acquire new bases for interpreting events. And even for the many who do seek actively to enlarge the variety of human beings with whom they are capable of communicating there are still difficulties.

Cultural myopia persists not merely because of inertia and habit, but chiefly because it is so difficult to overcome. One acquires a personality and a culture in childhood, long before he is capable of comprehending either of them. To survive, each person masters the perceptual orientations, cognitive biases, and communicative habits of his own culture. But once mastered, objective assessment of these same processes is awkward since the same mechanisms that are being evaluated must be used in making the evaluations.

46. The examples of birds and fish are used to _____.

    A. show that they, too, have their respective cultures

    B. explain humans occupy a symbolic universe as birds and fish occupy the sky and the sea

    C. illustrate that human beings are unaware of the cultural codes governing them

    D. demonstrate the similarity between man, birds, and fish in their ways of thinking

47. The term "parochialism" (Line 3, Para. 3) most possibly means _____.

    A. open-mindedness          B. provincialism

    C. superiority              D. discrimination

48. It can be inferred from the last two paragraphs that _____.

    A. everyone would like to widen their cultural scope if they can

    B. the obstacles to overcoming cultural parochialism lie mainly in people's habit of thinking

    C. provided one's brought up in a culture, he may be with bias in making cultural evaluations

    D. childhood is an important stage in comprehending culture

49. Which of the following statements is TRUE according to the passage?

    A. Individual and collective neurosis might prevent communications with others.

    B. People in different cultures may be governed by the same cultural norms.

    C. People's visions will be enlarged if only they knew that cultural differences exist.

    D. If cultural norms are something tangible, they won't be so confining.

50. The passage might be entitled _____.

    A. "How to Overcome Cultural Myopia"

    B. "Behavioral Patterns and Cultural Background"

    C. "Harms of Cultural Myopia"

    D. "Cultural Myopia—A Deep-rooted Collective Neurosis"

## IV. Translation (30')

A. Translate the following words and phrases from Chinese into English (51-60) or vice versa (61-70).(10')

51. 没收          52. 误机          53. 退票          54. 三轮车          55. 市区高架路

56. 林荫道        57. 马术          58. 音乐大师       59. 花车巡游        60. 博物馆

61. fresco        62. Confucianism          63. waterside pavilion          64. winding path

65. magnolia      66. valid certificate      67. embroidery                  68. ticket both

69. sunstroke     70. first aid

B. Translate the following passages from Chinese into English (71-72) or vice versa (73-74).(20')

71. 旅游宣传广告通常采用的方式有报纸、杂志以及电视广播。旅游宣传的最有效手段莫过于游客的口碑，通过旅游者向他们的朋友介绍和推荐旅游景点。

72. 上海是一座充满魅力的大都市。它不仅是中国近代史的缩影和新中国改革开放的窗口，也被誉为21世纪最具有活力的国际大都市。

73. With most of its residents being immigrants, Shanghai has a mixed culture. People from various places made their own contribution to the city's culture. As they enjoy their own cultures, they help mold the Shanghai character of inclusiveness. The inclusive and open character makes Shanghai a gigantic receptor of modern technological development.

74. In terms of Chinese cuisine, people will naturally dwell on four main cuisines in China. Known as Shandong Cuisine, Guangdong Cuisine, Huai-Yang Cuisine and Sichuan Cuisine, they represent cooking styles of different regions of China. They are unique for their distinctive flavor of salty, fresh, sweet, hot and spicy accordingly. As a country with a vast territory and various nationalities, its cuisines can be much more than what we have described above, due to the wide range of flavors of Chinese culinary culture.

## V. Question and Answer (5')

75. Please list five pillar industries in Shanghai.

## VI. Writing (15')

Write a composition of 150-200 words on the giving topic:

What is the best quality a tour guide should have?

## 参考答案

## I. Listening Comprehesion (15')

Omitted

## II. Grammar and Vocabulary (20')

| 16 | 17 | 18 | 19 | 20 | 21 | 22 | 23 | 24 | 25 | 26 | 27 | 28 | 29 | 30 |
|----|----|----|----|----|----|----|----|----|----|----|----|----|----|----|
| B | B | A | C | B | D | B | C | D | D | B | D | D | B | A |

| 31 | 32 | 33 | 34 | 35 | | | | | | | | | | |
|----|----|----|----|----|--|--|--|--|--|--|--|--|--|--|
| D | C | B | A | B | | | | | | | | | | |

## III. Reading Comprehension (15')

| 36 | 37 | 38 | 39 | 40 | 41 | 42 | 43 | 44 | 45 | 46 | 47 | 48 | 49 | 50 |
|----|----|----|----|----|----|----|----|----|----|----|----|----|----|----|
| C | C | D | D | B | D | B | A | C | B | C | B | C | A | D |

## IV. Translation (30')

A. Translate the following words and phrases from Chinese into English (51-60) or vice versa (61-70).(10')

51. confiscate    52. miss the plane/miss the flight    53. return a ticket

54. tricycle    55. downtown viaduct    56. boulevard/avenue

57. horsemanship    58. virtuoso    59. parade    60. museum

61. 壁画    62. 儒教    63. 水榭 / 近水楼台    64. 曲径

65. 木兰    66. 有效证件    67. 刺绣    68. 售票处 / 售票厅
69. 中暑    70. 急救

B. Translate the following passages from Chinese into English (71-72) or vice versa (73-74).(20')

71. Tourism advertising usually takes the form of newspapers, magazines and television broadcasts. The most effective means of tourism promotion is word of mouth, and the tourists may introduce and recommend tourist attractions to their friends.

72. Shanghai is a fascinating metropolis. It is not only the epitome of modern Chinese history and the windows of new China's reform and opening up. It is also known as the most dynamic international metropolis of the 21st century.

73. 由于大部分居民是移民，上海具有了混合的文化。来自不同地方的人都为这个城市的文化做出了自己的贡献。他们在享受自己的文化的同时，也帮助上海形成了包容的特性。其包容性和开放性使上海成为现代科技发展的 一个巨大的受体。

74. 说起中国菜，人们自然会想到中国有四大主要菜系，即鲁菜，粤菜，淮扬菜和川菜。它们代表中国不同地区的烹饪风格。它们别有风味，特点分别是咸，鲜，甜和辛辣。作为一个地域辽阔且多民族的国家，也由于中国饮食文化的多样性，它的美食远不止我们上面所描述的这些。

## V. Question and Answer (5')

1) Electronic information product manufacturing

2) Automotive manufacturing

3) Petrochemical and fine chemical manufacturing

4) Fine steel manufacturing

5) Biomedical manufacturing

## VI. Writing (15')

Open

# "中级导游员等级考试" 模拟题

## 一、词汇翻译（请用所报考语种翻译。每小题 1.5 分，共 45 分）

| | | |
|---|---|---|
| 1. 文化遗产 | 11. 市场份额 | 21. 河姆渡遗址 |
| 2. 游牧民 | 12. 现象 | 22. 流感病例 |
| 3. 假山 | 13. 自然景观 | 23. 主题乐园 |
| 4. 青铜器时代 | 14. 廉价航空 | 24. 家用电器 |
| 5. 游轮 | 15. 高血压 | 25. 随身行李 |
| 6. 车展 | 16. 购买力 | 26. 退款 |
| 7. 世博会 | 17. 吉祥图案 | 27. 飞行线路 |
| 8. 游乐园 | 18. 症状 | 28. 客栈 |
| 9. 传染病 | 19. 审美标准 | 29. 常委会 |
| 10. 游览胜地 | 20. 社会治安 | 30. 食谱 |

## 二、段落翻译（请用所报考语种翻译。每小题 5 分，共 25 分）

1. 农历正月十五是中国的传统节日元宵节。在元宵节人们扶老携幼，呼朋唤友，来到灯会猜灯谜。在现代社会，灯笼有着各种复杂的设计，其中大多数的灯笼都被设计成动物的形状。元宵节又叫小年，因为它标志着新年庆祝活动的结束。

2. 四川乐山的沫若堂是 1992 年为纪念世界文化名人郭沫若而建的一组建筑群，在郭沫若诞辰 100 周年之际落成。堂前塑有郭沫若铜像一尊。郭沫若资料研究中心也建于此。

3. 在许多外国人的眼里，京剧就是中国戏曲的同义词。两百多年来，艺术家们不断努力与创新，使京剧成为一门综合性的表演艺术。京剧融唱、念、做、打于一身，成为中国传统文化的瑰宝。同时，观看京剧也成了来华游客的一大乐趣。

4. 去年开始的全球经济下滑对我国经济和旅游业的实际影响已明显显现。就旅游业而言，今年 5 月共有 175.69 万境外游客来华旅游，与去年同期相比下降了 17%，较 4 月份的 191.17 万人次也下降了 8.1%。

5. 自古以来，丝织品就是中国的传统出口产品之一。公元前 2 世纪的西汉时期，中国就开始向韩国、日本和西欧出口优质丝织品。现在，中国可以生产上百种丝织品，有数千种花色图案，深受世界各国人民的青睐。

### 三、旅游应用文写作 (10 分)

你叫李明，是一家旅行社的顾客服务部门经理。两星期前，你社的一名导游接待过来自 × 国的旅游团。其中一位名叫 ×××（姓名自拟）的游客来信投诉：

1. 行程中安排的就餐环境差；

2. 司机态度粗鲁、喜欢按喇叭。

请用所报考语种就以上投诉内容给 ××× 游客写一封回信，回信要求语言规范，行文流畅，格式正确，字数为 150~200 词，并包含以下内容：

1. 感谢客人来信并对他表示歉意，对他遇到的问题表示理解；

2 解释问题产生的原因；

3 告知问题的处理办法；

4 承诺下次不再发生此类情况；

5 再次向客人致歉。

### 四、文化专题解说写作 (20 分)

用所报考的语种就所给题目写出一篇 400~600 字的导游解说词。要求语言规范，内容切题，条理清楚，有一定的思想深度，符合导游的语言要求，能反映中国茶文化悠久的历史、对世界的影响以及独有的特点。

题目：中国茶文化

## 参考答案

**一、词汇翻译**（请用所报考语种翻译。每小题 1.5 分，共 45 分）

| | | |
|---|---|---|
| 1. cultural heritage | 11. market share | 21. the Hemudu Ruins |
| 2. nomad | 12. phenomenon | 22. flu case |
| 3. rockery | 13. natural landscape | 23. theme park |
| 4. the Bronze Age | 14. low-cost airline | 24. household appliances |
| 5. cruise ship | 15. high blood pressure | 25. carry-on bag |
| 6. auto show | 16. purchasing power | 26. refunds |
| 7. World Expo | 17. auspicious pattern/lucky pattern | 27. flight routes |
| 8. amusement park | 18. symptoms | 28. inn |
| 9. infectious disease | 19. aesthetic standard | 29. standing committee |
| 10. tourist attraction | 20. social security | 30. recipe |

**二、段落翻译**（请用所报考语种翻译。每小题 5 分，共 25 分）

1. The 15th of the first lunar month, also called the Lantern Festival, is a traditional Chinese festival. On the Lantern Festival, people young and old will come to the lantern show to guess riddles. In modern society, the lanterns have a variety of designs, most of which are designed in the shape of animals. The Lantern Festival is also called the small year because it marks the end of New Year celebrations.

2. Moruo Hall in Sichuan Leshan is a group of buildings built in 1992 to commemorate the world cultural celebrity Guo Moruo. It was completed on the occasion of the 100th anniversary of the birth of Guo. In front of the hall, there is a bronze statue of Guo Moruo. Guo Moruo Research Center is also built here.

3. In the eyes of many foreigners, Peking Opera is the synonym of Chinese traditional opera. Over the past two hundred years, artists have made great efforts and innovations, so that the opera has become a comprehensive performing arts. With singing, speaking, acting and acrobatics fighting all in one, Peking Opera has become a treasure of traditional Chinese culture. At the same time, watching Peking Opera in China has become a great pleasure for tourists.

4. The global economic downturn which started last year has actual had a clear impact on our economy and tourism. As far as tourism industry is concerned, in May this year, a total of 1,756,900 foreign tourists travel to China. Compared to the same time last year it went down by 17%. Compared to 1,911,700 visitors in April it also fell by 8.1%.

5. Since ancient times, silk has been one of China's traditional export products. During the Western Han Dynasty, the 2nd century BC, China exported high-quality silk to Korea, Japan and Western Europe. Now, China can produce hundreds of silk, with thousands of colors and patterns favored by the peoples all over the world.

三、旅游应用文写作 (10 分 )

**Sample**

Dear Mr. Smith,

We've received your letter sent last Sunday. In your letter, you complained that during your trip the dining conditions were poor and the driver was very rude and honked his horn continuously. We feel very sorry for that and at the same time we are very grateful to your telling us the unpleasant things happened during your trip.

At meal time when there are too many people in the restaurants you have to wait for a long time, and they are very noisy, it will make people sick. So we fully understand how you feel. We have told the guide to try to find better places next time and he promised to do so. As for the rude driver, we have given him a fine of 1,000 yuan and made him promise that he will be nice to our customers, otherwise he will be fired.

Many thanks again for your letter, so we know the problems existing in our management. We do apologize for what happened to you due to our poor management. We promise we'll improve our management and try to provide the best service to all our customers. We also guarantee that such kind of things will not happen again.

All the very best to you!

Yours faithfully,

Li Ming

Customer Service Manager

四、文化专题解说写作 (20 分 )

## Chinese Tea Culture

Tea-drinking is a nation-wide custom in China. It is a daily necessity for the Chinese to have three meals and tea a day. When any guest comes, it is a custom to present a cup of tea to him/her. There are numerous tea-houses in every town and city.

Tea-drinking is an art, a skill in China. In some places the way of making tea is very complicated. And the tea utensils—the teacup, tea saucer, teapot, tea tray—are works of art. There are hundreds of famous teas in China and there are a great many famous springs and streams to provide water to make tea. And the tea fields or tea mountains are also marvelous sights to add beauty to the scenery.

Tea drinking in China has a history of four thousand years. It can be traced back to the Zhou Dynasty (1100 BC–221 BC). Tea was discovered by Shennong and became popular as a drink in the State of Lu because of Zhou Gong.

As the legend has it, Shennong, a legendary hero, tasted hundreds of wild plants to see which were poisonous and which were edible, so as to prevent people from eating the poisonous plants. It is said that he was poisoned seventy-two times in one day but was saved by chewing some tender leaves of an evergreen plant blossoming with white flowers. Since he had a transparent belly, people could see how the food moved throughout his stomach and intestines. When they saw the juice of the tender leaves go up and down in the stomach as if it were searching for something, they called it "cha", meaning search in Chinese. Later it was renamed "cha", which has the same sound of the present one.

It is said that the literary artists of Ancient China were inspired either by tea or by wine. Those who were fond of wine were said to write in a passionate and heroic style; those who preferred tea tended to be sentimental and romantic.

At present, people still keep drinking tea as their daily drinking. Studies show that tea can have effects on some modern illnesses. To those groups who have to work with computers for a long time, drinking a cup of tea can help them to build up a wall to the computer radiate gradually. To those people who may find too much fat, drinking tea can help them to re-create a new balance in their bodies. And to those aged people, drinking tea is also a good way to keep a calm mood for a longer life.